Ike:
The memoir of Isom "Ike" Rigell

by Ike Rigell

© Copyright 2017 by Ike Rigell

ISBN 978-1-63393-514-3

Published by

 köehlerbooks™

210 60th Street
Virginia Beach, VA 23451
800-435-4811
www.koehlerbooks.com

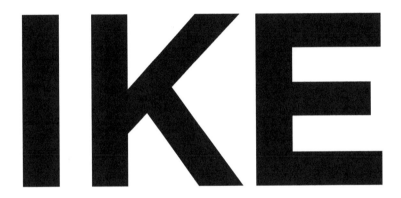

IKE

THE MEMOIR OF ISOM "IKE" RIGELL

VIRGINIA BEACH
CAPE CHARLES

TABLE OF CONTENTS

DEDICATION

I have been blessed with a wonderful family, whom I love dearly, and I dedicate this work to them. I want to give special recognition, though, to two: Mary Beatrice Rigell, my saintly mother, and my beautiful wife, Kathryn Rigell, God's gift to me 63 years ago. Through the years, we have been richly blessed by the wisdom and prayers of these two precious women.

I also must express my deep appreciation and thanks to my daughter, Amy Rigell Hendricks, and my granddaughter, Lindsey Rigell Burke, for making this work possible. Without these two beautiful and talented individuals and their unlimited patience, gentle guidance, advice, encouragement, organizational skills, and the time they sacrificed to this work, it would never have been completed. I am forever indebted to them for their devotion in making this project not just a dream but a reality. I am convinced that by divine appointment they enabled me to complete this work. Amazing Grace—oh, how God has blessed me.

The Dream Team. Me with my granddaughter, Lindsey Rigell Burke (L), and my daughter, Amy Rigell Hendricks (R).

The "Dream Team" hard at work on my book in my "office" at my house. If you look carefully you can see all of the photos and memorabilia from my life on the surrounding walls. My granddaughter, Lindsey, and my daughter, Amy, did much of the work on the book from their homes in Virginia, but also made several trips down to Florida to work on it with me as well.

FOREWORD

My father, Isom "Ike" Rigell, lived an extraordinary life during a very important time in our country's history. Ike was born in 1923 and grew up during the Great Depression, the youngest of three children. His father passed away from pneumonia when he was 2 years old. Little Ike, as he was known, was raised by his widowed mother with the help of his uncles and grandparents in the small town of Slocomb, Alabama. My father experienced firsthand the power, influence, and importance extended family can have in a young person's life. I am grateful that he passed this core value on to me and my siblings.

My father graduated from Slocomb High School in 1941 (three brick buildings housed all twelve grades). He was 18 years old with no prospects for a job, and he made the decision to join the Marine Corps and serve his country. For the first time in his life he traveled more than 125 miles from his home. After boot camp and completing Combat Field Telephone School in San Diego my father was assigned to the 6th Marine Defense Battalion stationed on Midway Island. He was there operating a field telephone switchboard on the morning of December 7, 1941, when the Japanese attacked Pearl Harbor. After 17 months on Midway Island, he returned to the United States for R&R and reassignment. He was then assigned to the newly formed 4th Marine Division and was sent back overseas where he participated in all four landings of the 4th Marine Division: Roi-Namur (in the Marshall Islands), Saipan, Tinian, and Iwo Jima. While serving on Midway Island, he was operating a small combat telephone switchboard that made the connection to Col. Shannon, the commanding officer of the Marine Garrison on Midway, that the Japanese had bombed Pearl Harbor.

My father served four and a half years in the Marine Corps with one thirty-day leave. Though he spent four Christmases away on deployment, he never lost sight of his family at home. Many brave young men of his generation served as my father did, but only a few have the opportunity to share their personal story. My father's memoir is a voice for all the servicemen he served alongside.

After the war, and under the guidance of his cousin, Bill Rigell, my father enrolled in Georgia Tech on the GI bill and graduated in 1950 with an electrical engineering degree. A few years later, he was working at Redstone Arsenal in Huntsville, Alabama, when he fell in love and married my amazing mother, Kathryn Gillespie. Together they moved to Cape Canaveral, Florida, where my father worked as part of the Army Ballistic Missile Agency's original launch team. During those early years in our nation's space program, my father was an integral part of the elite launch team that included Dr. Wernher von Braun, Dr. Kurt Debus, Dr. Hans Gruene, and Rocco Petrone.

My father's career spanned 30 years with NASA. He served as Chief Engineer and Deputy Director of all Apollo launches, including Skylab, and as Director of Launch Operations for the Apollo-Soyuz Test Project (ASTP), the historical mission between the United States and Russia. After retiring from NASA, my father continued his work in the space program for the next ten years as Vice President of Florida Operations for the United Space Boosters Inc. (USBI).

Today, my father has a room in his house that is filled wall to wall with historical space-related memorabilia, photographs, and awards he has received over his career. One award that stands out to me is the Lifetime Achievement Award, which was presented to him in 1969 by astronaut John Young from the National Space Club. My father still resides in Florida's Space

Coast, where rocket launches can be seen from his back yard. At 95 years old, he is an honored and active member of the NASA Alumni League.

In the summer of 2010, my father brought me an extra-large notebook overflowing with handwritten pages he had compiled and saved over the past ten years. It chronicled his life's journey. He asked me to help him organize and type his memoir. I was a little overwhelmed with the project because there were so many stories spanning so many years, and they were hard to read because they were all in pencil. As we got started organizing the pages by events and years, and as the stories started to take shape on my computer, I developed a very strong sense of purpose.

I live in Virginia Beach, Virginia, and my visits to my parents' home in Florida took on new meaning as my dad and I began to work on his memoir project. I visited more often, and each time I would bring with me new sections I had typed, ready for his review and proofreading. Dad loved the anticipation of my visits, for it gave him incentive to write down more and more of his personal story, and that he did. My dad was always present growing up, but the experiences he was writing about in his memoir were all new to me. He never spoke at length, or in such detail about his years in WWII until now. In the early days of working on my father's manuscript, I set up my laptop on a makeshift desk in the family laundry room. Even in those humble surroundings, compiling my dad's story, I knew I was working on something of great significance.

My father's memoir has been a work in progress for many years. I recall taking road trips with my parents where I would drive and my dad would sit in the front passenger seat. Stories from his past would just come spilling out. He'd share stories that were laugh-out-loud funny, and I would listen in amazement as I heard for the first time where he'd been and what he had gone through in his life. He'd later handwrite these stories on paper, and my job would be to type them and save them on the computer. I would marvel as I'd read his stories, in awe that this humble, devoted family man I knew as a great, fix-anything-with-duct-tape kind of father had such a remarkable life journey.

Parts of my dad's memoir came by way of me transcribing recordings he made on his microcassette player. I believe those were some of the harder memories for him to share, because he had to go back and relive horrifying personal experiences as a young Marine in active combat during WWII. I found this note written in my dad's journal about his time in the war: "Thousands and thousands of ordinary young men [were] caught up in a daily environment where they accomplished very heroic deeds to help or even save another's life while in grave danger to their own life and even at times the cost of their own life . . . they were not looking for hero status."

In 2011, while my brother, Scott Rigell, was representing Virginia's 2nd Congressional District in the United States Congress, my mother, father, and other family members were invited as Scott's guests to Washington, D.C. Due to Scott's position in Congress, our family was invited to attend a private reception at the home of General James "Jim" Amos, then Commandant of the United States Marine Corps. My father, wearing his Iwo Jima survivor hat, was seated with his walking cane, which is embellished with a Marine Corps emblem, propped up beside him. General Amos respectfully bent down on one knee to have a conversation with my father. It was a very moving experience.

My father proudly wears his Marine Corps hat every day, and I am grateful for the complete strangers who reach out to him and thank him for his service. It happens every time I am out with him in public, and it makes me proud to be an American, and it makes me appreciate everyone who has served our country.

This book chronicles my father's remarkable life journey. It is about him being at the right place in history at the right time, but it's also about making right choices. My father grew up in a Christian home, and his faith in God has always provided strength and direction in his life. My father will tell you that his life is a reflection of his mother, Attie Rigell's fervent prayers for him.

My father is a memorable man, and his story will inspire you to face your life with courage, humility, and humor. His story is insightful. It includes details of a young man's firsthand experiences from the trenches of Iwo Jima to the trials and successes that went into making our nation's great space program. My dad is part of, and truly exemplifies, the Greatest Generation.

My father will tell you today that his deepest regret is that he did not spend time hearing the life story of his mother, grandparents, aunts, and uncles. So this book is his gift to the children of the Rigell family, to the generations here now, and the generations to follow. But it is also a gift to you, the reader. May you be inspired by reading this book to explore and record your family roots, for everyone has a unique and remarkable story to share.

The following is one of my father's favorite Bible verses. Years ago, my mother and father lived with me and my two young boys. My father would recite Psalms 19:14 with the boys every day: "Let the words of my mouth and the meditations of my heart be always acceptable to you, oh Lord, my strength and redeemer."

My father always closes his conversations with "Bless you," so it is my prayer that you will be blessed by reading his story.

—Amy Rigell Hendricks

Sgt. Rigell and Marine Corps Commandant General Amos at the Marine Barracks in Washington, D.C.

"For even when we were with you, we commanded you this:
If anyone will not work, neither shall he eat."

—II Thessalonians 3:10

INTRODUCTION

"Are you a survivor?" she asked.
"Pardon, I don't understand," I replied.
"Are you a survivor?" she asked again.
"Well, yes, I guess I am a survivor," I answered.

On June 30, 2001, Kathryn, my beautiful and faithful wife of fifty-nine years, and I had the privilege of attending the commissioning ceremony of the new amphibious assault ship, *USS Iwo Jima,* in Pensacola, Florida. Our invitation instructed us to enter the main gate, where we would receive further instruction on parking and seating for the ceremony. We were in a long line of bumper-to-bumper cars, and I could see the ship docked about three-quarters of a mile from the main gate. I could see most of the cars being directed to parking lots just inside the gate, and a few cars being directed on down toward the ship.

A steady drizzle had been falling all morning, so when we reached the traffic attendant at the main gate, I rolled down my window for further directions. With a big smile and water dripping off her poncho, the attendant said, "Are you a survivor?"

I didn't understand her question, so I asked her to repeat it. Again, with her big smile, she repeated, "Are you a survivor?"

"Well, I guess I am a survivor."

"Oh, you get to go on down to the ship to park." So she told me to proceed toward the ship and I would get further instructions down at the dock. As we drove toward the ship, we passed many people walking in the drizzling rain with umbrellas and raincoats; some even pushed baby carriages.

Being a survivor is nice and brings you some perks, I thought. *But why am I a survivor, not only of Iwo Jima, but of many other situations as well?* I think almost everyone will ponder that unanswerable question at some point.

We were seated on the dock just in front of the ship, and by this time we were accustomed to the steady drizzle as we waited for the ceremony to begin. I was seated next to a fellow Marine from the 4th Marine Division. I did not know him during the war; he was a machine gunner in the 23rd Regiment and had served in all four invasions by the 4th Division. He'd come through all the invasions unscathed. The 23rd Regiment bore the brunt of most of the toughest situations we encountered, and a Marine gunner is a prime target.

Having survived four invasions with no wounds is a good story, but one with a sad ending. His younger brother-in-law enlisted in the Marines and was assigned to the 5th Marine Division. The 5th Division's first action of the war was the invasion of Iwo Jima along with the 4th Division. My new friend's brother-in-law was killed instantly just as he landed on the beach on D-Day. My friend was not aware of this until after the battle. That comes back to the unanswerable question, Why do some survive to an old age and some perish early in life?

That day made an impact on my thinking that increasingly occupies my thoughts as I get older. *For what purpose did my God choose to make me a survivor, and, more importantly, am I fulfilling the purpose for which I am here?* My focus and desire now is to fulfill whatever mission my Lord has for me with the remaining time I have on this good earth. This subject of survival will come up later in these chronicles.

I am age ninety-four at the time of this writing. As you reach the latter years of your life, you increasingly reflect on your early years and recall regrettable things that you've done and also things you have left undone that you now wish you had completed.

One of the things left undone that I regret the most is not getting the life stories of my mother, my grandparents, and older aunts and uncles. They were available, and I blew it. Unfortunately, when I had the opportunity to collect this data, I was not interested. But if any of my heirs have a desire to know how it was to grow up in the 20th century, I wanted to make it available.

Another regret that bothers me also falls into the category of things I should have done that I left undone. I can look back today and am vividly reminded of a number of people who made a profound and positive influence on my life. My deep regret is that I never thanked them or expressed my appreciation for their influence, timely support, and guidance at critical times in my life. These special people will be identified in the chronicles that follow, but it saddens me that they have all died without my acknowledgment and thanks for what they meant in my life. I strongly urge anyone who reads this to flash back over your life and identify those who were there at the right time and place to provide you the lift you needed to proceed in the right direction. This is not something to put off until a better day. Go do it!

One message I must convey up front, and I want to make this very clear, is that these chronicles will naturally describe the conditions that I grew up in during the Great Depression as very primitive and harsh compared to today's world. However, describing my daily life growing up in that environment is not to invoke your sympathy or receive any accolades for surviving in such tough times. I will not try to impress you with the "old-timers' tales" about how I had to walk five miles to school in a foot of snow every day, uphill both ways. The truth is, I walked a block to school, passing my grandparent's house on the way, came home for lunch, and then most days after school my grandmother was out on her porch to greet me with a biscuit and jelly or honey.

I enjoyed a very happy childhood. Since my early childhood years were all during the Great Depression, I had no reference for what life would be like in a booming economy. I was six years old in 1929 at the start of the Great Depression, and it lasted through the 1930s, so to me everything was normal. As I get older, my experience reveals to me that true happiness and contentment comes from within and not from the outside. I like a quote from Will Rogers: "I grew up in the depression, but I was never depressed."

That brings me to the point of explaining why I am taking the time and effort to document my journey on this good earth and to talk about personal events and the cultural environment that influenced and shaped my thinking and actions during the past three quarters of the 20th century. These chronicles will be somewhat introspective, but focusing on me is not my primary objective. Rather, I want you, the reader, to feel like you are experiencing the particular situations discussed.

1923-1941
EARLY YEARS

PARENTS

FATHER

In April 1925, my father died of pneumonia. I was 27 months old at that time and, of course, could not grasp the meaning or the impact on my life.

I am revealing something that I have been silent about all these years, never, ever mentioning this to my mother or anyone. Whether these events ever happened as I describe them, I cannot say, but I can say that to me they are real.

The first scene I recall is of my daddy holding my hand as we walked up to the porch at my grandfather's house. He lived four houses down the street from our house. My grandfather was sitting in a rocking chair on the porch, and they were carrying on a conversation. We were on the way to my father's store to get some candy, so the day had to be Sunday.

The next scene, just as real as the one described above, is not easy to write about. It occurred in what we called the front room of our house. This was a corner room with windows on each side facing a wraparound porch. There were two doors to this room, one from a wide central hallway in the house and one door to the outside porch. There was a fireplace, and my father's casket was against the wall, centered under the window.

People were shoulder to shoulder, milling around the room and coming in and out of the two doors. I was aimlessly wandering around the room. All I could see were legs and knees; no one even knew I was there. It was like walking in a thick forest of giant redwood trees.

I experienced this vision before I learned, years later, that in those times, in rural areas, it was standard that when a person died, the funeral home embalmed the body and took it back to the home so friends and relatives would come pay their respects. Later, the casket would be taken to the church for the funeral service. One reason for this procedure was that there were no funeral homes in the small towns. The nearest funeral home to us was in Dothan, Alabama, about sixteen miles away, and most people did not have transportation.

Also confirming this vision I had was a seemingly unrelated story my sister, Mary Jo, told me a couple of years before she passed away. We had never discussed it prior to that. This story was from the time that she was a student nurse in Dothan, Alabama. The hospital she worked at was adjacent to a funeral home. Here is her story as she told it to me:

"Me and one of my friends, another student nurse, were leaving work one day and we ran into two of our friends that worked at the funeral home. They were just leaving to take a body out to a home in a rural area. They asked if we would like to ride out with them and we said sure. So they rode in this hearse out to this home in the country. As they pulled into the yard of this home, there were many people gathered in the yard and on the porch. It was obvious that they were waiting for the hearse to arrive. One of the guys said, 'You watch, someone will come up to the casket and say, "Ella Mae, speak to me just one more time."' They took the casket inside of the house and me and my friend went in the house with them. They opened the casket and sure enough one of the first ladies to come up and view the body said, 'Ella Mae, speak to me just one more time.'"

I cannot recall for what reason we were talking about Mary Jo's days as a student nurse in the Dothan hospital, but I know it had nothing to do with my father's death. After the death of my father, there were only two more family deaths before I left Slocomb at the age of eighteen. Grandfather McCaskill passed away when I was five years old. He was living with us when he passed away, and I have no memory of a viewing in our home. Grandmother Rigell passed away when I was twelve years old, and I know there was no viewing at my grandparent's home.

When Mary Jo told this story I was inwardly very emotional, but outwardly apparently I showed no emotion. Understand that until I heard this story I had no reference or any knowledge that it was the culture in that day for some people, especially in small towns and rural areas where funeral homes were not readily accessible and transportation was a problem, to have the funeral home bring the body to the home for a viewing for family and friends. To me, this confirms my memory, or "vision," as I call it, of seeing my father's casket at our house when I was only two years old. I still never told Mary Jo about my vision, even after she told me that story. Maybe I should have shared it with her at that time—I don't know.

I would like to share one other memory having to do with my father from when I was young. It was standard practice for our whole family to be in church Sunday morning and many Sunday nights. One of the popular old gospel hymns you would often hear was *In the Garden*, and the lyrics went something like this:

> *I come to the garden alone . . .*
> *And He walks with me*
> *And He talks with me*
> *And He tells me I am his own*
> *And the joy we share as we tarry there*
> *None other has ever known*

To me, the meaning of "He" in the old hymn was my earthly father. In my young mind, he would be holding my hand again as we enjoyed a walk. Don't think for a moment I am placing my daddy as God. I am saying the words in this song are comforting even today.

MOTHER

The older I get, the more I look back, and the more I look back, the more I marvel at what a remarkable lady my mother was.

At 31, she became a widow with three children ages 2, 3, and 5. We were an average, middle-income family. My father and my grandfather owned a general merchandise store. My father had some life insurance. I don't know how much. For a few years, my mother received mortgage payments from a house my father had sold. My grandfather McCaskill received a small pension because he was a Confederate veteran of the Civil War. Fortunately, the house we lived in had two extra bedrooms we could rent out. Our house was on a corner lot, and we had an L-shaped porch facing the streets. Both bedrooms had an outside door to the porch, a fireplace, and interior doors that opened into a hallway accessing the dining room. During the school season we rented these rooms to teachers, who also had their meals with us, and other teachers would join us for meals.

There were no restaurants or apartments in our town, so all the teachers, most of whom were single, had to find meals and rooms to rent. During the summers, between school sessions, we were always able to rent these rooms, mostly to Alabama Power and Light crews working in the area.

My mother had to prepare the menu, buy the groceries, and cook three meals a day, seven days a week for a large dining table full of people. The cooking was done on a wood stove. We had no refrigerator and had to buy ice daily.

I cannot recall the exact year, but my grandfather Rigell got my mother a job as a clerk in the largest store in town. It was owned by his friend Charlie Segrest.

That is when Johnnie Mae Jackson came to work fulltime for us. Johnnie Mae did our washing and also washed the clothes for our boarders. Johnnie Mae's older sister, Lulu, worked for my grandmother Rigell. Johnnie Mae was a jewel; I truly believe she was sent to us by our Lord. She just took over and ran the household and did all the cooking and cleaning. Johnnie Mae was a favorite with our boarders, who were always complimenting her on her delicious meals.

When my mother went to work, she was the only female store clerk in our town. In that era, the women in the workforce were mostly schoolteachers and nurses. That changed in World War II; I'll cover that subject later.

My mother was an expert seamstress who made all the

dresses for herself, grandmother McCaskill, and my sisters, Mary Jo and Florence. We did not have many clothes like people today, but we always wore good clothes and enjoyed good food.

My mother made sure we were in Sunday school and church every week. Several times a year we would visit the little Presbyterian country church, Immanuel, that my grandfather McCaskill helped found. Sometimes my mother would play the old church organ. What pleasant memories I have of this little country church and the sweet sounds of an old organ and gospel songs.

In our little country town, much of our social life centered around the church. My mother once told me that I gave her a hard time about going to church. It was not that I didn't want to go; I did not want to dress up. I wanted to wear my overalls to church. Back then, men, women, and children all had Sunday church clothes. They would think it horrible to see people going to church in the casual clothes so common in today's world. We all had one Sunday outfit for winter and one Sunday outfit for summer—that was it. All women would be wearing hats.

My mother was always active in a lady's prayer group, and I thank God every day for my Christian heritage.

My parents, Isom "Ike" Rigell, Sr. and
Beatrice "Addie" Rigell.

JOBS

"If you like what you are doing, it ain't work."

I read that statement recently and reflected on my many jobs, from my first job at a very early age to my retirement at 68. Work was not a dirty word in the environment in which I grew up. II Thessalonians 3:10 was a reality. "If you don't work, you don't eat." It was that simple. There were no government social programs to entice one to avoid working.

In the 1930s, the challenge was finding work. It was not a time one could be selective and hold out for the most desirable job. One took any job available. One of the most devastating circumstances that a man can face is when he cannot provide for the basic needs of his family because of extended unemployment. I consider myself blessed that I never had to experience this situation.

My grandfather, Joe Rigell, instilled a strong work ethic in my life from a very early age. Next to my mother, my grandfather Rigell was the most influential person in my life, and I take comfort in saying this influence was all positive. My grandfather McCaskill died when I was 5 years old, so I did not have the opportunity to know him during my formative years. However, as I grew older, I learned to really appreciate him. He joined the Confederate army at age 15 and participated in a number of battles. He was a very devout man and the founder of a little Presbyterian church called Immanuel. He worked in the turpentine business and also had a farm.

My first paid job was at the local blacksmith shop. When I was around 8 or 9, I would often walk from my house down a dirt road to town. On the way was the village blacksmith's shop near the railroad track. The blacksmith was a good man named Fes Youmans. His shop was in an old building that in better days was a nice barn. It looked more like a junk yard, with a dirt floor and pieces of plows, wagon wheels, and old farm machinery parts scattered around the shop and property. Mr. Youman was also the local gunsmith, which provided much work in hunting season. Most gun owners considered their needs an emergency situation.

In one corner of the shop there was a forge, heated by coal and operated by the constant turning of hand crank bellows to provide enough oxygen to increase the temperature to the desired level. I was fascinated watching Mr. Youman turn the crank with one hand and try to keep the iron object in the center of the hot coals. When the iron was red hot and glowing, he would use a pair of tongs to remove the object from the fire and place it on the anvil. He would hammer the iron into the shape he wanted and, with sparks flying, thrust the hot iron into a tub of water to harden it, generating steam as it touched.

One busy day, he asked me if I wanted to turn the crank for the bellows. I answered, "Of course." I felt big, I felt like a man, and I felt important. I got on an old stool he placed by the crank and started cranking. I liked what I was doing, so I didn't consider it as work. For my services that day he gave me a dime, which in that period was a valuable coin. I'm sure I ran all the way home to show my mother my first payday.

It was not only the dime that thrilled me. It was a certain feeling that I had done something worthwhile and to the best of my ability. For some time after this, during busy times at the blacksmith's shop, I earned several dollars, a dime at a time. This was the first of many jobs I had as a teenager, and I am proud to say I never had to ask my mother for spending money. If you subscribe to the theory that "if you enjoy what you are doing, it ain't work," I never worked at the blacksmith's shop.

One other vivid memory I feel compelled to relate from my

time at the blacksmith's shop was a rather significant incident that occurred one day during the height of the dove hunting season. Dove shooting was serious business, not only for the enjoyment from a sports aspect, but because it provided a favorite dish on the table.

One of the prominent men in the church came in the shop very upset that his gun had malfunctioned in the middle of a big dove shoot. He wanted his gun fixed immediately, and he was using words that, in my young and innocent mind, I didn't think church people used. It was not uncommon to hear words like that, and it was in the daily vocabulary of many of the boys at school. It had a profound impact on me because I did not expect the language from a prominent church person.

As I get older, I often ponder why certain seemingly insignificant events stay in our memory when other, more significant events are erased. I believed it was etched in my memory that day that sometimes people respond and act according to the environment they are in.

This reminds me of a saying I picked up years later from my Uncle Gus Brown, one of the most interesting storytellers you would ever meet.

"You can never tell the depth of a well by the length of the handle on the pump!" he would say about judging other people. This is well-said, and there is much wisdom here. The true measure of a person is whether they are the same no matter the environment they are in.

The next job on my list was real work. I did not enjoy anything about it except getting paid. It was cotton picking by hand, no machinery, and I did it for the money.

During a short period in the summer months when the fields were snow white with cotton, the farmers wanted it picked immediately. They recruited all available help, from the very young to the very old, including boys, girls, men, and women, white and black. There were no itinerant workers available, so the work force was the local population. My sisters Mary Jo and Florence and I were among the workforce. Most of our cotton picking was for our neighbors, Frank Stewart and his wife. For our small town, they lived in what was considered a big, nice house across the street from us. Frank Steward owned a farm out in the country, where his sharecroppers worked the land. When cotton picking time came, Mr. Stewart would load all the kids he could pack in his car. He'd take us out to the farm early in the morning and pick us up in the late afternoon.

When we left home in the mornings, we had to be prepared to stay all day. We took a fruit jar full of water and a lunch, typically sandwiches of some kind, biscuits and jelly, sausage and biscuits, and maybe a sweet potato. The first thing you do when you get to the work site is find a good, shady spot—usually a thick bush—to store your water jug and lunch. Restroom facilities were plentiful, behind any big tree or thick bush. This met or exceeded all EPA rules at that time.

There were some advantages to getting an early start. The cotton would weigh a little more when it was still covered with dew. You were paid by the weight of cotton you picked—around fifty cents for a hundred pounds. I could pick about 150 pounds a day, depending on the thickness of the cotton on the stalk.

Each picker would go to the end of one row and come back on another row. Each pulled a tow sack, about fifteen inches in diameter, made of heavy, rugged cloth with a strap to go over your shoulder. As you picked, you put the cotton in the tow sack, and you dragged this sack along as you moved down the row. When the sack became heavy, you took it to the weigh station. This was either a cotton house on the edge of the field or, more likely, a cotton wagon conveniently located near the pickers. Your cotton would be weighed there and entered into a ledger. Pay day was when the farmer took his cotton to the gin, which was usually on Saturday. There were two cotton gins in our town, and on Saturdays there would be long lines of wagons and a few trucks lined up waiting their turn to be emptied. The wait was usually so long the mules would be unhitched and tied to a hitching post near the gin. We kept up with Mr. Stewart, and as soon as his cotton had been ginned, he would take the receipt and go across the street to the bank and receive his money.

Mr. Segrest, the man who owned the gin, also owned the bank. When Mr. Steward came out of the bank, he had already figured up how much each of us had picked and the exact change he needed to pay us. Of course, we had already figured this out, too, and had spent much time pouring over the Sears Roebuck catalog. Most of our new wealth was targeted for new "going back to school" clothes.

Picking cotton was work. I didn't enjoy it, but I'm glad I had that experience. I subscribe to the belief that there is something positive to be learned from every experience in life. My times in the cotton fields taught me that if you want something, you must work for it. The old adage is true. "There are no free lunches." And I learned the more consistent you are in your work, the more rewards await you. Another way to say it is, "The harder you work, the luckier you get."

Another one of my earliest jobs was that of a paperboy. As best as I can recall, my career as a paperboy lasted about two or three years. My first paper route was delivering *The Grit* when I was about 9 or 10 years old. This was a weekly paper and, if I remember correctly, it cost a nickel. I received a very small amount of money from this job, as the rewards were in the selling of enough papers to select an item from their little catalog. The catalog contained all the items a young boy would want but couldn't afford to buy, like a baseball, glove, knife, football, camera, flashlight, etc.

I think I was about 12 or 13 when I got the job delivering the No. 1 daily paper in our area, *The Montgomery Advertiser*. This paper route covered our entire town, including the black town, where I had three or four good customers, and I had to have a bicycle. (I'd delivered *The Grit* on foot, but my customers were primarily in my neighborhood). I would say when I started the delivery of *The Montgomery Advertiser,* there were no more than three or four bicycles in town, and it was a pretty big deal back then to own one. I bought one of these used bicycles. As stated above, my paper route took me all through the black town. I would like to make it clear that there was no concern for safety going through the black district—absolutely none.

I delivered the papers no matter how adverse the weather conditions. Paper boys then did not throw papers. You got off your bike, went up the steps, and placed the paper at the front door. The only thing I disliked about the paper delivery job was collecting the money at the end of the week. I learned a little bit about human behavior, and that was the better off people were, the harder it was to collect their money. Actually, my best paying customers were black.

It became harder and harder for me to keep my old bicycle in good running condition, so I decided I needed to buy a new bike. There were no bike stores in our town so the only source for items like this was a good old reliable Sears catalog—it had everything in it. The catalog had several pages of bikes, and I think I almost wore out the bicycle pages thumbing through them to make my big decision. The one I selected was not the most expensive, but to me it was a beauty. It had balloon tires, and that was a new feature. No one in town had a bike with balloon tires. All of my paper route was on dirt roads or dirt sidewalks, and the balloon tires were more suitable for dirt roads then the standard narrow tires.

I couldn't wait for my bike to come in. I think I waited about four days. Then I would try to go down to the railroad depot every afternoon to meet the train. It was with great anticipation that I stood waiting to see them roll that bike out of the Railway Express car onto the loading dock. This went on for several days, and I would sadly leave the dock, hoping the next day it would be there. I never could understand why it took so long, but finally it came!

I was a little disappointed in the way it arrived, however. I was looking for it to come in ready to ride. I would even leave my old bike at home every day and walk to the depot so I could ride the new bike home. Much to my chagrin though, it came in a wooden frame with the handle bars and pedals packed separately. It would require some work to remove the wooden frame and assemble the handlebars, basket, and pedals.

How was I going to get this thing home? I wondered. Then I got the answer: The big store where my mother worked was only about two blocks away. I knew the store had a grocery delivery wagon that would deliver my new bike.

I need to explain the delivery wagon. People with a telephone could call in to the store and leave their order, and it would be delivered by this delivery wagon, or you could walk in the store and make your purchases and get them delivered by the delivery wagon. It was pulled by a mule, and the driver was a black man named Dennis. Everyone in town knew and loved Dennis; he was a fixture in our little town. Sure enough, my mother called

Dennis, and he was very pleased to solve my problem.

Fortunately, I had all the tools and the know-how to unpack and assemble my bike. You can imagine how excited I was to take my first ride. Many of my friends came over to take a spin on my new bike. I was happy to accommodate them.

I almost forgot one interesting job I had in the banking business at a very young age. I need to give a little background on how I got this special job. I think I was about 9 or 10 at this time. My grandfather Rigell would frequently take me downtown with him. As I mentioned earlier, my grandfather was good friends with Charlie Segrest who owned the bank, the largest general store in town, as well as the cotton gin, the fertilizer plant, and farmland. When I went to town with my grandfather, he would often stop in the bank to do some business, or if Mr. Segrest was not busy, my grandfather would go in his office and visit.

On this occasion, Mr. Segrest was giving my grandfather a little walk through the bank to show him all the new remodeling, which included marble floors and marble counters. The bank was a small building with only one teller window. One man, Mr. Harry Harris, ran the bank, and he had only one helper, a young lady.

"We have got to get somebody in here once a week to polish the new marble floor and counter," Mr. Segrest said as he showed my grandfather around.

"Sonny boy, you can do that, can't you?" my grandfather immediately said.

"Yes, sir," was all I could say, so I was hired on the spot. I started my new job the next Friday afternoon after the bank closed.

Polishing the marble floor, which was not a large area, and polishing the counter were not a big deal, but cleaning the two spittoons by the teller window was. Back in that era most men either smoked or chewed tobacco, and some did both. Of course, when you chewed tobacco, you had to spit tobacco juice frequently, and public places provided spittoons for this purpose.

The bank had two nice brass spittoons conveniently located for their tobacco-chewing customers. The brass spittoons were about twelve inches in diameter and about five inches high with a brass cover that sloped down to about a four-inch hole in the center. The only problem was these tobacco juice spitters were not very accurate, so there was tobacco juice all over the floor around these spittoons, resulting in a very nasty situation to clean up. That particular part of this job was worse than picking cotton. I cannot recall exactly, but I know my career in the banking business did not last very long. I think I got busy with some other jobs and gave it up.

During my high school years I had a part-time job working in a store downtown. My good friend, Mr. J.T. Boyette, owned a store that sold a number of things: seed and feed, Philco radios, pecan shellers, and incubators for raising little chicks. Mr. Boyette was a good man, and I could not have been treated any better. I was the only employee at the store and many times Mr. Boyette would be out and I would run the store by myself. During the planting season we were real busy in the seed department.

The Philco radio was one of the top brands during this time, and we were the only dealer in town. All the radios were AM, which meant you had to tolerate a lot of static in bad weather. All radios, tabletop and console, were in a wooden case and treated as a piece of furniture. There was no electricity out in the rural areas, so the radios we sold to the farmers had to be battery operated. We had a battery charging operation to support these radios. The owners had to have two batteries, one to keep the radio operating while the other was being charged.

While I am on the subject of radios, I should mention that during this period, when I was not busy in the store, I built our first radio. I ordered a kit from a catalog and mounted these components on a small board. It was crude and did not resemble a radio, but it worked beautifully. I had fun when some of my customers came in and thought they were listening to one of those fine Philco radios; I pointed out my crude contraption was the source of the beautiful music and they could hardly believe it. I proudly took my "beautiful treasure" home and placed it on the mantel over the fireplace. That is the only radio we had, and it was working when I left to go to the Marines.

We had a pecan sheller in the back of the store. Mr. Boyette would buy the pecans from the local people, process the pecans through the sheller, and sell the shelled pecans to a wholesale dealer in the nearby town of Dothan. This was a pretty good moneymaker.

Another part of the business were the incubators for raising the small chicks. This was a pretty good business. We not only sold the baby chicks to the local townspeople and the farmers, but we shipped a lot of them. There were special boxes made for this purpose.

I need to say I learned how to play checkers while working for Mr. Boyette. You could always find a checker game underway on the sidewalk on the main street in town. All the storefronts on Main Street had a wide covered sidewalk, and we were no exception. Mr. Boyette was a good checker player, and when we were not busy he wanted a checker game with me. At first I really didn't want to play checkers, but since he was the boss, I agreed.

The more I played, the better I liked it and the better I got. It wasn't too long before I began to win some games, and the more I played, the more games I won. Word soon got around that I was a pretty good checker player, and more and more of the good checker players in town would come over to challenge me. Eventually I was considered one of the best, and maybe *the* best, player in town. I do not intend to be bragging here, but that is just the way it was.

I didn't play checkers after I left for the Marines except on the ship going to Iwo Jima, and I really don't remember that. After the war, Buck Horton, a sailor on the boat, got in touch with me. He commented on how I'd beat everyone at checkers. I told Buck I didn't remember playing checkers on the boat to Iwo Jima, and I still don't. I will be talking more about Buck later.

The store Grandpa Rigell and my father
owned in Slocomb, Alabama.

THE GREAT DEPRESSION

I read where the Great Depression was one of the most studied periods in the history of our country. If you would like to know the cause, just ask the experts, either an economist or a professor. You will receive a different answer from each of the esteemed experts. If you would like to know how long the Depression lasted, again ask the experts, and you will receive a different time. I will not bore you with my expert opinion on these questions. You can decide which expert you choose to believe. I'll just stick to the story of how the Depression affected me and the environment in which I lived.

Herbert Hoover was elected President in 1928, and since he was president in 1929 when the stock market crashed, he was given credit for our economic disaster. But I believe this event would have occurred no matter who was president. In my view, no one event triggered this problem. Rather, several things had been building up, and they all came together at the right time for the bubble to burst.

We had been living above our means in the Roaring '20s. Investors were investing big time, and most of it on margins, so when the crash came, they not only lost their fortune. They were deeply in debt.

Some economists talk about the gold standard being a factor, but I do not know enough about that to form an opinion.

President Hoover did sponsor some government intervention like tariffs, which made things even worse. People thought Franklin Roosevelt had all the answers, so in 1932, he was elected president.

Roosevelt sponsored several programs to get the economy back on track, but the Supreme Court ruled some of these unconstitutional. Probably the largest was the Works Progress Administration (WPA). This plan was to put men to work in all kinds of projects, some very worthwhile and some a total waste of money. The Tennessee Valley Authority was one of the good programs. Cleaning out a ditch in front of our house, which I'll describe later on, was a waste of money.

Another Roosevelt program was the Civilian Conservation Corps (CCC). I was a little more familiar with this program, as several of my friends joined. This program was for unemployed men between the ages of 17 to 28. The CCC fed, clothed, and housed them. It employed them mostly in unskilled labor jobs, like planting trees and building trails, lodges, and shelters in national parks. Many of these structures are still standing. They received a small salary—about $40 a month—and most of that had to be sent home. At the height of this program, there were several hundred thousand young men in the CCC.

I was 6 years old when the stock market crashed in October 1929. I think that you would not expect me to be sensitive to the fact that many people woke up that morning rich and went to bed deeply in debt. There were reports—and probably some exaggerations—on the number of investors that got wiped out financially and jumped out of tall buildings in New York and other large cities. One joke of the day, though a little morbid, was that when a man would check into the hotel, the clerk would ask, "Do you want a room to sleep or jump?"

I said that I would not comment on why the Depression lasted so long, but I changed my mind. I have some thoughts that are valid, so I want to express them. It lasted because of continued government intervention both by Hoover and Roosevelt, and it only ended when we mobilized for WWII.

It proves the old axiom that what we learn from history is that we don't learn from history. President Obama followed the same mistakes as Roosevelt. He raised taxes and ran up the national debt by spending enormous sums on worthless projects.

Good intentions don't always end in positive results. For example, President Obama got his docile subjects in Congress to pass a more than $800 million stimulus bill. It was a total disaster. It did nothing for the economy and increased our national debt by almost $1 billion.

If you don't think that was a repeat of history, listen to this. President Roosevelt's close friend and Secretary of the Treasury Henry Morgenthau made these statements to Congress in 1937: "We have tried spending money. We are spending more than we have ever spent before, and it does not work. And I have just one interest, and if I am wrong . . . somebody else can have my job. I want to see this country prosperous. I want to see people get a job. I want to see people get enough to eat. We have never made good on our promises. I say after eight years of this administration we have just as much unemployment as when we started and an enormous debt to boot!"

Just think of the significance of these honest words eight years after the Wall Street crash, after an enormous amount of taxpayer dollars were poured into projects that were supposed to jumpstart the economy. The man in charge is agonizing over real people without a job and without enough to eat. From 1932 to 1936, federal spending skyrocketed 77 percent and the national debt rose by 73 percent. The top tax rates tripled, but that did not resolve the problem.

In my opinion, Roosevelt, on the domestic side, was a total failure. He listened to too much bad advice. On the foreign policy side, and when it came to the war, I would give him an A. He did, however, make one serious mistake in the Pacific concerning Gen. Douglas MacArthur, which I'll discuss later.

During the 1930s, the country was strongly isolationist. But Roosevelt saw early on the dangers of Hitler's ultimate intentions and tried to warn and prepare us to deal with this menace. The 1941 Lend-Lease Act to save Great Britain was smart and timely. This provided US military aid to foreign nations during the war.

As an added note, the South was predominantly made up of Democrats who thought Roosevelt could do no wrong. But I need to say there is no similarity between the far-far left Democratic Party today and the Democratic Party of that era.

I have no memory of one day living with plenty and the next

day having nothing. Maybe we were like the people in some of the old country songs about the Depression:

Somebody told us Wall Street fell
But we were so poor that we couldn't tell
The cotton was short but the weeds were tall
But Mr. Roosevelt's a-gonna save us all
Another old country song from that era went like this:
Five cent cotton and forty cent meat
How in the hell can a poor man eat

Fortunately, and by the grace of God, I lived in a decent house, and we always enjoyed tasty food. I didn't have many clothes, but the ones I owned were good. What money we had went for necessities; "discretionary funds" was not in our vocabulary.

My entire growing up years, from age 6 to 18 when I left home to join the Marines, were lived in the Great Depression. I had no reference of living in so-called "good times" that I could compare it to. The environment I was living in was perfectly normal. On a happy occasion when you had a spare nickel to splurge and buy an ice cream cone, you had to agonize and make a big decision. What ice cream flavor are you going to select? Believe me. This was real.

In my mind, the Great Depression dispels the myth of today that if you grow up in poverty, you are a victim and not responsible for some criminal act you may commit and that it is society's fault and no fault of your own. Some idiots tried to make excuses for the terrorists who carried out the attacks of September 11, 2001 because they grew up in a poor environment. The truth was that most of them came from upper-middle class families. Their ideologies were poor, but economically, they were not poor. Based on that kind of thinking, my generation would be known as the "worst criminal generation" rather than the "Greatest Generation."

Compared to our society today, we were literally crime-free. People left their car keys in the car, and in my 18 years in Slocomb, I don't recall hearing of one stolen. Nor can I recall an armed robbery. Many people never locked their doors at night, and no one thought about locking their doors when they left home in the daytime. We did lock our doors at night. However, with five outside doors to our home, I am sure we sometimes forgot at least one. House break-ins were something you just did not worry about.

I recall only one murder in our small town in all my growing up years. This murder was never solved, and people talked and speculated about it for years. Maybe the reason it went unsolved is because our law enforcement did not have much practice in solving murders.

In any society, there will always be some petty thievery occurring. About the only business our little jail in Slocomb had was some guy having a little too much moonshine in public and maybe engaging in a fist fight with another moonshine partaker. We had no drug dealers, and young blacks in jail were almost unheard of. In our small town, we would read about gangsters on the national scene, like Dillinger, Bonnie and Clyde, and Baby Face Nelson who were robbing banks and shooting law enforcement. But that was not because they were poor and hungry; they were just plain gangsters.

Like a hurricane sweeping through your area, the Great Depression left its physical and psychological mark on our culture. Marriages, childbirths, and divorces were down. College enrollment and school spending were down. People used home remedies and nonprescription medicine rather than visit doctors, all due to lack of money.

Forty percent of all farms in Mississippi were on the auction block. The interesting thing here is that the good neighbors of these unfortunate farmers would not bid on these farms because they did not want to take advantage of them.

There were very few government relief programs at this time and no unemployment payments. In 1932, only one in four needy families received any government relief. The people hardest hit were those who lost their homes and farms and the unemployed who rented. This group had nowhere to go, and they ended up in shantytowns called Hoovervilles, crude shelters made of cardboard, scrap lumber, and tin. The sanitation situation in these shantytowns was deplorable; it is the same situation we see today in refugee camps in the Middle East.

When the stock market crashed, we had two small banks in our town. One closed and never reopened. The other bank managed somehow to stay open. Nationwide, stores and many businesses, small and large, closed. Many farmers could not pay their debts and lost their farms. Fortunately, our home was paid for, so this was not a problem for us.

During this period, unemployment at times reached 25 percent. Men were desperately trying to find work of any kind. We would read and see pictures in the newspapers of soup and bread lines as long as two city blocks. These lines were not made up of bums. They were well respected middle and upper-class citizens.

To put this in perspective, a loaf of bread cost a nickel. Just imagine if you are hungry and did not even have enough money to buy a loaf of bread.

An observation that sticks in my mind that illustrates the severity of the Great Depression was when I came home from school one afternoon and saw about a dozen men across the street from our house with picks and shovels cleaning out a ditch that did not need cleaning out. As I looked closely, almost in disbelief, I recognized one of the men was the father of one of my good friends who just a few days earlier was the owner of a prominent business in our town. It was now closed. He was a sharply dressed man in coat, tie, and hat. As he worked, he was still wearing his hat and his white shirt and nice pants. People had to swallow their pride and do anything to help feed their family. None of the people were looking for a free handout. They were just looking to survive.

As I have mentioned earlier, during the summer and before my grandfather Rigell closed his livery stable, he would often take me to town with him. Here is a typical day. His place was popular for men, farmers, and townspeople to get together, to chew tobacco and spit, take out their pocketknives and whittle on some wood, and talk. They would be sitting around several old chairs and some old wooden nail kegs.

I would sit there silently and listen. I was between 8 and 11 years old and did not understand much of what they were talking about, which was predominantly "hard times." I had no frame of reference for what life was like in "good times." These men had clear memories of when they had respectable jobs and money in their pockets. Some of them probably had owned a nice home or a farm. I don't recall much about their conversations, except for one little story with a little humor to it.

It went like this:

Sam: "Times are getting better now."

Homer: "Sam, how come you say that?"

Sam: "I saw a rabbit run across the road, and there were only five men chasing it. Used to, you would see about a dozen men chasing that rabbit."

One of our family friends, Mr. Bronson, had a truck with a large stake body, and for several years during the citrus season in Florida he would haul about a dozen unemployed men to the citrus area of Florida to pick fruit. He then hauled the citrus from the groves to the packing house. I had never heard of this small town prior to this, but the packing house was in Mims, Florida. I never dreamed years later I would be a proud and happy citizen of Mims, Florida. Mims in that era had two of the largest citrus packing plants in the state.

In today's world, unemployed, able-bodied men would never do this fruit picking job. That would be beneath their dignity. Government handouts would be more lucrative than fruit-picking. The "Greatest Generation" had more pride than to take a government handout when work, no matter what type, was available. It's sad we don't have more people thinking like that today.

Although they were older than me, I knew several of the guys in this fruit picking program. As I mentioned above, Mr. Bronson was a friend of our family, and he would bring these guys home to Slocomb for a few days during Christmas. He also brought oranges, grapefruit, and tangerines that he passed out free to his close friends, including us. This was a real treat for us at Christmas because this was the only time we would have citrus fruit. Even if you could afford to buy the fruit, it was not available in our local market.

There was an interesting result caused by the Great Depression that I have never seen addressed. Maybe this is just my own theory. It has to do with the effect on wildlife. Almost all men and boys were hunters and fishermen, not only for the sport, but to put another dish on the table. I went hunting many times for dove, quail, and squirrels with one of our boarders, Mr. Herschel Lindsey, who was our high school math teacher and a great hunter. I do not know if we had endangered species programs back then, but if we did, I think squirrels would have been on it. We did not hunt deer because there were none in our area. The last time I visited my old hometown, squirrels were running all around in the neighborhoods, and deer had made a tremendous comeback. I would predict if we had another Great Depression, these squirrels and deer would quickly be consumed.

I cannot emphasize enough how important hunting and fishing were to our society during the Great Depression—not only from the sporting aspect but also in terms of adding a wholesome variety to our dinner table. Unless some member of the family or friends went fishing, we had no seafood. It was not available in our small market. Other than fresh fish, our only source of seafood was canned salmon and tuna, so fresh fish was a precious commodity. No fish that we caught was too small for the frying pan, and "catch and release" was not in our vocabulary; we lived by "catch and eat."

I must modify slightly my statement that "we could not buy fresh seafood;" the exception was oyster season and, to us, any month with an *R* was oyster season. We looked forward to oyster season, when my friend T. E. Hall would open his oyster shack and serve super fresh oysters from Apalachicola Bay, 15 cents a dozen, along with an RC Cola. What a treat!

It was common to hunt possums and raccoons, and if you killed more than you wanted, you could take them to the black town and quickly sell them for twenty-five to fifty cents. Nothing was wasted. People ate a lot of biscuits and made their own bread, and they bought flour in twenty-five and fifty-pound cloth sacks. Women made underwear out of these cheap cloth sacks. You had to be careful here, as one flour brand had this written on the sack: "World's Best—Best by test."

I believe this era did make our generation stronger. I believe the circumstances that we were in made our family stronger, and the stronger the family, the stronger the nation. I'm speaking of black families and white families.

We all depended more on our families and friends to survive than we did the government. I can say this with authority: In the environment in which I lived, there was no need to depend on the government. We had no soup kitchens, no bread lines, no government-sponsored school luncheons. In fact, we had no school cafeteria. I don't know what the situation was in larger towns.

We enjoyed some significant advantages over city people. Most people in our town had a large garden like we did, and most of them, also like us, had chickens. My grandfather Rigell always kept one or more good milk cows in his barn behind his house. That was the source of our milk, and at times I was the one to churn the milk into butter.

I think one positive trait of my generation is that we were not a bunch of whiners. In fact, I think my generation was more stable in many respects than today's generation even though there is no comparison in material wealth. On a physical standard of living comparison, people today on welfare live far better than the upper middle-class of the 1930s. But are they any happier? My observation is they are not nearly as happy. In fact, I would say there are many more dysfunctional families today than when I was growing up.

One of the positive traits I acquired during this era was if you want something, you've got to work for it. I can never thank my grandfather enough for instilling in me that hard work is a virtue. I cleaned spittoons, picked cotton, cleaned up baby chick poop, delivered newspapers, rain or shine, along with some other odd jobs, but it was worth it, and I enjoyed the fruits of my labors.

BARTERING

During the Great Depression, the unemployment rate reached 25 percent, which means many people did not always have enough cash to purchase their basic needs. To help overcome this problem, people would resort to bartering at every opportunity.

Here is a good example of bartering. My grandfather Rigell was a professional trader in his later days. He would trade livestock for a truckload of corn. My grandfather, his hired hand, and I would shuck the corn and put it through a corn sheller, a device that separated the corn kernels from the cob. The sheller was operated by turning a hand crank, which was my job. The corn would drop down into a container, and we would empty the container into cloth bags. We would then load the corn on the truck and take the corn to a grist mill to be ground into meal. There was a water wheel grist mill on a little creek a few miles from Slocomb. My grandfather would then pay for the grinding by giving the miller a part of the meal.

The best part of this project was getting to head out on a route my grandfather had selected to sell the meal. We would visit a number of small towns and some country stores north of Slocomb. My grandfather, always as far back as I can remember, had a late model truck, but he never did drive. He had a regular hired man to drive so there would be three of us in the truck, me in the middle with the gear shift lever between my legs. I had to move my legs for the driver to change gears. This was before automatic gear shifts were on the scene. There was also no A/C back in those days, but I don't recall that being a problem. With the windows down, we got plenty of fresh air.

I always looked forward to these trips. It was really a big deal for me just riding in a vehicle all day, and having lunch on these trips was truly something I looked forward to. We always ate in some little country store, and I had to make some big decisions.

For drinks, I had a choice of a Nehi soda—orange, strawberry, or grape—or a Coca-Cola. Since a Nehi was in a larger bottle than a Coca-Cola, I had to pass and just decide on flavor of drink. Lunch would be a can of Vienna sausage, a can of potted meat, or maybe a can of sardines and some cheese and crackers. We would share a big slice of cheese cut from a big block of cheese mounted on a turntable, with a special movable knife to cut any size piece you wanted. My grandfather would pay the country store a certain amount of meal for our lunch.

I have since enjoyed some great meals in a number of four- and five-star restaurants all over the world, but I can truthfully say I have never enjoyed a dinner better than I enjoyed those meals in those country stores. It sure would be nice if I could relive a day like this. It reminds me of a saying I heard one time, "I grew up in the Great Depression, but I was never depressed."

Here is another example of bartering. The largest grocery store in my town—the store where my mother worked—had two Rolling Stores. A Rolling Store was similar to a FedEx vehicle, with an aisle down the center and shelves on either side stocked with the basic needs of the farmers. On the back of the vehicle was a small porch with a chicken coop on one side and a fifty-five gallon drum of kerosene on the other side. There was no electricity in the countryside at this time, so all farmers needed kerosene for their lamps. The Rolling Store had a regular schedule like a school bus, and people would be waiting at the side of the road with their chickens and eggs to exchange for their purchases.

I was a good friend of one of those drivers, and I made trips with him occasionally. I did it for the fun; there was no pay for this. At one stop he delivered a couple of hundred-pound bags of sugar to a guy. I commented that he sure did use a lot of sugar. My friend laughed and said he was one of the biggest bootleggers around there and added that he had two or three more good customers like that. I would add here everyone knew who the bootleggers were, but catching them in action was a very difficult job. We lived in what we called a "dry county," which means all alcoholic drinks were illegal. This was a good thing for the bootleggers, and they thrived.

A little more on bartering: The larger grocery stores in town had chicken houses in the back. People would bring their chickens in to exchange for their purchases. A commercial chicken truck would come by about once a week and buy the chickens from the store. Occasionally, in the transfer of the chickens from the chicken house to the truck, a chicken would escape. The workers never bothered to chase the escaped chicken, so little kids would hang out around there, catch it, and go in the store and barter the chicken for candy.

HOG KILLING

One big event that I always looked forward to in my early years was when my grandfather would announce the day for hog killing. This was an exciting time for us children as well as the neighbors, as everyone in the immediate neighborhood would be involved in this activity. It was truly a festive time, right after the first cold snap came through (now you would probably refer to a cold snap as a cold wave). My grandfather always had livestock around: hogs, cattle, horses, and even occasionally a Billy goat.

Several hogs would be butchered on hog killing day. One hog at a time would be brought out of the hog pen, and someone would shoot the pig between the eyes with a .22 caliber rifle. The hog's throat would then be cut to drain the blood, and the pig would be hung up on an "A" frame (the "A" frame was just like the frame you see on a playground for swings). They would pour scalding water on the pig to make it easier to take the hide off. Then the hog would be butchered. You would end up with hams, pork chops, bacon, and the meat for making sausages. The intestines of the pig would be used for two things: first as casings for the sausage and then to make chitlins. Many people like these chitlins, but I never had a taste for them. Very little of the pig was wasted; they even used the meat scraps to make something called souse. Souse looked like some of the cold cuts you see in the deli.

My grandfather had a smokehouse in his backyard, and some of the meat would be placed in the smokehouse. We always had plenty of bacon, pork chops, and ham. In that era no one had a home freezer. There was an ice house in town, and the ice house had freezer lockers that you could rent and store your meat. At home, we kept food cold with a block of ice in the refrigerator. You had to replenish the ice every day. That was accomplished by buying a block of ice from the "ice truck" that came by every morning. The ice truck had 300-pound blocks of ice, and the iceman, using an ice pick, would chip off any size block of ice that you wanted. As I recall, a twenty-five cent block of ice would fill up the ice compartment in our refrigerator. That would be sufficient for keeping the food cool and having enough ice for iced tea.

While I am on the subject of hogs, I will document my experience in the livestock market place. We had a large, fenced-in backyard, and in the back part of the lot I had a pig pen where I always had at least one pig. My grandfather was in the livestock business, so I got a little pig from him every year. He would sell me the little old pig for usually about fifty cents. I wondered then why he did not just give me the pig. At the time, I could not understand his reasoning for selling me the pig. Now, I understand. He was teaching me that there are no "free lunches."

I fed the pig mostly scraps from the table. Since we had boarders, we always had plenty of food on the table, so the leftovers went to my pig. I would raise the little pig until he got large enough to take to the market and sell it. My grandfather taught me how to read the commodities in the newspaper, so I would really follow that information when it was time to sell my pig. My grandfather also taught me how to judge the weight of livestock so I could make a good guess on the weight of my pig and have a pretty good estimate of how much my pig was worth.

DOVE HUNTING

This story is about how I received my undeserved reputation as a super dove hunter. From 12 years old until I left home for the Marines, dove hunting was one of my favorite sports. I was a pretty good shot, but I had a much better reputation than I actually deserved.

A little background is necessary as to how my excellent reputation came about. One of my favorite dove hunting locations was on the edge of town along a ditch where the runoff came from the "salty brine" of the cucumber pickling plant. The cucumber pickling plant was an open structure with the floor about 10 feet off the ground and up near the top of the pickling vats.

There were about 15 to 20 of these wooden vats; they were circular and about 10 feet in diameter and about 12 feet deep. The structure was open, essentially just a roof and a floor with a small office and a large room filled with tons of salt. The vats were filled with a very salty brine. The fresh cucumbers were dumped into the brine and they soaked there for many days until they were loaded into railroad tank cars, which were on a railroad spur line adjacent to the pickling plant. The opening on top of the tank car was at about the same level as the floor of the pickling plant.

If you observed how these cucumbers were transferred from the vats to the tank car, you might lose your appetite for pickles. The workers, black and white, would roll up their pants to their knees, and, barefooted, they would stand on an adjustable platform in the vat, and the brine with the floating cucumbers was all around their feet, up to their knees. At the end of the day they would come out with very clean feet, as they had been soaking all day in that brine. They would dip the floating cucumbers in a net just like a shrimp and then dump the cucumbers into a wheelbarrow, which they moved over a temporary platform to the top of the tank. Then they dumped them into the tank car, which was loaded with fresh, salty brine.

When the vats were empty, they opened a valve at the bottom of each vat and let the salty brine run down the ditch I mentioned above. A present-day EPA guru would have a heart attack if he or she observed something like this.

Late in the afternoon, the doves would come in from the nearby fields to feed along this ditch. Many days during the dove hunting season when I could accumulate the 15 cents needed to buy five shells for my .410, I would head for this location. I never considered the danger then, but many days there would be several shooters very close together, and due to the high weeds in that location you could not see the other guys. One day I was down there with my five shells, and apparently divine providence was smiling on me, because in a brief time I hit five doves. Hard to believe because doves in flight are not easy to hit.

When I expended my last shell, I came out and ran into one of my friends, Mr. Red Sullivan, a local merchant. He said, "Ike, who is in there with you?" I said, "Nobody, I was by myself." He said, "You mean, you knocked all those birds down, and you didn't miss a shot?" I said, "Yes, there was nobody in there but me." Mr. Sullivan spread the word that I never missed. Fortunately, he wasn't there the days I shot five times and maybe only got one or two birds.

SCHOOL DAYS

I have many good memories of my schooldays in Slocomb. The Slocomb School Complex was located on my street, just one block away. My aunt Etta Justice's house was adjacent to the schoolyard, and my grandparents Rigell's house was right across the street from Aunt Etta's, so I passed them on my way to school.

The School Complex consisted of three buildings: a nice brick grammar school (grades one through six) and the junior high (grades seven through nine) and the high school (grades ten through twelve) next to it in the same building. The third building was a wooden structure, which housed vocational type courses: home economics courses for the girls and agricultural and shop activities for the boys. None of these buildings had air conditioning, but I do not recall that being a problem. In the hot weather, we just opened all the windows; in the winter, we had a big coal burning stove in the corner of the room.

One school principal was head of all of the grades, and he did this job without a secretary. Some of the senior students would be assigned to help in the principal's office. All the facilities were serviced by one janitor, a black man named James.

In my school, the average class size was forty to forty-five students, which means we had a total in all grades of approximately 500 students. Just think, one principle, no secretary, and no teacher assistants, and we had one coach for all athletic programs. Compare that to today's school system, with several more principals and assistant principals; many more teachers and teacher's assistants; assistants for the assistants; counselors, truant officers and security officers.

Back to James. Everyone, including students and teachers, loved James and, whenever practical, the students would assist James by sweeping the floors and starting fires in the furnaces on cold winter mornings. James lived about a block from the schoolhouse in the middle of a white neighborhood which, though unusual, was not a problem.

Most of the teachers were women, and in this era all teachers were among the highest respected people in the community, especially in small towns. In our town, which I think would be typical, the teachers were the only people in town with a college education other than the doctor and pharmacists. They also could count on a paycheck every month, which during the Great Depression was something many people were deeply concerned about.

I enjoyed all of my school years from the first grade through the twelfth grade. I think we all looked forward to the end of the school year and the summer vacation, but we were all very excited and eager to start the next school year. We lived only one block from our school so that at noon we could come home for our dinner—the big meal of the day in that era. We called our evening meal supper, and it was usually leftovers from dinner.

Even during the height of the Great Depression, we always had plenty of good food on the table. That was for a couple of reasons. One, we had our super good cook, Johnnie Mae. Secondly, we always had at least two teachers board in with us, plus two or three more for dinner during the school year. So we had to maintain our reputation for serving plenty of good food with the teachers.

I have fond memories of my Granny Rigell waiting on her front porch for me after school in my early school years. She always wanted to know how my day went, and she would take me back to the kitchen for some goodies: a biscuit and jelly, a biscuit and honey, a piece of pie, or maybe a piece of fried chicken. All of my Rigell cousins always said I was Granny Rigell's "favorite grandchild." Maybe so, I don't know. My thoughts are that if I was special in her sight, it was because I was the son of the boy (my father) she lost at such an early age.

The following scene is so real in my mind today, and I recall it with great sadness but also as a precious memory. When Granny Rigell was in her last moments, I was told that she wanted to speak with me. I went to her house and went to her bedside. She squeezed my hand faintly and said, "Be a good boy." Those were the last words she spoke to me, and a very short time later she went home to Jesus.

Grandfather Rigell was my father figure; I cannot say that strongly enough. Most of the time he wore a coat and a vest, and in his vest pocket he always had a small notebook and a stubby pencil. My grandfather called me "sonny boy."

"Sonny boy, come over here, I want to give you a little problem to work," he would say, and I knew what was coming. He would hand me the notepad and the pencil.

The complexity of the problem, of course, would vary with my level of schooling at that time. The problems he would give me to solve would be practical ones that I could relate to at a young age. I did not realize it, but I was absorbing the things I learned in school that have a real application in daily life.

A typical problem would go like this: "I sell you a pig for fifty cents. You raise the pig until he weighs 150 pounds, and you sell him for five cents a pound. You have spent $1.75 for feed. How much money did you make?"

This was a real-life example.

My grandfather was a no-nonsense man. One day when I was about 7 or 8 years old, my mother sent me to my grandfather's barn behind his house to get a load of cow manure in my little red wagon.

"Sonny boy, what are you going to do with this cow manure?" my grandfather said when he saw me.

"My mother is going to put it on her flowers," I replied.

"I know. Attie (my mother) and Etta (his daughter who lived across the street from my grandfather) are always working with them old 'furns' (ferns) and ought to be planting something to eat," my grandfather said.

We all had big vegetable gardens, but my mother and Aunt Etta were also big flower ladies.

Slocomb was in a very rural area and had the only local high school. There were several elementary and junior high country schools in the surrounding areas that would bus their students to our high school after these students completed the ninth grade. These country schools were all the same design: wooden structure, outdoor toilets, no auditoriums, and the only athletic facility was an outdoor basketball court.

Little leagues in football and baseball were unheard of in those days, with the exception of the American Legion baseball team. We had only this one baseball team in our town, so we had to go to surrounding towns to play. The American Legion people would provide the transportation. Riding in a car to another town was a big deal, not only because we would get to ride in a car there, but also because we would get a cold drink after the game. One Hartford player, Early Wynn, went on to be a Major League Baseball star.

Basketball, though, was the primary sport in the surrounding schools. They played basketball year-round and maintained very serious competition among these many rural schools. Once a year they would come to our high school gymnasium for their yearly basketball tournament. The enthusiasm these people would bring to our town would rival the Super Bowl. This tournament would last a couple of days, and the fans would pack our gym with standing room only.

Every year, our Boy Scouts of America troop would set up a couple of tables in the school hallway just outside the gym and sell hotdogs and RC Colas. Our Scoutmaster during this period was also our school principal. We had no restaurants in our town, so we Scouts were the answer to some very hungry folks. We raised enough money at this event to send us to a Panama City Beach campground for several days during the summer.

At the beginning of every school year, our coach would eagerly look over the crop of potential basketball and football players from these rural schools who were enrolling for the first time in our tenth grade class. I need to explain something here. All these guys were seasoned basketball players, but almost none of them had ever seen a football or a football game. Our coach was looking for raw athletic potential with the hope he could entice them to try out for the football team.

Here is a good example of that. A student from one of the rural schools already had a reputation as a super basketball player, even before he enrolled in our high school. There was no question he would be a starter on the basketball team, but he had never seen a football game, knew nothing about football, and had never had a football in his hand. This boy's name was Howell "Red" Swan, and he entered the tenth grade at Slocomb High the same year I did.

When I was in the ninth grade, we got a new football and basketball coach. His name was Cleveland Bridges, and this was his first year of coaching. In the small schools, like Slocomb, there would be only one coach for all sports. The coach also had to teach a couple of classes, usually some easy courses like Social Sciences. Toward the end of my ninth grade year, Coach Bridges came up to me in the hallway one day and asked me if I planned to go out for football next year.

That was an easy question for me to answer, as I had been waiting and dreaming of this for several years. "Yes, sir," I said.

I was flattered that he talked to me about this. We had no junior varsity in those days, but us guys would get together and choose up teams and play tackle football during our recreational period. At times, Coach Bridges would come out and watch us play. Of course, he was scouting for potential prospects.

When the next school year began, the day I had been eagerly waiting for arrived, and I was there on the first day of practice for the football team. Football teams were different back then. High school, college, and professional football players were much smaller. In high school, I weighed 145 pounds, and there were plenty of high school and college players my size. In fact, when I was at Georgia Tech one year, we had a national championship team, and several players were under 200 pounds. One of the star players was 135 pounds.

The year I went out for the team, 1939, happened to be the same year the school got new uniforms, including new helmets. What a change! The pants of the old uniforms were a canvas type material, and the hip pads were built into the pants. The new pants were made of a slick rayon type material, and the hip pads, like today, were separate. The old helmets were soft leather with some padding. The new helmets were the hard plastic type like we see today, although we did not have the face guards, so getting a bloody nose or black eye was not uncommon.

One of the most anxious times in my young life was when Coach Bridges called the team together not long before the first game to pass out the new uniforms. The anxiety was based on the fact that the school could only afford to buy fifteen new uniforms, and there were twenty-two of us on the squad. Coach Bridges made my day when he called my name for one of the new uniforms. My jersey number was fifty-four. I have never forgotten that number. In fact, when I watch a game today, I pull for fifty-four on both teams. Back then, your jersey number did not indicate your position.

Just think about it. We had one coach. He had to cover every position, and he was dealing every year with several new players who had never seen a football game. Today, high schools typically have coaches for every position and their new players usually have a background of several years in organized leagues with good coaching. But one thing is common with most players from all eras, they love the game.

I want to go back for a moment to Red Swan. He was a natural born athlete and he was eager to play football, although, as mentioned earlier, he knew nothing about the game. At one of our first practice sessions, Coach was looking for a new punter to replace the one who had graduated. Coach handed Red the football and told him to kick it. Red took the football and held it 90 degrees from the normal position and kicked it. Of course, it did not go very far. Coach now had to do a little basic coaching. He gently told Red he was holding the ball the wrong way. When Red and I graduated three years later, I am sure he could have played college football, basketball, and baseball.

In a small school, in a small town, being on the football team is a big deal, and of course all the guys enjoyed the attention that it brought. But we also just liked the game. Coach waited till the day of the first game to announce the first-string players. For some, like the guys who were on the team the previous year, it was obvious they would be on the first string. But there were several positions where there was a real question.

When the coach called out the names for the first-string team, I was greatly disappointed. I thought from our practice sessions I had a good chance to make the first team. I want to point out that in small schools like Slocomb, where you only had sixty or seventy guys in high school, you had to scrape the bottom of the barrel to field two teams. In those days, you did not have an offensive and defensive team. You played the eleven best players both ways.

Fortunately, I did not have to wait long before I got some action. Coach Bridges sent me in during the first game to replace one of our guys. At that moment, we were on defense. My position was halfback, which in today's world would be a running back on offense and a defensive cornerback. I had only been in the game a couple of plays when I had the opportunity to make one of the best tackles that I ever made in the three years I played football.

One of their running backs was making an end run. I was the only one facing him, so I had to make an open field tackle. It was just me and him. I still remember that moment. To say I was excited would be an understatement. I lowered my shoulders and met him head on. The timing was just right. I lifted his feet up in the air, and he landed ka-punk! From that time on, I played every minute of every game for the next three years. I have good memories of those high school football days.

Basketball was a different story. Let me say you did not have to be seven feet tall in those days to play basketball in high school and college. Naturally, the boys coming in from these rural junior high schools dominated our basketball squad, because they played basketball year-round. I went out for basketball and made the squad. I never made the first team and never expected to, but the first-team guys needed some players to practice and I was one of them. I enjoyed practicing with these guys, and occasionally I would get to play a few minutes in a regular game.

I enjoyed my school years. In a small town, much of your social and everyday life center on your school activities. However, we did not have yearbooks in those days, and that would've been nice. We did not have a senior prom. I'm not sure this is a bad thing, though. I think in today's world it is much overdone.

I don't recall being worried, but in the spring of 1941 when I graduated from high school, I faced the same daunting questions that thousands of eighteen-year-olds were facing at that time: "Now what?" Like most of the others, my options were limited. The Great Depression of the 1930s was still hanging on. The economy had improved in the last decade, but the unemployment rate was still in the 12 to 14 percent range.

In our rural area, there were very limited opportunities for full-time employment. Community colleges did not exist anywhere in our area. For financial reasons, attending college did not seem like a viable option. Coach Bridges, offered to try to get me and my friend, Red Swan, scholarships at his alma mater, Birmingham Southern, a small school in Birmingham, Alabama, which today is known as the much larger Samford University. I could try out for baseball and football, and Red, I am sure, could have made it in baseball, football, and basketball. Even with scholarship help, I did not see how I could go to college, since I had absolutely no money.

About a month before graduation, one of my best friends, Horace "Gator" Jones, and I were spending the afternoon in Dothan, Alabama. Dothan, population 16,000, was the largest town in our area. As we walked past the Dothan Post Office, we saw a sign you could not miss. It was a large sign in the middle of a wide sidewalk that said, "Join the Marines—Visit the recruiting office inside the Post Office."

"Let's go and check this out," I told Gator on an impulse. He was wrestling with the same question I faced about life after graduation.

We went inside, where the recruiting sergeant gave us an exciting sales pitch. It was not overly hyped; I would say it was pretty straightforward. After a lengthy discussion, we left with a bunch of brochures and some parting words. We both were definitely interested, we said, and we would be back after talking it over with our families. We hitchhiked back to Slocomb to spread the news. I would add that hitchhiking in those days was a very normal and very safe way to travel. No teenagers had a car.

I sought out a number of people for advice on my decision to join the Marines. Of course, number one was my mother. I am not sure how she really felt, but I know she prayed about it.

"If you are sure this is what you want to do, go ahead," she told me.

One of my grandmothers, Granny McCaskill, was living with us at that time, and I know she was praying for me. She had a private prayer closet, and often I could hear her praying out loud. Grandpa Rigell, whose advice I valued, said the same thing as my mother.

"If you are convinced that is what you want to do, go ahead," he said.

He had a very strong work ethic, and I knew he did not want me hanging around doing nothing. I discussed this with my friend, Coach Bridges, and several businessmen that I knew well. I did not get any really negative input.

"Why don't you join the Navy?" a couple of them asked me.

That had entered my mind, as a couple of my buddies on our football team were joining the Navy. One of the deciding factors was that the Navy required a six-year enlistment but the Marines was four years.

To end this chapter on my school years, I want to note that I had the honor and privilege of being chosen as the Slocomb High School alumni of the year in 1976. It was an honor I was proud and humbled to receive, and I want to make mention of it as I reflect on how much I enjoyed my school years in Slocomb.

YOU ARE A PRODUCT OF YOUR GROWING UP ENVIRONMENT

As far as our relationships with blacks during the early years of my life (1923 to 1941), we were the product of our time. You tend to accept as normal the culture you are exposed to in your early years. For example, if I had grown up in the wine-growing region of France, a daily drink of wine with meals would be perfectly normal, whereas in my culture, this would be unthinkable.

Today, the filth that is on TV, in the movies, and in national magazines is considered normal for teenagers since they have no other reference. However, to the senior citizens, these things are totally abnormal. They are a product of their time, and I don't see many young people on a crusade to eliminate that track.

Likewise, we look back in history and wonder how our ancestors treated the Native Americans. We tend to think we could never be part of anything like the injustices inflicted on the Cherokee in the Trail of Tears, when they were relocated from their native land in the East to Oklahoma. But we must remember that if we were living in that era, we would probably subscribe to the common feeling that many Indians were pawns of the British, French, and Spanish. We would probably think their goal was to inflict damage on our frontier settlers, and that they were a threat to our westward movement. Also, true or not, one argument for the relocation of these Indians is that it would save them from meeting their demise at the hands of white settlers.

There are some in every generation who have a calling to advance a minority population faced with some injustice. They are willing to make whatever sacrifices necessary to be an activist for their cause. Unless you happen to be one of those few, then you willingly accept the status quo. I accepted without question the relationship between blacks and whites in that era. So did everyone I knew.

If you had the subconscious feeling that the black population was being denied proper freedoms, your reaction was to be especially nice to those blacks you had some contact with. In most cases, they were the blacks who worked for you.

I readily admit that it was natural to accept this white superior position because that was the environment I grew up in. Another factor that tended to minimize your concern for the black population was that many whites were in the same economic condition during the Great Depression.

There was absolutely no integration in my growing up years. This word was not even in our vocabulary. There were no protests or demonstrations and no confrontations between whites and blacks. I will limit that observation to my experience in a small southern town. I do not believe this scenario held up for some of the larger cities, especially in the North.

The cultures of the black and white communities are vastly different today compared to the first half of the twentieth century. Segregation in the South meant exactly that, separate schools. Separate drinking fountains were not a problem since we had no drinking fountains. Churches were 100 percent segregated. Blacks did not have access to the better jobs, and this was exacerbated by the fact that during the Great Depression, 25 percent of the white population could not find a job. This caused many white workers to accept lower class jobs that would ordinarily be filled by blacks.

Whites were always addressed by blacks as "mister" and "missus." I don't recall whites always addressing black men as "boy," as is commonly portrayed in the movies of that era. We referred to them by their first name, and we usually knew all the blacks in our town by name.

Blacks always came to the back door of white homes. You never saw a white and black person of the opposite sex together.

Blacks had no opportunity to exploit their natural athletic abilities. Sports, amateur and professional, were segregated except for boxing and baseball when, in 1947, Jackie Robinson broke the color barrier with the old Brooklyn Dodgers. I was a great fan of Joe Louis, one of the greatest boxers of all time, in part because he was born in Alabama.

One of the people outside of my family who had a great influence on my life was Johnnie Mae Robinson, whom I mentioned earlier. Let me correct this statement. Rightly, I must say *inside* my family. Johnnie Mae was a black woman whom I affectionately called "Collardhead." Around 1930, when my mother went to work in a general store downtown, Johnnie Mae was hired to essentially run our household. This entailed a myriad of jobs such as cooking, taking care of the house, washing clothes, and making the soap to wash the clothes.

Washing clothes in those days involved more than dumping a basket of clothes in a washing machine. Washing started with building a fire under a big black iron pot, pouring in lye and other ingredients, and boiling the mixture to make wash soap. Then you would dump the clothes into boiling water, stirring it constantly with a wooden paddle. Then you would rinse the clothes several times in galvanized tin tubs and hang them on a clothesline for sun drying. Finally, the clothes were ready for ironing with a flat iron heated on the wood burning kitchen stove or placed in front of a fireplace.

Cooking was no small chore for our household. My mother, my grandmother McCaskill, three children, a number of boarders, and school teachers who boarded at other places all ate dinner at our house. Collardhead's good cooking was well known around town.

Collardhead had unwritten authority, and she used it to tell us children what and what not to do. All of my extended family and our boarders loved and respected Collardhead. She had a demeanor that demanded respect, and she was not hesitant to call your attention to anything she felt was offensive. For example, she wanted people to call black people "black people" instead of Negroes.

I can vividly recall sitting at our large boarding house dinner table and hearing the word Negro. It was not intended in an offensive manner, but just using that word would trigger Collardhead if she heard it. She usually did, as she was in and out of the dining room refilling dishes or drinks. She immediately came to the dining table to refill a dish whether it needed it or not and, in a very curt voice, would say "black folks." That was all she had to say. I can tell you it was very effective and everyone got the message, especially the one who used the term Negro.

After I moved away from Slocomb, I always made it a point to see Johnnie Mae when I returned. One of my cousins there always kept in touch with her.

On my first visit to Slocomb after we landed the first man on the moon in 1969, I went over to see Johnnie Mae. There were several people around, and she called me aside and said she wanted to talk to me privately. She was calling me "Mr. Ike." I don't remember her addressing me this way before.

"What is it you want to talk about, Johnnie Mae?" I asked

"Mr. Ike, I know you folks didn't put no man on that moon," she said. "If the good Lord had wanted a man up there on that moon, He would have done it. Now, Mr. Ike, I want you to tell me how you all faked them pictures to make it look like the moon."

"Johnnie Mae, those pictures were real. We did not fake it. We actually put men on the moon," I said.

Johnnie Mae did not accept that at all. "Now, Mr. Ike, you know me, and you know I ain't going to tell nobody," she said. "You know you can trust me. I just want to know how you faked it."

That dialogue continued for several minutes with neither of us convincing the other. Johnnie Mae passed away before my next visit to Slocomb, and she went to her grave thinking that I did not trust her enough to let her in on one of NASA's big secrets.

It has since entered my mind that maybe I should have made up some scenario on how NASA faked that moon landing rather than let her think I did not trust her enough to keep our secret. That compares to some of my relatives in Alabama that blamed any adverse weather conditions they experienced on "firing them rockets at Kennedy Space Center."

I want to throw in another personal thought related to what I have just written. I've always wondered, but never really understood, why people think and do what they do. How do you explain this? There were three groups—Catholics, Jews, and black people—in the environment I grew up in that, as individuals, were all loved and respected, but as a group they were considered a negative. I never understood this. Let me add another little tidbit: All of my family and all the people I knew were staunch Democrats. I only knew one Republican in our town, Mr. L. A. Carroll, and he was one of the most respected citizens in our community. He was an accountant, and my sister, Florence, worked for him until she moved to South Carolina.

The only conclusion I can make is that human nature is very complex, and you are largely a product of your environment. Fortunately, the environment can slowly change and you change along with it, and sometimes it is certainly for the good.

Johnnie Mae Jackson
was a big part of our family.

GUNS, THE CONSTITUTION, AND THE SECOND AMENDMENT

In my early years, I was taught, and I still believe, that our Constitution is the greatest document next to the Holy Scriptures, and it is the greatest document ever created by the mind of man. I thank my God for our Founding Fathers. I want to make a point here supporting some of my following comments, which is that most of the framers of our Constitution were solid Christians. Those that were not had a profound respect for Christian principles, and they supported these principles in their contributions to the Constitution.

In my growing up years, I cannot recall any issue concerning the interpretation of the Second Amendment of our Constitution. As I pause and look back over my 94 years on this good Earth, I marvel at what a non-violent world I grew up in and how this could be when I grew up in a world where gun ownership was so common and natural, even from a very early age. I never heard of needing a permit to carry a concealed weapon; in fact, I need to clarify these words—I did not look on my guns as weapons. Guns were used to hunt game and target practice but certainly not to commit a crime and shoot people.

Comparing the environment in which I grew up and today's

environment in 2017, we live in a violent society. It is very unsafe to travel in certain parts of any city, especially at night. There are armed guards at our banks, and metal detectors and security measures are a considerable expense for many businesses and entertainment and sports venues. If we listen to the "far left liberals," the reason for this violence is guns, and if you interpret the Second Amendment as preventing us patriotic citizens from having the right to gun ownership, then we would all be living in "la-la land." In my view, common sense is not a common virtue with the far left liberals. I have never heard these liberal people explain why the city of Chicago, with the most restrictive gun ownership laws in the country, has the distinction of being the most violent area in our country.

Using a little common sense, it appears to me there are only two factors involved—people and guns; if we had far more guns when I was growing up but almost no violent crime, then to explain why things are so different . . . it must be the people. It does not require a "rocket scientist" to figure that out. So, why is our society today so different than it was when I was growing up?

You could write volumes on this subject, but I will make an effort to offer my thoughts as concisely as possible. First, and fortunately, we were not "politically correct." We were not concerned about offending someone if we offered a prayer in school. In fact, the deterioration of our society began in the 1960s when an assault was made on the Constitution regarding prayer in school. We respected authority back then, especially those in education and law enforcement. The curriculum in our schools was positive; you learned to respect and value the Judeo-Christian principles on which our country was founded. We were not taught that we were victims and the government owed us a living and moral standards were whatever we chose to make them. Our school system today is a total, total disaster. Believe it or not, at one time, Hollywood made decent and entertaining films. Today, Hollywood is a cesspool. Cesspools do not smell good, period. I mentioned above that the non-Christian framers of our Constitution supported strongly the principles of Christianity, whereas today non-Christians and some Christians have nothing but disdain for this wonderful document.

The war on poverty, instituted by President Johnson in the

1960s, contributed to our dysfunctional society today because poor young girls were paid to have babies out of wedlock. This was a disastrous "war" on poverty, and sadly poverty won. Billions and billions of dollars have been poured into this horrible war, and we have more poverty today than we did back then. This program completely destroyed many, many families. Maybe it was designed with good intentions, but it had horrible consequences. Our nation, today, is morally bankrupt. There is no limit to the filth, vulgarity, and obscenities that our young people are exposed to via TV, radio, music, and the public media.

If our culture had changed overnight from what it was when I was growing up to our current environment, there would have been an armed revolution, but, absorbing these cultural changes in gradual doses, we end up in amazement, saying, "How did this happen?" What bothers me the most is wondering, if this trend continues, what the world that my grandchildren and great-grandchildren grow up in is going to be like. It bothers me just to think about it.

Now, having said all of this, why did I, living in a world of guns and poverty, not grow up to be a "born-again" criminal? According to the liberal left-wing folks, I was in a perfect environment for this, and furthermore it would not be my fault if I had lived a life of crime since, in their way of thinking, I was a victim.

The answer to this is the message I have tried to preach in other parts of my story: You are influenced by the culture in which you grow up. Fortunately, in the culture I grew up in, guns were for hunting, providing food for the table, and target practice. Life was sacred. Taking another person's life, other than in war, was unthinkable. Sadly, in today's society, life is cheap, from the unborn up to any age.

Sorry, I could not resist getting on my soapbox for a little while; back to growing up with guns. In our culture, us kids did not have many toys. Most recreational activities for men centered around playing cowboys and Indians, "war," and games like dodgeball, kick-the-can, hide-and-seek, baseball, football, and others. As we got older, our choices for recreation strongly gravitated to hunting, fishing, and sports like baseball and football.

My earliest memories of playing with other kids involve

pretending to be cowboys or Indians and "playing war" in general, where we had good guys and bad guys. We would choose sides, but the little guys that wanted to join the games always had to be the Indians or the bad guys in the war games. Toy guns were the most sought-after toy because to play cowboys and Indians you needed a toy cap pistol. A typical cap pistol used a roll of caps, and each contained a minute amount of gunpowder; when you pulled the trigger on the pistol, the hammer would hit the cap and explode the gunpowder, resulting in a "pop" and a little smoke, and you would declare your enemy, the Indian, deceased. Each time you pulled the trigger, it advanced the roll of caps so it would fire every time you pulled the trigger. The ultimate dress for the cowboy/Indian game would be two pistols with a holster on either side and a cowboy belt with chaps.

For the general war games, it would be either the North versus the South or WWI, with the good guys, us, fighting the bad guys, the Germans. For these war games, we needed a gun in addition to a pistol, so with a little ingenuity we came up with a gun that was standard equipment for us little soldiers. Usually it required a bit of adult help. We would take a one-by-four about three feet long and, with a saw, shape it, maybe a little crudely, like a rifle. On top of the gun, where the barrel met the stock of the gun, you cut three notches about three-quarters of an inch deep. That meant your gun could be loaded with three "rubber bullets," a.k.a. rubber bands. Then you took these heavy rubber bands, about six inches in diameter and about one inch wide, and stretched them from the tip of the barrel to one of these notches so you had the stored energy of this heavy rubber band ready to be released, just like having stored energy in a bullet ready to be released.

You released the rubber band by using your thumb to push it up out of the notch, and then it flew away to hit your enemy. The helpful thing about the rubber bands was that they were free, but you had to make them first. This was before the invention of tubeless tires; all tires had an inner tube made of heavy, strong rubber the same size as the tire, and all us kids had to do was go down to the garage where they worked on cars and pick up an old discarded inner tube. We could make many "rubber bullets" out of one old inner tube.

There was a large field across the street from our house, and at times we could make our wargames more realistic by setting small patches of grass on fire so we could chase our enemy through the smoke. I better be careful here—the EPA might learn of this and retroactively place a large fine me.

I have always been a history buff, and at an early age I read everything I could get my hands on, which I must say was very limited. If you read about history, you are likely reading about wars. I read about Napoleon, Charlemagne, the Crusades, and, of course, the Civil War and WWI. In my youthful innocence, war had a certain romantic image and a noble purpose: the good guys defeating the evil enemy forces. I did not see the horrible carnage and suffering of not only the military but also the civilians, women, and small children all wars produce.

Back to my personal guns, my first real gun was an air rifle. Maybe an adult considers it a toy, but to a very young kid it is a big gun. I bought this air rifle from a friend who was a couple of years older than me, and he in turn bought a .22 rifle. He let me shoot his .22, which was really a big thrill for me.

My next step up in the gun world was a real shotgun from Grandfather Rigell. He gave my cousin, Bill Rigell, a .410 shotgun when he turned 12 years old, and he told me he already had a .410 for me when I turned 12. Bill was 3 years older than me, so I had 3 long years to wait before I could take this gun home. Happily, during this waiting period I had numerous opportunities to shoot this gun. Grandpa Rigell had a large tract of land behind his house, and when I was at his house he would take me back in his pasture and let me shoot my gun. He really made my day when we went out for target practice.

I cannot remember exactly how we arrived at this, but, after many times target shooting, Grandmother Rigell let me take the gun for target practice when my grandfather was not there. Apparently they both trusted me enough to let me be on my own with the gun. My first big—and I emphasize big—event when I took the gun out alone was when a rabbit hopped up just in front of me. I was so startled I did not have time to shoot before he disappeared in a brush pile. It was a large stack of dead bushes ready to be burned. (Back then we did not know you needed a burn permit to burn your own bushes.) I quietly eased up to this brush pile and I looked real close and I saw this rabbit. With adrenalin flowing and my hands shaking, I aimed at this rabbit only a few feet away and pulled the trigger. At that moment, my hunting record was 100 percent. I had some game for every shot I had ever fired. I proudly carried my rabbit back to my grandmother and asked her if she would cook it for me. She readily agreed and later I enjoyed a rabbit feast. A couple of days later, I was at her house and she did not know I heard her laughingly telling her neighbor about this event and how she had a problem dressing this rabbit as the rabbit was so mangled because he was so close, almost at the end of my gun barrel, when I shot him. I could not have been older than 10 or 11 at that time because sadly, very sadly, Grandmother Rigell passed away when I was 12.

I don't recall that back in those days a birthday was a big deal. I don't remember birthday presents or birthday cakes, but I do remember anxiously waiting for January 10, 1965, when I could visit Grandfather Rigell and leave with my treasure, my most prized possession, my own .410 shotgun. I had been diligently saving my pennies, nickels, and dimes to buy ammunition. One shell cost 3 cents and it was a big deal if you could save 75 cents to buy the whole box of shells.

My hunting career started immediately when I was 12. I know it sounds a little risky now, but I would go out hunting with friends my age or a little older as a normal event. If my friends did not have their own guns, they had access to their fathers' guns, but I say again I cannot remember—and I have pretty good memory—a gun being used in our community for committing a crime such as an armed robbery or shooting another person. We just did not think like that, so I'll just reinforce what I said before; the problem today is people, not guns.

I end my discourse on guns with a sad note. I wish it were possible to undo something I did. It is hard to believe I was so stupid, utterly stupid, but when I enlisted in the Marine Corps I sold my cherished treasure, my .410. I would pay any price now to retrieve that gun, but of course that is impossible. Stupid, stupid. I am, however, proud to say I carried on the tradition of giving my sons, David and Scott, shotguns when they were 12 years old.

As I said, I never considered my .410 to be a weapon, but as a Marine I immediately got introduced to real weapons. First, in boot camp, the old reliable '03 Springfield; then, as a wire chief, a .45 pistol and a Thompson submachine gun and later a carbine.

Unfortunately, today we live in such a violent and dysfunctional society that more and more people feel they must carry a concealed weapon for self-defense, and I do not disagree with them. I do not think I am wrong by identifying our current society as dysfunctional when a six-year-old innocently taking a toy gun to school makes national headlines and the little kid is sent home in disgrace.

I still ponder the question I posed above. How did we get from a non-violent, peaceful society to the current dysfunction (or whatever word you want to use to describe this mess we are in)?

CHRISTIAN HERITAGE

I thank my Lord every day that I have been so blessed with a strong Christian heritage. I firmly believe that the greatest thing you can do for your children and grandchildren is to leave them a Christian heritage.

On my mother's side, the McCaskills came over from Scotland as very devout Presbyterians. It is very sad to see so many liberal Presbyterian churches today, but the Presbyterian church of my McCaskill grandparents was rock solid.

About seven miles outside of Slocomb, there is a small cemetery on the church grounds where my McCaskill grandparents and other relatives on his side of the family are buried. For me, this is a special place, and I visit this little church and cemetery whenever I am in that area. In my younger years, we would visit this little church several times a year, and sometimes my mother would play the organ.

On my father's side, the Rigells had a strong Baptist background. One of my uncles, Dr. William Rigell, was a Baptist preacher, and my grandfather Rigell served for a number of years as a deacon in the Slocomb Baptist Church. In our little town there were only two churches, Baptist and Methodist. If you were going to church, those were your options. There was a Holiness Church on the outskirts of town, and we called those people "holy rollers," as they were very active and loud in their services.

Occasionally, you would you hear someone make some negative remarks about Catholics and Jews. I never knew why. I did not know, nor had I ever seen a Catholic, and strangely, we had one Jew in town and everyone seemed to love him. His name was Barney Bloomingfield, and he owned a local store. He later moved the store to the larger town of Dothan, and when people would go there, they would visit Barney. I never did see nor know a Catholic until I was in boot camp, and then I met many of them. I did not observe anything wrong with them. In fact, I admired their dedication in attending church services. Some of the best friends I ever had were these Catholic guys.

When I was growing up, it was not a question of if you were going to church every Sunday morning and evening. You just knew you were going to church. It was an accepted part of life. There was also not a question of what you were going to wear to church, because in those days people had what we called "everyday clothes and shoes," and we had one outfit we called our "Sunday clothes and Sunday shoes."

During the summer, both churches had what we called a "Revival." The Revival would last a week, and everyday there would be a service at noon and a service at night. A visiting preacher would be called in for all of these services. During these revivals, the Baptist folks would attend the Methodist revival, and the Methodist folks would attend the Baptist revival.

For the noon service, most of the businesses in town closed so their employees could attend the noon service. Whether the business owner was a Baptist, Methodist, or non-church person, he would close for both revivals.

There is one big difference today in the way people honor Christianity. I do not know if we had more of what we call "born-again Christians" back in those earlier times than we do today. But I do know that the non-church going people honored and respected the churches. A good example of this is just what I mentioned above, when the non-church going business owner closed his business to permit his employees to go to church. Contrast that with today's environment where the media and Hollywood ridicule and slander Christianity.

My Grandfather McCaskill. He and my Granny McCaskill came to live with us in 1925, after my father died. He was a Confederate soldier out of South Carolina.

My Granny McCaskill. She was a saintly lady.

Grandpa and Granny Rigell.

The Rigell brothers. (L-R:) Frank, Ed, Ike, and William.

1941—1945
WAR YEARS

MARINE CORPS

Several days after I had first talked with the Marine recruiter in Dothan, I made up my mind that I wanted to enlist. I felt pretty good about my decision since I had the backing of my family and friends.

I would frequently check with my friend, Gator Jones, to see if he had made the decision to go with me. I got the distinct impression that he had lost his original enthusiasm for this venture. This was confirmed one day when Gator told me his parents said no. I was disappointed that I would not have my friend going with me. Gator would not admit it, but I think his decision not to go was more his than his parents.

In the meantime, one of my friends, Winton Justice, indicated an interest in going with me. I encouraged him to visit the Marine recruiter in Dothan, which he did, and he came back and told me, "Yes, I am going." I was real happy to hear that. At 21, Winton was older than me. He was a very nice, quiet person and had one claim to fame in Slocomb: he was the best pool player in town. Winton faced the same problem as most men in our age group at that time, and that was a lack of job opportunities.

The big day came. Winton and I boarded that Greyhound bus in Slocomb, bound for Birmingham, Alabama, to be inducted into the Marine Corps. We had a nice little crowd of well-wishers to see us off. I never dreamed at that time that it would be almost two years before I returned. Our bus route took us through Dothan, where we had to change buses, then through Montgomery and onto Birmingham.

When we left Montgomery for Birmingham, every mile of my world got bigger and bigger. In all of my 18 years, I had never been farther than Montgomery, which was about 120 miles from home. The hills and small mountains around Birmingham were new and exciting. Also, entering a large city with multi-storied buildings and streetcars—and let me add *all paved streets*—was very interesting. I tried to absorb all of this new world. In hindsight, I think that having my mind occupied relieved me of some of the anxiety I had to deal with concerning a question always in the back of my mind: *Will I fit into this new environment?*

A Marine from the Birmingham recruitment office met me and Winton at the bus station and took us to the recruitment office where we did our official signing. The recruitment office was in the center of the business district downtown. They put us up in a hotel nearby, and this was my first time ever to spend the night in a hotel. This was a nice hotel with no air conditioning, but that was normal for that era.

Everything this country boy from Slocomb encountered was a new adventure. I can clearly recall that room, large with two ceiling fans and a couple of large windows overlooking a busy street. We opened the windows, and our entertainment was just watching the streetcars, automobiles, people, and traffic until it was time to go to bed.

The recruitment office provided us with meal "chits" for a restaurant across the street from the hotel. I am not sure why I still remember the name of this restaurant, Greenwood, but it is very clear. Again, I was in a new world. In my 18 years, I had only eaten in a restaurant one time, so to me, to eat three meals a day in a nice restaurant was a big deal.

The next day in Birmingham we were given a complete physical examination, including a dental checkup. We were joined by another recruit, whose last name was Lyons. I cannot remember his first name. We always called each other by our last names.

Winton, Lyons, and I all passed the physical examination, and Lyon and I passed the dental examination. However,

Winton was told that he required some dental work before he could be accepted. I was greatly disappointed when I learned that Winton had to return home for the required dental work.

It was now me and Lyons, and I wasn't sure how this "country boy" would get along with this city guy. Lyons was a couple of years older than me, and it was obvious he came from a much more affluent background. It turned out he was a very nice guy, and we became good friends. I learned a lot from Lyons in the few days we spent together.

BIRMINGHAM TO BOOT CAMP

When my friend Lyons and I boarded the train for San Diego, it was almost like a dream, traveling across this great land on a first-class train ticket. It was something I really looked forward to. With every click-click of the rails, my world would get bigger and bigger.

With Lyons leading the way, we found our reserved seats. It was a first-class Pullman coach inside a very long train with a coal-burning engine. In that era, trains were the prime mode for intercity and cross country travel. We were issued food vouchers, and it was a real treat for me to enjoy the dining car three times a day. The trip across the country took several days, and I kept my nose glued to the window as much as possible, trying not to miss a thing and also trying to keep up with exactly where we were.

All of it was exciting. The highlights were crossing the Mississippi River, seeing the oil fields in Texas, winding through those long curves in the Rocky Mountains, and watching the black smoke belching out of the engine as it struggled on upgrades and disappeared in a tunnel. There was never a dull moment for me on that trip. Lyons and I would get our daily exercise by walking the train from one end to the other, and I enjoyed the stops along the way where we could get off and look around.

"Let's not get too far," I told Lyons. "When the conductor yells 'all aboard,' I don't want to miss it."

Lyons and I got along real good. We talked some about our past, but more often about what lay ahead and what assignment we would like after boot camp.

Lyons was in ROTC when he attended Auburn, and after a couple of days on the train, he wore his ROTC uniform. I was impressed by this, and Lyons told me that with his two years of ROTC experience, they would make him a squad leader and he would get me in his squad. This sounded good to me. It erased some of my anxiety about entering this strange world alone without knowing anyone.

In a few pages, I will tell you how this turned out.

The closer we came to San Diego, the more my mind wrestled with what it was going to be like when the train trip ended. I had signed up for four years, but suppose I didn't fit in with a military lifestyle? You try to reassure yourself that this four year commitment was the right decision.

The train pulled into the San Diego rail terminal, and using the instructions given to us in Birmingham, we followed the prominent signs directing us to the Marine Recruit assembly area. We presented our papers to the Marine in charge. He greeted us in a friendly manner and told us to take a seat on one of the benches along with a number of recruits that had arrived on other trains. We waited there probably about thirty or forty minutes for another train to arrive. Lyons and I met some of the other recruits and asked them where they were from and whether they enlisted to get ahead of the draft. Turned out Lyons and I were the only ones from the Deep South.

When all the guys we were waiting for arrived, we climbed in the back of the big military truck parked nearby. There were two, maybe three trucks open in the back with benches on either side and suitcases in the center. It was only a few miles from the train station to the Marine Recruit Depot in San Diego.

I cannot describe my thoughts as our little convoy entered the main gate at the Marine base. As the guard waved us through, my mind was focused on keenly observing everything in view. I was trying to get some insight into what life would be like in this new world. We stopped for a traffic light, and a couple of

Marines were standing on the corner waiting to cross the street. One of them laughingly yelled, "Suckers, suckers!"

One of the guys in our group had a good answer. "Took them longer to get me than it did you," he said.

The buildings and grounds were impressive. The old Spanish type architecture was totally different from anything in south Alabama.

We passed the huge parade ground where a number of platoons of recruits were marching. That was impressive, especially the sounds: the yelling of the drill instructors and the clack-clack of the recruits Boondockers hitting the pavement. My friend Lyons explained a little about the close order drill and the role of a DI as we passed.

We arrived at our destination and were ordered to unload. Up to this point, all my encounters with the Marines were civil, from the recruit sergeant in Dothan, to the guys at the Induction Center at Birmingham, and the Marines at the San Diego train station.

Now came the culture shock. We were not moving fast enough for the corporal in charge. I had never been exposed to such fury.

"Let's move, move, move! Sorriest bunch of scum I have ever seen! Line up! Move, move, move!" he screamed at about 125 decibels.

I was just now thinking that is why I have such a bad hearing problem today.

He got us lined up and marched us into a building and into a large room, empty except for one desk. A sergeant was sitting at the desk. The corporal ordered us to stand at attention, look straight ahead, and not to talk. The sergeant still sitting at the desk took over.

"When I call your name, you answer questions 'yes sir' or 'no sir.' Do you hear that? I want a yes sir!" he said.

We gave him a big "Yes sir!" That was not good enough. We were slow learners.

It required three or four more "yes sirs" to satisfy him. He started calling names.

"Yes sir!" the recruit answered.

The sergeant asked each of them if they had any previous

military experience. Most said, "No sir," but three or four answered, "Yes sir."

"How much?" the sergeant asked.

"Four years Marine Corps, sir," one said.

"Three years in the Army, sir," said another.

All the time he was calling out names and asking questions, he talked pretty fast and never looked up at us. He kept his eyes focused on his list of names. All those with previous experience were told to step over to his desk. He still did not look up.

I was standing by Lyons in the first row.

"Any previous military experience?" he asked Lyons when he got to him.

"Yes sir."

"How much?" asked the sergeant.

"Two years ROTC, sir."

Dead silence. The sergeant pushed his chair back, walked around the desk and shouted, "Who said that?"

"I did, sir," Lyons said.

The sergeant got right in Lyon's face. "I did not say Boy Scouts. I said military experience. Have you had any military experience?"

"No sir!"

All this time, he had Lyons by the collar shaking him. My heart sank. I felt so sorry for him. At that moment I wished I was back in Slocomb.

When the sergeant got to my name, he pronounced it in a version I had never heard. I hesitated because I was unsure he was calling me. He shouted a second call in anger, and since no one else answered, I decided it must be me.

At the end of this introduction session, the sergeant went down the roster calling out names, splitting us into two groups. My friend Lyons and I were assigned to different groups. We had no time to say goodbye, and I never saw him again. I always wondered what happened to him.

As I mentioned earlier, the San Diego Marine Recruit Depot had many beautiful old Spanish type buildings surrounding a large parade field. The Marine Corps was in a rapid buildup at this time so all these nice buildings were occupied. The recruits were assigned to a newly constructed tent city. These were six-man tents set up in rows with boardwalks. The San Diego weather was ideal, so we kept the sides of the tents rolled up. It was not a bad setup.

The toilets and showers were at the end of the boardwalk, but to wash your hands and shave, you had to go outside. Water, cold only, was supplied through a long pipe with holes drilled about a foot apart, and a wooden trough would catch the running water. There were no glass mirrors so we had to use the small stainless steel mirrors, which was the standard issue for each Marine.

One of the first orders of business was to get a haircut, or more appropriately, a head shave. No matter how much hair you had, it took the barber about thirty seconds to have it on the floor. You had a sixth sense the barber really enjoyed what he was doing.

Getting your clothing allowance was another first day event. This included heavy hobnail shoes, which you had to get used to. Next came the shots. Rumors fly readily in the military, and one was that one of your shots had to be with a square needle. We received a shot for everything, so no matter where you would be sent, you were covered. Vaccinations were administered in a production-line fashion. The medics had set up a number of stations in a row, and we stripped down to our shorts. We went down the line getting vaccinations at each station, either in the arms or buttocks. Never did see the square needle.

No matter how old you get, you never forget your drill instructors. There were three for each platoon. The head DI was a Corporal named Allen, tall, slender, and ramrod straight. He was all military. He did not yell at the troops like the other two. He did not have to yell to get his message across. His demeanor commanded respect and attention. The second in command was a corporal also named Allen. Both were from Mississippi and no relation to each other. This DI was also a no-nonsense, in-your-face guy. Toward the end of boot camp, he did soften up a little, especially if he was the only one with us at the time. Both Allens had one hashmark. A hashmark is a stipe worn on your lower sleeve that denotes you have served four years.

Our tents were close to the parade ground, and many nights you could hear the hobnail shoes of a platoon hitting the pavement. That meant they had screwed up that day, or maybe the DI in charge that night wanted to see them suffer. My platoon had our share of these nightmare exercises.

Reveille came before daylight and was a real bugler (no recording). You had a very short time to dress for roll call. On the first roll call there was a missing recruit. One of the DIs went to his tent and found him sound asleep in his sack. The DI dumped his cot with him in it and poured a bucket of water on him. The six cots in the tent were positioned on the edge of the floor, so the guy actually landed on the ground.

Each tent had a bucket of water in the center of the tent. This water bucket was for extinguishing a fire in the tent, but apparently it had a good secondary purpose—to make sure you were out on time for roll call. This guy never missed roll call again. Neither did anyone else.

At first I was nervous answering roll call. All three DIs pronounced my name differently. I was never sure if they were calling my name or some other name. One day, not at roll call, I informed one of the DIs that he was pronouncing my name incorrectly. He informed me in no uncertain terms that my name was whatever he wanted to call me. I gave up on trying to correct how my name was pronounced. Even my buddies pronounced my name the same way they heard it from the DI. So my entire career in the Marines I was something like "Ry-gel."

Our third DI was a private first class with three hash marks. Yes, a PFC with over twelve years of service. We learned he had been a sergeant two or more times in the past. PFC Gemotes was a full-blooded Indian and had a real problem handling booze. Of the three DIs, he was the most physical. He would not hesitate to charge into you with a shoulder block during close order drill if you were not marching to his standards.

Apparently, on one occasion he observed that I was not marching up to his standards. We were in a close order drill exercise and he issued the command, "About Face." This was one of our first exercises under PFC Gemotes and I did momentarily get out of step during this maneuver, but before I could get back in the cadence he charged into me with a full shoulder block and I did not see him coming. I was in the outside column and I ended up colliding with the guy in the inside column. I think before boot camp was over most all of us had experienced a one-on-one with

PFC Gemotes. Actually, he was not a bad guy he was just doing his job.

He was very dedicated to the job and kept reminding us: "What I am teaching you will save your life someday." He was right.

In boot camp your world is limited to your platoon. You never interact with other units, and your only exposure to the outside world is at night when you can observe the shining lights on the hills of San Diego.

I experienced one freak problem in boot camp. One of the several inoculations we received I think was for smallpox. It is administered by a number of small needle pricks on the upper arm. This will result in an ugly-looking sore which forms a scab, and this is normal. My vaccination was healing as it should until one day I was putting on my full pack for a field exercise and the strap on my pack pulled across this spot and ripped the scab off. It did bleed some and did not look good, but I thought it would be ok so I said nothing about it at that time.

In a couple of days it really got infected, and I had to show it to the DI. He sent me to sick bay, where they cleaned the wound and put some medicine on it and said they were giving me a note for limited duty. It was painful to use my arm.

Still, I made a decision not to report this to the DI. Our platoon was scheduled to go to the rifle range at a camp a few miles outside San Diego. I knew limited duty status would keep me from going with my platoon and that I would be held back and reassigned to another unit. Going to the rifle range is a big, big deal in boot camp, so I could not think of delaying this and leaving my unit. I had made some real good friends.

This was probably not a wise decision, as I had no medication to fight this infection and it could have gotten much worse. Also, I could not ask the DI for any light duty assignments, so I really had to struggle daily at the rifle range to do everything the other guys were doing. The wound did finally heal with no further problem.

Toward the end of boot camp you start wondering what your assignment will be and where you will be stationed. We were given a form with a number of options. I requested a tank unit. As it turned out, this procedure was worthless, as no one I knew was assigned to the unit they requested. We were given an aptitude test, which was the main factor in determining our assignment.

Graduation from boot camp was certainly a big milestone in my life. We joined other platoons in the graduation ceremony on the parade field. The DIs were fiercely competitive; each one wanted to present the best platoon. In that era, families did not attend the graduating ceremony, and there was no leave after boot camp. You went immediately to your new assignment.

My assignment was Field Telephone School. I had no clue what Field Telephone School was all about. I didn't even know it existed. If I had known then what I know now, this would certainly be by far my first choice. I truly believe it is one of the many cases where my Lord was taking care of me.

The big, exciting thing we all had been looking for was a pass to go into the big city of San Diego. From our tents in boot camp we could see the city lights at night on the hills in San Diego. It was so near, but as far as getting there, it was like being on another planet. These guys would talk about how they could not wait until they could find a good restaurant serving pizza, meatballs, and spaghetti. I had never eaten or even heard of these dishes. I kept it a secret, but I was looking for some good old southern fried chicken and country ham. They would later find what they were looking for. Sadly, I found no southern fried chicken or country ham.

TELEPHONE SCHOOL
TO MIDWAY

F ield Telephone School was located on the base but was a totally different environment from boot camp. In fact, I enjoyed this phase of my service. The classroom and living quarters were housed in a beautiful facility of Spanish architecture. This was the only period in my four years and four months of active duty that I had the pleasure of sleeping on a real mattress. There was a good mixture of classroom and field operations and a period of physical fitness every day. Some of this time was organized activity, but there was some free time to play ball and to participate in other activities of your choice.

Boxing was a popular national sport during this era, and one of my classmates, Bob Clements, had done a lot of amateur boxing. He was our unofficial boxing instructor. There were regular boxing matches between the Marine units, the Navy, and the Army. These matches were very popular and well attended. These guys operated on a much higher skill level; some of them had professional experience. Bob Clements and I were good buddies, and he will appear a couple of times later in my story.

I enjoyed Field Telephone School and graduated number one in my class. I do not note this in a boastful manner. Fortunately, my background prepared me for this assignment. There were two distinct aspects of the school program: learning the basic theory and principles of electricity and applying this knowledge to combat field communications.

In my teenage years I had a part-time job working with the only electrician in our town. His name was Bennie Patterson, and he had limited experience in this area. He was enrolled in a correspondence course to become a licensed electrical contractor. This included electrical equipment for experiments, so he could apply what he learned from the written portion of the course.

When Bennie was not on a job, which was much of the time, he would work on his correspondence course. He had one room in his house set up for the lab and study room. I essentially took the course along with Bennie. I was not seeking any credit. I just enjoyed working with this material, and I was eager to learn all I could. This experience really paid off, as I had an easy time in Field Telephone School. In fact, I was a popular guy at night, as I could help many of them struggling with their homework.

At our graduation, we received our future station assignment. I, along with a number of others, was assigned to report to the Marine barracks at Pearl Harbor. My friend Clements was in this group. I could not be more pleased with this assignment to the Hawaiian Islands. This was truly a big deal, as very few people could afford to make trips overseas. The barracks had to be cleared for the next class, so all the guys with overseas assignments were loaded in trucks bound for a large Navy ship docked a few miles away in the harbor at San Diego.

Again, my world got much larger. I had never been on a boat of any kind, and to walk up the gang plank of this huge ship was awesome. It was a totally different world for me and also for all the guys in our group. It was several days after we boarded before we sailed. They continued loading cargo and bringing on more troops: Army, Navy, and other Marine units.

We were permitted to have liberty most nights to go into downtown San Diego. We had a curfew which was strictly enforced. The night before we sailed, Clements and I got a pass to go into town. We first visited the USO, which was a popular place for servicemen. It was a little quiet that night, and we decided to leave. The USO was a large building with a porch facing the street, and the porch was about fifteen steps above the level of the sidewalk, The steps were very wide, so heavy traffic up and down was not a problem. Clements and I were standing at the top of the steps discussing where to go to get a good civilian meal; the food for the troops on that ship was not Michelin rated.

As we were standing there talking, we heard some noise in the distance. It sounded like someone shouting, and it kept getting louder and louder. Soon we saw four drunken sailors staggering and shouting and coming our way. We could not decipher their words until they were directly in front of us on the sidewalk. Then we got their message: "All Army and Marines out of the USO. The Navy is taking over!"

One of them who appeared to be the leader staggered up the steps and stood about two steps below, right in front of Clements. "Army and Marines out!" he shouted. "The Navy is taking over!"

"Just knock the hell out of him," I told Clements.

That was very bad advice, and I am glad Clements remained calm. The guy could hardly stand up. If Clements had hit him, it could have killed him, as his head would have hit the steps. Fortunately, the Navy Shore Patrol arrived with a paddy wagon and loaded all of them. They were still shouting!

This is not the end of the story of the sailor that confronted us on the steps.

The next morning, I woke up early and was up on deck to see the tugboats easing this big ship out of the harbor into the open sea. I experienced some mixed feelings. I was excited about going to Hawaii, but as I watched the shore becoming fainter and fainter, I wondered when I would see it again. I also thought of my mother and how she was accepting all this as it surely meant I would not be home anytime soon.

This cruise was certainly not in the deluxe class. In fact, it was not even the "El Cheapo" tourist class. The ship was loaded to its full capacity with Army, Navy, and Marines. Over the next four years, I would be on a number of Navy ships, and fortunately they were all several grades above this vessel.

There were so many troops on board that there was almost a constant chow line. The line would wrap around the ship, and it passed the portholes looking into the officers' dining room. We saw orderlies, who were almost all Filipinos, in fresh uniforms serving fancy food on white table clothes with real china. You had to put this scene out of your mind as you picked up your metal tray and passed down the line as the cooks tossed something on your tray.

I don't know why we were all so eager to get in the chow line, I think maybe we were hoping that this time it would be something good. This was my first introduction of navy beans for breakfast. I have been on many Navy ships, and all served beans for breakfast, but I never got used to this dish for breakfast. Beans are a poor substitute for grits.

There were some black army soldiers on the ship. I never saw them in our chow line, nor did I see them in the mess hall. I don't know where they ate or when they ate. They slept in compartments separate from the other troops. Integration had not arrived at this time.

One day, I went over and sat down on the deck by a black soldier from Mississippi. I was interested in their operations. I struck up a conversation with him.

"What unit are you in?" I asked him.

"I just don't know," he replied. "Half of our outfit is on this ship, half our outfit was sent to Samoa, and half our outfit is still in the states."

I guess the military can be confusing at times. I asked his rank.

"I am a private. I should be a sergeant, but I just don't take no shit," he said.

We had several more chats before landing, which I enjoyed, and I'm sorry I never saw him again.

I think it was the second day out at sea, Clements and I were sitting on deck near one of the hatches.

"Do you see what I see?" Clements said, and he pointed to the hatch.

Two sailors were coming out of the hatch, followed by a SP (Shore Patrol) with a .45. The SP is the Navy military police. One of those sailors was the sailor that confronted us at the USO. Apparently, the night they picked him up at the USO, they put him in the brig on this ship. Many of the sailors on the ship were not part of the crew but going to Pearl Harbor for their assignment. The SP was taking them out for sunshine and exercise. He never saw us, and I don't think he would recognize us if he looked right at us. I had the urge to go up to him and say, "All sailors and soldiers off the ship. The Marines are taking over!" But common sense said no.

It was not so pleasant on this overcrowded ship, but I had something exciting to look forward to—Hawaii. Visiting Hawaii in today's world is no big deal, but to an 18-year-old country boy who had never traveled beyond the cotton, corn, and peanut fields of south Alabama, it was a big deal.

I think it was about the fifth day out at sea when there was a PA announcement that we would make landfall off Diamond Head. Everyone was up early the next morning to get a glimpse of Diamond Head, one of the most famous landmarks in the world. It is an extinct volcano rising about 750 feet above sea level and is right next to Waikiki Beach, one of the most famous beaches in the world. Honolulu is located right by Waikiki Beach. Honolulu and Pearl Harbor are located on Oahu, one of the five islands in the Hawaiian chain. Remember this name, Oahu. To my great embarrassment, you will hear more on Oahu later.

We sailed smoothly into Pearl Harbor. The tugboats came out to direct us to the dock. This was very interesting to me, and we passed many ships tied to the docks. Marine trucks were waiting to take us to the Marine barracks. My assumption that I would be stationed in Hawaii was short-lived. After a roll call at the Marine barracks, the sergeant started calling out names for further deployment.

My name was called for the 6th Defense Battalion at Midway Island. There were about a dozen of us in the Midway group and about the same number assigned to Wake Island. Some were not assigned at that time, and my buddy Clements was in that group. I lost contact with him, but fate would bring us together again in about eighteen months. That story will come later.

The next day, the Marines assigned to Wake and Midway Islands boarded a Navy ship bound for Wake and then Midway. This ship and this voyage were nothing like the voyage from San Diego to Pearl Harbor. Again, there was only about a dozen in the Midway group and the same number in the Wake Island group. We were the only passengers on this large ship, and we enjoyed the upgrade. We ate with the crew, and the sleeping quarters were the same as the crew. We had access to the ship's library and the ship store, and we were allowed to go to the galley twenty-four hours a day to get a cup of fresh coffee. I was never seasick and in fact found I really enjoyed the seas.

There was one big difference headed west out of Pearl Harbor. After dark absolutely no smoking was allowed on the decks. Somehow you could sense a more serious atmosphere on this ship. It turned out it was up to us, the passenger Marines, to enforce this no smoking rule. Almost everyone smoked in that era, so it did require some effort to see this rule was not violated.

Right after we boarded this ship, the sergeant in charge of our group called us to assemble and gave us our instructions on our guard assignments. After he finished his lecture, he said to go to the bulletin board and we'd see our post and hours listed for today and tomorrow. I went to the bulletin board and my name was not listed for any of the stations, but down at the bottom it had "Supernumeraries." Under Supernumeraries, my name was listed along with another guy's name I slightly knew. This word was not in my Slocomb vocabulary, so I did not have the foggiest idea what a supernumerary was supposed to do. I found the other guy whose name was with mine, and I was hoping he understood this. Turned out he didn't know any more about this than I did.

We knew we had to find out what this meant, or we could be in real trouble. We decided we had no choice but to go talk to the sergeant. Being fresh out of boot camp, you were not inclined to talk to a sergeant because you still were thinking all sergeants were like DIs. We needed some clarification on what we were supposed to do, so we had no choice. The sergeant was very civil and spoke to us with no put-down attitude. He said that means you are on standby, and if something happens to one of the guys assigned to a post, you will be called. What a relief. We could now go out and enjoy the salt spray.

Later I looked up the meaning of supernumerary in a dictionary, and one definition was "not needed." This tended to lower my ego.

The atmosphere on this ship was totally different than on the ship from San Diego to Pearl Harbor. There were so many troops packed on the ship to Pearl Harbor that it was a little chaotic at times. On the voyage to Wake and Midway things were in order. You could just sense a more serious tone. This voyage was in strict blackout, whereas in the first voyage all the lights were on at night. The abandon ship drill on the first voyage was chaos. I am not sure any of us would have been saved if there was a real problem on that ship. This time, everything went smoothly on the abandon ship drill. The ship's crew knew what they were doing.

There were about twenty-five Marines on the ship assigned for duty on Wake or Midway. I am sure the person making these assignments did not realize this would be a life or death decision for this group of Marines. A number of us had the same classifications: we'd just graduated from Field Telephone School, and all of us were privates.

Only two of the telephone guys were in the Midway group. My name was on this list along with a good friend in my telephone class, Mort Harkins. The significance of this assignment decision was that two months later, in December 1941, the Japanese attacked Wake. The Japs also attacked our garrison at Midway on the night of December 7th, but they made no attempt to land that night.

This first attempt to capture Wake was repulsed by this small Marine garrison, but the Japs came back on December 21st with a larger force and captured or killed all of our troops there. The prisoners, Marines, and contractors were taken to China and used as slave labor under unimaginable hardships. At that time parts of China were occupied by Japan under a brutal military rule. Later, it was learned that on the way to China, five of the Marines were beheaded on the ship. I have pondered many times how I escaped that fate.

After unloading the supplies on Wake, the ship headed for Midway Island. Unlike Wake, the lagoon at Midway was large enough and deep enough to dock a large ship. I don't know how to describe my feelings as the ship was pulling into this dock. I had no idea what life would be like here and even less knowledge of how long I would be here. We immediately heard the same comments the Wake Marines used in greeting the newcomers.

"You are going to get your ass worked off," they told us.

It turned out they knew what they were talking about, which

I'll describe later. The living quarters at this time were Quonset huts, with about fifteen to twenty men to a building, depending on rank.

There were no natives on Midway, and there were no women. Besides the Marines and sailors, there were several hundred construction workers building various structures and fortifications. Some nice looking barracks were under construction and almost ready to move into, and we were looking forward to that. However, it would turn out that was not to be during my time on Midway.

Parallel with building the barracks, they were very busy building fortifications, including underground living quarters. Midway is nothing but sand, so we had no caves or tunnels for defense purposes like we would later encounter on Saipan, Tinian, and Iwo Jima. The personnel bunkers were designed somewhat like a submarine, with an aisle down the center, bunks stacked three high on either side, and an entrance on either end in an L-shape so a shell could not directly enter the bunker. Some structures were heavy timber and some concrete, and all would be covered by several feet of sand. There were lights but no indoor plumbing. The toilets were out in the bushes and for a shower we could use the new barracks bathrooms.

The Marine garrison at Midway was a very diverse group. Many of the senior enlisted men were career military and had served in China. Then there were regular enlisted raw recruits like myself and a number of draftees. Many of these had some college credits and some were college graduates. Recently, in 1940, President Roosevelt had signed the first peace-time draft in United States history. Initially, this Selective Service Act required all men ages 21 to 35 to register with the local draft board. The age bracket was later expanded from 18 to 45 years of age. The tour of duty would be twelve months.

After the war started in December 1941, the draftees, like the regular enlisted, were in for the duration of the war. When drafted, you had no choice of which branch of service you would be assigned, but when you volunteered ahead of your draft call-up, you could select the branch of service. All the draftees in our group had volunteered for the Marines. We had a well-educated group. Most of the officers were from the Naval Academy or

Ivy League schools. Patriotism was not a dirty word in the Ivy League schools in that era.

If half the stories those old China Marines told about their service in China were true, it had to be a wild place. The top sergeant in our wire group was an old China Marine named Bill Haley, a tough Texan with a big handlebar mustache. He talked gruff, but I got along very well with him. My immediate boss was a big, red-headed Irishman from Oklahoma named Luther Hutchingson. Hutch and Sgt. Haley were very close buddies, and they took care of me. I was a smart, hard worker, and they put me up for promotion as early as they had the authorization.

I don't recall it being mentioned at my level, but there was a sense of urgency. You could feel in the air the need to prepare for an attack by the Japanese Naval forces. At our level, we were not aware of the growing atmosphere of hostilities going on in the diplomatic world between Washington and Tokyo. In hindsight, you could see we were headed to war with Japan based on their empire-building activities in the Far East and their belligerent attitude on the diplomatic front.

One duty I had occasionally was manning the lookout tower, a high tower located near the center of Sand Island. There are two islands in the Midway lagoon: Sand and Eastern. I was stationed on Sand Island. I did not like to climb heights, especially this watch tower on a windy dark night. I did take this assignment seriously. I did not want to miss anything. This results in a bit of strain in the daytime while you are scanning 360 degrees for aircraft and watercraft.

On Midway, the sky always has some gooney birds flying out over the surrounding ocean, and those large birds with such a wide wing span can momentarily look like an aircraft. At night as you scan the ocean, your imagination comes into play, and you are sure you saw a light flash. You don't want to miss anything, and for sure you don't want to send a false alarm, so it was a little nerve racking.

The lookout tower for some strange reason was located very close to the radar station. In fact, from the crow's nest on the top of the tower, you looked down on the rotating radar antenna on the roof of the radar building. In the military, there is never a shortage of rumors, and one rumor that certainly got our attention was that close exposure to this powerful radar beam would make you sterile. Of course, we have living proof that is not true, but at that time radar was a new word in our vocabulary.

Radar was a new invention and was first used effectively at that time by England. They would use radar to pick up the German planes coming across the English Channel to bomb targets in England. The radar control room was a wooden building surrounded by sandbag walls several feet thick and up to the level of the roof, which had to be unprotected due to the large antenna.

One pleasant memory I have of watch tower duty was getting a snack at midnight from the mess hall, which delivered food to all of the outposts via an old 1935 Ford truck. The truck had no cab and a flat body with no sides. I can still hear that old truck chugging slowly along as it approached the tower. We were in a strict blackout mode so the driver had to go slow. As much as I disliked climbing up and down the tower, I looked forward to climbing down to meet the "meals on wheels." It was always the same, a peanut butter and jelly sandwich and the chance to fill your canteen with coffee. At that time, to me, this was like eating at a five-star restaurant. I had never eaten a peanut butter and jelly sandwich that tasted as good.

Maybe the journey on this old truck was what made it special. The truck was not a military vehicle, and I never knew which outfit claimed ownership. Our communication guys used it at times. One thing that made it special was that it was one of the very few vehicles on this island.

The military aspect of everyday life on Midway was minimum. I am referring to inspections, formations, and those type of activities. There was a sense of urgency to get the island ready for an attack. We did have classes on the nature of the Japanese military, their thinking, and their weapons.

Sometime in late November 1941, we had a special event. There was a high-ranking Japanese ambassador, Kichisaburo Nomura, staying overnight at the Pan-Am Lodge. He was a passenger on the China Clipper on his way to meet with Secretary of State Cordell Hull at the White House. The China Clipper was a large, four-engine seaplane designed especially for mail and passenger service in the Orient. It required ten to twelve days to make the journey. The flight was from Honolulu with stops for refueling and service at Midway, Wake, and Guam and on to Manila or Hong Kong. At Midway, the Clipper would land in the smooth waters in the lagoon, and small boats would ferry the passengers to the dock for an overnight stay at the Pan-Am Lodge. This was a small but nice motel-like structure which would provide overnight accommodations for the passengers and crew. We called it the "Gooney Bird Lodge."

Diplomatic issues between the US and Japan were increasing in hostility. In fact, things were not going well at all in the diplomatic discussions with Japan. The US had established an embargo on our trade with Japan because of their actions in China and other parts of the Far East. We had stopped exporting oil to Japan. That really angered them.

Col. Shannon wanted to impress this Japanese ambassador with the strength of our Marine garrison on Midway so he had all the troops, with our field packs and weapons, march single file past the front of the Pan-Am Lodge. We would then circle around behind the lodge and march again by the front. We made several rounds so it would appear our manpower was several time larger than what we actually had. Col. Shannon assumed that the Japanese ambassador would be observing all he could about our military strength on Midway.

As it turned out, many days later, on the afternoon of December 7, 1941, as Ambassador Nomura was engaged in a heated discussion in Washington D.C. with Secretary Hull in Washington, the Japanese bombed Pearl Harbor. This attack was the worst defeat our naval forces had ever experienced.

This special Japanese envoy and the Japanese ambassador had set up a critical meeting on Sunday afternoon, December 7th. As they met, Secretary Hull was slipped a note that the Japs had attacked Pearl Harbor. Due to the time zone difference, it was early afternoon in Washington when the attack occurred. The Japanese diplomat claimed they were unaware of this surprise. I don't think that question was ever answered. That was a good indication of what a treacherous and evil enemy we faced.

The morning Pearl Harbor was attacked, I was on duty in our command center. I had operated the switchboard before, but never alone. I guess Corporal Hutchingson thought a quiet

Sunday morning would be a good time to let a raw recruit operate the system alone. I knew the technical side of this system as well as anyone, but I was not prepared for the human aspect I was about to encounter.

In this field telephone system, all calls have to be routed through the switchboard. No direct calls are possible. I received a signal from the Officer of the Day to connect him to Col. Shannon. I was totally unprepared for a call like that. In my experience as a trainee, I had never connected a call to Col. Shannon's line. In fact, the jack to his line was painted red, and I had gotten the impression that you don't mess with that line. It was understood he will call you, you don't call him.

Here I am, early Sunday morning and some lieutenant wants me to wake up the Commanding Officer. I don't recall my exact words, but it was something like this: "Sir, I am not supposed to call Col. Shannon."

He replied in a much stronger voice. "I have got to talk to Col. Shannon. The Japs have bombed Oahu."

It still did not register with me that he was talking about Pearl Harbor. I need to explain, Oahu, pronounced, "Ah-who," is the island where Pearl Harbor and Honolulu are located. In my many discussions with others on Pearl Harbor or Honolulu, we never referred to Oahu. I am sure I had seen Oahu in writing, but I was not familiar with the pronunciation "Ah-who." So to me, when the lieutenant said Japs had bombed Oahu, I thought he was referring to some place in the Far East, like Indonesia, where the Japs were operating.

I guess I was still trying to stall this call to wake up the commanding officer, and to put it mildly, he was getting impatient with me. Then he came across loud and clear.

"The Japanese have bombed Pearl Harbor," he said.

I couldn't make that connection fast enough. I knew then that the United States was at war with Japan.

It was hard to accept the fact that our great nation suffered such a devastating defeat by what most people thought of, at that time, as a third rate country. We quickly had to recognize that we faced a nation with a powerful navy, air force, and army.

From my studies, the Japanese military expected this surprise attack to be a blow so devastating that we would accept a peace treaty on their terms, meaning the Japanese Empire would be supreme in the Pacific Rim and in the Central Pacific and in complete control of all their newly gained territory. This would include a large part of China, Korea, Manchuria, Philippines, Formosa (present day Tinian), plus islands in the central Pacific.

The following is an excerpt from *Marines at Midway* by Lt. Col. R.D. Heinl, which documents how the message that Pearl Harbor had been attacked was received at the Officers' Mess that morning. Lt. William R. Dorr would have to be the guy who called me, and I am surprised he did not say, "I had trouble from that stupid telephone operator, but I finally got the message to Col. Shannon."

> *On Sunday morning, 7 December 1941, I was at breakfast in the officers' mess with the other officers of the Battalion when Lt. William R. Dorr, officer of the day, came into the mess, and told us a message had been received from Pearl Harbor, which stated that the Japanese had attacked Oahu. We all thought he was joking and said so, but Lieutenant Dorr stuck to his story and added that he had awakened Lieutenant Colonel Shannon and informed him of the contents of the message.*
>
> *Shortly afterward Lieutenant Colonel Shannon and Major Archie O'Neil came into the mess, confirmed Dorr's report, and told all battery commanders to alert their men and have them ready to man battle stations within the hour.*
>
> *My feelings at that time and that of nearly all the other officers I am sure, was that this was a realistic war game. I believe that Lieutenant Colonel Shannon also doubted that the warning was a report of a real attack.*
>
> *We notified our men to be ready to march to the batteries in light marching order within an hour and hurriedly finished breakfast. As I recall, Dorr said the message from Pearl Harbor had been received about 0700. The siren sounded for*

*general quarters at about 0900, at which time all
batteries were marching to their positions.*

We also received a message that day that the Japs were attacking Wake Island, so we fully expected we would be next. We were in a full alert status. The day passed quietly, but sometime after dark I was on standby in our bunker when we heard some explosions. We all went outside. Due to the surrounding bushes, we could not see the horizon. A new bunker was under construction right next to our bunker, and the bulldozers had excavated a large amount of sand for the foundation. My friend Harkins, and I climbed up on the mound of sand to get a better view. We observed flashes offshore and flashes near the seaplane hangars, which were only a short distance away. We were up on our observation perch a few moments when our gunnery sergeant came charging out of the bushes.

"We are giving them hell, ain't we, gunny?" I yelled.

He stopped and looked up at us. "You stupid idiots, we ain't fired a shot! Get your ass down and follow me."

He was panting, almost out of breath. Just as he said that, a shell burst very close to our position and shrapnel went zinging by and some pieces ricocheted off a bundle of rebar, drawing sparks. I don't remember just how Harkins and I got down off that perch on the sand pile, but we did it in record time.

The gunnery sergeant got all of our troops together and made sure we understood our assignments. No one knew the size of the Jap forces, so you had to be prepared for the worst, which would be a landing force. That didn't turn out to be the case. Some accounts said there were two ships out there, and some record four ships.

At the time, I did not know the difference in sound from incoming or outgoing artillery rounds. The flashes we observed offshore were the Japs firing, and the flashes on shore were the incoming bursts. I guess I was fixed on the thought that "we would do the sending and the Japs would be receiving."

When our guns opened up, the Japs retreated. We had one, maybe more, scout planes flying that day. (I never knew why they did not spot these ships. Maybe it was poor visibility. Our radar at that time could not detect surface objects.)

We closely followed the situation on Wake. They were being attacked daily, and on December 11, 1941, the Japs made an attempt to land on Wake. They were repulsed by the Marines on Wake, and the Marines inflicted heavy damage to their naval forces. This was later noted as a historic event, as it was the only time in the war where an amphibious landing force was repulsed.

After this defeat, the Japs came back with a much larger force. The Marine garrison was hopelessly outnumbered and outgunned. They were forced to surrender. I saw a documentary a couple of years ago on this battle, and several survivors interviewed very emphatically stated they wanted to keep on fighting.

I admire their courage, but when you see the forces the Japs had amassed for their assault—men, air, naval—there is no way they could have survived. The situation on Wake was of the utmost interest to us troops on Midway, because after Wake fell Midway. It was the outermost American outpost, and we were the next potential target for the Japs. Wake Island is 2,300 miles due west of Honolulu, and Midway is 1,250 miles northwest of Honolulu.

I personally had special feelings for the troops on Wake. Not too many weeks earlier I was with those guys on the ship. I did not know any of them real well. In fact, I can't even remember a single name. I again ponder a question raised earlier: Why was I not in the group assigned to Wake?

I have thought on this, and I don't normally ask questions like this, but as I explained to Kathryn, how was it that I was assigned to Midway and some guys, with the exact same credentials, were assigned to Wake? If I say the good Lord was looking after me, then does that mean the Lord was not looking out for the guy who, in a sense, took my place on Wake? Her answer was God had a plan for your life, and that is it.

I accept that.

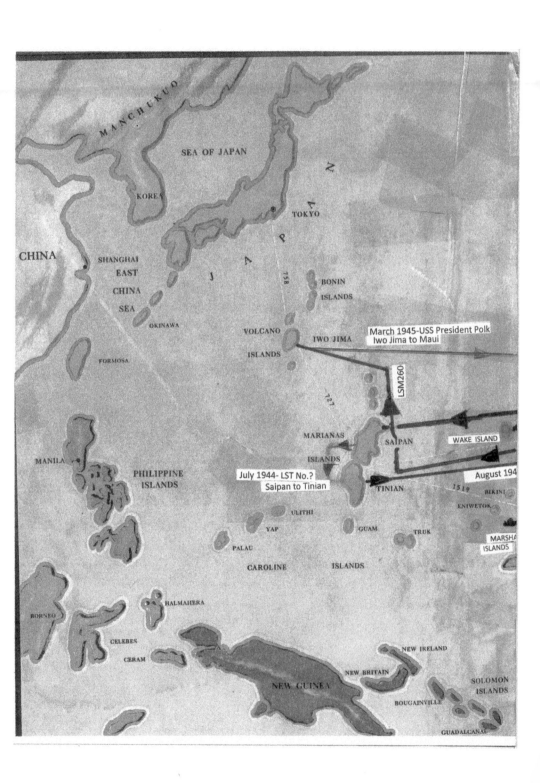

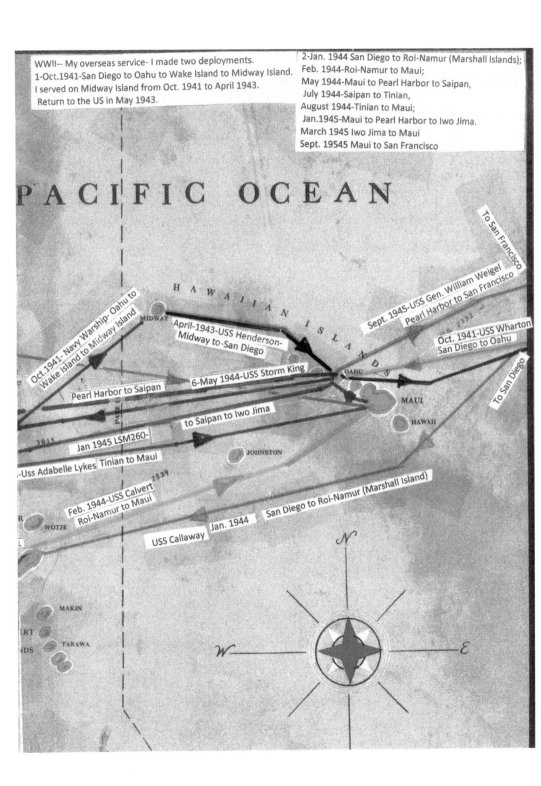

WWII-- My overseas service- I made two deployments.
1-Oct.1941-San Diego to Oahu to Wake Island to Midway Island.
I served on Midway Island from Oct. 1941 to April 1943.
Return to the US in May 1943.

2-Jan. 1944 San Diego to Roi-Namur (Marshall Islands);
Feb. 1944-Roi-Namur to Maui;
May 1944-Maui to Pearl Harbor to Saipan,
July 1944-Saipan to Tinian,
August 1944-Tinian to Maui;
Jan.1945-Maui to Pearl Harbor to Iwo Jima.
March 1945 Iwo Jima to Maui
Sept. 19545 Maui to San Francisco

PACIFIC OCEAN

HAWAIIAN ISLANDS

To San Francisco

Sept. 1945-USS Gen. William Weigel
Pearl Harbor to San Francisco

Oct. 1941- Navy Warship- Oahu to
Wake Island to Midway Island

April-1943-USS Henderson-
Midway to-San Diego

Oct. 1941-USS Wharton
San Diego to Oahu

MIDWAY

6-May 1944-USS Storm King

OAHU

To San Diego

Pearl Harbor to Saipan

MAUI

HAWAII

to Saipan to Iwo Jima

Jan 1945 LSM260-

JOHNSTON

-Uss Adabelle Lykes Tinian to Maui

Feb. 1944-USS Calvert
Roi-Namur to Maui

San Diego to Roi-Namur (Marshall Island)

USS Callaway   Jan. 1944

WOTJE

MAKIN

TARAWA

N

W   E

Highest In Class

Ison A. Rigell, above, private in the United States Marine Corps and son of Mrs. Mary Rigell, of Slocomb, has been graduated from the Field Telephone School at the Marine Corps Base at San Diego, Cal., with the highest mark in his class. Private Rigell, before entering the Marine Corps, attended Slocomb High School where he took an active part in athletics, earning three letters in football and two in basketball. Upon the completion of his high school work, he joined the Marines at Birmingham and was then transferred to California.

This was published in the *Dothan Eagle*, which was the paper for southeast Alabama, including Slocomb.

DOOLITTLE'S RAID

The spring of 1942 was a low point in our history. We had not recovered from the devastating defeat at Pearl Harbor, and with the loss of Wake Island, Guam, and the Philippines, the Japs were cruelly expanding their empire throughout the Pacific Rim. Nowhere could we claim a victory. At a meeting in late December 1941, President Roosevelt pressed his military leaders to find a way to bomb the Japanese homeland. This would provide a desperately needed boost to our morale and cause the Japanese population to have some doubts about their leadership, as they had been assured the homeland of Japan would never be attacked. A brilliant Navy captain came up with a clever idea where we could, at least, temporarily take the war to the Japanese homeland.

I was on Midway Island at this time, April 1942, and of course we had no knowledge of this plan. However, we would later learn this plan did have a profound effect on us troops on Midway Island. I will explain that later. The captain had observed that the Navy had outlined a carrier deck on an airstrip at Naval Station Norfolk, in Virginia, for practicing takeoffs and landings.

The plan was to load one of our aircraft carriers with our B-25 bombers and, from the northern Pacific Ocean, slip up on Japan.

The bombers would take off from the carrier, bomb cities in Japan, and fly to friendly areas in China unoccupied by the Japs.

Our B-25 bomber was a twin engine land-based bomber. It could take off from one of our aircraft carriers, but it was not possible for a B-25 to land on a carrier. The military proved the B-25 could take off from a carrier by painting the outline of a carrier flight deck on one of our airstrips at Eglin Airbase in the Florida Panhandle and making practice takeoffs. There was not much room for error, but they proved it could be done. The military put out a request for volunteers for a very special and dangerous mission, which they did not disclose to the volunteers. The response was overwhelming. They got all the right people, and they went into an intensive training program. Gen. Jimmy Doolittle was their leader.

Our aircraft carrier, the USS Hornet, was selected for this mission. In early April 1942, the Hornet, its flight deck loaded with 16 B-25 bombers, sailed out of San Francisco with their escort ships. They sailed in radio silence, and when they were still 250 miles away from their designated takeoff point, they encountered a Japanese vessel. The escort ships immediately sank this Japanese ship, but they knew it would have already alerted the mainland. This posed a real problem for Gen. Doolittle. Our cover had been completely blown.

At best, this was a very dangerous mission. It was unclear if they would even have enough fuel to reach the occupied Jap territory in China. Gen. Doolittle knew that by the time they could reach the designated point for takeoff, the Japanese fighter planes would be waiting for them. Taking off at this point meant running out of fuel and having to bail out almost certainly in Japanese-occupied China or maybe even in the ocean.

Despite the odds against them, Gen. Doolittle made the decision: "We go now."

It should be noted this was the first time any of the crew had taken off from the deck of an aircraft carrier. The plan was to fly in at a low altitude and spread out and bomb five cities. The reason they selected five cities was to make sure the Japanese propaganda machines could not hide this operation from the Japanese masses. These brave airmen took off and did their job. They dropped their bombs on all five cities. They hit their targets.

From a military standpoint, the damage would be considered minimal, but from a psychological standpoint, the damage was enormous. The Japanese had been assured by their leaders when the war started, the Japanese homeland would never be touched, so this was a tremendous embarrassment. From our side, the boost in our morale was tremendous; we bombed the Japanese homeland.

Due to having to take off over 200 miles before the designated point, it appeared some of the planes would not be able to reach the coast of China. Here is where a little divine intervention occurred. They encountered a storm between Japan and China, which was very unusual for this time of the year. The winds were fortunately pushing them toward China, resulting in fifteen of the sixteen planes reaching China. Then, one by one, as they ran out of fuel, they crashed. This was in the middle of the night. Just imagine yourself up there in the dark having to bail out, having no clue where you were.

Eight of our airmen were captured by the Japanese in China, and three of them were executed. One plane made it safely to Vladivostok in the Soviet Union, and this crew was interned for about a year before being released. The Japanese army in the area of China where our planes crashed made a concentrated effort to find any Chinese citizen that helped our airmen escape, and they indiscriminately and cruelly punished many suspected in aiding our downed airmen.

I mentioned above that at the time of the raid, US troops on Midway had no knowledge of how this operation would have almost immediate consequences on our small Marine garrison. Of course, we quickly received the good news about the raid, and believe me, it did help our morale, as that was the first good news we had since the start of the war.

Here is how our troops on Midway Island would be affected by this operation. As already mentioned, Midway was the furthest US outpost flying the American flag west of Pearl Harbor looking toward Japan. The Japanese High Command was profoundly embarrassed by the fact we could bomb their homeland. To make sure this could never happen again, they made the decision to extend their defense perimeter to guard the Western Pacific Ocean approaches to Japan. To accomplish this, they needed Midway Island.

They could see another advantage in capturing Midway, and that is they anticipated what was left of our Navy would be forced to leave Pearl Harbor to try protect Midway. In this scenario, their navy, which at this time was so much more powerful than ours, would have an excellent opportunity to destroy our naval forces in the Pacific. They thought we would then be ready to sign a peace treaty, which would leave Japan with all the territory they had captured, which was enormous.

The Doolittle attack was on April 18, 1942. They immediately developed a plan to send a powerful convoy of several battleships, cruisers, destroyers, ships for the assault troops, and four aircraft carriers to capture Midway Island in early June 1942. That resulted in the battle for Midway Island, which proved to be a disaster for the Japanese. I want to state something I will repeat again later: I thank my Lord for those talented people that broke the Japanese code, and I thank my Lord for those brave Navy and Marine pilots, many of whom lost their lives, who saved our butts on Midway.

Now this is not the end of the Doolittle Raid story. There is truly an amazing spiritual story about one of the crew members who was captured and spent forty months being tortured and abused in a Japanese prison in China. Jacob DeShazer, a 27-year-old farm boy from Oregon, was an enlisted crew member of one of the planes that ran out of fuel. He bailed out and was captured the next day by the Japanese in China. It is hard to imagine how some human beings can be so cruel to other human beings, and unfortunately all prisoners captured by the Japanese in WWII were treated the same.

DeShazer said at times it was hard to keep your sanity due to the mistreatment by the guards. At one time the Japanese did respond to a request by these prisoners for a Bible, and DeShazer devoured this book, reading it over and over. God had his hand on DeShazer, because only God could cause DeShazer to forgive these evil guards. He made a vow, if God permitted him to live through the war, he would return to Japan, preaching the gospel of forgiveness. The Holy Spirit must be on this man to think like this. This is the closest example that I know of a real person following Jesus's prayer on the cross—asking forgiveness for those people because they did not know what they were doing.

Jacob DeShazer survived the war, and in 1948, in obedience to his commitment in that Japanese prison cell, he returned to Japan to preach the gospel. One day at a railroad station in Tokyo he was passing out tracts describing his conversion in that Japanese prison cell, and one Japanese man came by and took one of them. This man happened to be Mitsuo Fuchida, the former leader of the Japanese attack force on Pearl Harbor. He was the one who shouted that famous Japanese war cry, "Tora, Tora, Tora," as they began the attack on Pearl Harbor. It was the Japanese code word for a complete surprise with no opposition.

Fuchida, like all former Japanese military, was now a civilian. He had moved back into his little village and was trying to make a living for his family by farming. The Holy Spirit had his hand on Fuchida. He could not believe this man, DeShazer, after all the suffering he had experienced as a prisoner, was back in Japan preaching forgiveness. Fuchida said a peace came over him, something he had been seeking but never experienced. This prompted him to buy a Bible, and like DeShazer, he just devoured it.

"I read this book eagerly," he said.

He read Luke 23:34, the prayer of Jesus at his death: "Father, forgive them; for they know not what they do." He said he was impressed because he was one of those for whom Jesus had prayed.

I can tell you this spoke to me, because after the war I had real trouble forgiving the Japanese, and I had suffered nothing like DeShazer. In fact, I could not understand why anyone would buy a Japanese product, especially cars. But one day, several years ago, it occurred to me that I had a real problem in forgiveness. I had repeated the Lord's Prayer many, many times without realizing what I was saying, and I suspect many Christians are guilty of the same thing. This is what the Holy Spirit revealed to me.

I prayed, "Lord forgive me of my trespasses as I forgive others of their trespasses."

Think about what I just said. "Lord if I do not forgive others of their trespasses, don't forgive me of my trespasses." Oh, Lord, thank you for giving me the "light" that I may never be guilty of any unforgiveness again.

There is much more to this amazing story, and I would encourage you to read *From Pearl Harbor to Calvary* by Mitsuo Fuchida. When Fuchida gave his life to Christ, since he was a well-known Japanese war hero, it made headlines in Japanese newspapers. "Pearl Harbor Hero converts to Christianity," It read.

His old military comrades tried to tell him this was a big mistake, but he remained steadfast in his faith and stated he would give anything if he could retract his actions many years ago at Pearl Harbor.

Fuchida and DeShazer became good friends. Fuchida spent the rest of his life spreading the gospel in Japan and the Far East until his death in 1976.

BATTLE OF MIDWAY

On May 3, 1942, Adm. Nimitz made a trip to Midway to confer with Lt. Col. Shannon and Cmdr. Simard on our capability to hold Midway against a major Japanese assault.

In real estate, commercial and residential, the location determines the value. This fact is even more important in military conflicts. It determines whether you lose or win a battle.

Midway, a tiny sand pit in the middle of the Pacific Ocean, had no natural resources, no potable water, and no mineral resources, and by real estate standards was worthless. Yet both the US and Japan saw the possession of these few hundred acres of sand as absolutely vital to achieving victory in the Pacific.

It was very logical to assume the occupation of Midway was a prime objective of the Japanese war plan. In this May 3rd meeting, Adm. Nimitz told Col. Shannon what reinforcements he could provide, which included a squadron of Marine dive bombers, some additional troops, and four tanks. Then Adm. Nimitz asked Col. Shannon if he could hold the island with these reinforcements. Col. Shannon's response was, "We can hold this island until hell freezes over."

Obviously, none of us troopers were privy to the information in this meeting; I only learned this later in doing some historical research. However, I would add that if Adm. Nimitz had posed this question to any of us troops, we would have, with confidence, given the same answer as Col. Shannon.

Knowing what I know today though, with some regret, I would have to give a different answer. Based on our experiences on Saipan and Iwo Jima, we knew all too well that the rugged terrain of caves, crevices, ravines, and high ground gave the defense forces a great advantage. Although with a very high cost of lives, despite this grave disadvantage, the invading forces still won.

Now compared to Saipan and Iwo Jima, Midway had no high ground, no caves, no crevices, or ravines. The Midway landscape greatly favored the invading forces, and the terrain was a big minus for the defending forces. Our largest guns were five inches, and the enemy, with cruisers and battleships with eight and sixteen inch guns, could position themselves out of range of our 5 inch guns and pulverize the island. Even with the additional dive bombers, we would be no match for four aircraft carriers loaded with dive bombers and fighter planes. We could give a good account for ourselves in a battle with the invading forces, but in my view now, we would all have been killed or taken as prisoner.

Sometime in late May 1942, all the troops were called out in formation. Our officers gave us very detailed information about a very large Jap task force that was on the way to attack and capture Midway Island. There were four aircraft carriers in this armada, and they were supported by battleships, cruisers, and destroyers—a very formidable force. We were all amazed at the very detailed information they were passing on to us. We were not aware that the Navy intelligence group had broken the Japanese military code.

There is some interesting background information on how our intelligence derived that Midway was a target of this Japanese task force. Our intelligence people knew all about the task force, but they were not sure of the target because, in coded messages, the Japs always referred to the target as AF. We were not given this background information at our briefing. I later read what was going on behind the scenes in trying to identify target AF.

The Navy had an intelligence group stationed in Hawaii and another intelligence group in Washington, D.C. There was much jealousy between these two groups, and from the research I did, the people in Washington always thought they were superior to the group in Hawaii. However, my research shows that the group in Hawaii was always superior to the group in Washington, and it was certainly true in this case. The group in Washington was convinced that the code AF was the Aleutian Islands, and that that was where the Jap Task Force was headed. The group in Hawaii was convinced target AF was Midway Island.

These opposing opinions created a great dilemma for Adm. Nimitz, the overall commander. Adm. Nimitz only had three aircraft carriers to face this large Japanese task force. It would be a total disaster if he placed the carriers to intercept the Jap task force headed for the Aleutian Islands and the enemy task force actually went to Midway and vice versa.

Fortunately, there was one clear-thinking Navy lieutenant in the intelligence group in Hawaii that came up with a clever way to identify target AF. It was a very simple plan: Send an open message that the Japs would read.

"Desalination plant on Midway Island is inoperative, and they have only two weeks of water," the message said.

Then they waited. Sure enough, the Japs took the bait. The Japs sent a coded message to their task force: "The desalination plant at AF is down, and they only have two weeks of water."

I would add a little personal touch; I would not be here today if those Washington "weenies" had their way. Our aircraft carriers would have been up in the Aleutian Islands, and we would have been in big, big trouble on Midway.

Now, back to our briefing. They had the names of the aircraft carriers, battleships, cruisers, and other ships in the task force. They had the names of the top leaders, and interestingly enough, they told us where the assault troops for landing on Midway were being loaded.

It did not mean anything to me at the time, but some of the assault troops were being loaded at Saipan. At that point I had never heard of Saipan. I mention this because exactly two years later, in late May of 1944, I was on a troopship headed for an assault on Saipan. You never know what the future holds.

As previously mentioned, in late spring of 1942, Midway was the furthest station toward Japan that was flying the

American flag. The Japs had captured Wake Island, Guam, and the Philippines, and taken American prisoners in all of these locations. Word was getting out about how brutally our prisoners were being treated. One of my friends from Slocomb was captured in the Philippines and spent the war working in a coal mine in Japan.

We were told what day—June 4, 1942—and the exact time to expect the first wave of the enemy bombers, and sure enough, at the expected time our radar picked up the incoming planes and the air raid siren sounded.

Let me say that is an eerie sound you don't ever want to hear. Our strict orders were that unless you were manning an anti-aircraft gun or had some other specific assignment that required you to be topside, you had to go into a designated underground bunker. Right on time we heard from inside our bunker our anti-aircraft guns in action, and you could clearly hear the dive bombers and the exploding bombs.

The bunker I was in did not have any bombs land really close by, but several were close enough to shake the ground. I think everyone had the urge to go out and see what was going on. A few guys did this, and got a bit of satisfaction firing their rifles at the dive bombers. It was tempting, but I obeyed the orders and stayed underground until the all-clear signal.

The damage we suffered the first night of the Jap attack on Midway was not extensive. They did set the seaplane hangar on fire and did some other structural damage. I commend Col. Shannon for having prepared the troops so well for such an attack. I can appreciate now why we had been busy night and day since I arrived building fortifications and pillboxes, setting up landmines and barbed wire on the beach, and living in underground bunkers. I think, looking back, we had done everything we could to prepare for war, although I will say none of us really expected it to come at that time.

We were expecting a second wave of bombers followed by the landing of Jap troops, but neither of these ever happened. Providence intervened, and although we did not know it at the time, our Navy and Marine pilots were doing a miraculous job destroying the enemy task force out in the ocean north of Midway. Unknown to the Japanese, Adm. Nimitz had three aircraft carriers and supporting ships to intercept and destroy the Japanese task force.

Our Navy did destroy the Japanese task force, but sadly it came at a very high price. The initial attack on the Japanese task force was by a squadron of torpedo bombers. Unfortunately, these were old, slow planes that were no match for the Japanese fighters, called Zeros, which came out to meet them. Every one of our torpedo bombers were shot down by the Zeros, and all of the flight crews were killed except one pilot. He was shot down and was later picked up out of the water by one of our ships.

None of our torpedoes made a hit on a Japanese ship, but fortunately, as the Zeros were engaged with our torpedo bombers, the dive bombers from our aircraft carriers found the Japanese aircraft carriers. The carriers had their dive bombers on the flight deck busy loading them with bombs for the second attack on Midway. When the action was over, our pilots had sunk three of their four carriers and later, they sunk the fourth carrier.

While all of this action was going on, some of the Jap bombers did attack and sink one of our aircraft carriers, the Yorktown. I can never thank those brave Navy and Marine airmen that attacked and sank those enemy carriers enough. I am here today because of their sacrifices, and I thank my Lord for them.

The day after the Japanese bombed us, I had the first opportunity in several days to get a shower and get cleaned up. There were some nice new barracks ready, and although we were not allowed to move in, we could use the heads. The "head" is a nautical term the Navy and Marines use for the toilets, washbasins, and showers. One of my buddies, Mort Harkins, and I went over to one of the barracks to take a shower and get cleaned up.

As you entered, there was a door immediately on your left that led to the head on that end of the barracks. The door opened inward and to the right, and as I opened the door I was looking at the opposite wall where there was a row of sinks and mirrors above the sinks. I was startled because directly in front of me was the back of a Jap pilot in his flight suit. He never turned around to look at me, but I could see his face in the mirror, and then in the mirror I could see a Marine with a rifle. He had been blocked from my view by the door when it was open; it obscured my direct view of the guard, who I did not know. He immediately told us that we couldn't come in there right now.

"We just wanted to come in and take a shower," I said.

He said we could go on down the hall and use the other door as it opened directly into the shower area, but he told us not to come back in that area. The prisoner never turned around to look at us, but I could see him looking at us in the mirror. He did not appear to be wounded.

We knew that our ground anti-aircraft guns and our aircraft had shot down a number of the enemy planes, and the word was that we had captured a number of enemy pilots. I never did know exactly how many were captured, nor did we know where they were keeping them. I assume these prisoners were taken back to Hawaii for more interrogation by our intelligence people as quickly as possible.

That was my first view of the enemy.

History records the battle of Midway as the turning point in the war with Japan. Up until this time, the Japanese had enjoyed tremendous success in expanding the Japanese Empire, and as a result of the tremendous losses suffered in this battle, the enemy was forced to go into a defensive mode and abandon any further plans for expansion.

The enemy not only lost four of their very best aircraft carriers, but also hundreds of their most experienced pilots. Most of these pilots had participated in the attack on Pearl Harbor. I need to say it again: Those brave Navy and Marine pilots saved every man on Midway. I would not be here today if it were not for their bold action in destroying this Japanese armada.

I think it is safe to say that after the battle of Midway, we troops on the island could live in a little more relaxed fashion. We even naïvely thought we would be permitted to come out of our dugouts and live in those nice barracks, but that was not to be. The only enemy encounter we would experience during our remaining days on Midway was the occasional Jap submarine surfacing at night and lobbing a few shells from their deck guns. They would then submerge before our artillery could respond. To my knowledge no one was ever wounded by these sub attacks, and there was very little material damage.

Now our daily thoughts and focus were not on an impending attack from the enemy, but how long we were going to be isolated out there on this tiny island. The very name of our unit, 6th Defense Battalion, defined who we were. Our job was to defend. The enemy comes to us, we are stationary, and we cannot go on the attack.

Our country was now ready to go on the offensive. Our first offensive move in the war in the Pacific was in August 1942, when the 1st Marine Division landed on Guadalcanal. I don't say this in any kind of heroic context, but I do think that every Marine and sailor stationed on Midway at that time envied those troops involved in the Guadalcanal campaign. I do not know how to describe the thinking at that time concerning wanting to be in a vital role in defeating the enemy. It is such a contrast to the thinking of so many people today with their anti-American attitude. The country was united then; everyone was willing and eager to do and go wherever needed to defeat the enemy.

We had no word and could not get any information on how long we would be on Midway, and I do not think our commander knew any more about the subject than the troops. It turned out that after the battle of Midway, it would be eleven months before we would be relieved in May 1943. As I recall, the notice came very suddenly and just a few days before we boarded a ship that would take us to Pearl Harbor, the first leg of our journey back to the good old USA.

I will say a few words about our lives on Midway in the last eleven months. One plus thing I would say about the military in WWII is that they did a good job of delivering mail to the troops. If you do not have good mail service, you will have a big morale problem.

We received mail on a regular schedule. It was delivered from Pearl Harbor by a Navy PBY, which is a large seaplane. On the scheduled day for the mail plane we would be watching the skies for its arrival, and then later in the day waiting for "Mail Call." There was one negative thing about outgoing mail though. It was all censored, and there was hardly anything you could say other than, "Don't worry, I'm okay." You could not say where you were. The people writing you addressed your mail to a P.O. Box number in San Francisco. It was a military P.O. Box, and they would forward it to your unit no matter where you were.

Back to everyday life on Midway. As I previously mentioned,

we were still not allowed to live in those new barracks. Our underground dugouts were still home. We had developed our communication system to a point where it was very reliable, and keeping it in good operation was not a problem.

Our daily entertainment was watching the gooney birds. Midway is home to thousands of gooney birds. They are in the air and all over the ground. Gooney birds, like an airplane, have to get up a little speed to take off, and when they land, they must take a few steps to stop. It is amusing to watch the immature birds and their first attempts to take off and land. They do a lot of tumbling, but like a little kid learning to walk, they get up and try it again.

Another gooney bird story: A few years ago I signed up for a military tour back to Midway, and it involved taking a Navy plane from Pearl Harbor. A few days before the scheduled departure, the trip was canceled by the Navy because the daylight trips were becoming too dangerous due to encounters with the gooney birds. For safety reasons, all flights to Midway required landing and taking off at night. A gooney bird is a very large bird, and I guess it could bring down a plane. I was very disappointed, as I really wanted to visit Midway.

I may have mentioned this before, but there was one big difference in serving with the 6th Defense Battalion and the 4th Marine Division. In the 4th Division, if you are a telephone wire man, that is all you do. On Midway, due to the small number of troops, you had to take on other tasks as required. I was assigned to the watchtower, and another assignment which was certainly out of my area of experience was serving as Corporal of the Guard. I only got called upon to do this one time, but that was enough. That was more than enough. The Corporal of the Guard reports to the Officer of the Day. The Officer of the Day takes care of all the routine matters that come up during the day, and he makes the judgment call of taking any significant issues to the attention of the commanding officer.

When I was on duty as Corporal of the Guard, I received a call from the Beer Garden that they needed some help, as there was a disturbance. The disturbance was that "Yellow Hair" was on a rampage. That was about the worst news I could get. I knew what that meant.

I did not know "Yellow Hair" personally, but I think everyone on the island had heard about him. He was a full-blooded Indian and, sober, he was one of the nicest people you would ever meet. But when he was full of booze, you did not want to be anywhere near him. Yellow Hair was not a tall guy but he was built like a tank, and he was certainly someone you would not want to tangle with. There was a limit of two beers per night at the Beer Garden, but with a buddy system operating there was no way to enforce that. I don't know how many beers Yellow Hair had consumed. I would also like to mention this was not the first time Yellow Hair had been on a rampage at the Beer Garden. I did have an assistant with me that night, Bob Heuser. Bob was a pretty big guy, but I still dreaded confronting Yellow Hair.

Bob and I took off for the Beer Garden, and we began to hear some loud voices. But as we got closer, we could tell the voices were not coming from the Beer Garden. We were still operating in a complete blackout on Midway, so we could not see exactly where these voices were coming from. The voices seemed to be getting fainter. We went on into the Beer Garden, and to our great relief everything was quiet inside. We talked to the guy who had called us, and he said some of Yellow Hair's friends had calmed him down and were trying to get him back to his dugout. I don't remember if I said it but even if I didn't, I'm sure I was thinking, "Thank you, Lord, for taking care of this situation."

One thing we all did on Midway that was not good was that most of the time we wore no caps, hats, or jackets. We did not know any better. I would say we all got more sun than we needed.

It was a very happy, happy day when we received word that we were going to be relieved, and when we were back in the USA, we would have a 30-day leave. As I mentioned earlier, the first leg of our trip home was to Pearl Harbor.

I guess you would say there was a small concern about encountering a Jap submarine, but since we were headed home, I don't think that bothered anyone.

When we arrived at Pearl Harbor, we boarded another Navy ship that took us to San Diego. We were transferred from the ship to the Marine base.

I think we overwhelmed their administrative staff. We all needed more clothes, and of course we wanted a pass to go to downtown San Diego. We finally got these things taken care of, and we went downtown and rented a large reception room. We stocked it with all kinds of good food and drinks, and anytime day or night, you had access to our VIP lounge.

The first night in San Diego, I was walking down the sidewalk with several of my buddies, and I heard someone behind me calling out, "Ike, Ike."

I initially thought it was one of my Midway Marine buddies, but as I turned around to look, all I saw was three or four Navy guys. At first I did not recognize any of them until one got a little closer. He was my old Slocomb classmate, "Gator" Jones. If you remember, "Gator" was with me when I first visited the Marine recruit sergeant in Dothan.

One thing that threw me off a little bit in immediately recognizing "Gator" was that in the two years since I last saw him, he had grown about five or six inches. When we graduated from high school, he was not much taller than me, and now, two years later, he was 6'3". "Gator" and I broke off from our friends and went up to our hospitality room in the hotel and did a lot of catching up. He was just out of boot camp, and he brought me up to date on all the big news from Slocomb. I did not see "Gator" again until after the war when we returned to Slocomb.

After several days in San Diego, I received my orders for a 30-day leave and then to report to Camp Lejeune. This would be my first leave in my two years in the Marine Corps. I also never had a dress blues uniform, and I just had to get my dress blues before I showed up in Slocomb.

I received a first-class train ticket with meal tickets for the diner. This was a big deal for me as I love trains, especially when they are first-class. The first leg of the trip was from San Diego to Birmingham, Alabama by train. The second leg of the trip from Birmingham to Slocomb was via the Greyhound bus. In that era, interstate and intercity travel was by rail and Greyhound bus. I stayed overnight in Birmingham to visit my sister Mary Jo, who was a nurse at the area hospital. While I was there, I bought her a nice new nurse's watch.

It was a little strange feeling when I stepped off that bus in Slocomb almost two years after I had boarded for a world unknown. I soon observed that, physically, Slocomb had not changed. There was a notable change in the population; all of the males my age and a little older were gone. They had either been drafted or had volunteered for the service and were in training camps across the country.

Many women and some of the older men were working full-time in the shipyards in Panama City, Florida. Most of these people from Slocomb and the surrounding countryside commuted every day from Slocomb to Panama City in old school buses. Panama City is about 90 miles from Slocomb, and it would make for a long day. However, these people were making more money than they had ever dreamed about.

I want to say something about civilians in wartime. Maybe this is not the best place to insert my thoughts on this subject, but I'm doing it anyway. In all the wars we have experienced in our brief history, the War for Independence and the Civil War are the only wars where the terrible devastation and suffering of the wars falls on the shoulders of the general population.

Unless you are a Gold Star mother, a war is not as real to the general population as it was in places like the South in the Civil War and Germany, France, London, and Russia in WWI and WWII. I would also include the territory in the Pacific Rim occupied by Japan in WWII. In these situations, you see everything you have completely destroyed, your children dying of starvation and having absolutely no medical attention.

Unfortunately, in war, dying and living in misery are not limited to the military battlefield. I am convinced we should, if possible, avoid having to go to war. I am also convinced that the only way to avoid war is, to quote an old Latin adage: "If you want peace, prepare for war."

That means we should always have such a powerful military force that no country would dare attack us. That also means we should honor our military people and pay them well. The world will always have people like Stalin, Hitler, Putin, and Kim Jong-un in power, and the only thing they understand is power. The best investment we can make for our future generations is a powerful military force.

Okay, off my soapbox and back to Slocomb. It was hot weather, but I could not let that bother me. I had to wear my dress blues uniform. I was treated like a hero although I had not done anything heroic. I happened to be the first serviceman from our small town to return home after serving in a combat zone. The war in Europe was still a year away, and as I said earlier, all of the local men in the draft age range were in training camps across the country. I received the royal treatment. For example, one of my uncles and several businessmen offered me the use of their cars for my social activities. This was somewhat of a sacrifice, because gasoline was rationed and this would limit their travels.

I found our house needed a new roof, and I had saved some money, so I went out to find a contractor. This proved to be a little difficult, as much of our industrial capability had been converted to wartime production and roofing was not readily available in our town. With the help of one of my uncles, I did find a roofing contractor in Dothan who could do the job for us. I felt good about that.

My thirty days in Slocomb just flew by too quickly. Again, I was stepping on that bus, headed for Camp Lejeune and then who knows where. I tried to think positive, but you must be realistic because you really have no clue about what lies ahead.

I arrived at Camp Lejeune on time, but my papers had not arrived and they did not really know where to assign me. Camp Lejeune at that time was nothing like it is today. It was a little chaotic; buildings were being constructed, some of the roads were still mud, and many of the troops were living in tents. I was assigned to a barracks called the Casual Company for arriving troops that they did not know what to do with. I found there were about a hundred guys in the same situation that I was in. All the guys that I got to know in this group had been serving overseas and were sent home for leave and further assignments.

Now, the Marine Corps was growing at such a fast pace that on the home front things got a little chaotic especially in the paper world. None of us coming from overseas had a full allotment of clothes, and since we belonged to no organization on the base, we couldn't find anyone with the authority to issue them. We also had the same problem in other areas, such as laundry and getting a pass to go to downtown Jacksonville. We were almost nobodies.

When I checked in the barracks, all the lower bunks were

occupied, so I found an upper bunk, and for the next several days I did not see the guy in the lower bunk. I finally asked one of the guys where he was. I did not catch on at the moment, but later I did understand.

"Oh, he is on leave," the guy told me.

This turned out to be the same kind of leave I would be taking in a few days.

Here is the environment we were in: an old gunnery sergeant who should have been retired was living in a room in the corner of the barracks. Every morning before daylight we had to get up and muster for roll call. Many of the guys in the barracks had been there for days waiting for their future assignments, so they had worked out a system. They would take turns answering roll call for their buddy still sleeping. The old gunnery sergeant either never caught on or didn't care.

After roll call we had close order drill, which we all hated. This drill was without weapons, and this was the only period in my Marine Corps service that I was not assigned a personal weapon. After the drill exercise, we were marched to the mess hall for breakfast. We were free until we were marched to the mess hall for lunch, followed by a period of exercise, and then we were free until we were marched to the mess hall for supper. All this under the supervision of the old gunnery sergeant.

Initially, I did not know anyone in this Casual Company. Then after I was there a couple of days, my old friend from Field Telephone School, Bob Clements, checked in. I was very glad to see this old friend. He had served in Guadalcanal, which was our first offensive battle in the Pacific and a very tough campaign.

One night Bob and I got to talking. I think it was after a couple of beers when Bob said he would like to visit Slocomb. He had heard me talk a lot about my tiny home town. In much of my military experience, I was one of the few guys from the Deep South, and these guys from other parts of the country were intrigued when I talked about it. We knew all the guys in the barracks were working the system of taking a few days off and have their buddies cover for them. I don't remember how we did it, but we did get a weekend pass, and we decided to stretch that a little bit and take a short trip to Slocomb while we were covered by our friends in the barracks.

So we took off via the Greyhound bus. We arrived in Atlanta and had to change buses there. Before we exited the bus, we noticed there was an Army MP checking the papers of all the military troops on the bus. I guess our heart rate went up. What were we going to do now? We had no choice. We had to exit the bus.

We tried to act like we didn't see the MP and walk on by him, but that didn't work. He stopped us and wanted to see our papers. Clements did the talking, and he told the MP we were Marines on a secret mission. The MP didn't exactly buy that. He said we should have some paper to show that we were on official leave and also noted that we were out of uniform.

"What do you mean by that?" Clements asked.

"Your tie should be tucked in your shirt," the MP said.

We were in our summer uniform, which was khaki just like the Army. The Marines wore their tie out just like we do today, and the Army wears it tucked in. To please the MP, we tucked our ties in our shirts.

Clements had our bus tickets in his hand for the remainder of our trip. "Furlough Rate" was stamped on the back of the tickets for all servicemen in big letters.

"See there," Clements said, "this shows we are on official leave. We must hurry, or we are going to miss our bus."

We quickly took off. At that time the bus station was very crowded with people shoulder to shoulder, and we got lost in the crowd. The poor MP, a very young guy, apparently did not know how to handle a situation like this. Fortunately, he just stood there and didn't pursue us. The rest of our trip we were very concerned, but we never encountered another MP.

We couldn't have enjoyed our short stay in Slocomb any more than we did. We again received royal treatment and stayed a day longer than we had planned, which turned out to be a big mistake.

We arrived back in Jacksonville and were very happy that we had taken this short trip. We expected to come back and get in our old routine again. Unfortunately, that's not exactly the way it turned out. When we entered the barracks, our buddies told us our papers came in the day before and they were looking for us. I went from a sergeant to a corporal.

Was it worth it? Would I do the same thing again? I don't know the answer to this question. You have to know what is in your mind at that time to understand why you're doing something that normally you would never think about doing. Two thoughts influenced me. One, I was certainly sure I was going back overseas and might not come home again. The other is you felt the chances of doing this without a problem were very high because it was such a common thing in the barracks. I never heard of anyone having a problem. So it doesn't bother me now, and I like to go back to Romans 8:28: "And we know that all things work together for good to them that love God."

My only concern was my mother would be hurt if she knew I had been demoted. Fortunately, my sister Florence was working in Slocomb at that time and was living with my mother. I contacted Florence and explained the situation to her. She is a very smart girl, and she handled it beautifully. She always picked up the mail at the post office, and my letters had to be from Cpl. Rigell instead of Sgt. Rigell. She would give the letter to my mother without the envelope, and all the letters to me from my mother Florence addressed as Corporal. This worked, praise the Lord.

My orders were an assignment to the 4th Signal Co., 4th Marine Division just activated at Camp Lejeune. This would be my home for the remainder of the war. In hindsight, I don't think I could have had a better assignment. Again, praise the Lord. Later in the 4th Signal Co. my rank of Sgt. was restored.

LEJEUNE TO ROI-NAMUR

In the late summer of 1943, the newly formed 4th Marine Division transferred from Camp Lejeune, North Carolina to Camp Pendleton, California via troop trains. The train I was on was not too bad, but it was not in the class of the train that I traveled on from Birmingham, Alabama to San Diego for boot camp.

Both trains were coal burners, but the Pullman car and the food on the recruit train was first-class and the food on a troop train was "troop train class," meaning it was one star. Our train took the southern route, and when we arrived in New Orleans, we were put on a side track for several hours. We never knew why there was the hold-up. The train was so long that the cars on the rear, where I was, ended up in a nice residential neighborhood. In a very short time after the train stopped, people in this neighborhood came out to greet us. Of course, we could not get off the train, but we could open all the windows and have nice conversations. Some even brought sandwiches and something cold to drink, but no alcohol. As best as I can recall, we were on this train three or four days before we reached our destination of Camp Pendleton, California.

Camp Pendleton is a very large Marine base just east of Oceanside, California. To our pleasant surprise, we were assigned to some very nice new barracks. As it turned out, we did not get to spend much time in these barracks in our four or five-month stay. We immediately went into a very vigorous and active training program. Most of this occurred in the boondocks, which meant sleeping on the ground. I recall the temperature in the daytime was very pleasant, but the temperature at night was cool, especially when you're sleeping on the ground.

Some weekends we could get back to the barracks, and most of the time we could get a weekend pass, which meant going to Los Angeles for the weekend. On Friday afternoons, the Pacific Highway at Oceanside would be lined with Marines hitchhiking to LA. As I have mentioned earlier, hitchhiking was very common and very safe. It was not uncommon for a vehicle to stop and apologize to the hitchhiker that he was only going a very short distance. This meant: "I know you're going to LA, and if I were going that far, I would gladly give you a ride."

We knew we would be going overseas soon, but we did not know when or where. There was always much speculation though. Obviously, we were not very good at this, because we never even got close in our predictions. This reminds me of one of Yogi Berra's famous quotes: "It is always hard to make predictions, especially about the future." (Yogi Berra was a Hall of Fame baseball player with the New York Yankees).

I think sometime in early December we did what we judged to be our dress rehearsal for deployment. We loaded up everything we had and headed on trucks to San Diego, and boarded troop ships. Leaving the harbor at San Diego we sailed north up the California coast, just north of Oceanside. In full battle gear we climbed down the rope ladders on the troopship into our landing craft, which was a combination of Higgins boats and AmTracs. Then we made an assault on the beaches and moved inland to the training grounds of Camp Pendleton. This exercise was about as realistic as you could get. We had the infantry, tanks, artillery, and all the supporting units.

A natural question we were pondering at this time was whether we would spend Christmas in the US or on the high seas. Of course, if we were still in the US at Christmastime, it would be our strong desire to get a pass for home. Christmas is always the time you miss your family and friends the most. During the war, I missed spending Christmas at home four times. Deep down, we knew getting a pass to go home for Christmas would be out of the question.

In the early part of January 1944, my platoon, as well as other platoons, were called out in formation. Our captain announced he would call the name and address of the next of kin for each Marine. He wanted verification that his records on this subject were complete and correct. We did not initially pick up on the significance of this event. Later, we understood that when they call for the verification of this data, get ready. You are about to leave for the next operation.

Shortly after this event, we received the order to leave. We were going to San Diego to board ships, and we were all convinced that we would not be going up the coast and landing like we had done before. When we pulled out of the harbor at San Diego, we joined a large convoy and sailed due west. The troops did not have the foggiest idea of where we were going. At this time in early 1944, the Japs owned the central and Far East Pacific Ocean west of Hawaii, except for Midway. Somehow, we convinced ourselves that we would be going to Hawaii and then on a mission to capture an unknown island.

It was not until we passed the Hawaiian Islands that we were told our target would be the tiny islands of Roi-Namur. Roi-Namur is connected by a causeway and is part of the Eniwetok Atoll, which is a part of the Marshall Islands. When I say Roi-Namur is tiny, I am being very generous. These islands are measured in acres and not square miles. Roi had an airfield, but Namur was considered the main island, and that is where most of the enemy troops were located.

I want to add a little thought here that just came to mind. It was eighteen days from the time we left the harbor at San Diego until we landed on Roi-Namur. After you have been on a crowded troopship eating beans, cream of wheat, substitute eggs, and milk, you are ready to land almost anywhere.

February 1, 1944 was the day when all of my training and who I was would now be fully tested. This was where the rubber meets the road.

As I climbed down the rope ladders into a bouncing landing craft, I tried to think of all the positive things I could. Being young (21 years old) helps. The younger you are, the more you have a false and unjustified sense of immortality. One thought that I latched on to was this: "No matter how hard this coming battle is, there will be people who survive, and I will be one of them."

I also thought about the fact that some troops were landing ahead of my boat. None of the guys around me were showing any emotion, and somehow that was a comforting thing too. One thought that is always in your mind, even after you have landed, is that you absolutely do not want to do anything that would let your buddy down. Another negative thought you have to suppress is the fear of suffering some terrible, disfiguring wound.

Tarawa was also fresh on our minds. Our 2nd Marine Division had recently suffered terrible casualties in capturing Tarawa, primarily because of inefficient pre-landing bombardment by our ships and planes. Fortunately, from the hard lessons learned at Tarawa, the pre-landing bombardment of Roi-Namur was greatly increased. As I recall, our Higgins boat landed pretty close to our scheduled landing time, and there was no incoming artillery on the way into the beach or after we landed. There was some scattered mortar fire, but almost all of the resistance our troops encountered was small arms, machine guns, and grenades.

My unit landed on Namur, which was the most heavily fortified. The landing beaches on Roi-Namur were on the lagoon side of the island. The planners for this campaign did a super job. As I stated above, we landed on the main islands, Roi-Namur, on February 1st. However, because these islands were so small, we could not use our artillery. To overcome this problem, some of our troops landed on several of the very, very small adjacent islands with our artillery the day before. The Japs did not anticipate any landings on these smaller islands, and they were lightly defended. Our troops had no problem taking over and setting up our artillery for close-in support for our assault on Roi-Namur the next day. In spite of the tremendous pre-invasion bombardment by our ships and planes, it is remarkable how many of the enemy survived. They may have been dazed, confused, and disorganized, but they were still a dangerous enemy.

When our landing boat hit the beach and the bow door was dropped, I had no idea what to expect as we scrambled out. Each man was looking for a place to find some cover. The terrain reminded me of Midway. Just a sand spit with heavy foliage in the middle of the ocean, without any natural defense features like the ones present on Saipan, Iwo Jima, and other islands.

Fortunately, there were plenty of bombshell craters all around us and no artillery shells zinging in like we would encounter later on Saipan and Iwo Jima. There was some sporadic small arms fire and a few rounds of mortars. We were able to get organized, set up our communications command post, and start stringing our telephone lines out to the various combat units. One good thing about this operation was that all of the combat units were where they were supposed to be (this would be the only time during the war this would be the case), and all were very close by. You almost did not need a phone. We could yell, we were so close together. We could see and hear our artillery as it was giving close support for the guys on the front lines, and, of course, we could hear our machine guns and small arms firing up ahead.

The whole operation seemed to be going according to the plan, and I think all of our units reached the 0-1 Line on or before their scheduled time. The 0-1 Line is the point where you want to advance to on the first day and dig in for the night. I know some units reached their objective ahead of time and requested permission to advance beyond the 0-1 Line.

One scene on Namur that made a lasting impression was, by far, the largest single explosion I would see during the entire war. All the buildings had essentially been destroyed in the pre-invasion bombardment except one very solid concrete structure. One moment it stood out very boldly, and the next moment there was a large crater filled with water where the structure had been. I learned later the structure was where Japs stored their bombs and torpedoes. I never did know what set off the explosion—whether it was one of our bombs or artillery or if the Japs set it off. This blast was devastating. Chunks of concrete and metal were flying in all directions. We suffered a number of casualties from this blast, some from concussions and others from falling debris. I heard some of our Marines in the landing crafts still coming onto the beach suffered some casualties. One of the officers that was up close to the blast reported the smoke was so black, he could not see his hand in front of him.

We knew the Japs were noted for their Banzai attacks, and our troops were about to experience this head-on, crazy death charge by these sake-filled enemy soldiers. This particular Banzai attack occurred at night, and it was raining. Our troops on the front line in this sector had a field day mowing these charging enemy troops down with their machine guns, BARS, grenades, and other small arms. Our artillery firing from the nearby islands kept the scene lighted by star shells. (A star shell explodes several hundred feet in the air and releases a flare, and suspended by a parachute, it slowly drifts down to the ground and lights up the area like it is daylight). Some of the Japs in this charge did not even have a rifle. They had kitchen-type knives strapped to long bamboo poles. It was a horrific scene the next morning in this area, as you could hardly take a step without stepping on a dead Jap.

Another scene comes to my mind from our last day on the island. The battle was over, and we were on the beach waiting for a Higgins boat to take us out to the troopship. Several of us guys were sitting around enjoying (ugh) hopefully our last K-Ration (a piece of hard chocolate, a little piece of cheese, some crackers, and four cigarettes) meal for a long time. We were among some scraggly palm trees, most with only the trunk remaining. Dead Japs were scattered all around us on the ground. Some had obviously been killed in the pre-invasion bombardment, as their bodies were bloated like they were about to explode out of their uniform. Some had been killed in the invasion battle. I should add that during this time, I was sitting on a sixteen-inch shell, a dud from one of our battleships. That did not bother me at all.

I want to say something here that I think is significant. I looked at these enemy soldiers just like I would today look at a dead possum or coon roadkill. I honestly don't think I looked at them as human beings. It was well known how brutally and inhumanely the Japanese treated the prisoners and civilians in the territories they occupied.

In the battle of Roi-Namur, we lost 197 Marines and sailors, and over 500 were wounded. By World War II standards this would be described as "casualties were light." In today's world it would be described as enormous. The way I see it, if you lose one man, the casualties are enormous. If you don't believe that, then go talk to a Gold Star mother.

MARSHALL ISLANDS
AND MAUI

After our invasion and capture of Roi-Namur in the Marshall Islands, we sailed to Maui, which would be our home between operations for the remainder of the war. Our leaders could not have selected a more perfect location for our preparation for the next operation. Maui is a beautiful place with an ideal climate, and we were very well received by the natives.

In fact, I don't think we could have been accepted any better, and we always looked forward with pleasure to returning to Maui after an operation. In the 1940s, Maui was not on the tourist map. Pineapple fields, sugar cane fields, and cattle were the main industries.

We lived in a huge tent and camp city in the middle of a pineapple field. After you have been sleeping in a foxhole or on top of the ground for days, a clean cot in a tent looks and feels like pure luxury. We take so much for granted in today's world. We forget how blessed we are. We live and act like we deserve all the luxury around us. The poor on welfare today live in more luxury than most of the world's population in that era.

I read in our 4th Marine history book that in our one year and nine months overseas, a little over four months of that time was spent on the water. The Marine Corps is part of the Navy, and we certainly did our part living with our sailor friends. We quickly learned the Navy lingo and how to make the most out of days at sea on a very crowded troop ship.

At Camp Maui, we were on a very busy schedule integrating new replacements and new equipment. The terrain was perfect, with plenty of beaches for training for the next amphibious operation. We trained hard and were on maneuvers much of the time, but our commanders were very generous in giving us liberty to visit the small villages with little mom-and-pop stores and restaurants where you could get one of the very best steaks you have ever eaten for ninety cents. It was their custom to put a "sunny side up" egg on top of the steak.

The base provided bus service to most of the little villages on the island, and frequently we would check out a vehicle from the motor pool to go sightseeing in some of the remote areas, including a trip to the rim of Haleakala Crater, an extinct volcano. That was an interesting trip up a winding road to the summit at a height of 10,000 feet. My first time to see a pheasant was on the road up the mountain. We would flush a number of these beautiful mountain birds out as we traveled.

When we were not training, sports were a high priority in all branches of the military. Football, baseball, and boxing were all very popular, with some great rivalries between the Marines, Navy, and Army. I played on our baseball team. The services were segregated at that time, but one Navy team we played had a black player and he was the first minority any of us had played against. None of us had any problem with that; in fact, there was not the slightest indication from anyone that this was a first experience for us.

One special event we looked forward to on our return to Maui after an operation was the lottery to select some lucky guys to spend several days at the Royal Hawaiian Hotel on Waikiki Beach in Honolulu. At that time, the Royal Hawaiian Hotel and Waikiki Beach were world-famous landmarks. For the duration of the war, the Navy took over the Royal Hawaiian Hotel for R&R for the submarine crews when they returned from assignments and allocated a number of rooms to the 4th Division. Each unit was allocated so many rooms based on their size. Our company was allocated two rooms with four Marines.

The rooms were assigned by a lottery system, and it's a little hard to believe, but my name and that of my closest buddy, Jerry Foley, were drawn twice. I still think our captain had something to do with that on both occasions, and some of our buddies had the same suspicions. Our captain never said anything to indicate he fixed the lottery. I did have a good relationship with our captain, and my team and I had successfully completed some of our toughest assignments.

On one of these trips to Honolulu, I made my first flight in an airplane. Jerry's brother-in-law was a pilot in the Air Force, and he was stationed at nearby Hickman Field. He invited us out to have lunch at the Officer's Club, which was a big deal for us enlisted men. He then offered to take us for a flight around the island. That was another big event for me. I don't recall the name of the plane; it was some kind of cargo plane with seats down each side and small windows. Visibility was limited, but it was still exciting and something to talk about.

After the flight, we went back to the Officer's Club for refreshments, and we were enjoying all this activity so much that time slipped up on me and Foley. We suddenly realized we were due back at the dock in a very short time. We had to catch the small boat at the dock, which would to take us to the large boat anchored in the harbor, which would then take us back to Maui. If we missed the boat, we would be in big trouble. I don't recall exactly how this happened, but there was an Army general in the club that heard of our plight and said he had a car and a driver and would see that we got back to the dock in time to catch our boat.

Fortunately, the driver seemed to know the shortcuts from the airfield to the hotel, where we picked up our baggage, and then on to the dock. We made it just in time; we were the last ones to board the boat. I regret I never got the general's name so I could thank him for this act of kindness. He saved me and Foley from a lot of grief.

In our camp on Maui we lived in six-man tents, the same as we had in boot camp and Camp Lejeune. The tents had wooden floors built about a foot above the ground, and we slept on cots. When we arrived for the first time, not all of the facilities were complete. One of the main items on this list was no hot water system. Our source of water for showers and bathing was a mountain stream with ice cold water. I don't think you ever get accustomed to ice cold showers, but this was still better than the environment we had been living in with no showers.

The only commercial telephone (connecting to the outside world) was at the Camp Headquarters. It was our platoon's responsibility to install telephone communications with the various units in the camp. In the combat zones all of our telephone wire was laid on the ground, but in camp we still used combat wire. However, some lines had to be on poles or trees due to the road traffic and foot traffic on pathways and sidewalks. One of our initial assignments was to install a line to the chaplains' tents. The Catholic and Jewish chaplains were in the same tent. We discovered what you might call the "motherlode" when our guys first entered to connect the phone.

There must have been fifteen to twenty bottles of booze on the floor, some full and some partially full. This was too tempting for these poor thirsty wiremen. Beer was available at the Beer Garden, but booze was a prized, rare commodity. The thought process was this: A wireman on the inside of the tent could ease two to three bottles under the tent flaps, and a couple of buddies outside could slip these bottles under their jackets and take off. The chaplains would never miss these bottles, thinking the other chaplain had consumed what was missing.

It did not stop after this initial discovery. From time to time, when one of the guys would get real thirsty, he would disconnect the line to the chaplains' tents and wait for a report from the chaplains that their phone was out of order. The thirsty guy would then reconnect the wire and follow the standard procedure: call back to the switchboard to verify the phone was working correctly. A special job like this required three men: one to go inside the tent to make the call to the switchboard and pass the booze under the tent flap, and two guys outside to collect the booze and slip it under their jacket.

We could sense when we were getting close to departure for the next mission. We would study maps of the Pacific and speculate on where our next landing would be. Our leaders did a super job of keeping the plans for the next invasion a secret. To my knowledge, we were never successful in predicting the next target area.

This is a Christmas card I sent my mother from Maui.

My wire team on Camp Maui in 1943.
They were a great crew. (Squatting:) Jim Fuller,
(Standing, L-R:) Tom Becker, me, Larry Mason,
G.P. Foley, and Steve Cosby

Maui Rest Camp, 1944—
(Kneeling, L-R:) Foley, Bonifer, Mason, Charles
(Standing, L-R:) Becker, Early, Wood, Cosby,
Billingsley, me, Plaskon

The Honorable Mrs + Mr I.A. Rigell

Got your care Package and was Very Pleasd
with the Contents

We Havent Had our Air Conditioneor once
this Summer. Thats How Far North we Are.

We Are Both in Pretty good shape For Being
So old and out of Shape. Helen Had Her Toe
Operated on, get the stiches out To-morrow

Talking About Memores. I Still think of all
the good Times we Had, And some that were Not
So Much Fun, the Best Part we made it
And All in one Piece.

the Memory thats starks My mind is the
Time the Brig. General Picket us up And Took
us Back To the Royal Hawair Hotel. We wire About
2 Hrs Late And Been Talking (Drinking) with Somme Air
Force Plots that Had Landed on Iwo. He was A
good Man As He could of Turned us In or worse
He Just said Good Luck And God Bless you.

Hope Too See one of thess Days But
will Never Forget All our good Times
Semper Fi
G. F.

Letter from G. P. Foley, my best foxhole buddy.

SAIPAN

Our first operations from our base in Maui were the invasion of Saipan and then Tinian in the Marianas Islands. No one had predicted Saipan as the next invasion. I was sure our next target would be Turk, a heavily fortified Jap base in the Central Pacific.

It is difficult to go back in your mind and identify just how you felt or what you were thinking as you were packing your equipment and loading the trucks for the trip to the harbor where the ships were waiting. We always had a very small skeleton crew that was assigned to maintain the camp until we returned, and to my knowledge no one, of course including me, wanted to stay behind no matter how much we were concerned about the coming battle. I think we all felt the same. You had to go.

I don't recall discussing our next operations specifically in this context, but we all knew it had to be tough because it would be closer to Japan and more heavily fortified with guns and men. It would also have rougher terrain.

I recently learned something of interest concerning Saipan and Midway Island. Back in May 1942 when the Japanese were assembling that huge armada to capture us on Midway, the assault troops were from the Japanese military forces on Saipan. So the tables were turned; according to the Japanese plans, we would meet their Saipan troops on the beaches at

Midway, and it turned out—by an act of divine providence, I am convinced—we met these same troops on the beaches at Saipan two years later in June 1944.

The first week of May 1944, we loaded all of our equipment for the next operation. Our destination was unknown. It was a slow journey with military vehicles of every description. Along the route to the port, we passed through a number of little towns. When the natives learned of our departure, they lined the roadway, waving and giving us a good, friendly send-off.

As our ship moved out into the open sea and Maui was fading in the distance, you could not escape the question: "Will I have the pleasure of seeing this beautiful land appear on the horizon again?"

Returning, we were always up on the deck searching the horizon for the first glimpse of land, which resulted in loud yells of joy.

The big moment we were anxiously waiting for after we joined the convoy in the open sea was the briefing on the coming mission. Our officers would assemble the various units on deck, break out the maps, and go through the battle plans. This would be in great detail, including all the available data: the strength of the defending forces, their known gun emplacements, the beach conditions, and the pre-invasion bombardment by Navy ships and aircraft. We were hearing all of this for the first time. I was always impressed with the detailed information concerning the enemy in these first briefings. Despite having so much information, we still encountered many unpleasant surprises on every mission. There is some truth to the old military saying, "All well-laid plans work beautifully until the first shot is fired."

I want to describe the type of troop ship I was on so you can get a better picture of what it was like. Troop ships were very uncomfortable, as they were super crowded with troops and equipment. Trying to sleep soundly several decks down in a musty, crowded compartment was not a pleasant experience. Several guys from my crew and I found a way to solve this problem. We took the pads from our bunks down in the lower deck, where we found a little partially secluded place by the super-structure on the top deck to spread them. That is where we slept. You can't get any fresher air than that. We were a little surprised the Navy did not tell us we couldn't do that, but I assume they must have had enough compassion to let us enjoy the fresh air.

Our location on the deck was a perfect spot. Due to the surrounding equipment, we could tie up a couple of ponchos for a roof, which afforded some protection from the rain and the sun during the day.

We also noticed some guys from another unit found a unique way to wash clothes: get a long rope from the ship's rope locker, tie your dirty clothes on, and throw them over the rail at the stern. The clothes are bounced vigorously in the churning water from the ship's propeller. In a few minutes they would be spotless; left too long, they would be in shreds. Again, we were expecting the Navy to say, "You can't do that," but they let it pass.

All I can say about the food on a troop ship is simply that you would not eat there again if you had a choice. In Navy lingo, a dining room is a "mess hall," and maybe the name fits. I have not figured this one out: how all the troops complained about the food ("the chow" in Navy lingo), yet much of the day was spent in a slow, winding chow line to pick up a metal tray and hold it out for a Navy mess cook to slap something on. For example, for breakfast we would be served navy beans (ugh), powdered eggs, and powdered milk.

One morning, as I looked down the serving line, I thought I had hit the jackpot. I am really going to dine this morning, I thought. I saw a big food container of what I assumed were grits. Then as I got closer, to my horror, I observed them putting the grits in a little cereal bowl, putting sugar on them, and pouring powdered milk on them. Then I was shocked—disappointed is too mild of a word—to learn the dish was not grits but something called cream of wheat, which I had never heard of and hope I never hear of again. I will have to admit there was one new dish they served on occasions that I liked. Actually, I first discovered this dish in Marine boot camp. It was called S.O.S., or "*sh--* on a shingle," which is thin sliced corn beef in a sauce poured over a piece of toast. Not bad. In fact, real good.

Every day on the ship is about the same: exercising, standing in chow line, and attending daily briefings on the overall mission. Much of it you had been taught before, such as how the Jap solider thinks, recognizing the weapons expected to be encountered, aircraft, tanks, gun fortifications, and, of course, a briefing on details unique to the operation. This included climbing down the rope ladders to your assigned landing craft, departure time to head for the beach, exact location (hopefully) of your boat's landing spot, and carrying out your assignments when you hit the beach.

Every day, rain or shine, we had an organized exercise session, and as all Marines know, you had to make sure your weapon was kept clean-clean. Even with these mandatory daily assignments and added time in the chow line, there was still plenty of free time. During this free time I did some reading. On every troop ship I was on, we had access to the ship's library, which by necessity was very limited. It was about the size of a large closet, but I always was able to find something worth reading. I would also do a lot of thinking; your mind goes back home, to your family and friends and what it will be like when you return. Also, your mind cannot escape thinking about how the next few days are going to unfold.

I confess there would be fleeting moments I'd be up on the bow of the ship, facing the wind with a little salt spray in the air, and blank out about what my buddies and I were about to encounter. You could actually enjoy the moment, especially if you love the sea like I do.

I always found it interesting to walk around the deck and observe all the ships in the convoy. As far as you could see, ships of all sizes and shapes moved silently through the water, maintaining their exact position relative to the surrounding ships. It gives you much comfort to be surrounded by those big ships; it takes away any fear of enemy submarines.

We enjoyed a good position in the convoy. However, one day our ship had to temporarily move to an outside position to take our turn in anti-aircraft gunnery practice. For this exercise, the Navy used a small airplane from one of the carriers in the convoy to tow a wind sock behind the plane to act as a target. It would be like shooting at one of those advertising signs towed by an airplane at the beach. These young sailors on the gun crews would be really excited, and we would be standing by the gun turret giving encouraging words.

"I would not want to be the pilot on that plane!" we would say.

We had one little bit of entertainment on most days, and that came from broadcasting from Japan. Tokyo Rose, a name given to her by the GIs, was actually an American citizen of Japanese ancestry. She was visiting relatives in Japan when the war broke out. Japan used her to broadcast a program to our armed forces in the Pacific. The purpose of the program was to demoralize our troops, but it had the opposite effect. The radio signal could be picked up by the ships in the Pacific, and it would be put on the ship's PA system. Tokyo Rose acquired a good listening audience. She played the latest US wartime songs and talked in a seductive voice with messages like, "You are sent out here by your cruel leaders, you will die, and your girlfriends and wives are living it up with someone else back home. We know where you are going, and we are waiting for you." It utterly failed as a demoralizing effect on the troops. Instead it was a big, entertaining joke.

When we occupied Japan, our military searched for and found Tokyo Rose. Her real name was Iva D'Aquino. The military kept her in custody for a year, and she was released for lack of evidence. Later she tried to return to the US, and this caused a big public uproar which resulted in the FBI stepping in and making a more detailed investigation of her wartime activities. Tokyo Rose was charged with eight counts of treason, and she was convicted of one. Later, in 1974, key witnesses in the trial claimed they were forced to lie during testimony. Tokyo Rose was released. In 1977, Tokyo Rose was pardoned by President Ford, but I don't recall this making the news at the time.

On the ship to Saipan, there was one very special, spiritual event that I truly believe was providentially arranged. Every night after the last serving in the mess hall, the tables were cleared, and one of the Protestant chaplains would hold a church service. This was not a pre-planned event. This chaplain, a true man of God, saw an opportunity to have a captive audience to preach the word. Every night there would be movie in the mess hall. Normally, the movie was shown on deck, but because of the total blackout it had to be shown in the mess hall, and the mess hall was much too small for all the troops that wanted to attend. So to get a seat for the movie, you had to come early, and the chaplain would move in and hold a church service.

From his sermons, I judged he had to be a conservative Southern Baptist. His sermons were "hell, fire, and brimstone." He did not hold anything back. I had heard sermons like this all my life, but I would guess 70 to 80 percent of the audience had never heard anything like it. I know some of them didn't want to hear it. There would be interruptions at times with some of the guys yelling, "Hey, we want the movie, we're here to see the movie, get this over with!"

This never seemed to phase the chaplain. He just stayed on course. It is my recollection that these interruptions did taper off the nearer we got to the day for climbing down the rope ladder to the landing craft. We had no movie or service the last night before landing. I did not mind missing the movie, but I did miss the service. I was not at all as spiritually-minded as I should have been during this period of my life, but I always attended services in the military.

I found it hard to sleep soundly the last night before landing. Your mind is occupied with thoughts of, "Will I make it out alive and without a serious wound?" I would try to fill my thoughts with all the positive things I could think of. *Pre-bombardment helped make the area safer. I'm not in the first wave of Marines to hit the beach.* I also thought back over the past year since I enlisted, and I got some comfort in knowing I'd had the best training possible.

All night long before landing, there was the never-ceasing boom, boom of the big guns of our warships bombarding the target. On the night before the invasion, my buddies and I had to give up our "on-deck penthouse" and move to our bunks several decks below. You could clearly hear the big guns even there, and since it was hard to sleep, I went up on deck to view the fireworks. It was awesome. You could observe the flash of the big guns on our warships and see the shells exploding on the island. You hoped every shell landed on a vital target. Sadly, we learned later it didn't exactly work out like that, even though they did inflict damage.

The most unforgettable sound that I remember from our shipboard operations on landing day was from the huge electrical winches that lowered the landing craft from the ship down into the water. I can't describe this particular sound. It was the most mournful sound I have ever heard. I first heard the sound of these winches when we were training offshore at Camp Pendleton, California. It was the same on all the troop ships I was on.

Not often, but at times through the years, a mental picture will come briefly to my mind of a landing boat being lowered into the water with a bunch of anxious Marines on the deck, awaiting their order to climb down the rope ladder. I realize this sounds morbid, and with great reluctance I complete this scene: There is also a picture of a coffin being lowered into the earth in a cemetery. This event does not keep me awake at night. It is just a fleeting scene during the day, and I often ponder just why this particular scene appears.

On the landing day, the cooks would send us off with a good, special breakfast: steak and eggs. You had to savor this meal because you didn't have any idea when you would sit down to a good hot meal again. I really can't recall the nature of our conversation as we were waiting to climb down the rope ladder to our assigned landing craft. One thing we would do as we were waiting for the boarding call was check each other out, making sure we had all required equipment and it was properly secured. The day we landed on Saipan, the sea was so rough, the landing craft was bouncing around. Climbing down a rope ladder with your full battle gear is not the easiest task in the world.

There was one funny event in our operation that morning. Let me explain, this was a very serious event and certainly not funny at the time, but later, in a safe environment and since no one got hurt, I got a good laugh out of it. The event I describe happened to my good buddy, "Smiley Johnson." I was in a different landing craft than Smiley, so I wasn't an eyewitness to this event. I first heard about this from my good buddy, "Cotton" Billingsly, after we returned to Maui.

When Smiley was descending the rope ladder into the landing craft, he slipped and fell into the water with his full battle gear on. Between a bouncing landing craft and the big ship, he was in a lot of trouble. A couple of sailors from the ship jumped overboard and got him back to the rope ladder and saved his life. Cotton went through boot camp with Smiley and said he did not know how they let Smiley pass the swimming test. Swimming was not his thing. Smiley lost his rifle in this event, but things had to keep moving. They got him in the landing craft, and he hit the beach soaking wet with no rifle. Part of our landing gear was two hand grenades, so Smiley did at least have those.

Smiley had a gruff voice that made him sound much older than his nineteen years, and he was always bitching, especially about the Navy. Of course, in the military a little bitching is a natural and maybe even healthy disease. After this event, Smiley's sergeant, Bill Cassell, told him, "If I ever hear you bitching about the Navy, I will break every bone in your body." Bill will be mentioned later. Underneath all that gruff façade, Smiley was a really nice guy, one of the best liked in our unit. There was another Smiley Johnson in the 4th Division, a star football player at Notre Dame, but sadly, he was killed on Saipan.

As I was nearby watching these rockets being launched, I didn't realize that this was the beginning of a long career of launching rockets myself, although in a friendlier fashion later.

Saipan, July 1944—
(Kneeling) Steve Janoski, Frenchy Des Roberts, Larry Mason
(Standing): me, Ed Shannon

HITTING THE BEACH

Before we left the troopship, we were getting reports over the loudspeakers from the troops that had already landed on the beach, and it was not exactly good news. In most sectors they were taking pretty heavy fire. We could observe some of that from the waterspouts right off the beach where some of the Jap artillery and mortar shells were hitting all around our AmTracs and Higgins boats swarming in on the beach. We lined up on the deck, waiting for the signal to take the rope ladder down to our landing craft. The sea was a bit rough that day as the Higgins boat bounced around, so we had to be real careful descending the rope ladder into the boat. After we were loaded and moved away from the troop ship, we circled around for a little while until the coxswain received the order to position our boat for the departure to shore.

You do not know what awaits you when the bow door opens. What I had feared was now happening. Our boat hit the beach right next to one of our AmTracs that had been knocked out. In fact, there were several disabled AmTracs along the beach on either side, and in the sector where we landed, there was pretty heavy incoming artillery and mortar fire. There had been some scattered palm trees along this portion of the beach, but all that remained of most of them was a stub of a trunk because of the heavy bombardment by our bombers and Navy guns.

We landed just to the right of a large structure that had been a sugar mill. It had a tall smokestack that was still standing, and some thought the Japs had a lookout in the top of the smokestack. I never knew if that was true or not, but I doubted it because at that time the Japs controlled all of the high ground, including one peak in the center of the island, Mount Tapatchau. It was 1,154 feet, so high that they had a complete view of all the beach.

We exited the Higgins boat as fast as we could, and every Marine made a mad dash to find some cover as some pretty heavy stuff was coming in. Every man was on his own. I have to say I was about as scared as you could get and dove in the first hole I could find, which looked to be a bomb crater from one of our planes in the pre-invasion bombardment. Right behind me came one of my buddies, Tom Becker. Looking to the right and left down the beach was not a pretty sight. Several AmTracs did not make it; some got hit in the water and never made it to the beach.

There were troops from other units landing in the same sector, so our immediate problem was to locate our wire platoon commanding officer, Lt. Mattingly. We decided we could not just sit there hunkered down in this bomb crater, so we started moving inland. We were afraid to stand up straight, so we made short dashes from hole to hole, bent over as low as we could get, and we did a little bit of crawling. I'm not sure how it happened, but we finally had most of the wire platoon together. We were still pretty much pinned down with the heavy artillery and mortar fire, and we could hear the machine guns and small arms firing up on the front line, but we were far enough behind that we were not receiving any small arms fire.

There were no Japs confronting our troops on our landing. The Jap commander's battle plan was to pull his troops back, giving them well-hidden gun positions on the higher ground, where they were in position to destroy our landing forces. As best I can recall, our unit went ashore in the late morning. I believe by then we had several thousand Marines ashore, including the 2nd Marine Division that landed on our left.

At the time my landing craft hit the beach, troops from all units were pouring in up and down the beach. With all the troops scattering for cover, it was a little hard to keep our unit together and advance up to our rendezvous point. If we perceived any lull in the firing, we moved inland. Our initial objective was to keep our unit together, and considering all the confusion, we did a pretty good job. In our sector, a steady stream of artillery and mortar with some occasional small arms fire continued throughout the day. It was frustrating to have to sit there and be fired upon. We couldn't fight back because we could not see our enemy. It was different in the sector to the right of our position. In their sector, the 25th Marines not only encountered heavy artillery and mortar fire, but also heavy small arms fire and hand-to-hand encounters.

Things were not going as well as planned. By late afternoon we were told to dig in for the night, although we had not advanced as far as planned. We received word that the Japs on the northern tip of the island were planning to get in small boats and come in on the beach and attack us from the rear. We were not sure if this was fact or rumor. Influenced by this information, my best buddy, Jerry Foley, and I dug a two-man foxhole, one of us facing the front and the other facing the ocean. We did hear that some of the Japs tried this and were intercepted by our Navy, but we never did know whether that was true or not.

If we thought we were already receiving heavy artillery and mortar fire, we were in for a surprise. Come night fall, all hell broke loose. The Japs didn't have to contend with our air cover at night, so they pulled all their guns out of the many caves and unloaded on us. I am serious about this. If Foley and I had known what was in store for us that night, we would have made a much deeper hole. We sat in that foxhole all night, facing each other with our knees pulled up in front of us and the top of our helmets about level with the ground. A heavy round would burst close by, shaking the ground and causing the sand from the walls of our foxhole to trickle down.

Artillery fire is higher velocity than mortar shells, and artillery rounds have that distinctive sizzling sound as they whiz over. The longer you can hear the sizzling sound, the safer you are, but if the explosion comes about the same time as you hear the sizzle, it is too close. If the explosion is the first thing you hear, it could very well be the last thing you hear. At times during the night there would be a lull in the firing, and you just hope for whatever reason that lull continues. Then you hear that dreaded sound—a loud pop up overhead and the whole area lights up like daylight. This is called a "star shell," when the shell pops open and it releases a bright light that floats down to the ground on a small parachute. When this happens, it is bad news because you know a new, heavy barrage is coming your way. You are scared and helpless. All you can do is try to get lower in your hole and pray and hope daylight comes soon.

Sometime during the night, a little piece of shrapnel from a nearby mortar shell landed on my chin. I felt it hit, but it really was painful for only a minute or so. I did feel the wound with my finger, and there was a little blood, but it was nothing that required any immediate attention. Foley and I, and I'm sure all the troops, were looking forward to daylight when our artillery spotters and aircraft spotters could locate and knock out these guns that were giving us so much trouble. It was a long night, and when daylight came, the firing did greatly subside.

I found I did have more blood from my little wound than I was aware of. I had dried blood from my chin down my neck and onto my undershirt. Foley suggested I find a corpsman and get him to put something on it so I would not get an infection, as there was dirt all over my face. We found a corpsman and he cleaned up my chin and put some iodine on the little wound and covered it with a Band-Aid. As we were leaving, Foley said, "Ike, you got yourself a Purple Heart."

"What do you mean? You don't get a Purple Heart for something like this," I said.

"He took your name, rank, and serial number, and that means you are on his Purple Heart list."

I thought Foley might be right, so I went back and asked the corpsman, "Did you put me down for a Purple Heart?"

He asked me my name, and I told him. He looked in his little book and said, "Yes, you're down for a Purple Heart."

I told him to take my name off the list because I couldn't accept a Purple Heart for this little wound. He said something like, "Well, if you say so, I'll take it off," and he did mark my name off the list.

I knew I could not face my buddies later with a Purple Heart for this minor thing when others around me would have serious wounds. I would like to note that all of the medical personnel, doctors, and corpsmen serving the Marines and Navy personnel were highly respected. They were right up there with our guys on the front lines.

I don't think anyone got any sleep on that first night, but with a little boost of energy from a "nice" breakfast of K-Rations, we were ready to face the day. "Nice" is not exactly the word I would use to describe the K-Rations, but I will leave it at that.

On day two on Saipan the artillery rounds were still coming but nowhere near the steady barrage we experienced the night before, and the small arms fire really came alive. During the night I could hear bursts of machine gun fire, and as far as I could tell, we were far enough behind the guys on the very front lines that the small arms fire did not reach us.

We were not burdened with "Rules of Engagement," as our troops in Iraq and Afghanistan have had to contend with. The only rule I heard was, "If it moves, shoot!" Later, I'll give you an example of that simple rule.

My division's urgent job upon landing in Saipan was to establish telephone communication between the commanding general's post and all operational combat units. We strung no wire on the first day we landed because there was just too much confusion. We didn't know the exact location of any of the command posts or exactly where the front line was.

According to the prepared battle plans, if every unit met their objective for the day, you would know the location of the units. But we found the old saying to be very true: "Your battle plans work perfectly until the first shot is fired. Then throw your plans away." As far as I knew, no unit was where they were supposed to be on the map. The teams would take off in the direction where they expected to find the command post for the unit they were looking for, only to find nothing.

When the war started, the standard field combat wire was a heavy, insulated twisted pair of wires on a spool about twenty inches in diameter and six inches thick. It required two men to string it off the spool. Later, a smaller, lighter combat wire was developed. Put on a smaller reel, it could be handled by one man. We had use of this improved wire for the first time in Saipan.

Describing a typical day in the combat zone is impossible, because there is no such thing. As best I can, I will record a few events from my experience from each battle I was involved in.

Some days from that era are a complete blank, but some events I vividly remember.

For example, I remember hitting the beach in Saipan, but I have no memory of boarding the troop ship to return to Maui. I can recall, on all operations, when we climbed up the rope ladder on the troop ship, sailors crowded around wanting to buy souvenirs: Jap rifles, pistols, flags, anything Jap.

One experience I recall was when my crew was assigned to run a line to one of our units located on our left flank. At that time, our command post was near the center of the island where the terrain was very rugged. We thought we had a good fix on their location. Judging from the map, this would be a rather long line. We thought we would start off in a Jeep and go as far as we thought safe and then walk to look for the command post. It was not easy to locate, and there was no way you could make a straight shot to the post.

There was a very visible code number stamped on the back of every Marine's jacket. Our plan was to move toward the front line until we started seeing Marines with the code number of the unit we were looking for. The code numbers were not complicated, and we knew them all. My code number was 112, and my unit retained that same number throughout the war. When we began to see Marines we were looking for, we would ask for the location of their command post. Much of the time it would require a number of inquiries.

I need to clarify something. You could never start out at point A and run a direct line to point B, because you never knew the exact location of point B. If you did that, you would just be stringing wire all over the island as you wandered around searching for the command post. On this assignment we purposely took the long route to find the command post. As mentioned earlier, we were located near the center of the island in rough terrain, so we started out in a Jeep on a road parallel to the front line and headed down the hill toward the beach where the terrain was much flatter. You will see this is a significant point as this story unfolds.

By the time we located the unit and set up to lay the line, it was late afternoon. That was a concern because, if at all possible, you always wanted to be back to your home base by nightfall.

But you also never leave a job unfinished, so sometimes you would come back in the dark.

I think that motivated our desire to get going on the most direct path back to our base. The method to laying a combat wire line is simply walking along with the spool; the wire unreels and lays on top of the ground. The only time we buried a line was in areas where tanks or other heavy vehicles might cross.

We completed our job and headed back to our command post. Our trip was uneventful except for one positive event. We came across a little clearing, and it appeared to be an abandoned Jap field kitchen. There was a thatched roof shelter with benches and a fire pit with various stones scattered around. In plain view was a brightly polished Jap military bugle with a red tassel. As soon as I saw the bugle, I knew I wanted it, but it was so visible I had to consider it was part of a booby trap. I can't recall what I did to convince myself it was safe to pick this bugle up, but I did. There was a bunch of stuff laying around. I found another item that looked interesting, but I wasn't sure what it was. I found out later it was an opium scale, like something you would find in a chemical lab. Along with the bugle, I brought that little scale back. Unfortunately, I can't find it today.

We did accomplish our task and made it back to our base. We had connected the line to the forward unit, and everything checked out. We felt really good about getting back to have some C-rations and dig in before dark. That good feeling about a job well done lasted only a few moments. As we were getting our C-rations ready, Lt. Mattingly came up to me.

"That line you just laid is out. Get your team and troubleshoot it," he said.

This is bad, bad news you hope you never hear. The whole team heard what Lt. Mattingly said, so I did not have to round up a crew. In troubleshooting a line, you just follow the wire until you find the problem. The main problems are usually caused by a tank tearing up a wire, artillery and mortar fire, or a wire cut by the Japs. When the Japs cut a wire, you had to be concerned they were setting up an ambush attack.

To avoid this situation, when we would string the wire, we'd tie it every couple hundred feet to a bush, rock, or whatever was available. As you walk along, you pull the slack out of the wire, and if you can pull it taut, you can proceed to the next tie point. If you can keep pulling the wire, soon you will have the end of a broken wire. Then you have to be creative on how you safely restore communications.

So our team started out following the line. We had only gone a very short distance when we came upon a line of Marines digging fox holes. I couldn't identify their unit because their jackets were off. It was hot, and they were working hard digging in some pretty hard ground. They were spread about ten feet apart, and our line ran between two of the foxholes. As we were passing between them, one of the Marines digging said "Hey, where are you guys going?"

"We are troubleshooting this telephone line," I said.

"Where does that line go?" he asked.

"The 24th Regiment Command post," I answered.

"When did you guys put that line in?" he asked.

"A couple of hours ago," I told him.

I cannot adequately tell you how shocked we were at his next statement.

"I don't know how you got that line in," the Marine said. "*We are the front line*. There is no one out there in front of us but Japs. Our orders are to shoot anything that moves. If you guys go on out there, you better sing a merry tune. Our orders are to shoot anything that moves," he said again.

I knew exactly what that meant: The slightest bit of noise, and they would blast away. That was standard practice.

We had to stop and rethink. In reconstructing our path to run this line, we concluded this is what happened. The unit that we ran the line to had advanced much farther that day than we realized. They were operating in much more favorable territory than the rugged center of the island, and they had made great progress that day. This resulted in an "L" shaped front line, with the tip of the long "L" where we started our return trip back to our base in the center of the island. Actually, our journey that day was like a triangle. We started parallel to what we thought was the front line, then took a right turn on the long leg of the triangle and returned to the starting point. Then we unknowingly compounded the problem by our desire to return to our base as soon as possible. We took the most direct path back. We further concluded our line had been cut by the Japs, as most of our return path was through heavy growth and we saw no tanks operating in this area.

Most definitely the path we took laying our line took us through some territory you could call "no man's territory," and some of our path had to take us through Jap-held territory. As I recall on our return trip, we did not feel any degree of elevated danger. We could hear the mortars and artillery going both directions, which was normal both day and night on these small islands. None of the mortars or artillery fell anywhere near us.

I concluded from all the data that it did not make sense to proceed any further to repair this line. We went back to our base and asked our old Gunnery Sgt. Guy Reynolds, a Marine veteran with four hash marks, to go with me to explain our situation to Lt. Mattingly. I told Lt. Mattingly I thought it would be suicide to try to retrace our steps and fix this line, and I further advised him that our chance of getting this line fixed tonight was close to zero. Lt. Mattingly and Guy agreed with my position, but Lt. Mattingly said he had to talk to Maj. LaLane for approval. He came back after a few anxious minutes.

"This line has to be working," he said. "They expect a big counter attack in that area tonight."

I never knew if the decision to "go" was made by the major or higher. I was in a tough spot. I could very well appreciate the value of having this communication line working tonight, but I was still convinced it would be suicide to send our crew out on this mission with zero odds of getting it repaired. Lt. Mattingly, a really good Marine, was not willing to go back and have another session with the major, and I understood that. My concern was how to "sing a merry tune" to safely get back though our frontline guys digging foxholes. I was convinced we would not get back to that point.

As we were about to end our discussion and start out again, Foley said, "How about we just run a new line?"

We all latched on to this thought, and after a short discussion we all agreed, including Lt. Mattingly, that this was the logical way to go. In fact, we came up with a very good way to get this job done. We got another crew to go with us, so we had two Jeeps, and we took the same route, parallel to the front line near the beach and left toward the front line.

Since they had advanced the front line farther than we originally thought, we were able to proceed closer to the front line than on our previous trip. When we had gone as far as we could with the Jeeps, my team proceeded on foot to the command post. The other team, from that point, started laying the line back to our base. We reached our destination without any problems, and when we connected our line and made a test call back to our base, we were happy to hear a voice on the other end.

The team laying the line with the Jeep made really good time and were there waiting for our call. It was getting dark, and we made it back to our departure point where we left our Jeep safely. The danger in that situation was probably more from friendly fire than enemy fire. It was a great relief to know this second line was intact and working, as there was a counter attack in that sector later that night. If the order to find the original line had not changed, we would have followed it, of course, while trying to stay alive. I don't think we would have met either one of these objectives. I believe we would not have make it back to "sing a merry tune" to our friends on the front line. Praise the Lord.

I want to say something about friendly fire. In all wars, unfortunately, there are going to be some casualties from friendly fire. General Stonewall Jackson was killed by friendly fire in the Civil War, and in the war in Iraq and Afghanistan there were a number of friendly fire incidents. On Saipan, I got caught in friendly fire a couple of times. In one case, one of our fighter planes was strafing the enemy front lines and assumed the frontline was straight when it was not. Some parts of the line were more advanced than other sections, and apparently, as he was coming out of his dive, he still had his finger on the trigger. His bullets were hitting the ground all around us, and we were well back from the front line.

In the other case of friendly fire, one night I was asleep in a little ravine parallel to the front lines. Even though I was not in a foxhole, I felt I would be protected from anything coming from the front line. I was jolted awake by a super-loud explosion, and even before I opened my eyes, I seemed to see a very bright light. A few more rounds came in, but not as close as this first burst.

After things quieted down we determined these shots, which

were pretty big stuff, came from one of our ships offshore. There were no Japs in that direction with big guns like these. Again, I think it was just a case of poor communication; it was not really clear where the front lines were. I certainly would not fault the people on the ship or the fighter pilot for making a mistake like this.

Unfortunately, this is just the nature of war, and I strongly disagree with some of the people who wanted to court-martial those troops in Iraq and Afghanistan involved in friendly fire.

Around the third or fourth day of the Saipan campaign, we had a little extra special excitement. We heard the planes roaring and we looked up, and there were a number of aircraft going through all kinds of gyrations: diving, climbing, figure eights, and weaving in and out and around each other. In all my four years during the war this was the only aerial dogfight I witnessed. In fact, I think the local war sort of came to a standstill as we all stopped what we were doing and watched this aerial combat.

This dogfight took place at a pretty high altitude, and we could not be sure which planes were ours and which planes were the enemy. Two or three were hit, and they began to smoke and lose altitude. Although we really weren't sure, we claimed those to be Japanese planes.

The Japanese had no aircraft carriers close by, so these enemy planes were land-based planes coming from one of the islands still held by the Japanese, which could have been Guam. Fortunately, after the battle of Midway, we had complete superiority and control of the airspace. However, on Saipan, we did have a couple of nights where we were visited by Jap planes. They dropped a few bombs in our area, but they were not really close. They made several passes, and you could hear them whistling down. Then some smart a-- in a nearby foxhole started making sounds like a bomb coming down.

Some guy nearby yelled, "If you don't cut that sh-- out, I am coming over there and ram a bayonet up your a--."

He was silent after that.

27TH ARMY INFANTRY

T he battle plan for capturing Saipan called for the 2nd and 4th Marine Divisions to land side by side, and the 27th Army Infantry Division would remain on board the ships and be called in if necessary. It was obvious from the time the first troops hit the beaches at Saipan it would be much more difficult than anticipated. As a result of the unexpected fierce opposition, the 27th Army Division was called in to relieve some of our units operating in some very rough terrain.

I received an order to run a telephone line to one of those units that had moved up to the front lines. As I mentioned, we had to take several factors into consideration to determine how we would get there: distance, type of terrain, and the reliability of the information about their location and the activity in that particular area. Evaluating all the best data available, we decided to start out in a Jeep and go as far as it was safe. On this mission we had a crew of five. We moved along a dirt road that only a vehicle like a Jeep could negotiate.

As we rounded a sharp turn on the road around a clump of trees, there was an open area, and the road led downhill to a bridge. Beyond that, it was heavily wooded. As we approached the bridge, we observed a line of soldiers hunkered down in the ravine on either side. These were the first soldiers of the 27th

Army Division that we had encountered, and I asked the driver to stop. I wanted to find out the location of their command post.

Just as I started to talk to these guys, they begin to yell, "Get the *bleep* Jeep out of here! Get that *bleep* Jeep out of here! You're going to draw fire, and the Japs are right up that hill!" At that time, it was quiet in this sector. Of course, we could hear the mortars and artillery in the distance, but none of it was falling near us, so we really weren't concerned.

I was trying to carry on a conversation with these guys. I told them our mission was to install a telephone in their command post with a line back to the 4th Marine Division communication center. They were still yelling at us to get that *bleep* Jeep out of there, but one soldier did say their command post was under the bridge. We were really surprised, as we thought their command post would be at least a half mile farther up the road. We still did not sense any danger, so I told the soldiers as soon as we connect the telephone, we would be out of there.

Our crew was still in the Jeep. As they started to dismount and get our equipment running, all hell broke loose. We heard a sizzling sound and an explosion right in back of us, and all of us except the Jeep driver hit the ground. He was trying to make a U-turn and get back around the corner behind the trees, and he ran into a ditch and stalled the Jeep.

He jumped out and took cover behind the Jeep. In rapid succession, several more rounds came in. None were any closer than the first. Fortunately, this was unusual. Normally the first round of mortars and artillery were used to adjust their sights as necessary to zero in on the target, which in this case was us. The other three guys in our crew were thinking the same thing. We should get up and make a dash for the safety of the ravine or stay flat on the ground.

In my position, I could turn my head without raising it off the ground and look up and see the clearing on the hill. I saw a Jap tank move out of the trees into the open area and smoke when it fired. There appeared to be a second Jap tank hidden in the trees on the edge of the clearing. I could see smoke when they fired from this position too.

As suddenly as it started, the firing ended, and the visible tank retreated back into the trees. I do not know how many rounds they sent our way, nor how long this lasted. At the time it seemed like an eternity, but in reality they got off a few quick rounds and went back into hiding before some of our forward observers or our spotter planes could get a fix on them. After a few minutes we felt it was safe to make a dash for the ravine. We were thankful that none of us were hit and that our Jeep was not damaged.

Then one of our guys noticed the back of Sgt. Steve Janoski's jacket. It had a diagonal rip about a foot long from the right shoulder toward the left hip. One of the guys pulled Steve's jacket up to look at his back. There was a red streak the same length as the rip in his jacket. There was no blood but apparently a piece of shrapnel streaked across Steve's back. You would have to say it was a miracle that this piece of shrapnel did not hit a half-inch lower.

Normally there would be only one sergeant going on a mission with a crew this small. Steve and I were really good buddies, and on Maui many times we would go on liberty together. Steve is in the only photo I have from our operation on Saipan. I think he retired that jacket, and I suspect he took it home after the war and framed it. That is what I would have done.

We had to admit that the soldiers knew what they were talking about when they told us "get that Jeep out of here or you are going to draw fire." To the soldiers' credit, they did not tell us "we told you so" or laugh at how we were scrambling around when that first shot fired.

We had to push the Jeep to get it out of the ditch, and we quickly drove around the other side of the bridge where there was some cover. We connected the phone in their command post under the bridge and laid the line back to our communication center without any other problems. When we returned to our base, we went to our next assignment, and the thought did not occur to me until much later that I would not be writing this material if we had not stopped and asked those soldiers for directions to their command post. If we had continued over the bridge up that hill, we would have been right in the middle of the Jap tanks. I want to thank You again right now my Lord for Your mercy and grace that has allowed me to enjoy all these years. Your wonderful blessings are without limits. Praise Your holy name!

One added comment about the 27th Army Division. I thought the 27th was doing a pretty good job. However, they were apparently not advancing fast enough to please Marine Gen. "Howling Mad" Smith, the commanding general of the overall Saipan operation. Gen. Smith was a legendary figure in Marine Corps history, and from what I understand, the title "Howling Mad" was well earned. He relieved the commanding general of the 27th Division and replaced him with another general. I am not sure that was justified, as those 27th guys were working in some very tough territory, and toward the end of the battle the Japs made one last Banzai charge in their sector.

MORE SAIPAN MEMORIES

Normally there were more than two of us on a troubleshooting team, but for some reason it was just Foley and I on one mission. As we were moving through the bushes, we noticed a dead Japanese officer just ahead of us. We did a quick take, trying to determine whether he was dead or if this was a booby trap. We could not see any wounds. He was stretched out in his nice uniform with a pistol on his side. It looked really suspicious, and we could not see his hand on the other side.

We got behind a big rock so we could safely peek out for any movement. We were trying to figure out how we could make sure that it was not a booby trap. We really wanted that pistol; a pistol was a prize souvenir. As we waited, a couple guys from another unit came barreling through the bushes and rushed over to this dead Japanese officer and, of course, they got that pistol. They rolled him over and searched him, and I don't know what else they found.

We wanted to yell out to them, "Hey, that's our pistol! We found it first."

We knew their response would not be very favorable, so we just sat there quietly and little bit remorseful that we didn't barrel in first. However, in hindsight, I think we did the prudent thing.

Another event, one that could possibly have some connection to my present hearing problem, occurred one night on the way back to our command post, after we had installed a line out to one of the forward units. I have mentioned before that we always really dreaded having to work on a line or connect a line after dark. One real potential problem in these situations was exposure to friendly fire, because at night "shoot anything that moves in front" was a common order. The second problem was getting lost, which was really easy to do.

On this occasion, we only had to worry about friendly fire. We had a good reference point to get back to our command post. We were following a little narrow gauge railroad that the Japanese had installed to all the sugar cane fields to haul sugar cane back to the sugar factory near our camp. The sugar factory had been completely destroyed, but the big smokestack still remained, and our command post was nearby.

As I recall, our team that night was Jerry Foley, Tom Becker, Steve Cosby, and myself. As we quietly walked along the railroad we heard some very faint voices. At first we were unable to distinguish if the voices were friend or foe. As we listened, we could faintly make out a few words that convinced us these voices were Marines, but we were unable to actually hear what they were saying. We were very quietly discussing among ourselves whether it was better to call out to the Marines and identify ourselves or quietly continue on our pathway.

As this little thought process was underway, all hell broke loose. There was a tremendous explosion right in the vicinity of where the voices were coming from. It turned out this was a battery of our artillery, our big guns, 155 mm. They just cut loose a salvo. I think it was four guns, and once they opened up, you could expect many more salvos to follow. We were so close to the guns, we really weren't in any physical danger because the elevation of the barrels put them well above our heads. But the noise was deafening. We took off as fast as we could safely travel in the dark along that railroad track, and we were some distance away before they cut loose with the next salvo. I don't recall if any of us suffered any temporary hearing problems.

When I went to the audiologist years later to check on hearing aids, I was asked if I had ever been exposed to loud noises in my career. I answered that yes, back in my military career, I had been exposed to a certain amount of really loud noise, but that I really didn't connect that with my present condition because it had been so long ago. I could not make a statement that my hearing problem was service-connected. She told me that she processed many claims like this from veterans, and the VA paid for the hearing aids. She encouraged me to document my exposure to loud noises and then she would take that information and send a letter to the VA.

I commented to her that I didn't think I was eligible for VA assistance due to my income. Now I certainly did not classify myself as rich man at all, but my thinking was this program was set up for men who absolutely needed hearing aids and couldn't afford them. I didn't feel right in participating in this program. The audiologist told me she had processed a number of applications from some very prominent men in the community that I knew had a lot more money than I did, and they got the VA to pay for their hearing aids.

To end this story, I did get turned down by the VA because my income was over the maximum allowed. I don't know how these other guys who I know were much richer than me got the VA to take care of their hearing aids. They had to be a little loose with some of the information they provided the VA. I do not regret that my claim was denied.

As our front line advanced, we pushed the Japs right up to the end of the island. This was rugged territory full of caves, and at the very end of the island was a cliff called Marpi Point with a sheer drop-off a couple hundred feet down to the rocky ground right at the beach. We had Japanese interpreters with microphones pleading for the military and civilians to peacefully surrender and they would be treated well. It was obvious that they were not going to win; it would be futile to continue the fight. Their options were clear: They could surrender and be well treated, they could continue the fight and be annihilated, or they could commit hari-kari, which is suicide. The battle of Saipan did end with a massive banzai charge by the Japs, which was one way to commit suicide, as our machine gunners and riflemen on the front line mowed them down.

Unfortunately, the Japanese military had brainwashed the

native civilians to the extent that they believed jumping off this cliff was a better choice than surrender. They had convinced these people that the Americans were just a bunch of barbarians, and the treatment they would receive from us would be worse than death. Our combat photographers took some graphic pictures of these people, civilians and military, committing suicide by jumping off the cliff and smashing themselves on the rocks below. In the haze of war this did not appear to be a big event, but later in 2012, when I had the opportunity to return to Saipan, we went up to the edge of the cliff at Marpi Point and my thoughts were far different than they were as a 21-year-old back in 1944.

Two of the most effective weapons that we used on Saipan were the flamethrowers and the rockets. As telephone guys, we never operated any of these weapons, but we could observe them in action. There are two types of configurations for the flamethrowers: One was a heavy fuel tank carried on the back of the flamethrower infantryman, and the second was a flamethrowing tank that could shoot out a flame for some distance. These weapons were especially effective in wiping out the enemy hiding in the many caves on Saipan. It would consume all oxygen in the cave. In my book, every one of those flamethrowing guys was a hero.

The rockets I refer to were clusters of rockets launched from the back of a recon vehicle. Recon vehicles were a military version of a big pickup truck. Back when we were training at Camp Pendleton with live ammunition, I heard we had this new weapon. We could hear them in the distance, but I never had the opportunity to observe them up close. On one of our trips to install a telephone line, my crew came upon a recon vehicle getting ready to launch the rockets. This rocket-launching vehicle had a bunch of tubes, I'm guessing forty or more, and we stopped, not very close, but close enough to get a really good view of the launch and observe the impact. They fired in sequence, swoosh-swoosh-swoosh-swoosh. The impact appeared to cover an area large enough to obliterate everything in that sector. It would have to be terrifying to be on the receiving end of these rockets.

There are a number of major events that occurred in the Pacific that changed the course of the war and actually either saved my life or saved me from becoming a prisoner. One happened during the initial landing phase of the invasion of Saipan.

The Mariana Islands, Guam, Tinian, and Saipan were extremely important to the Japanese. They considered these islands the inner circle of their defense. They knew that if we controlled them, we would have the capability with our long-range B-29 bombers to bomb the Japanese mainland. They could not tolerate this. On June 12, 1944, we began the pre-invasion bombardment of Saipan from our aircraft carriers. The Japanese high command response was to assemble a powerful task force to come to the rescue of Saipan.

Their plan was to destroy the naval task force supporting our Saipan operations and, of course, wipe out our invasion forces on the island. US troops on the ground did not know all this was taking place. Fortunately, we had broken the Japanese naval code, and our high command was aware of the enemy plans and the powerful strength of their task force. Adm. Nimitz, the supreme commander in the Central Pacific, whom I have the utmost regard for, developed a plan for our naval forces to intercept this Japanese task force.

History records the battle of the Philippine Sea, better known by its nickname, "The Great Mariana Turkey Shoot." The loss ratio inflicted upon Japanese aircraft by American pilots and aircraft gunners was so disproportionate that one carrier pilot came back and said it was just like a "turkey shoot." Due to our superior equipment and training, this turned out to be a disaster for the Japanese. They lost between 550 and 645 aircraft and three fleet carriers. By comparison, we only lost 29 aircraft and suffered damage to one battleship. The Japanese task force had no choice but to retreat, which saved our butts on Saipan and left the Japanese navy in a very weak condition.

SAIPAN CANE FIELD

You are always glad to see daylight in a war zone, but you never know what the day is going to be like. The following story I describe is as real to me today as it was 71 years ago.

Early in the morning we would gather for our daily assignments. My wire crew's first assignment that day was to lay a line to one of our combat units on the front line. This was early in our campaign on Saipan, and our communications command post was still located in its original, well-camouflaged position not very far inland. We did have a big disadvantage though. In front of us, toward the front line, was a large sugar cane field that had recently been harvested. It was completely bare, so it provided no cover at all.

The unit we were going to run the line to was located directly across the cane field, so naturally, the shortest distance to our target would be directly through it. The alternative was the long way around this large field, which would provide cover in the bushes and trees that surrounded it. The Japs still held all the high ground on Saipan, and there was much rugged high ground in the central part of the island.

We opted to take the short cut across this open field even though we knew we would be visible to the enemy. We rationalized there had to be more important targets available for the Jap artillery and mortar troops than the four of us; if they fired, it would expose their positions.

Foley, Cosby, Mason, and I headed out across the open field to locate the command post of the unit where we were to connect the phone. We made it without receiving any enemy fire and we felt good about our decision. We felt it would be safe to go back the same way we came. In cases like this, we had to wander around searching for the command post, so we had to lay the wire on the return trip for a direct path back to the command post.

We found the command post we were looking for without too much trouble, and then we started on our return path directly across the open field. Everything was going fine until we were about halfway. In rapid succession, several mortar shells fell all around us. The first shots were over us and off to one side, but the next rounds were much closer. Of course, when the first mortar exploded, we all hit the ground. I hit the ground as flat as I could with my arms stretched out in front of me, my weapon in hand. A telephone wire chief's weapon at that time was a Thompson submachine gun .45, and I was holding it with the wooden stock of the gun perpendicular to the ground.

I wasn't aware until later that a small piece of shrapnel was embedded in the stock of my gun. It is my belief that by a divine act of Providence, none of us suffered any wounds that day.

I think I've said this before, but you can have a fine weapon to defend yourself, but in situations like this it is useless. There is nothing you can shoot at. You just have to lay there and take whatever comes. You are thinking that the enemy has full view of where their mortars are landing in reference to where you are, and you know as they make adjustments, they can put one right on the target. You are the target. Then for whatever reason, the firing stops. No more shots.

Maybe since there was no movement from us, they thought they had wiped us out, or perhaps one of our forward observers had spotted them and called our artillery or aircraft to wipe them out. Or maybe there was another reason the enemy stopped firing, which I describe below.

Now here is something very special about this event that I still treasure. Sometime later, I cannot recall exactly when, but I had a very vivid revelation that at the exact time that I was lying on the ground with those incoming mortars exploding all around us, my mother was at home on her knees praying for my safety. I know my mother and other members of my family were in constant prayer for me during those days. But until now I never had the vivid revelation that at this very crucial, exact time, my mother was on her knees talking to Jesus. This scene is always on my mind.

There is another related part of the story that I think is worthy of documenting. Every day late in the afternoon, all of our wire crews came in and reported on their day's assignments, and it was always interesting to hear their daily experiences. I wasn't aware of it in real time, but I found out that one other wire team had a similar experience crossing this same open cane field that day. One of my good buddies, Cotton Billingsley, was in the crew that got hit that day in the cane field. He and his sergeant, Bill Cassell, were wounded.

Cotton lived in Richmond and, after the war, he would often be asked to speak to the Marines in training at Quantico, Virginia about his experience. In one session he talked about the event I have been writing about, and a colonel asked Cotton if he received any award for his efforts to save Sgt. Cassell that day. Cotton told him no and said he had never thought about getting any award for what he did. The colonel encouraged Cotton to document this event and request a review for a possible award, which he did. Cotton stated in the letter that I was the only one still alive that could vouch for what happened. Unfortunately, as far as I know, Cotton's letter was never acted upon.

I would add, shortly after this event, we advanced our communications command post across this cane field, as it was standard practice that as the front line advanced, we would also move forward.

THE BATTLE OF SAIPAN

There are a few events here from what I would call the sights and sounds of the battle of Saipan. I had nothing to do with the first three events described. I was just an observer, and maybe you could call me an accessory to the fact, but I was not a participant.

The first event is gruesome, and I don't know why this scene stays in my mind. I really would like to forget it, but it is not something that keeps me up at night. I don't wake up and have nightmares or anything like that. One of my early assignments on Saipan was to lay a line to a unit that took us over a rather high ridge. We were moving along through the bushes near the top of the ridge and suddenly, right in front of us, was a dead young lady. I would judge to be in her mid-20's, and she appeared to be a Chamorro (a native of Saipan). There was a dead baby in her arms, and they were pretty badly decomposed with maggots.

Obviously, she had been killed days earlier during the pre-invasion bombardment either by the Air Force or the Navy. It would be nice to have a delete button, like on a computer, to rid yourself of any unpleasant scenes like this.

I have another gruesome memory that I will describe. Again, I don't know why this particular sight remains in my memory, but since I have no erase button it is there. We were laying line and came across a dead Jap soldier. He had just been hit by one of our flamethrowing Marines. He was lying on his face, and all the clothes on his back had been burned off. All you could see was just a mass of burned flesh. After he had been hit by the flamethrower, he had defecated. This defecation was fresh with no signs of burn. Strange sight, I had absolutely no compassion for a dead Japanese soldier.

I'll share the final image that stands out in my mind. One day, we heard that some captured prisoners were being held in a stockade down toward the beach. Naturally we were curious and wanted to take a look. There were about seventy to eighty prisoners of all ages, some women but mostly men. I think it was a mixture of Chamorros and Japs. I really didn't see anyone that had on a Japanese soldier's uniform, but some would use civilian clothes to infiltrate our troops. They were enclosed in a regular wire fence with Marine guards around them. We walked right up to the fence to get a close look. Inside the fence there was a Japanese girl who I would judge was in her early 20s. She was sitting on the ground in such a position that indicated she might be wounded, but there were no visible wounds. I will never forget the face of that girl. She was shaking her fist at us and screaming. Of course, we could not understand the words, but the hatred expressed in her voice and the expression on her face is indescribable. I have never seen hate in anyone's eyes remotely near the extent of the hatred displayed by this girl. Somehow this thing sticks with me and I don't have a delete button.

A final, little event comes to mind, and I don't know why I would remember this. It was sort of a non-event. While at our base camp, someone noticed some light red smoke coming from the Japanese side of the front line. The wind was blowing it right in our direction. In the military, rumors were not hard to start, and so word swiftly spread: "The Japs have started a gas attack on us!"

Each Marine had come ashore with his required equipment pack called 782 gear. The 782 gear pack contained a canteen, foxhole shovel, K-Bar knife, a gas mask, and other survival gear. After a few days on the island many of the Marines began to discard their gas masks, as they were cumbersome and we had not experienced or even heard anything about gas attacks. Seeing red smoke coming from enemy lines resulted in a mad scramble. Guys were trying to remember where they had left their gas masks and, if that didn't work, where they could find another one. Fortunately, this colored gas quickly dissipated, and things returned to normal.

I think every recruit will agree that the most unpleasant thing in basic training is learning how to use the gas mask. Looking back, this event seems a little bit funny, but at that time it was not.

NAVAJO CODE TALKERS

Saipan was the first operation for the Navajo Indian code talkers, and the history is very interesting. They had an unwritten language of extreme complexity, making it unintelligible to anyone without extensive exposure and training. The language has no alphabet or symbols and is spoken only on the Navajo Indian reservations. The son of a missionary who had spent years working with the Navajo tribes brought this to the attention of a Marine general.

The Navajos could transmit and interpret a coded message within seconds. The coding and decoding machines at that time required about thirty minutes to do the same job. This resulted in recruiting 300 or 400 Navajos to train and use as code talkers. They had to invent words in common use by the military that did not exist in the Navajo language. For example, iron fish meant submarine. I would see the code talkers from time to time, but I never knew one personally.

Several summers ago, Kathryn and I traveled to Monument Valley, Utah, in our airstream. We were on a Navajo reservation way out by a little village in the desert. There we came upon a Burger King, and next to it was a big sign that said, "Navajo Code Talker Museum." I could not pass this up, so we stopped. I wanted to meet a code talker.

It turned out the owner of the Burger King was the son of one of the code talkers. Unfortunately, the son was not in that day, and I learned his father had passed away a few years earlier. In the little museum there was a Jap rifle, a Jap uniform, a Jap sword, and a few other items from the battlefield. According to all the reports I heard, these code talkers did a super job, and I was sorry I did not get to meet this code talker's son.

FIELD KITCHEN AND C-RATIONS

Saipan was the only campaign we had with the support of our field kitchen. As I recall, the field kitchen came in five or six days after we landed, and when we had the opportunity, we could get a hot meal. Saipan was also the first operation where we had C-rations. Over all of our maneuvers and training, we had K-rations: a piece of dark chocolate, cheese, crackers, and a little pack of four cigarettes. After about the second meal of K-rations, you've had enough.

I remember during the Marshall Islands battle we supplemented our K-rations with coconuts we found. I guess we overdid the coconuts and coconut milk diet, because many of us suffered from diarrhea. C-rations were a great improvement over K-rations, but after a few days C-rations even got a little old. I think it was on Saipan that we were first introduced to Spam. At first it was a real treat, but after a while you got Spammed out.

As soldiers, we had strict orders not to eat any food unless it was issued by the military. One day Foley, Becker, and I came across the entrance of a little cave with big piles of canned goods. It obviously was a food storage cave for the Japs. Of course, the labels were written in Japanese but some had pictures describing the contents, and one had pictures of orange slices. Our mouths just watered for these oranges. We rationalized that nothing could possibly be wrong with these oranges since they were in a sealed can. We decided to inspect one. We got out our trusty K-Bar and opened a can (a K-Bar is like a hunting knife issued to a soldier or Marine, and next to your rifle it is your most valuable possession).

The can was full of juice and orange slices, and it was just too tempting. We had to taste it. It was delicious! It turned out these were Mandarin oranges, which I'd never seen or heard of. We did supplement our diet with a few cans of Mandarin oranges, and we suffered no ill effects.

END OF THE BATTLE OF SAIPAN

On July 9, 1944, the battle of Saipan was declared secure. It was over. In reality though none of these islands in the Pacific were ever completely secured. Because of the brainwashing of the Japanese military, a number of stragglers would hide out in the caves and bushes rather than surrender.

I just cannot remember how it felt when the battle was over. The biggest thing on our mind was the coming invasion of Tinian just a few miles south, which had been put on hold while we captured Saipan.

BEST BUDDIES FROM BATTLE OF SAIPAN

Mentioning my buddy Foley earlier in this section brings some sadness. The events I am writing about occurred in June and July of 1944 and are now being retold in September 2012. Several weeks ago, Foley's wife, Helen, called and gave us the news that he had passed away. Not only was Foley my best buddy in the service, he was the last surviving member of our unit that I could communicate with.

One other good buddy is still living, but sadly he has developed such a bad case of Alzheimer's that we cannot communicate. With Foley gone, it closes a chapter of my life that I miss. Fortunately, I still retain memories of the good times and the difficult times. I can't explain it. Memories of difficult times are meaningful when you feel like you are doing something that is good and beneficial. After the war, Foley and I stayed in close contact along with several other members of our unit.

Foley and his wife Helen made two trips to Florida to visit us. On one visit, they were accompanied by three other guys from our unit, all from New York. Sgt. R. P. Wood, a super guy and not afraid of anything, had recently lost his wife. Larry Mason and his wife came. Larry was an Ivy Leaguer and later an executive with Merrill Lynch. Joe Bonifer came. He was a retired owner of a butcher shop on Long Island, New York. I was working with USBI at the time, and I arranged for them to stay in a large condominium our company owned on Cocoa Beach. This was before the terrorist attacks of September 11, 2001, so I had passes that allowed me to take them all over the Space Center where access to the general public was typically not allowed.

TINIAN

L ate in June 1944, the 3rd Marine Division recaptured Guam. Guam was in our possession at the start of the war, but the Japanese had captured it along with Wake Island in early 1942. The only target now left in the Mariana Islands was Tinian, which actually had the best airfields in the central Pacific.

The Japanese troops on Tinian knew we were coming and therefore had several weeks to prepare their defenses. Most of their work had to be done at night because we had complete control of the airspace.

Our high command developed a brilliant plan for the invasion of Tinian. Geographically, there was one section of the beaches that was ideal for landing and staging the assault on the island. The plan called for a heavy pre-invasion bombardment of this sector of the beach, and we sent a number of troop ships and supporting warships right offshore. It appeared to the Japs that we would be coming in on this sector of the beach.

In the meantime, the plan called for our underwater frog men to remove and disarm the underwater and beach mines from a very small sector on the other side of the island, and that is where we actually went in. It turned out to be a brilliant plan. It could also have very easily turned into a disaster if the Japanese had not been fooled.

One big new experience for me during this invasion was that our team went ashore in an amphibious tractor (AmTrac). My platoon went ashore in Higgins boats during the two previous invasions.

Tinian was the only invasion where we knew the target ahead of time. We received briefings on the battle plan before we boarded the Landing Ship Tank (LST). I had never been on board an LST. It has a main top deck and a large space below for tanks, AmTracs, or whatever kind of vehicle they want to transport, and bow doors for the vehicles to exit. I cannot recall clearly whether we were on board this LST at night and landed during the night, or whether we spent the next full day on the LST and landed on the following day.

What I do remember well was the order to board our assigned AmTrac. We went below and found our AmTrac, and in just a few minutes all of the track drivers were starting their motors. We expected the bow doors to open, and we would get out of there. For some reason, I never knew why, there was a delay that resulted in a real problem—exhaust fumes!

Many guys were yelling, "Get these bow doors open!"

They were using a few extra words that I won't repeat here. I felt I was about to get sick. Some of the guys probably did. You would be ready to hit the beach just to get out of that environment.

I mentioned earlier the frogmen cleared a very narrow section of the beach for us to land, and we knew all the beaches were heavily mined. After the AmTracs had gotten off the ship, they maneuvered around to get their position for the departure to the shore. The AmTrac I was in developed a steering problem. An AmTrac has tracks like a caterpillar; you steer it by slowing down one tread and increasing the speed of the opposite tread. Whatever mechanical problem this particular AmTrac had caused it to veer to the left. The driver could not keep the vehicle in a straight line. It got so bad that at one time we were in an area by ourselves. The driver was desperately trying to get us back in the declared area and had to make a 360 degree turn to get us back in position. Our guys were yelling at us and using a few choice words to our crew. Of course, it wasn't the fault of the AmTrac crew. They were doing the best they could.

Before we hit the beach, the AmTrac crew was able to get

us back into the cleared area. In spite of the good work by our frogmen, a few of our AmTracs did encounter some mines, and we suffered some casualties. The reception, however, was not anything like it was when we first landed on Saipan.

The decoy landing plan had worked beautifully. The Japs had pulled most of their heavy guns and mortars to the other side to protect the area where they had anticipated our landing. In our particular area, we only encountered small arms fire and some mortar fire when we went to shore. It was not anything like our initial landing on Saipan. Maybe there was some scattered artillery but I just don't remember that. Our orders the first day were to get organized, set up by our communication center, and string some lines out to the infantry command post.

By nightfall we had several thousand Marines ashore and had established our beachhead according to the plan. But as night came and darkness fell, there was a marked increase in small arms fire and mortars. In fact, all night long visible tracer bullets went in all directions. It was more small arms fire than I had ever been exposed to at one time. The terrain on Tinian was much more suitable for tanks and other heavy equipment than the rugged terrain on Saipan.

It was a great day when we were told our job on Tinian was over and we could go back to our overseas home on Maui. Once there, people everywhere treated us super. They would line the streets and roads to welcome us every time we returned from an operation.

Each time we were gone, improvements were made in our Maui camp that made life a little more comfortable. Although we would immediately go back into a heavy training schedule for the next operation, we did find time to participate in and enjoy other activities. We had pretty good food, regular mail service, outdoor movies, and entertainment groups from time to time from the main island. We had liberty on most of the weekends, and we could visit little towns and villages, and on occasion we could check out vehicles from the motor pool to explore some of the remote places on the island. I enjoyed playing on our company baseball team. We played other units and divisions and teams from the Navy and Army.

IWO JIMA

W hether you are engaged in official duties or off-duty, the thought of the next operation and whether you will make it is always in the back of your mind. You constantly think of home and your loved ones.

We were never given any advance information about our departure date for the next operation. However, you could sense when our departure date was near. We were told to be ready, and that the announcement could come at any time. Toward the end of December 1944, we were in this mode, and we didn't know whether we'd be spending Christmas on Maui or on board a ship headed for our next operation.

In late January, we received the order to load our equipment and head for the port at Kahului, Maui. A landing ship (LSM-260) was tied up at the dock waiting for us, I had never seen or heard of a LSM. Maybe LSMs had been used in other operations, but they were new to us. A LSM is like a mini-LST with bow doors opening on the beach. You know when a seagoing vessel has only a number and not a name, it has to be small.

I did not know it at the time, but LSM-260 would be my home for the next six weeks. Prior to this trip the longest sea voyage I had experienced was approximately three weeks, and this was the only ship that I was on that we had the opportunity to mingle with and make friends with the crew.

As I recall, we had about forty-five Marines, two small amphibious vehicles that we call Weasels, and several Jeeps on board. We had only used these Weasels in our training exercises preparing for the Iwo Jima invasion. They were neat little vehicles made with rubber tires for land operations and a small propeller for the amphibious mode. We figured it was going to be somewhat of a luxurious ride from the LSM landing craft and then up on the beach as far as we could go.

We'd also never left a landing craft riding on a Jeep. This all sounded really good on paper, but unfortunately it did not turn out like that. These wheeled vehicles were a big mistake. We left the harbor at Kahului and sailed over to Pearl Harbor, where we tied up at one of the piers along with many, many other ships preparing to convoy to our next destination.

While docked at Pearl Harbor, we were not allowed to leave the ship, so we had plenty of time to watch what was going on around us: ships being loaded at the adjacent piers and coming in and out the harbor. One day, several of us were standing at the rail, watching them load a cargo-type ship tied up at the adjacent pier. One thing really got our attention. They were loading white crosses. The railroad-type shipping containers very common today for shipping goods did not yet exist.

All cargo was placed on a large heavy rope net that is spread out on the dock. Then a crane would pick up the four corners of the net and drop it into the cargo hold of the ship. At first we made a feeble attempt to make light of this scene by saying things like, "Hey, Becker, I see one with your name on it," and "Hey, Mason, your name is on that one."

After a few minutes, those comments just didn't go over so well, so we watched silently for a little while and then drifted away. We had had enough.

I cannot say this scene bothered me a great deal, but it did linger in my mind. I'm sure it did for the other guys too. Silently, I wondered how they determine how many of these things you need. I still don't know the answer to that question.

Sadly, the next time we saw these crosses, they would not be in a cargo net but upright in the ground with a name on them. It did not occur to me when I wrote the above story, but these crosses had to be for the 5th Marine Division. Our 4th Marine

Division used wooden tombstone-type grave markers. You can see this in one of the 4th Division cemetery photos on Iwo Jima I included.

After a couple of days at Pearl Harbor we joined other ships and made some practice landings around the Hawaiian Islands. Then we returned to Pearl Harbor to refuel and resupply. We pulled out of Pearl Harbor and took our position in the convoy headed toward our next destination. We didn't know where. We found it was much more comfortable traveling in this little LSM than it was traveling on an overcrowded troopship. We did not have to stand in long chow lines, and I would say the quality of the food on the LSM was well above the quality of the food on a crowded troopship.

Another positive thing on the LSM was that because it was one of the smallest ships in the convoy, we had no fear of a submarine attack. No Jap submarine commander would waste a torpedo on our small ship with so many very large ships surrounding us. The only negative thing that I can say about traveling in the smaller ship was that if you encountered some rough weather, you'd get bounced around much more than if you were in a much larger ship. On our journey to Iwo Jima we ate mostly peanut butter and jelly sandwiches for a couple of days, as our cooks were seasick.

We got along extremely well with the crew, and I made a lifelong friend. It turned out to be one of those "small world" things. His name was Buck Horton. He was from Montgomery, Alabama, and I found out one of his cousins was the valedictorian in my high school class. Buck got in touch with me a few years ago, and Kathryn and I have had the opportunity to visit Buck and his wife in Montgomery on a couple of occasions. Of course, we relived our journey from Maui to Iwo Jima.

I can say that of all the ships I was on during the war, LSM-260 was the only ship I was ever attached to. In fact, I think 260 was kind of special to all of the Marines onboard. After the bow doors opened and they put us off on the beach at Iwo Jima, I never saw 260 again. In one of our postwar visits, Buck gave me the interesting history of 260 after we departed on the beach. They got battered up pretty badly and had to go back to San Francisco for repairs and then went to Japan with the occupation forces.

Once your ship cleared the harbor, you anxiously awaited the brief from the officers on your destination and the battle plan. Prior to this time, there was always constant speculation on what your next target would be, but as I recall, we never got it right. I guess this indicates that the high command was much smarter than us troops. Our target was always a surprise, and this time was no different, as our captain pulled out a detailed map of Iwo Jima. My memory is not clear enough to say whether I had actually ever heard of this forsaken bit of land in the far Pacific. If I had heard of it, it certainly didn't register that it would be a part of my life forever.

Why Iwo Jima? In real estate, commercial or residential, location, location, location determines the price and the value of the land. This is even more true in the military world. Unfortunately, in the military, you must pay a higher price in human lives for the most strategic territory. We had to pay a heavy price to gain possession of the strategic airbases on Tinian and Saipan, but it put the vast industrial complex on mainland Japan within the range of our B-29 bombers.

Unfortunately, to reach the mainland of Japan, our bombers had to fly directly over Iwo Jima. Iwo Jima is about 600 miles from Tokyo. We were suffering heavy losses of our B-29 bombers, because from Iwo Jima the Japs could warn the mainland that our bombers were on the way. They could also intercept our bombers with fighter planes. Many B-29's crippled on the bombing run over Japan could not make it all the way back to our bases on Tinian. Many B-29's and their crew were saved as a result of our capture of Iwo Jima.

The first leg of our journey from Pearl Harbor took us to the Kwajaleim Atoll (a large coral atoll of forty islands) in the Marshall Islands. We had captured the small island of Roi-Namur early in 1943. The next leg of our journey took us to Saipan and Tinian, where we anchored offshore for a day or two for refueling and operations. We had captured these islands in June and July of 1944.

Our LSM was anchored offshore on Tinian very close to the end of one of the runways. Day and night we could see and hear our B-29 bombers taking off to bomb Japan. These planes were so heavily loaded, you could just feel them struggling to gain altitude as far as you could see. I saw one crash on the beach in a great ball of flame. That really hurt. The other planes just kept taking off in sequence, and you could just imagine how those airmen were feeling as they flew over this terrible scene. At this time there were thousands and thousands of airmen stationed on Tinian, and it was classified as the busiest airport in the world.

We departed Saipan and Tinian on February 16, 1944, and three days later we arrived at Iwo Jima. I had my first glimpse of Iwo Jima at first daylight on February 19th. The island was being constantly bombarded by our battleships, cruisers, and destroyers, and the planes from our aircraft carriers were bombing the island without ceasing.

The landscape on Iwo Jima is certainly one of the most unfriendly looking on the face of the earth: black beaches, no greenery, and a few small tree trunks with the foliage blasted off in the pre-invasion bombardment still standing. It looked like hell, and it smelled like hell. Parts of the island had sulfur fumes that oozed out of cracks in the surface.

I could see nothing but smoke and dirt and debris flying in the air. It seemed every inch was being bombed. It appeared to me we had enough firepower to wipe this little island off the map. We naïvely thought no one could live under that type of bombardment; surely taking this island would be a cakewalk because no one would be left to defend it. The aerial photographs we had made did not reveal the vast network of caves and underground facilities that the Japanese had constructed on Iwo Jima. While we bombed them, the enemy would just retreat underground and suffer no personal damage. We learned the hard way about these underground tunnels and caves.

It had to be an awesome sight that morning for the Japs to look out over the ocean from their well-camouflaged position on the island. Ships of every size and description in all directions as far as you could see, many of them belching smoke as their big guns sent huge projectiles to explode on the island.

In the meantime, they were doing some counterattacks, and you could see waterspouts around the ships as their incoming shells hit the water. I think most of them did hit the water. I heard one LST took a direct hit, but I do not know if others were hit. I did not observe any.

Our ship's radio was listening in on the communication link from the guys on the beach back to the general's command post, which was on board a ship near us. The first report that we heard sounded like good news. In fact, we had expected light resistance.

However, bad news came. As soon as the beach got a little crowded with men and equipment, the Japs raked the beach with all the firepower they had. A big surprise resulted in a very serious problem: trying to navigate people and vehicles in that volcanic ash on the beach. There were several terraces from five to ten feet high running parallel to the beach, and it was very, very difficult to move in this type of terrain. These were rather steep inclines, and you would take one step forward and maybe slide back two steps trying to climb up in this heavy volcanic ash.

They quickly learned that wheeled vehicles could not negotiate this beach area at all. We were in standby mode for an hour, waiting for our orders to head for the beach when the message came over the loudspeakers on the ship that no more wheeled vehicles would attempt to land there. Our nice laid out plans to come ashore with all of our equipment aboard a vehicle was now down the tubes.

We had to hastily develop a plan to select our priority equipment and remove it from the vehicle. We had to manhandle it to get it ashore, and that also meant going up those terraces slipping and sliding. This decision to have no more wheeled vehicles come ashore completely changed our departure time. The more reports we got from what was happening on the beach, the worse it sounded. Our guys had almost no cover, and trying to dig a foxhole in that volcanic ash was a real problem. Very soon the beach was clogged with men and equipment, and the best targets for the Japanese big guns was the area along the beach. They took advantage of this.

In one of my visits a few years ago with my friend, Buck Horton, a member of the crew on LSM-260, we were reliving our experience. Buck maintained that we went ashore late in the day on February 19th. Sometimes after sixty years it's a little hard to remember some things clearly, but as I recall, we were not ready to go in before dark, and we did not make it in that day. After dark the Japanese pulled some more of their big guns and mortars out of these hidden caves, making it a very tough night for our guys that were ashore.

We anticipated drawing some heavy fire when LSM-260 approached the beach. Our LSM was much smaller than the LST's, but it still was much larger than the Amtracs or Higgins boats, so we were afraid we were going to be a good target for the Jap gunners. We were surprised when we were able to come ashore from 260 without drawing heavy fire. At all times on Iwo Jima, there was mortar and artillery fire going back and forth in all directions, but for some unknown reason none of this was real close to us. We learned quickly that the lull in fire in our particular area would not last very long.

Our first objective after we came ashore was to find a suitable location for our communication center. That did not look very promising initially because the sector we were supposed to set up in was almost completely out in the open. But I do believe that Providence had something to do with this when we discovered an abandoned Japanese anti-aircraft gun position. This was a circular pit about twelve to fifteen feet in diameter and about four feet deep. The gun had been removed, and I would assume it had been relocated to one of their caves or heavily camouflaged positions behind their front lines. It was really out in the open, and I'm surprised it could escape all of the heavy bombardment from our ships and aircraft.

There was a tunnel on one side of the wall about four feet in diameter, and it led to a little room at the end of the tunnel, which was about twenty-five feet long. This appeared to be a room that housed the gun crew. Directly opposite this tunnel there was a similar tunnel, again the same size, about four feet in diameter, and this tunnel terminated in a room which appeared to be where they stored their ammunition. The Japs left nothing behind, no ammunition, nothing. We could not ask for a better setup than this for our initial communication center. It provided a protected area for our switchboard and members of our crew when we were not out on a mission.

On Iwo Jima you could very easily be caught in a sector that was experiencing heavy mortar and artillery fire. I don't think anyone can say that they're not very afraid when caught in heavy mortar and artillery fire, and it's very frustrating. Besides being scared, there is nothing you can do about it except try to get as much coverage as you can. You can't shoot back because there's nothing in range that you can shoot at.

At night they would bring their heavy guns out of the caves, some of them on rails, and they would bring other heavy artillery and mortars out of camouflaged positions in the rugged terrain they occupied. We had one special name for a heavy Spigot Mortar that they would launch at night. I cannot remember our name for this big mortar, but the sound of it chugging along is still fresh in my memory. When you first hear it, it appears it is coming right at you. You feel quite relieved as it passes overhead; you cringe as you know what will happen in a few seconds. There is a big ball of fire somewhere behind you, followed by the sound of the explosion. You know that the island is so crowded with equipment and men, it is going to do great harm wherever it lands. After a number of nights hearing this rocket flying over, it was finally silenced. Our front line troops had apparently overrun their launch site.

There were a couple of very unusual and strange events that I recall from my experience on Iwo Jima. The first event I describe happened late one evening while several of us were gathered around talking and preparing to warm some food with some Sterno cans. We were just outside of our command post in the old abandoned Jap anti-aircraft position. All was quiet in our immediate sector, no artillery or mortar fire, and we were far enough behind the front lines that we were not in any danger from small arms firing.

Suddenly a mortar shell landed right at our feet. It was so close that we were fortunate it did not strike one of us directly. When it exploded, it showered us with that volcanic sand. Of course, we hit the ground fully expecting follow-on shots. To our great surprise they did not come. That lone shot was all there was. I do not recall how long we waited. We communicated with each other, and again, to our great surprise, no one was injured. We should've all been killed or badly wounded.

Then we discovered why we weren't. This mortar round was defective. Rather than explode into many fragments as a mortar shell should, it had just enough explosives to split the shell but remained in one piece. It was like if you cut a watermelon and open it up and still it is in one piece because all of the rind has not been severed. I just have to believe that divine Providence was with us.

Back at the factory where this mortar was made, someone, maybe a slave prisoner, deliberately or by mistake made an error in the explosive charge in this mortar shell.

The mortar crew that launched this particular mortar shell had many in their stockpile to select from but by divine intervention picked up this defective mortar to aim at us.

Another thing that can't be explained is that no mortar crew can be accurate enough to hit a small target like our little group on the first shot. A mortar team's first shot is always to get a reference point from which to make adjustments for following shots to hit the target. Normally, the first shot is long or short and could be on either side of the real target. Back in the chapter on Saipan, I described a situation where our crew was the target of a Jap mortar crew and their mortars were hitting all around us.

Another unusual event that I witnessed seem to defy the laws of physics. On one occasion, as my crew was laying a telephone line near the edge of the runway, we watched a P-38, one of our best fighter planes, come in for a landing. About the time the wheels touched the runway, the propeller came off and started spinning toward the opposite side of the runway. We could see some guys in that general area begin to scramble because it was headed directly toward them. The amazing thing was how long the propeller stayed up right. It finally tilted over, but it still had enough momentum to endanger those guys in that area where it was headed.

It appeared to fizzle out before it reached those guys, and as best we could tell, no one was injured by this freak accident. While we are talking about airplanes, before we left the island we did witness a number of our crippled B-29 super bombers safely land on our newly captured airfields.

I think this would be a good time to mention a group that probably never did get the recognition they deserved, and that is the Navy Seabees. In all the islands we landed on, Seabees were right behind us. They could have a heavily damaged runway back in operation in record time. I am reminded right now of a picture in our 4th Marine division history book of a bulldozer on the edge of the airfield on Iwo Jima that is blown over from hitting a landmine. Some photographer caught this scene just as the mine exploded. My wire team was close by when this happened. We weren't directly looking at it, but we heard the explosion. We looked over at the bulldozer, and there were several guys rushing toward it to help the driver.

Artillery and mortar fire were much more constant on Iwo Jima than any previous battles we had experienced. I remember a story from a motivational speaker at one of our national conventions who was blinded from a second wound on Iwo Jima. It was a sad and unusual case. He was on a stretcher, along with a number of other wounded Marines on the beach waiting to be evacuated to the hospital ship offshore, when a mortar shell landed close by. He suffered a shrapnel wound that destroyed his eyesight. Despite this tragic story, he still maintained such a positive outlook on life and I enjoyed hearing him speak.

I mentioned earlier that our ship, LSM-260, did not get hit when we went ashore. After the war, when I was visiting my friend Buck Horton, a member of the crew on LSM-260 told me that after they let us off, they were used to bring supplies from the bigger ships offshore back to the beach. They got hit a couple of times when they came in.

Buck told me one funny little story where he almost got into real trouble. They were at the beach with the bow doors open, and supplies were being unloaded from the ship. Buck and one of his buddies stepped off the ship to see if they could find some souvenirs. While they were out, the Japs suddenly opened up with some heavy artillery fire. The captain of the ship closed the bow door and pulled out. Buck and his buddy were left stranded on the island and had to spend the night there. Their ship came back in the next day, and they were able to get back aboard. Buck and his buddy were pleasantly surprised that they did not get a court-martial for this event.

One afternoon I returned to our command post from a mission, and one of the guys said, "You should go in there and take a look at Tony R."

We were still using the abandoned Jap anti-aircraft gun position as our command post, and when he said "in there," he meant the little dugout room the Japs had made for their gun crew. I went through the tunnel to the little room where Tony was. It was dimly lit, but I could see that Tony was in trouble. It had been raining, and he had his poncho and his helmet on. He had a strange blank stare and was shaking pretty badly.

I do not remember exactly what I said to Tony, but he gave no response. He just sat there with that blank stare. Tony was a young Marine, a tough little Italian guy from the Bronx. Tony was evacuated and rejoined our unit later back on Maui. I don't know if he suffered any long-term problems from this experience. I heard a statement the other day that I think applies to Tony and other cases like this, and especially our veterans from the wars in Afghanistan and Iraq, and the statement was, "All wounds do not bleed." Sadly, I would add these wounds seem to be more difficult to treat as well.

On Iwo Jima we found it much harder to keep our telephone lines to the forward units intact. Also, in this operation we had more problems that occurred at night. It was absolutely essential that we keep our lines intact, day or night. We were always concerned that an ambush was waiting for us as we followed our lines troubleshooting a problem, especially at night. Sometimes the Japs would hide in a cave or tunnel and come out behind the front line.

I mentioned my friend Buck Horton earlier in this chapter. I wanted to conclude this chapter with an excerpt from a paper he wrote for the Library of Congress. The paper begins with his enlistment in the Navy and his service on a ship that participated in the Normandy invasion. We pick up his story back in the States and on his trip to Iwo Jima on LSM-260. I think you will find it interesting to hear about these historic events from his perspective as well.

Excerpt from Buck Horton's paper for the Library of Congress:

"After arriving in San Diego I was assigned to another landing ship, LSM-260 (LSM Group Fourteen, Flotilla Five, built in NY). It was brand new and was designed to land cargo on the beaches of the South Pacific. Unknown to us the destination would be Iwo Jima, one of the hardest fought battles of the war.

"We moved up the coast to San Francisco and anchored in the San Francisco Bay for a few days. It was another staging area for hundreds of ships. Our next destination: Honolulu and beyond.

"After passing beneath the Golden Gate Bridge, we headed out to sea where we joined up with a huge convoy of ships, including all types and sizes. The water was very rough and the waves (swells) were fifty feet high. Many times, we couldn't see any of the other ships because of the high waves. Most of the crew, including me, became seasick. This was the only time I actually threw up during my time in the Navy.

"Somewhere along the way, I think it was in Hawaii, we brought a squadron of Marines and their equipment on board our ship. They were well trained and combat experienced and they fit right in with the rest of us. There was a corporal, Ike Rigell (whose son Scott, at the time of this writing in 2011, is now a freshmen in Congress), and one officer in charge of these Marines. I hardly ever saw the officer. He stayed holed up, for the most part, in the officers' quarters. It was obvious from the start that the corporal was in charge. Ike and I became close friends. He was from Slocomb, but he was not typical. I found out the hard way that he was unbeatable at the checker board. Checkers, like chess, is a game of total skill with no luck involved. His keen mind was so far ahead of the rest of us, and those of us who were foolish enough to challenge him soon found out that his mind worked beyond any of us. I don't think I ever even got a 'king' playing against him.

"We left Hawaii with the main convoy of 880 ships and their crews, and 110,000 Marines. We took a southward course and briefly crossed the equator. It was only after we were at sea, with no chance to blab our destination, that we found out that we were now part of an invasion force assembled for the Iwo Jima invasion.

"Our mission would be to drop off the Marines and their equipment when they called us into the beach. For a long time, I never knew whether my friend, Ike, had lived or not. It took several years to find out. We have had two very emotional face to face meetings in the last year.

"I don't remember the exact date or time (February 19, 1945) that we first landed at Iwo. I do remember we were there from the beginning. Our first landing location was at the extreme north end of the landing area, probably the most dangerous spot of all the landing areas. That remained our designated landing for the remaining time we were at Iwo. There was nothing between us and the enemy except for about two hundred feet.

"The Japs were entrenched in deep caves they had carved in the hillsides. We couldn't see them but they could see us. We were so close to the enemy that they could hit us with a good slingshot, and any other weapons they had. They would roll out whatever their weapon of choice was and start shooting at us. This continued for several weeks until the Marines finally drove them out with flame throwers.

"Once, while sitting on the beach unloading supplies for the fighting Marines, a Marine parked his tracked vehicle near our starboard bow and asked permission to use our 'head' (toilet). He said he hadn't had a decent movement since landing on the beach. We said sure, come aboard. The head was located along the starboard side, the side exposed to the Japs. While sitting there, tending to his business, the Japs decided to roll out some of their heavy artillery and we took several direct hits. One penetrated the bulkhead, just a few inches from where our guest was seated, leaving a two-inch hole. He was unharmed but very scared. He came running out and said, "You can have this thing, it is safer on the beach!" However, unknown to him, his vehicle had taken a direct hit and was totally destroyed.

"Along about the second or third week, we were sitting on the beach unloading supplies during a time when I was not standing any kind of watch. It was a bright, sunny day and as peaceful as any Sunday afternoon in the park. Knowing that we would be there for quite a while, a fellow seaman and I decided to once again take a stroll away from our ship. Big mistake, again.

"We started inland hoping to find some souvenirs to take home. I did come across a Jap officer standing upright in a small round hole, deep enough to afford him some sort of protection but not enough. He was dead. I looked down at him and saw both a sidearm and a sword attached to his belt. I wanted them really bad but I was afraid that he might be booby trapped so I gave up.

"We continued on inward, reaching a small bank that led up to the airstrips on the island. We climbed to the top and stood up. All hell broke loose. The Japs must have been planning an all-out attack with mortars on the beach. We were around three hundred feet from our ship when it all started. We had no choice but to run for our lives. I don't know which way my buddy went. I found myself running as fast as I could toward my ship, and the mortar rounds continued at an all-out pace. I knew I couldn't make it back to the ship so I dove in a well-rounded foxhole belonging to a Marine. With his hospitality I stayed there until things quieted down.

"After things were quiet, I left my new Marine friend and headed back toward my ship. Problem was, things had gotten so rough on the beach that they had backed out to sea. There I was with no ship. Eventually our ship came back and dropped the front landing ramp. We were greeted by a very angry skipper.

"Another time while the ship was sitting on the beach, I was asleep in my bunk (remember, we stood four hours on and four hours off watch, plus helping with other unrelated duties to our watches). When we could get a chance to get a little sleep, we took it. The general alarm sounded, waking me from a dead sleep. The boatswain's mate came running through our quarters screaming that the Japs had just broken through and we would have to back out to sea again. In my semi-trance, I envisioned that the Japs had already stormed our ship. I thought I would have to fight my way to the battle station. It turned out that only one Jap had come running onto the beach, screaming at the top of his lungs. He was soon killed.

"Along at about the end of my time at Iwo, I was asleep again. We were sitting on the beach unloading supplies when a LCI sitting next to us lost control. His starboard stern swept around and, with the waves' help, dug several gaping holes in our port side below the water line. My sleeping quarters were flooded with seawater. The general alarm sounded and I awoke to find water already up to within a few inches of my bunk. There was no real danger to me; after all, the bow of the ship was already sitting on the beach. The damage control crew took over and fashioned a system to seal off the gaping holes. They took mattress pads and large plates of steel, and pulled them all together with draw bolts and formed a watertight gasket.

"This ended our tour at Iwo. We sailed back to Guam, where they replaced the gaskets with welded-on plates. Our entire port side was already heavily damaged from the banging we took while tied up to the cargo ships. The starboard side was full of bullet holes as mentioned earlier.

"From there we went back to Hawaii, and then onto San Diego, as the repairs were too extensive for them to take care of in Hawaii. While there, they replaced our entire port side and repaired the holes in our starboard side."

I am so thankful that Buck and I were able to reconnect several years after the war, learn that both of us had survived, and continue our friendship. I am also glad that he has the opportunity to share his story as well.

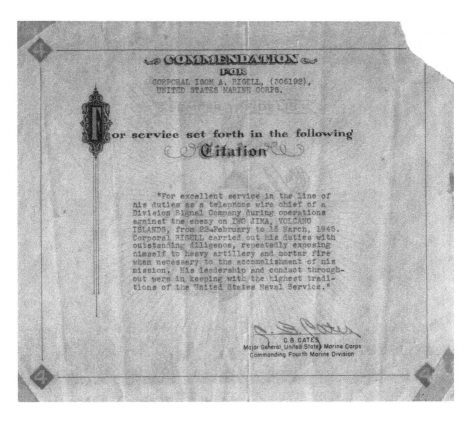

A Letter of Commendation I received from Major General C.B. Cates for excellent service on Iwo Jima.

Divine services on Iwo Jima—Catholic, Protestant, and Jewish.

Here I am listening to a sermon at a
church service held on Iwo Jima.

FLAG RAISING

I think any time you mention Iwo Jima you have a mental picture of the flag raising, which occurred on the fourth day of the battle. Facing the beaches where we landed, the 5th Marine Division was on the left, and the 4th Marine Division was on the right. The plan was for the 4th Division to go inland and swing to the right, and the 5th division would go inland across the narrow neck of the island, capture Mount Suribachi, and then swing to the right and advance parallel with the 4th Division.

While there was still very stiff enemy opposition on all fronts, Lt. Col. Chandler Johnson, 5th Marine Division, gave the order to send a patrol to the summit of Mount Suribachi. Lt. George Schrier was selected to lead this forty-man patrol. Col. Johnson gave Lt. Schrier a flag and told him if he reached the top to raise it.

Note the colonel did not say "when" you reach the top. He said "if" you reach the top. I got this little tidbit from the well-documented book, *Flag of Our Fathers*, by the son of one of the flag raisers, James Bradley.

Marine Sgt. Louis Lowery, a Marine combat photographer representing the magazine *Leatherneck*, accompanied this patrol up the mountain. Surprisingly, they encountered little resistance on the way up, but on top of the mount several Japs charged out of their caves. They were immediately eliminated. Fortunately, there were some metal pipes scattered around that had been part of a rain-capturing system destroyed by our pre-invasion bombardment. The patrol raised this flag, and it was photographed by Sgt. Lowery.

The raising of the flag was immediately observed by all the troops on the island as well as the nearby ships offshore. The ships began to blow their whistles and sound their horns, and the men on the island began waving their helmets and shouting.

One thing I read about this event that was dear to my heart was that Lt. Col. Chandler Johnson ordered one of his wire crews to install a telephone on the summit of Mount Suribachi. Seeing "Old Glory" flying from the summit of Mount Suribachi was really a much-needed morale booster, because capturing this island was much more difficult than anyone had anticipated. This was the first American flag to fly over Japanese homeland territory. All of the islands we had captured prior to this had not been original Japanese territory. Note that this was not the flag raising that became so famous because of the picture by the Associated Press photographer Joe Rosenthal.

Secretary of the Navy James Forrestal had just come ashore that day along with the overall commander of this operation, Marine Gen. "Howling Mad" Smith. The people who knew the General said he lived up to this title. I do not know why the Secretary of the Navy was present; as far as I know, that was highly unusual, but there he was. The report is that when he saw the flag, he told General Smith he would like to have it as a souvenir. Somewhere along the line, and I don't know exactly where, the decision was made to replace this rather small flag with a much larger one.

I don't know the details of this, but they came up with a much larger flag from one of the LSTs offshore. When they got the replacement, someone told Lt. Col. Johnson that the Secretary of the Navy wanted the flag that was first raised. Lt. Col. Johnson was reported to have the same disposition as Gen. Smith, and with a few choice words he said the Secretary of the Navy was not getting that flag. It belonged to his battalion.

Joe Rosenthal, the Associated Press photographer, was not present at the first flag raising. When he learned there would be a second flag raising with a larger flag, he asked if he could go along and photograph this event.

They found a larger, very heavy metal pipe, and it required several guys to raise the flagpole. During this raising Joe Rosenthal shot his famous photo. He had to send his negatives to Guam for development, and from there they transmitted the photos back to the US, so Rosenthal really didn't know exactly what he had captured on his negatives until much later. After the flag raising, Rosenthal asked all the Marines in that patrol to pose for a picture in front of the flag. Later Rosenthal was asked if the picture was posed. Rosenthal said yes because he thought they were asking about this picture and not about the actual "raising the flag picture," which he hadn't yet seen.

I assume we all saw the first flag, because the word-of-mouth passed quickly all over the island. That was very welcome news. In all military operations, you have a big advantage when you occupy the high ground.

My friend Buck Horton also writes about the flag-raising on Iwo Jima in his paper for the Library of Congress, and I wanted to share his perspective with you:

"We had seen the first flag go up and we were extremely proud that the American flag was now flying atop Mt. Suribachi. It was off to our left but easily within eyesight.

"While sitting on the beach, there was a sister LSM beached a few feet away on our port side. Their signalman informed me that the Marines had just borrowed a flag to be raised on top of Mt. Suribachi. I wondered why; after all, they already had a flag up. I didn't know what they wanted with a larger flag. Because of his tip I continued to watch Mt. Suribachi.

"I did see the first flag come down and the now famous flag go up. Never did I think that this would become the most remembered picture taken during WWII. I have an exact duplicate of this flag in my possession."

Unfortunately, it was not all downhill from then on as far as securing the island. Sadly, three of the six men in the flag raising photo would not leave the island. Neither would Sgt. Lowery, the Marine photographer.

During the battle, I never got up on Mount Suribachi, but I did on my return trip in 2012. I'll say more about that experience in my write-up on the return trip.

Feb. 23, 1945

(FX)—Feb. 24) MARINES HOIST FLAG ATOP SURIBACHI—UNITED STATES MARINES OF 28TH REGIMENT, FIFTH DIVISION, HOIST AMERICAN FLAG ATOP SURIBACHI, IWO JIMA VOLCANO, AFTER BATTLING JAPS TO TOP OF CRATER. PHOTO BY AP PHOTOGRAPHER JOE ROSENTHAL ON ASSIGNMENT WITH WARTIME STILL PICTURE POOL RADIOED BY NAVY FROM GUAM TO SAN FRANCISCO TODAY. (AP WIREPHOTO) (AWH-1945-JOER(BL) 1945

The iconic flag raising on Iwo Jima, on February 23, 1945.

END OF THE WAR

I can never forget August 6, 1945. We received the first report of the atomic bomb on Hiroshima. It was hard to comprehend that a large city could be completely destroyed with one bomb. We were on Maui, heavily involved in preparation for our next invasion. For the first time we knew in advance where we were going. After Iwo Jima, which was considered the first Japanese homeland victory, followed by the invasion and capture of Okinawa, there was nothing left but the shores of Japan. I learned later that one of the main objectives by the Japanese in their defense of Iwo Jima and Okinawa was to inflict such heavy causalities on our forces that we would settle a peace treaty more favorable than the unconditional surrender established by Truman, Churchill, and Stalin at the Potsdam Treaty in 1945.

There would be no negotiated peace treaty. The War in the Pacific had progressed to such a state that it was obvious, even to Japan, they were going to lose the war. They were still desperately hoping to end the war with a negotiated peace contract rather than an unconditional surrender, which was just unthinkable to them. Even though they were a defeated nation, they did have a vast amount of resources available for a very bloody encounter if we invaded. You can imagine all the planes—private and military—along with warships and available peacetime boats fitted with Kamikazes. Plenty were willing to sacrifice their lives to kill a few of the invading forces.

Japan was counting on those conditions to negotiate a peace treaty that would leave them with some influence in the Pacific—some of the empire that they had captured earlier. That was not acceptable to us.

Prior to the atomic bomb, our B-29 bombers flying from Tinian and Guam were devastating the Japanese industrial complex daily with conventional high explosive and incendiary bombs, eventually wiping out large cities like Tokyo. This was a massive air campaign. I learned after the war that in this period our airbase on Tinian was the busiest airport in the world, with hundreds of B-29's and thousands of airmen operating twenty-four hours a day, seven days a week. One raid on Tokyo by B-29's using incendiary bombs killed around 90,000 civilians and military, far more than the 40,000 to 50,000 obliterated at Hiroshima. We were suffering heavy B-29 losses in these raids. The capture of Iwo Jima helped minimize the losses by providing an emergency landing field for crippled bombers on their way back to Tinian and Guam. From our airfield on Iwo Jima, we could also provide fighter plane escorts to the B-29's on their bombing runs to Japan. I have read reports that our B-29's at that time were not the most reliable plane in the sky.

Back to the discussions we were engaged in on Maui. We were simply awed as we received more and more data on the vast destruction caused by one bomb. We figured the Japs would surely raise the white flag, even though we knew they were fanatics. One of our replacements after our Iwo Jima battle was a little guy named Ernie. I cannot recall his last name. Ernie was a private, just out of boot camp, and I would say we gave this little guy more respect than we would give an ordinary private. Ernie had a doctorate degree in physics and was a professor at a state university, possibly the University of Kentucky. I am not sure. I don't know why Ernie had not applied for Officer Candidate School, but it was not that unusual to see enlisted men with college degrees. Ernie was a good guy, and we would pump him for all the education we could absorb on the new atomic bomb. I don't think Ernie was a nuclear physicist, but he was so far above any of us in this area that we learned a lot from him.

One thing that bothered me, and I never did understand it, was what stopped the "chain reaction" of the atomic bomb? In other words, why didn't the "chain reaction" consume the atmosphere? Ernie somewhat alleviated my fears, but with all my vast Slocomb education, I still did not comprehend it. But I accepted Ernie's position that this was not a problem. I might add that good old Ernie looked more like a professor than he did a Marine. I don't know how it happened, but all of his uniforms were about two or three sizes too big.

When we dropped the first atomic bomb, we thought surely the Japanese would be willing to come to the table with a complete, unconditional surrender. We waited for the Japanese to respond. There was no response. Three days later, President Truman made a gutsy decision, which I greatly approved of, to order the second atomic bomb, which would destroy the city of Nagasaki. This sent a very clear message to Japan: If they did not surrender now, their entire nation was going to look like Hiroshima and Nagasaki. One thing I would like to point out is that this war was different from later engagements in Vietnam and the Middle East. In WWII we used all the resources we had. The theory was the sooner you could end the war, even at the cost of civilian lives, the better it was for us and the enemy. Lives would be saved the sooner you ended the war. I think this was proven with our conflict in Vietnam. We held back, and over a period of years we suffered more than 50,000 deaths with thousands more wounded. Some of the same things are happening now with our conflicts in Iraq and Afghanistan. Some of our troops get in real trouble by killing one or two civilians. Let me tell you, in a time of war, you don't have time to make distinctions between friend and foe. Also, we destroyed complete cities in Germany. In fact, Dresden, Germany, was wiped off the map by our bombers. The concept was, "Let's win the war and get it over with and save lives."

I am concerned we have cost the lives of some of our brave servicemen and women in the Middle East by the stupid "Rules of Engagement." Contrast that with some of the "Rules of Engagement" I mentioned on Saipan: "If it moves, shoot it."

We waited for a reply after we dropped the first atomic bomb over Japan. Nothing came, so Nagasaki got wiped off the map. We learned later that there was much conflict between the emperor of Japan and the Japanese military, which was actually running the show. Some wanted to continue the war even though they had seen the results of the atomic bomb, and others were ready to surrender. As I understand it, the emperor sided with the people who wanted to end the war. The white flag went up, and there was unconditional surrender.

There have been various publications about how cruel the Americans were to drop those atomic bombs. In my opinion, that is coming from people who did not know what was going on. They wanted to prolong the war. Again I go back to the loss of life. Some predicted invading Japan could cost 500,000 to a million lives. Another big factor, which our history confirms, was that the Potsdam Treaty laid out that after the war with Germany, Russia would enter the war against Japan, coming in from the north through Manchuria. If the Russians had participated more in the war with Japan, they would have had a seat at the peace treaty table and demanded that Japan be divided once it was conquered. In that case, you would have a communist North Japan, just like North Korea. Ending the war now gave Stalin no claim to Japan. Today Russia claims that the war with Japan ended not because of the atomic bomb, but because they entered the war. The Soviets did attack Manchuria, which had been occupied by the Japanese since 1931, and in fact they continued to attack the Japanese in Manchuria several days after Japan had surrendered.

There were conflicting views from our military about the plan for Japan once the war was over. Admiral Nimitz, head of Naval Operations, was in charge of moving toward Japan through the island hopping, which we did successfully (Marshall Islands, Guam, Saipan, Tinian, Iwo Jima, and Okinawa). Okinawa was a key operation in the march to Japan. This was where we first experienced Kamikaze pilots, which inflicted heavy damage on our Navy forces. The other path to Japan was through the Philippines and the island of Formosa. Japan had possession of Formosa, which today is known as Taiwan.

Now, the Philippines were a commonwealth of the US and we had considerable presence, both military and commercial, in the Philippines. Gen. MacArthur had been called out of retirement to head up our military forces there. After the Japs attacked Pearl Harbor on December 7, 1941, Gen. MacArthur had several hours' notice before the Japanese attacked his forces in the Philippines. Our main Air Force base in the Philippines was Clark Field and for some unknown reason our planes were on the ground all lined up like sitting ducks when the Japanese air force swarmed in and essentially destroyed our airpower in the Philippines. It appears to me Gen. MacArthur was completely asleep at the wheel, and I have never heard any criticism of his decision not to have our forces in the Philippines on full war alert. Remember, our commanders at Pearl Harbor, Army General Short and Navy Admiral Kinkade, were made scapegoats because they did not have our forces on full alert when Japan attacked.

During the Philippines campaign, when the Japanese attacked with their great forces, it was obvious we could not hold the territory because we were not in a position to send reinforcements. So Gen. MacArthur was evacuated secretly to Australia, and left in command to take the imprisonment was Lt. General Wainwright. Of course, he was a prisoner all those years instead of MacArthur. To MacArthur's credit, he did a good job after the surrender and occupation of Japan.

The peace treaty was signed in September of 1945 on the decks of the battleship *Missouri*, which was a very historic occasion. General MacArthur was in charge of reconstructing Japan and did a super job—in some ways too super. MacArthur brought in Dr. Demming, an American who was an expert in quality control. Dr. Demming had been trying to get the attention of American industries about better performance to turn out a better product. Most of his message had fallen on deaf ears. We were turning out some cars during that period that in some ways were substandard. You'd get a new car, and the first thing you'd do is take it home to put a water hose on it to see where it leaked. Doors would not close properly, and windshields were not installed properly. General MacArthur brought Dr. Demming over, and the Japanese listened to him, to their advantage.

Prior to the war they had been turning out nothing but junk. The only thing we imported from Japan was cheap junk type toys, and nobody had any respect for anything made there. But Dr. Demming turned that around. They began to turn out quality cars at a cheap price, and they began selling in America. At first, I completely revolted. I thought anybody who bought a

Japanese car was completely un-American. Of course, you had to change as time went on. Those are the facts of life.

After the surrender of Japan, there was a quick dismantling of our vast military complex. We had several million men in uniform. They did a very good job of getting people discharged and back into civilian life. In my particular company, I was the first one to be discharged. My four-year enlistment had been completed in June 1945, but it was toward the end of the war, and that didn't mean anything as far as getting out. I was immediately placed into the reserve position like most of the other guys, which meant you were in the war for the duration.

I mentioned I was the first one in our company to get the papers to report back to the US for discharge. That's because I was the only one in our company with previous experience overseas (my tour of Midway). The military had developed detailed criteria for who got discharged first, and one was the length of your service overseas. By that time I had accumulated well over three years. I got in the first contingent to go back home, and that was a great time. I had survived the war!

I am a history buff, and from my readings I learned that in all wars big mistakes are made by both the losers and the victors. Earlier I gave President Roosevelt an *A* for his foreign policies, I must modify that and award him an *F-* for one disastrous decision he made. In 1944, he held a Pacific strategy meeting in Hawaii with General MacArthur and Admiral Nimitz. Both noted military men had very divergent views on how to defeat the Japanese. Adm. Nimitz strongly favored continuing the island-hopping plan that he was on, and Gen. MacArthur strongly favored invading the Philippines. Roosevelt did not make a decision during the meeting, but later he did support Gen. MacArthur's plan to invade the Philippines, which turned out to be a very long and costly operation. This plan also called for the invasion and capture of Peleliu, which was a very fierce battle, and the 1st Marine Division suffered heavy casualties in this operation.

Remember Gen. MacArthur's famous remark when he was evacuated early in the war before the Japanese captured the Philippines: "I shall return." Gen. MacArthur was in some ways a brilliant man, but in my opinion he had an ego that at times clouded and overpowered logical thinking. He was strongly in favor of a land invasion of Japan where he would be leading the largest invasion force in history, greater than the Eisenhower force that invaded Normandy. In fact, Gen. MacArthur set his sights on running for president. His argument for his plan was that our control of the Philippines would cut off the Japanese from their recently captured possessions in the Dutch East Indies and other territories of the Pacific Rim. My point is that our Navy, with our submarines and complete control of the Western Pacific, was already accomplishing that without the necessity of engaging in a land battle for the Philippines. Apparently, Roosevelt did not have the courage that Truman later demonstrated when he removed Gen. MacArthur from command during the Korean War.

Fortunately, President Truman also had the courage and wisdom to use the atomic bombs to force Japan's surrender without the enormous casualties, US and Japanese, of a land invasion. The casualties from the atomic bombs on Hiroshima and Nagasaki were less than 200,000; that is a vast number, but compared to the estimated several hundred thousand casualties we would suffer in the invasion and the Japanese casualties, military and civilian, several times our own, clearly using the atomic bombs made sense. There are still idiots out there today that argue dropping these bombs was a horrible decision. I do not agree; I had a "dog in this fight," and I am convinced I would not be here today had President Truman not had the guts to use these bombs and end the war. Amen!

WARS ARE SENSELESS

War is senseless. Utterly senseless. For example, in 1914, at the start of WWI, two vast armies faced each other in trenches separated by a short distance referred to as "no man's land." During the next four years, each side took turns making suicidal charges against their enemy. Four years later, in 1918, after both sides had suffered millions of casualties, both military and civilian, and after unimaginable suffering on both sides, they ended up in those trenches where they started four years earlier. General Eisenhower and Civil War Gen. Sherman both stated, "War is senseless."

In all wars, it seems some soldier, sailor, or Marine expresses from the heart what war is all about more powerfully than professional journalists. In my reading of the history of WWI, this poem, *In Flanders Fields*, remains etched in my memory. This poem was written by Lt. Col. John McCrae, a surgeon in the Canadian army at the battle at Ypres, Belgium, in WWI. Read this carefully. It's very sobering. You cannot read this without asking why, *why*, do we have to do this.

In Flanders Fields

By John McCrae, Lt. Col. Canadian Army in Belgium in WWI.

In Flanders fields the poppies blow
Between the crosses, row on row,
That mark our place; and in the sky
The larks, still bravely singing, fly
Scarce heard amid the guns below.

We are the Dead, short days ago
We lived, felt dawn, saw sunset glow,
Loved and were loved, and now we lie in Flanders fields.

Take up our quarrel with the foe:
To you from failing hands we throw
The torch; be yours to hold it high.
If ye break faith with us who die
We shall not sleep, though poppies grow
In Flanders fields.

Two more poems that speak to my strong conviction that all wars are senseless are "From a Fox Hole Marine on Iwo Jima" and "Civil War—1865" by Walt Whitman. Carefully ponder the words in these poems, and you must agree.

From a Fox Hole Marine on Iwo Jima

Author Unknown—Written in WWII—1945

At last it's quiet on Iwo,
At last the battle is won,
And we who are left
Say a prayer of thanks,
Because our job is done.

In the shadows of Mount Suribachi,
Where crosses mark our dead,
We hear the names of our buddies,
And stand with bended head.

We recall good times together and
The sacrifices shared,
But we can't see why they had to die,
While the rest of us were spared.

So we say to you, truly,
Our hearts are filled with pain,
But we know some distant day,
We all shall meet again.

And if one should ask me how I know,
I would just reply,
We all met GOD on Iwo,
Not just those who had to die.

So to our loved ones back home hold your
Head with pride, for they are all true
Heroes, those who fought and died.

And to all mankind throughout our land,
Let us not forget their pain. This time
Let's build a lasting peace.
So, their death will not be in vain.

Civil War—1865

Walt Whitman

I see beyond the forest moving banners of
A hidden column.
Our dead brothers still live for us,
And bid us think of life, not death—
Of life to which in their youth they
Lent the passion and joy of the spring.

War is senseless—utterly senseless. The following pictures say it all. In the top photo, young Marines who are 18, 19, and 20 years old are going ashore on Iwo Jima. They go forward over this terrace with no cover ahead, and 22,000 Japs with every modern weapon of war wait for them. Some of these men will not see the sunset this day; some will not experience the sunrise the next morning. In the days and weeks ahead, many of their buddies will join them in our 4th Marine Cemetery on Iwo Jima, also pictured below. Never forget there is a grieving Gold Star mother for each marker.

Although I maintain all wars are senseless, I must qualify this statement by saying under certain circumstances, a nation must go to war. A perfect example of this is when the Japs attacked us at Pearl Harbor. We had no choice. We had to respond to this dastardly attack.

In the Bible, in Ecclesiastes 3:8, we get the words "a time for war, and a time for peace." Pearl Harbor fits the first part of that verse.

Young Marines going ashore on Iwo Jima.

The 4th MARDIV Cemetery on Iwo Jima,
March 1945. (National Archives)

CIVILIAN LIFE

DISCHARGED

I was discharged October 16, 1945 from Camp Lejeune, North Carolina, and at that time I did not have the foggiest idea what the future held for me. The best I could tell, Slocomb was pretty much just as I had left it four years ago, and that meant there would be no job opportunities. Even though I had no plans or direction for my life, I had perfect peace about what the future held.

I headed to Slocomb on the Greyhound bus, the prime method for intercity travel at that time. The route went through Atlanta, and my plans were to stop for a day or two and visit with my aunt Ann, my aunt Hortie Mae and her husband, Uncle Roy Hoskins, and my Uncle Ed and his wife, Myrtle. It was a pleasant surprise when I found out my cousin, Bill Rigell, and his wife, Grace, were now living in Atlanta. Bill had just been discharged from the Air Force, where he served as a lieutenant in the Panama Canal Zone during the war.

Bill had just enrolled at Georgia Tech and was working part-time in the administrative office. Bill immediately begin to work on me to enroll at Georgia Tech, which I'd never considered. I think a little divine providence was working here because before I knew it Bill had enrolled me, and of course I would be going to school on the G.I. Bill. When I enrolled, I learned I could not be accepted until the fall quarter of 1946. Georgia Tech, like all colleges at this time, were swamped with enrollment applications from the discharged G.I.s.

Georgia Tech had a priority system: Georgia veterans, followed by Georgia natives, and then out-of-state veterans. Of course, I was in this third category. I also learned I would have to take one quarter of remedial courses because my high school did not prepare me in the areas of math and science to enter a school like Georgia Tech. I had also been out of high school for four years. Taking those remedial courses turned out to be a good thing. I'm not sure I would've made it at Georgia Tech otherwise.

I stayed in Atlanta several days, and during this period my Uncle Roy and Uncle Ed spent some real quality time with me concerning my future. They felt very strongly that I should get a college education. I remember one thing Uncle Roy said to me, "Ike, you can go back to Slocomb and get some little job and make payments on a pickup truck for the rest of your life and live paycheck to paycheck, or you can sacrifice for four years to go to a good college and your lifetime earnings will be much greater," he told me. "A college education will open many doors that are closed to high school graduates."

Uncle Ed gave me the same advice. I am positive today that if I had not taken the advice of Bill, Uncle Roy, and Uncle Ed, I would not have enjoyed the good life, good jobs, and wonderful family that I have been so richly blessed with. They suggested that I go to Slocomb and visit a while and come back to Atlanta and live with them until I entered Georgia Tech. At that time Uncle Roy was a colonel in the Army stationed at Fort McPherson on the outskirts of Atlanta. I can tell you the officers in the military lived a good life. The officer housing was located on nice tree-lined streets surrounding a huge parade ground. Uncle Roy and Aunt Mae lived a couple of houses down from the commanding general's house. It was a nice, big, two-story brick house with a large front porch and beautiful white columns.

So I took their advice and went to Slocomb for a couple of weeks. I came back to Atlanta and moved in with Uncle Roy and Aunt Mae. Their son, my cousin Skeeter, was single at that time and he also was living there. He was the manager of an Army PX in downtown Atlanta. I got a job working at the Atlanta Train Station with Railway Express. This was before the days of UPS and FedEx. The railway system had special cars equipped to process and deliver regular mail and packages. My job was to help load and unload the Railway Express Cars. The pay was pretty good, but the working environment was miserable. It was winter, and I was working the night shift, and out on the loading docks it could get very cold. I think Uncle Roy sensed that I was not too happy, and he got me a much better job at Fort McPherson, where I could walk to work.

Fort McPherson had been designated as a staging facility to collect and dispose of the war surplus materials from military bases in the Southeast region now being closed. German prisoners of war were assigned to do the physical work. I was surprised to find that we actually still had some prisoners of war. This was in the early part of 1946. My job was to follow the instructions on how to process this surplus equipment. There were usually about four POW's assigned to my area. All of the POW's that I encountered could speak English, and it appeared to me these guys were in no hurry to go home.

I was not unhappy with this situation, but I did have a strong desire to spend the summer in Slocomb before I started school in the fall. So in the late spring of 1946, I went back hoping to get some little summer job there before returning to Atlanta.

As soon as I got back in town, I met one of my old baseball teammates, Chester Dykes. He told me he was going over to Geneva, Alabama, to try out for the newly organized Geneva baseball team. This would be Geneva's first entry in the old Alabama State league. He asked me to go with him for this tryout. I had not found a job yet, so I decided to go with Chester to Geneva and just observe the action. Chester encouraged me to join him in the tryouts but I had no desire to. Chester insisted and I finally agreed to participate. I really wasn't prepared to play that day. I didn't have a glove and I had no baseball shoes, but anyhow, I did it just to please Chester.

The manager asked us to come back the next day, and in the end, we both signed a contract to play with Geneva. The Alabama State League was a class D, the lowest ranking. But in a small town you receive a certain amount of prestige just being on the team.

My experience in playing ball in a minor league confirmed

my belief that unless you are pretty sure you have the natural talent to make it to the big leagues, you are wasting your time. We played six nights a week, and our road trips to the other towns in our league were in an old school bus. All the teams in the league had the same salary cap, and all the teams had the same player classifications. Each team was required to have so many rookies, so many limited service (three to five years), and the same number of veterans (more than five years). It was sad to see so many of these limited service and veterans returning year after year, hoping to be called up to the big leagues when, being realistic, you knew they would never make it.

Fortunately I had sense enough to judge my limitations. Geneva was a farm club on the St. Louis Cardinals, and a couple of times during the year they would send a scout down to evaluate the players. My manager told me to tell the scout that I was 20 years old. I was 23 at that time. The scout never asked me my age, and I'm not sure what I would have told him if he had. In addition to watching the games, the scout would put each player through various exercises in hitting, fielding, throwing, and running the bases and other exercises, depending on the position you played. After one scout visit, the manager told me and our first baseman that we would probably be called up to the Montgomery team next year. Montgomery was in a class B league and was a farm club of the St. Louis Cardinals as well. We had played Montgomery in a pre-season game, and my honest assessment was I could probably play in the league. But that was as far as I could go.

Playing baseball in a class D league completely destroys your social life. The games were at night, and after the game you traveled back to your home base in this old school bus. You'd sleep late the next day, and soon it was time to board the bus for the next game. I got tired of this demanding schedule and I resigned.

A couple of days later, I received a call from the Dothan team in the same league. They were looking for an outfielder. I had played several games against Dothan and I knew their team pretty well. I'm not sure why, but I ended up signing with the Dothan team. I do recall a couple of funny events during my short career in minor league baseball. One night one of our players, an old veteran with a beer belly who had bounced around in the minor leagues for several years, got caught in a rundown between third base and the home plate. It was obvious that he did not stand a chance of getting safely out. He stopped and yelled "Time." The poor rookie umpire in response yelled "Time." All actions stopped, and this old veteran walked back and stood on third-base and yelled "Okay." Both managers got into a pretty loud discussion on this event, and the poor umpire didn't know what to do. Many of the umpires in this league were recent graduates of an umpire school in Florida and they, like the rookie players, were hoping someday to get to the big leagues. Not sure this umpire ever made it to the majors.

On the Dothan team there was one old veteran, Ed Mitchell, who was a favorite of the fans, who played centerfield. When he was fielding a ground ball, he would on occasion catch the ball and make it appear it went between his legs. Then he would turn around and start running like he was chasing the ball. He still kept his eye on the runner, and if the runner took his bait and started for second base, he would turn around and throw him out at second. Surprisingly, sometimes this worked. When he made a hit to the infield and got thrown out at first base, he would continue to run full speed back to the dugout and make a good hook slide right there in front of the dugout. The fans loved that. Little things like this made the games interesting, but I was really glad when this season was over.

GEORGIA TECH TO TVA

I entered Georgia Tech in the Remedial Program in the fall of 1946. The Remedial Program was for one quarter of prep work with no credit, but it was a requirement for most veterans who had been out of high school for a while. Georgia Tech at that time had no female or black students. It was common in that era to have all-male schools, all-female schools and all-black schools. Georgia Tech had an enrollment at that time of about 3,500 students, and there were a number of foreign students.

This was the first year the colleges had a large number of veterans enrolled. I would say this resulted in a significant change in the environment in the classrooms, as the professors could not talk down to these veterans as they were accustomed to talking to the freshman just out of high school. I was not in the classroom when the following events occurred, but my cousin, Bill Rigell, who was then a sophomore, told me these two stories. You need a little background for the first story. In that era it was common for the men to use hair tonic and shaving lotion that had a distinct aroma. This veteran student had apparently used a heavy dose of hair tonic that morning and was sitting up in the front row. The professor came over near him and sniff-sniffed a couple of times.

"If I came home smelling like that, my wife would think I had been to a whorehouse," the professor said.

"My wife does not know what a whorehouse smells like," the veteran replied.

On another occasion, a veteran student asked the professor a question about the subject matter. The professor sarcastically said, "I've never heard such a dumb question in all my life."

The veteran replied, "One more crack like that out of you and I will throw your ass out that window."

This was at a time when many of the classrooms did not have air conditioning, and the windows were open. The professors weren't accustomed to being talked to like that. The veteran did receive a nice apology for that comment from the professor.

It was immediately apparent to me that I needed the Remedial Program. In one of the first classes, the professor said he would review logarithms for about five minutes. It was not a review for me; I didn't know what a logarithm was. It was my introduction to a slide rule, which I had never seen. A good slide rule is actually a manual computer, a powerful tool, and that was absolutely necessary in most of the classes at Georgia Tech. And like a computer today, it required much time to become proficient. You felt undressed if you did not have your slide rule strapped to your belt.

The Georgia Tech campus was not spread out like many college campuses. It was located very close to the downtown business district, and it was a short walk between the dormitories and the classrooms. A famous Atlanta landmark, the restaurant the Varsity, was one block away. Years later it was a favorite stop when our family vacations took us through Atlanta, and it is still going strong today. I think all of our children have pleasant memories of those occasions.

Under the G.I. bill, veterans received $75 a month, and of course, the VA paid for books and tuition. Most of the time it was very hard to stretch that $75 to the end of the month. The first day of every month you would find all the veterans at the little post office with their eyes glued to their mailbox. The door to the mailbox had a glass window, and if you were looking directly at your box, you could see the postman when he put your check in. As soon as you saw that check going in your box, you were out of there for someplace to get a good meal, something you probably had not experienced for several days.

I think my Uncle Ed and Aunt Myrtle sensed that maybe I was struggling to make ends meet, which happened to be a real good assessment. They had a nice home out in a good section of Atlanta with an extra bedroom, and they invited me to live with them. I accepted. Uncle Ed was the manager of a moving company with an office in downtown Atlanta, and Aunt Myrtle had a good position as a women's hat designer, also with an office downtown. Women frequently wore hats back in those days so hers was an important profession.

This arrangement worked out real well. I had breakfast there, and they had a maid who had dinner ready when they came home from work. They lived some distance from Georgia Tech, but Atlanta had a good streetcar service that made it no problem for me to get to school. About once a month, Uncle Ed would invite me and Bill to have lunch with him in a nice downtown restaurant. When I was living with Uncle Ed and Aunt Myrtle, I registered to vote for the first time. I registered as a Georgia veteran, and I received a lifetime Georgia driver's license I still have.

My cousin Bill was married, and he and his wife, Grace, had two young children. They used me as their babysitter from time to time, and I accused Bill of talking me into going to school at Georgia Tech so they would have a free babysitter. Actually, I enjoyed this little job, and I had real good relationships with Bill and Grace.

I should give a little credit to my sisters, Mary Jo and Florence, for my success in graduating from Georgia Tech. In my freshman year one of my required courses was literature, and although Georgia Tech was an engineering school, the professor had the attitude that it was the most important course in the school. So he piled an extraordinary amount of homework on us. I was having to spend so much time on the engineering courses, I was getting overwhelmed trying to keep up with the homework in this literature course. So I came up with a clever solution on how to deal with this problem.

My sister Florence was very smart, and she was also an avid reader, so it turned out she was the answer to one of my major problems in this course. The professor loaded us down with book reports, which I didn't think were that important. I also didn't have time to spend reading all these books. I talked to Florence and explained my problem. The solution was to give her the names of the books and the outline for the reports, and she would read them and send me the reports. I am happy to say she made an "A" on all of them. This probably saved me from having a lower grade in some of my engineering courses.

Mary Jo came to my rescue when I was graduating. I had no suit and no money to buy one. She found out about this and bought me a very nice suit for graduation. Mary Jo at that time was the head nurse at Georgia General Hospital in Athens.

In my senior year we were having a lot of lab work, and much of it a team effort. This was requiring longer hours at school more and more, so I had to move back into the dormitory. When I moved back in I got a job as a floor monitor. Each dorm had an apartment for a professor who was responsible for the dorm, and each floor had a student monitor. As a floor monitor, my room rent was free which was a big help.

I only had one problem during my tenure: If there were any disturbances, I had to take care them. I was also required to make a weekly inspection of all the rooms. I was in a new dorm and it had very nice, sturdy doors on the rooms. On one inspection I found that the two guys in this room had a little too much beer one night and destroyed the door. They had a life-size pinup of some glamorous movie star on the door and they had repeatedly thrown a hunting knife at the pinup. The result was a completely splintered door that had to be replaced. I turned my report in and these two guys were expelled.

Not long after I entered Georgia Tech, my mother sold our house in Slocomb and moved in with Florence and her husband, Russ Cothran. They lived in Spartanburg, South Carolina at the time, and their daughter, Diane, was about five-years-old. Russ was in the insurance business and Florence worked at a chemical company. My mother took care of Diane. I think every single person has an innate desire to have someplace that they can call home, especially during the holiday seasons. Mary Jo and I were very blessed that we had a place we could call home, and that was with Russ and Florence.

They received us so warmly and completely that we had a comfortable feeling of being at home. I can never thank them enough for how they took us in and how they took care of my mother. Later, Russ's job took him to Orangeburg, South Carolina, and that became home for me and Mary Jo.

I went to summer school one year at Georgia Tech, and for two summers I worked for an engineering company in Orangeburg. Russ knew one of the owners of this engineering company, and through him I got this really good summer job. One of the big projects was installing power lines out in the rural areas of South Carolina.

At that time, most of the rural areas in the south did not have electricity. I was in a surveying crew that established the route for the power lines and marked the spot for the power line poles all the way up to the meter on the house. This was a four-man crew, and the leader was a civil engineer graduate from the University of South Carolina. He had been working for this company a couple of years. He was a good guy to work for, and in fact, we had a real good crew and got along extremely well. This was a good thing because we lived together Monday through Friday. We were working in what they called the "low country" of South Carolina, down toward Charleston. We would leave Orangeburg early Monday morning and return late Friday afternoon.

Most of the time we were working out of a little town called Monks Corner. There was a large black population in this area, and they spoke a dialect I had a difficult time understanding. When we reached a home that was scheduled to have power, we had to get the name of the family living there to make sure we were at the right place. I soon learned one of the other guys in the crew had to verify the correct name. These guys had no problem understanding this dialect.

One day we had a house on our list to receive power that was about two miles off a main road through a thick forest of large pine trees. We finally came to a large opening in the pine forest, and before us was a large mansion, English style, with a guesthouse and a nearby landing strip. Our crew chief went up to the door of the main house and rang the doorbell. A butler in his full butler uniform came to the door and in a very distinct British accent said, "Who shall I say is calling?"

Our crew chief explained our mission and then asked the butler if we could have a drink of water. It was a very hot day, and we were all sweaty, and none of us had on a shirt. I would say we were not properly dressed for this environment.

"You must come around the back for water," the butler said.

We went around to the back of the house and were invited into a screened porch by a nice, attractive young lady. She was dressed in her maid's uniform, including a neat little maid's cap. She invited us to sit at a table on the back porch, and she brought us a big picture of ice water. She was very friendly. She told us the owner of the place was an elderly lady, the heiress of one of the big chewing gum companies. I can't remember which one. She was not at the house at the time as she had a house in Palm Beach, Florida and a house up north. The maid told us there were a number of large houses like this in the surrounding area. This complex did have electricity from a large motor-generator set on the property. A commercial power system would be much more reliable and eliminate the work involved in maintaining a motor-generator set.

People riding along the nearby highway would never dream such beautiful and large houses were nestled back in this forest. I felt really blessed to have such a great summer job that I enjoyed so much. The pay was good so I was able to go back to Georgia Tech with a few bucks at the end of the summer. This meant I could make a few more trips to the Varsity.

Two things I want to mention before I leave Georgia Tech. One is a big regret. One of the best friends I ever had was one of my roommates, John Harvey, of North Carolina. John was a cigar smoker like I was at that time, and we smoked the cheapest cigars we could find. Although they smelled good to us, nobody around us could stand the foul aroma of our cheap cigars. My regret is I didn't stay in touch with John after we graduated.

The other thing I want to record is that I did try to go to church on Sundays. I would take a streetcar to the first Methodist church near downtown Atlanta when I was living in the dormitory. When I was living with Uncle Ed and Aunt Myrtle, I attended a Presbyterian church out near where they lived. Both churches had excellent preachers.

Bill Rigell graduated from Georgia Tech a year before me. Bill was working for a chemical company in Chattanooga, Tennessee. Bill and I had become very close, and he wanted me to get a job in the Chattanooga area. I accused Bill again of trying to get me to stay close by so he would have a free babysitter.

Tennessee Valley Authority (TVA) had a sizable operation in Chattanooga and I applied for a job there. I went up for an interview, and I was told they had no openings in the Chattanooga office, but were hiring a number of engineers for a one-year training program. At the end of the program you would get a permanent assignment at one of the TVA facilities.

The training program was located at Watts Bar Dam near Dayton, Tennessee, about forty miles north of Chattanooga. This sounded interesting. I thought when I finished I could get assigned to the TVA Chattanooga office. I accepted this job and moved to Dayton and joined about a dozen recent engineering college graduates, mostly from the southeast. This move turned out to be a very good thing, as several of us in this training group became lifelong friends. I still stay in contact with some of these guys today but some are deceased.

A quick, funny story about my time living in Dayton. My mother called one night while I was working, and one of the guys, C.A. Reed, answered the phone. Back then, you could not dial direct on a long distance call. You had to go through an operator to complete the call.

Operator to C.A.: "Long distance call for Ike Rigell."

C.A. to Operator: "He is not here."

Operator to my mother: "He is not there."

My mother to Operator: "Do they know where he is?"

Operator to C.A.: "Do you know where he is?"

C.A. to Operator: "He is at the Watts Bar."

Operator to my mother: "He is at some bar."

My mother to Operator: "Does he know how long he will be there?"

Operator to C.A.: "How long will he be at the bar?"

C.A. to Operator: "He will be there all night."

Operator to my mother: "He will be at this bar all night."

I should note that on long distance calls like this, the caller and the person can hear everything the operator says to each party, but neither the caller nor the person receiving the call can talk to the other party.

C.A. said right after they hung up, he realized how this conversation came across to my mother: your son is out to some bar, and he is going to be there all night. When I came back to our house, C.A. was waiting for me.

"You better call your mother," he said. "I probably got you in trouble last night."

I promptly called my mother and assured her that I had been at work and not hanging out all night at some bar. The place I worked was literally called "Watts Bar."

TVA TO MY CAREER
IN SPACE

When I graduated from high school in June 1941, I could not have in my wildest dreams envisioned a rewarding career launching missiles and rockets into outer space. I do not recall the word "missile" being in our daily vocabulary, and the only time I heard the word "rocket" was when we sang our National Anthem, which in those days was often.

> *And the rocket's red glare,*
> *The bombs bursting in air,*
> *Gave proof through the night,*
> *That our flag was still there."*

Nine years later, in June 1950, I graduated from Georgia Tech. During the war I had been exposed to the word "rocket," but I never gave a thought that I would someday be a rocket man.

Two types of rockets were introduced in WWII. I had direct knowledge of one, and the other I had only read about. Actually there was no comparison between these two rocket systems. The rocket launcher was actually a military version of a big pickup truck with a rack of tubes on the bed of the truck. In each tube was a small rocket. I mentioned the following story in the previous section on Saipan, but it bears mentioning again.

One day my wire crew and I happened to be passing one of our missile rocket launcher vehicles when they fired a salvo. Swish, swish, swish, swish, until all rockets—about forty or fifty—had been launched. Moments later, we observed all hell breaking loose on a nearby hillside.

The rockets were dispersed enough that they almost covered the whole hillside. Dirt, trees, and anything else in the landing zone was flying through the air. I could not imagine any Japs in that area surviving. These rockets were very simple but extremely effective. The accuracy would be determined by the elevation of the tubes and the direction of the tubes. They were rather short-range, and they actually performed more like a sophisticated mortar.

The other rocket that I had read about but knew very little of was the German V-2 rocket. This was a devastating weapon the Germans fired across the English Channel into England, primarily London. These rockets traveled faster than the speed of sound, so there was no defense. You did not know the missile was coming in until it exploded.

The only similarity between these two rockets was the word "rocket." The Marine rocket I described was very simple, with no in-flight guidance, just a ballistic trajectory. The V-2 is a very sophisticated rocket with a gyroscope-controlled stabilized platform and steerable control vanes. I will go much more in detail on the V-2 later.

I think this would be a good place to put our short space history in perspective. Our country has an interesting history of about four hundred years, which began with the settlement of Jamestown in 1607. I would say the benchmark for the beginning of our history in space would be around 1953 (when we fired the first Redstone), which means we have a very short, but very productive, 60 years of space exploration. My generation will be the last, and only, generation that has lived through our space history.

In the early 1900's, there were three men who had the vision that we would someday travel in space beyond the Earth's field of gravitation. The first was Dr. Robert Goddard of the United States. The Goddard Space Flight Center in Maryland is named for him. The second was Professor Obert of Germany. The third was a Russian whose name I do not recall.

In Germany, at a very young age, Wernher von Braun was a protégé of Obert. In the 1930's, they had a small group of like-minded people that were very active in experimenting with liquid-propelled rockets. They had a real passion and vision for manned rockets traveling in outer space.

When Hitler started World War II in Europe this peacetime rocket project was converted to a military weapon system, which was later known as the V-2 rocket. At a very young age the brilliant Dr. von Braun was placed in charge of this project. At one time in the development program the funding was cut back severely to divert these funds to the German air force, which was having some big problems. Later in the war, after the German air force was almost destroyed, Hitler put a priority back on the development of the V-2.

Before the war ended, the V-2 was an effective and feared weapon, but it came too late to affect the outcome of the war. Who knows? It could have turned out differently if Hitler had put the priority on the development of these rockets from the beginning. Germany launched hundreds of these rockets at mainland England, mostly London.

The only way you could stop the V-2 was to destroy the launch site, and since the Germans had developed a mobile launcher for this rocket this was not a practical solution. The only sure way to protect England from these devastating rockets was to push the German lines in France and Germany far enough back that the Germans would not have control of any land within range of the V-2 rocket.

Toward the end of the war it was apparent that the Allies were going to overrun Germany. Dr. von Braun and his team were well aware of this. Since the V-2 manufacturing operations were much closer to the Russian front than the U.S. front line, they would be taken prisoners by the Russians rather than the U.S. or Britain. Earlier in the war, Germany had overrun much of Russia and the Russian people had suffered greatly, so the Germans knew the Russians would be looking for a little revenge. Von Braun had an easy decision to make. He loaded a long train with as many V-2's as he could, along with spare parts, documentation, and about

120 of his top missile team, and headed east toward the American lines. Von Braun had been made a member of the SS, and he had the authority to sign the right papers to get this train moving.

He did reach the American lines with the trainload of equipment and his team surrendered to the Americans. At the end of the war the Allies knew the Germans had a wealth of talent, not only in rockets, but in all areas of science and medicine. France, Britain, Russia, and the U.S. wanted to get their hands on these people. Germany had made some real advances in science, especially synthetic fuels, synthetic materials, and biological warfare.

Under the project named "Paperclip," headed by Army Gen. Toftoy, von Braun, his team of 120, and his trainload of rockets were transferred to Fort Bliss, Texas, adjacent to the White Sands Missile Proving Ground. Out of this group, von Braun was the youngest, but there was no question he was their well-respected leader. Von Braun was single at this time, but most of his team was married and had families back in Germany. Later the families came over to the U.S., and all of these people became good American citizens.

To bring this talented team to the U.S. at this time was a very smart move. After we had them settled though, we did a very dumb thing. For five years, from 1945 to 1950, we did not provide them with any meaningful projects to advance our capability in the development of an advanced rocket system. Years later, in a period when Russia was leading in the space race, von Braun remarked, "We lost five years—1945 to 1950."

In 1950, the Western world woke up to the fact that communism was becoming a real threat to our way of life. In 1950, Russia successfully tested their first atomic bomb. This sent a big shock wave through the Western world, and our comfortable feeling of national security went up in smoke.

Even though the Soviet Union had a much superior land force than we did after the war, the fact that we were the only nation with the atomic bomb made us feel that no nation would dare attack us. In 1950, communist North Korea, with the blessing of communist China and the Soviet Union, invaded South Korea, and this certainly added to our concern about the threat to world peace. Also, it was well known Western nations immediately did a vast disarmament after the war while the Soviet Union maintained their huge military capability. Our intelligence people learned the Soviets were feverishly working on advanced missile capabilities.

After the experience with the V-2 missile in WWII and the development of the atomic bomb, the weapon of the future would be long-range missiles capable of delivering atomic warheads.

After the surrender of Japan in August 1945, we immediately turned our awesome industrial capability from manufacturing tanks, airplanes, guns, artillery, and other military equipment into the production of automobiles, trucks, washing machines, refrigerators, stoves, radios, telephones, Jim Walters Homes, and other household goods. Jim Walters Homes were small, affordable, pre-fabricated homes that became popular for young families across the U.S.

During this period things were much different in the old Soviet Union, where they were maintaining the largest military force in the world. The Russian people were living in "third world" conditions. I can vouch for this. In 1982, Kathryn and I made our first trip to the old Soviet Union. People in rural areas and in cities were living in a very primitive environment compared to us. We observed women washing their clothes by the river and carrying water from one village well. None of the houses in the rural areas were painted. Small power lines ran through the village streets. I could judge from the size of the insulators on the power poles and the small transformers serving a row of houses that the only thing they could support were small light bulbs. I would say almost 100 percent of the vehicles we encountered in our journey through the Soviet Union countryside were government vehicles.

Fortunately our leaders in Washington became seriously concerned about the intentions of the Soviet Union and realized they had to respond. One of the smart things they did was move von Braun and his German missile team from Fort Bliss, Texas, to the Redstone Arsenal in Huntsville, Alabama, and task them with developing an advanced ground-to-ground ballistic missile that would be deployed in Western Europe.

This missile would be called the Redstone and would be developed totally in-house at the Redstone Arsenal.

This operation would be under the Army Ordinance Corps. Remember this was several years before the creation of NASA. This Redstone project would be a totally separate organization from the other missile activities going on at the Redstone Arsenal, which included the Field Service Division where I originally worked when I first moved to Huntsville.

In any military project, a military man is always the top guy. Maj. Gen. Bruce McDaris, a good man we called the "Big M," was our top leader. The top civilian under the general was von Braun. All of the technical first line and second line supervisors in the Redstone Project were Germans. The workforce was almost entirely made up of young engineers, and I would say this was the first job for most of them. This workforce reflected the culture at that time, which meant it was an all-white, male workforce. The vast majority came from colleges in the southeast: University of Alabama, Auburn, Georgia Tech, University of Tennessee, University of Mississippi, and University of Florida.

At that time, you could not go out and hire someone with several years of rocket experience. The only people with rocket experience were the Germans. I want to say very strongly that this environment worked extremely well. None of us had any resentment toward or problem with these Germans as our supervisors. In my experience, they were good and extremely capable people.

When I made our first visit to the Redstone Arsenal for a job interview, the Personnel Office (today they call it the Human Resource Office) sent me to the Field Service Engineering Department (FSED). The head of the FSED interviewed me and offered me a job right then. He said they had plenty of interesting work and really needed some good people now. I accepted this offer and did not follow up on interviews with other organizations, although we were aware there were openings in all of those organizations.

I returned to Dayton with the good news I was going to accept these new jobs in Huntsville and encouraged my fellow trainees in the TVA Training Program to follow me in my exciting new venture in the missile/rocket business. Eight of my friends followed me to Huntsville.

ARMY BALLISTIC MISSILE AGENCY (ABMA) - HUNTSVILLE TO COCOA BEACH TO TITUSVILLE

I n Dayton, five of us in the TVA training program rented a nice old home. This turned out to be a very good and enjoyable plan. We all got along extremely well, with no problems among us. We did much of our cooking and really enjoyed this lifestyle; economically, it really paid off.

All five of us made the move to Huntsville, and we hoped to get a similar setup. We must have received a little divine intervention, because when we arrived in Huntsville we responded to an ad in the local paper for a completely furnished home about five miles out in the country. It turned out this house was owned by Mr. Rubin Robinson, a cotton broker and farmer. He had just moved out of this house into a home in Huntsville. He told us his wife and daughter wanted to move into town, but he wanted to stay on the farm. Guess who won?

This place in the country was more than an ordinary farm. It was actually a plantation of over 1,000 acres. He gave us a key to go out and look it over. It was a large house with a screened porch on the front and on one side, a large kitchen, living room, dining room, and several bedrooms. It was completely furnished; if they took any furniture with them, it was not obvious. It had no air conditioning, but none of us had ever had it, so that was not a problem. It did have central heat from a coal-fired furnace in the basement.

There was a very small cottage just outside the back door to the kitchen, and one of Mr. Robinson's old employees, a black man named Walter, lived alone there. There was another little cottage on the side yard, and a single black lady and her young son lived there. There was a very large barn with several horses behind the house. There was also a very large front yard with several very mature oak trees. It was a very easy decision. We could not wait to get back to Mr. Robinson's office in town and tell him we wanted to rent this house.

We ended up calling it the "Old Soldiers' Home." The little boy who lived with his mother in the cottage on the side yard was named Mango, and we sort of adopted him. Some afternoons we would play pitch and catch and hit the baseball. Mango was right there with us, and any time a ball got loose Mango would eagerly chase it down. We bought Mango a little glove, bat, and a baseball. Anytime we came out the door, Mango was waiting for us.

One day I said, "Mango, do you play ball at school?"

"Nau, sur," he said. "They wonts lets me play."

"Mango, why won't they let you play?" I asked. I knew race was not an issue because at that time all schools were segregated.

With a sad face and a sad voice Mango said, "Every time I hits the ball, it goes so far, they loses it."

Mango apparently didn't suffer from a lack of imagination. I wonder whatever happened to Mango. Where is he today?

One day we decided we wanted to go down to Panama City, Florida, and do some offshore fishing. We arrived at the fishing docks late one evening as the fishing boats were coming back in to dock. One boat was unloading a big catch, and we talked to the captain about chartering it the next day. We ended up reserving it. We arrived at the boat early the next morning. We did not notice at first, but we soon discovered the captain and his first mate appeared to be drunk. In fact, I think they had partied all night; they were wearing the same clothes they had on the day before. As we pulled away from the dock, they turned the Marine radio on, and there was a constant announcement.

"Small craft warning: Do not venture out into the Gulf."

The captain told us they were going to take us out to the five-mile buoy.

"We will catch many big fish," he said.

As we moved out farther in the bay, the water was getting rougher and the radio was still blaring small craft warnings. We were convinced by this time the captain, his crew, and the first mate were half-looped. We held a little conference and decided we were going back to the dock even if we had to take over the boat. We told the captain in no uncertain terms what we were going to do. The captain was half-way sober enough now to offer us another option. We would just cruise around in the bay where the water was calm, and we could still catch a lot of fish. We agreed to try, so we got the fishing gear out and started trolling around in the bay.

To our surprise and delight, we started catching fish as soon as our bait hit the water. We did not know the name of the fish we were catching, but we were having much fun because these fish put up a good fight. By the end of the day we had the fishing box on the boat almost full. We were real proud of our catch.

When we got back to the dock, we bought a couple of garbage cans to put our fish in and went to the nearby ice plant to keep our prize catch iced down for the trip back to Huntsville.

The guy at the ice plant took a little wind out of our sail when he brought the ice out to our station wagon and started to pour it on the fish. He stopped and said, "What are you going to do with these fish?"

We thought that was a crazy question. "We are going to eat them," we said.

"That is trash fish," he said. "No one around here eats these fish."

We did not know what to do. We decided to put them on ice and carry them back to Huntsville and decide later. The next day, we told Walter to invite all of his friends to come up to the house and get some fresh fish. They came with pans and bags and took all the fish.

As long as we lived there, we ran into some of these people who took the fish. They thanked us and told us how much they enjoyed it. I later learned the meat on this fish was okay. The reason it was a "trash fish" was that it was very bony. A couple of those guys are still around. I do not think we ever have a telephone conversation without some comment about going to the five-mile buoy.

Life at the Old Soldiers' Home was good. One time we sponsored a record-breaking Tupperware party. One of the guys in our house, Rod Walker, had a friend working at the arsenal who was a Tupperware salesman on the side. This guy was also an ordained minister, but I don't think he had a church. We called him the Padre. The Padre pushed Rod to let him have a Tupperware party at our home. We did not know anything about this Tupperware business, but since he would furnish and cook all the food, we did not see how we could lose. All we had to do was invite a number of girls to attend the party.

We had a large dining room and kitchen, so we could accommodate a good number of people. We had about a dozen girls and us five guys, and the Padre did serve an excellent meal. Of course, after that, we had to listen to his sales pitch. We really didn't expect the Padre to sell anything, but it turned out later when all of his orders were in, they greatly exceeded any party he had ever given, and he had been doing this a long time. The host for the party receives gifts based on the sales at the party, and for months after that party we were still receiving little kitchen gadgets as a result of the party.

All of us guys in the house had handguns and shotguns. Fortunately, we had such a large yard and no close neighbors that we could safely take target practice in our front yard, which we often did. Almost always, Mango was there as soon as we walked out of the house with our guns. We had everything from a .22 to a .45, and when we were shooting with the .22 Mango would come up and say, "Shoot that old bigum. I wants to hear that old bigum."

We would make him happy by cutting loose with that .45. Life was good at the Old Soldiers' Home.

I actually enjoyed my short stay of a few months in the FSED, but the more we learned about the overall Army Missile Program, the more convinced we were that we made a mistake by not interviewing with some of the other departments at Redstone. It just occured to me that I should make a correction here. How can this be a mistake? If I had never been in the FSED I would never have met my wife, Kathryn. I can only explain it by recognizing my Lord had to be looking out for me.

I want to pause here and explain in more detail how my

Lord brought me and Kathryn together. My first job at Redstone Arsenal was in the Army Missile Field Service Division. Our office was in a large, brick, warehouse-type building down near the Tennessee River. The Army Ordinance Corps at that time was heavily involved in transforming the old WWII Redstone Arsenal facilities into the Army Missile and Rocket Center.

The building we were in was completely open, with no partitions or individual offices. Our Field Engineering area was adjacent to the Engineering Data Center. The majority of our engineers were young and single, and the Data Center personnel were mostly married women. All of these married women, in addition to doing their engineering data work, seemed to have a consuming desire to get all of us single guys married. We had a lot of work traffic with the Data Center, and we became good friends with all of these women. I was only in the Field Service Division for a few months before I made one of the best decisions in my life when I transferred to the Missile Firing Lab.

Fortunately the ladies in the Data Center did not forget me. A few weeks after I had transferred out of the Field Service Division, I received a call from one of my lady friends. She told me they had a new employee, a really pretty blonde they wanted me to meet. That sounded good to me. I told her I was in the process of leaving for Cape Canaveral, Florida, to launch our next Redstone rocket, and I would be gone for several weeks. When we returned, we always had a big celebration party, and I said I would like to invite this young lady.

Now here is where I think there was a little divine intervention in bringing me and Kathryn together. At this time we had hired a new man, Jim Finn. Jim was from Florida, and we brought him up to Huntsville for several weeks of training. At that time the little town of Huntsville was booming, and at times it was very difficult or impossible to get a room in one of the three hotels in town. We were able to get Jim a room in the YMCA, which was actually better than two of the hotels. The YMCA was located in a nice residential area directly across the street from a nice boarding house. Jim told me every morning when he was out in front of the YMCA waiting for his ride, there was a pretty young blonde across the street at the boarding house waiting for her ride.

"I must find some way to introduce you to this pretty young

lady," Jim said.

Fast forward. I made the trip to Florida, we launched our rocket, and I returned to Huntsville. I called my friend in the Data Center and told her I was back and would like to invite this young lady to our launch celebration party.

Let me make a little confession here. It is true that after each launch we had a celebration party in Florida, and another, bigger party later with our friends in Huntsville. But that does not necessarily mean the launch was successful. In fact, a good number of our early launches would be considered a failure. I will address that later.

Praise the Lord my lady friend in FSD arranged our date. As I was introducing Kathryn to my friends at the party, Jim Finn was a pleasantly surprised. He almost shouted, "Ike, this is the girl I wanted you to meet!"

I think it is a little interesting that in the missile/rocket business, it is good and desirable to have an alternate path so if one circuit does not operate properly the redundant path will save the day. Here I had a redundant path to ensure our paths would cross. Amen.

I am happy to say things seemed to go very well at our party, and when I took Kathryn home, I asked her for a date the next night. She said okay, as long as I would go to church with her the next morning. Needless to say, from then on as long as we lived in Huntsville, we were a regular couple every Sunday morning in the Huntsville First Methodist Church.

I would say from day one we were together at every opportunity. I immediately became her ride to work, and when my schedule would permit, we would have lunch at one of the two cafeterias at Redstone. I was playing baseball on one of the local teams. Kathryn was not exactly sports-minded, but she became my biggest fan. A few weeks after we first met, we both had the same thoughts. It was time for me to meet her parents, who were living in Jasper, Alabama, at the time.

We left work early one Friday afternoon to spend the weekend with her parents. Jasper was about a two-hour drive from Huntsville through back mountain roads with many curves. On one of these curves a car passed us at a high rate of speed.

Kathryn yelled, "That is my daddy!"

Of course, he did not recognize us. Needless to say, he got to Jasper long before we did. Her daddy was working for Alabama Power Company and had been on a surveying crew in Northeast Alabama and was headed home for the weekend. I was a little nervous about how I would be accepted by her parents, but praise the Lord, after meeting them I was perfectly at ease, and we really had a great weekend.

Four months after we first met, we both knew in our hearts it was time to get married. I think it is fair to say that we did not believe in long engagements. We took the big step and went over to the courthouse in Corinth, Mississippi, and were married by the Justice of Peace. The reason we went to Mississippi was because there was no waiting period in that state. I would have to say this plan worked rather well, as here it is 62 years later as of this writing, and we are still happily, happily, happily married. Jumping ahead a little bit, we did get our marriage vows renewed with our longtime pastor and dear friend, Peter Lord, in the presence of our family a few years ago.

At the time of our marriage, September 11, 1954, I was living with two of my old friends from the TVA program in a new, large apartment complex in Huntsville. I would say over 90 percent of the residents in this apartment complex were newcomers to Huntsville and were single or newly married couples. When I told my roommates I was getting married, they volunteered to move to another apartment available in the same building. This solved my housing problem. Kathryn and I made a trip to Chattanooga, Tennessee, and bought several pieces of nice furniture for our apartment. We received a generous discount from this furniture place, because the owner was a friend of Kathryn's mother and father. We only lived in this apartment for a few months and then moved to Florida as originally scheduled.

Kathryn knew before we married my job would require moving to Florida. This was fine with her. We both enjoyed living in Huntsville very much, and we both thought we'd move back at some time. Obviously, as the saying goes, "We got sand in our shoes." We never wanted to leave Florida, although we still have very fond memories of Huntsville.

I want to jump back now to my transition from the Field Service Division to the Redstone Missile Program, Missile Firing

Lab., which several years later, in 1958, was transferred intact to the NASA Launch Control Center.

Without getting into too much detail, I would describe the situation like this: The mission of the FSED was to manage the contracts of the various companies designing and manufacturing anti-aircraft missile systems. These were good jobs, but if you really had a desire for "hardware hands-on work," this was not it, and we all wanted the opportunity to get our hands on the hardware. All of this work was done by the contractors.

My first assignment in FSED was to attend a Nike Missile School at White Sands Missile Proving Ground in New Mexico. The Nike was a new anti-aircraft missile system under development. The Cold War with Russia was really beginning to heat up, and fortunately our leaders were beginning to respond to the Russian threat with expansions in advanced defensive and offensive weapons. I enjoyed my several weeks of school at White Sands Proving Ground. After I returned to Huntsville, I was sent on a similar mission to a school on the Terrier anti-aircraft missile system, which was being developed by Convair (present day General Dynamics) in San Diego, California.

To my pleasant surprise, the Convair facility was very close to the Marine Recruit Depot where I spent my boot camp days. To use an old southern saying, "The Marine base was only spitting distance from the Convair Facility." In case you don't know, "spitting distance" means it is very close. Like the Nike school, I enjoyed this school on the Terrier Missile. I learned things from both that were a great help in my work later on with other missile systems.

I was the only one from my department at the Nike school. In the Terrier Missile School there were two of us. I was joined by one of my old buddies, Bill Huff, from the TVA Program. We made the trip to San Diego in my vehicle, which at that time was a 1947 Chevrolet with no air conditioning, I might add. As I recall that did not bother us, but today I cannot think of making that cross-country trip, especially across the desert, without it.

Being government employees, they arranged for us to stay at the Navy Officers' Quarters at the San Diego Navy Base, which, again, was only "spitting distance" from the Convair Facility. What a difference this was from my living quarters ten years earlier when I was in boot camp just down the road. In boot camp, you go through the chow line and the cook throws something in your mess kit you can't recognize. Now compare that with the officer's dining room with tablecloths, china, silverware, and food served by men in white uniforms.

Huff and I really enjoyed the school and our living accommodations. We took a leisurely trip back to Huntsville. I have an especially fond memory of attending an Easter sunrise service on the rim of the Grand Canyon. Huff was a fine Christian man, so we were very compatible. We still keep in touch.

When Huff and I returned to our office in Huntsville, we found they had added several new engineers. They were young and single like us. We became a very close little group, and the more we learned about the overall operations at Redstone Arsenal the more we were convinced we were in the wrong place. This was confirmed when the Army sent a new career bureaucrat from Washington to head up our office. He turned out to be one of the most obnoxious people I have ever known. That settled it. We were getting out of there.

Fortunately, one the new guys, Jim Rorex from the University of Alabama, had an old family friend from his hometown in a high position in the Redstone Personnel Office. We received special treatment from him, and we immediately scheduled appointments for interviews in a number of the major organizations in the Redstone Missile Program.

My decision to move out of the FSED could not have been timelier. My first interview in the Redstone Project was with Dr. Hans Gruene in a newly formed organization called the Missile Firing Lab. The development and manufacturing of the first Redstone missile was well underway, although it was still a little more than one year from the first scheduled launch date. My interview with Dr. Gruene went extremely well and I received a job offer that day. The offers stated that at some time in the future, probably about a year, we would be required to move to the launch site at Cape Canaveral.

We were all single at this time and we looked forward to being a part of this first launch team in Florida. We found to our very pleasant surprise that we were getting in on the ground floor of this organization. There were less than ten members assigned to the Missile Firing Lab (MFL) at this time. Our leaders in the MFL were four Germans from the old V-2 Program. The head of the MFL was Dr. Kurt Debus, who reported directly to Dr. von Braun. Dr. Hans Gruene was his deputy and also head of the Electrical, Guidance, and Control Division. Karl Sendler was the head of the Instrumentation, Telemetry, and Tracking Systems, and Albert Zeiler was head of the Propulsion and Mechanical Systems.

I became good friends with all of these men. I would later become Dr. Gruene's deputy, and he would be my mentor until he retired. I took his place when he retired, and I had the pleasure of having lunch with him about once a month until he passed away.

I mentioned earlier that in a military project the top man will be a military officer. Capt. Rocco Petrone was assigned as the military leader for the Redstone Program. Rocco was a graduate of West Point and had a master's degree from MIT. He was a very smart, very capable, no-nonsense individual. Rocco was a big man, and he had played on the National Championship West Point football team during the war years. Some of our guys did not like Rocco's strict way of operating, but I had no problem with Rocco's methods. My service in the Marines prepared me for appreciating a well disciplined operation. Like most of us at that time Rocco was single, and he was dating a girl in one of the apartments where I lived. Rocco and I became very good friends.

When I signed up with the MFL, there was only one person other than Dr. Gruene in the Electrical, Guidance, and Control Division. His name was George Dannals, and he was Dr. Gruene's right-hand man at this time. George was a very sharp engineer, a graduate of Duke University, and our immediate boss. George and I got along extremely well and we became lifelong friends. A brief time later, two of my old TVA friends, Bill Chandler and C. A. Reid, joined me in the MFL and we enjoyed a long and successful career. Now in 2017, Bill Chandler, Bill Grafton, Reed Barnett and myself are the only surviving members of the original MFL team.

Fortunately, the timing of my transfer to the Missile Firing Lab (MFL) was perfect. At this time all the Redstone Arsenal organizations were going full speed in the manufacturing and development of the Redstone Missile, but the MFL was just getting organized. The only people in the MFL who had an office were Dr. Debus, Dr. Gruene, Zelier, and Sendler. All the troops were embedded in the various organizations working on the Redstone Missile.

Our job was to learn all we could about the Redstone, which meant most of the time it was up to us to decide where we would work that day. This meant some days I would be in the Qual Lab where the missile systems were being tested. I would follow the missile to the Static Test Stand. I also spent many days in the Astronics Lab, talking to the design engineers and observing them fabricating and testing the various flight black boxes. We troops in the MFL became lifelong friends with many of these young design engineers.

Some days I would accompany Dr. Gruene and George Dannals as they visited the top guys in the various organizations, getting detail test requirements for the pre-launch operations at the launch site. I loved what I was doing, and as I said earlier, "If you like what you're doing, it ain't work." I was having fun. I was learning so much every day, and I was collecting a vast amount of the technical documentation of the missile systems. In fact, if I could have, I would have taken some of the documentation home with me to study at night. At this time all of it was classified, and of course, we could not take it out of the gate.

The MFL was hiring personnel every day and sending them out to learn the missile systems as I have described. Some days I would be with some of these new people, but we never worked together as a team until we moved to Florida. I would add it was not only important that we learn the technical side of the rocket, but also that we became good friends with the designers. There was a big payoff in later years, as we would always have some major issues to resolve and we could do this on a friendly basis.

In the summer of 1953, the first Redstone Missile was ready to ship to the launch site at Cape Canaveral. Dr. Debus and Dr. Gruene had made several trips to the Cape to negotiate with the Air Force Eastern Test Range for all the logistical requirements and support for our operations at the launch site. They arranged for us to use the old WWII Navy Hangar-C for pre-launch pad operations and Block House Pad 3/4 for launch operations.

This little blockhouse reminded me of some of the fortified gun positions on Saipan and Iwo Jima.

I would say the available facilities were bare-bones, and you made do with what you had. We had no electrical or mechanical workshops. All we had were a couple of old military shop trucks. The only office space was a tiny space in the mobile launcher structure for Dr. Debus.

This was our first opportunity to work as a launch team. We did experience some first-time type problems, but overall it went extremely well. We launched our first Redstone Missile on August 20, 1953. What an exciting day that was. A few minutes before clearing the launch pad, I stood by the launch pedestal looking up at this huge missile with lox vapor coming out of the vent valve. It was seventy feet tall and five feet in diameter.

This thing is too big to fly, I thought.

Fast forward. In my wildest dreams I could never imagine that fifteen years later, I would be standing on the mobile launch platform of a moon rocket five times as high (350 feet), six times as wide (30 feet) and with a hundred times more thrust (75 thousand versus 7.5 million pounds), thinking the same thing. *This thing is just too big to fly.*

Sometimes, it is so good to be so wrong.

The moment we had worked so hard for finally came. George Dannals, our test conductor, called "Firing Command." This was a most critical moment. I was operating one of the control consoles, and like the other operators, I was glued to the displays on the console.

Of course, these were pre-computer days, and it was up to the console operators to make a decision if any of the information displayed on the console exceeded a predetermined "redline" value. Heaven forbid, but if this happened, you had to call "cutoff" immediately and stop the sequence. In the last few seconds before liftoff, the pressure is intense. Your eyes are glued to the various meters and lights. You certainly do not want to miss a problem, and on the other hand you certainly do not want to stop a good sequence. You're actually acting as a human computer. Years later, we could fortunately place this burden on computers.

Finally, that great moment came. The mechanical engineer on the propulsion console responded to this command by pressing the critical red firing command button. It had a special guard protecting it from being accidentally pressed. In this particular blockhouse, the consoles were facing a slot window with several inches of protective glass looking out to the missile on the launch pedestal. However, the console operators were seated and could not stand up to view the missile through the window until the "Liftoff" signal was given. Once the firing command button was pressed, a most critical responsibility now went to a flame observer standing behind the console, looking out to the missile.

The Redstone missile engine was very primitive compared with today's rocket engines. The Redstone engine required three steps: ignition, pre-stage, and mainstage. Each of the three stages had a distinct recognizable flame pattern for a good engine. To ensure we did not liftoff with a bad engine, the flame observer held in his hand a cutoff button wired with an extension cord into the electrical logic circuitry.

We had just the right engineer for this job. Albert Zeiler was the head of the Mechanical and Propulsion Department, and he was well experienced. He had the same job on the V-2 launches in Germany. Fortunately, never in the Redstone Program was it necessary to activate the cutoff button.

Our first launch was a failure, as it went out of control shortly after liftoff. In an effort to be as positive as we could, we classified all of our failures as a partial success if the missile got off of the launch pedestal. This turned out to be a standard press release statement for all of the missile programs at that time for the many, many failures experienced early on.

As in all walks of life, you can learn more from your failures than from your successes. From our limited view in the Blockhouse the missile lifted off beautifully, and everything looked good until it disappeared into some low-hanging clouds. Shortly after, the missile went out of control and crashed in the ocean about eight miles downrange. We received very good telemetry data from this short flight, which indicated the control vanes were slightly off the required "zero" position at liftoff. What caused it was the big unknown question.

Now here is the story and a big lesson we learned from this problem. We had a standing unwritten procedure before the final closure of a door on the missile. We would do what we call "kick the tires" and also double check everything we could on the inside and outside of the missile before the final closeout of the access doors. This included making sure cables were tightly connected and all loose tools and test equipment had been removed.

On this first launch we had some of the senior key design engineers from Huntsville supporting us in our prelaunch activities. One of the top German design engineers, a super nice guy and a very capable person, went up to von Braun and said, "I think I know what happened that caused this problem."

He told von Braun he was making a final closeout inspection and found a loose lock washer on a potentiometer mounted on the black box for the control system. He said when he was tightening this lock washer, he may have inadvertently moved the potentiometer slightly off of its zero position. Further analysis seemed to confirm this. Von Braun did not get angry with this man, in fact, he commended him for his honesty and rewarded him with a bottle of champagne.

It became a policy that lasted as long as I was out at the Space Center, and I would assume it is still in effect: If you inadvertently make a mistake that could cause or explain a problem, you confess it to the right people, and you will not be punished. Of course, the second part of that policy is that you are not to make the same mistake again. No matter how careful and how capable the launch team, these type of things will happen. The worst situation you could have is an environment where the individual is afraid to admit the error.

In those early days, after a launch we had to remove all of our consoles and equipment in the Blockhouse and on the pad. At that time we were sharing this Blockhouse and launch pad with another missile program operated by the Air Force. We would go back to Huntsville and follow the next missile to be launched through its assembly and verification process, which included a static firing of the rocket engine before shipping it to the launch site.

I must say the Brevard County we saw in 1953 was nowhere near the Brevard County of 2017. There were no interstates. The main road into Brevard County was the one-lane US-1. This was the main road through the Titusville business district, which was about two blocks long on what is now Garden Street to

South Street.

Cocoa Beach was mainly vacant land with four or five mom and pop motels and one very small grocery store. Cocoa Beach did have one restaurant called the Surf Club. It was popular and really first-class. People did not eat out as frequently as they do in 2017, so it was a very special occasion when we dined at the Surf Club.

Until the first part of our launch team moved permanently to Florida in 1955, most of us stayed in a place called Winslow Beach when we came down for a launch. This was a group of small cabins on the beach just north of the 520 Causeway. Mr. Winslow, the man who owned these cabins, also owned some of the surrounding land, including beachfront property. He wanted to sell us some of that land at what I recall as an enormous price of $200 an acre. We thought Mr. Winslow must have thought we were pretty stupid to pay $200 for that scrub wasteland. Fast forward to 2017. That land is probably worth that much for one foot of beachfront.

I can't have any regrets for not buying land like that when we first came to Florida. I might have gotten filthy rich, and there is no telling where I would be today. Thank you, Lord, for taking care of me every step of my life. Maybe I should add that none of us even had $200 at that time.

Our second Redstone rocket performed much better than the first one, but the third Redstone launch was a total disaster. In fact, we could not even use that old phrase, "partial success." The missile lifted a few inches off the launch table, and the engine shut down. The missile settled back down on the launch pedestal, tipped over, and exploded. That does not make for a very good day.

We in the Blockhouse a couple of hundred feet away were safe, but we did have a momentary scare. There was a little room underneath the launch pedestal that housed some of our ground control equipment, and from that room we had some large pipes going up to the launch pedestal which housed our large control cables and pressure lines to the missile. From this underground room we had a cable tunnel to the Blockhouse, and through a hole in the wall of the Blockhouse, the cables were connected to our control consoles. The hole in the Blockhouse wall was much larger than what was needed to get the cables through the wall.

This empty space was filled with packing material to prevent snakes, rats, and mosquitoes from getting in.

The blast from the explosion sent a pressure wave down the pipes into the underground room and tunnel and blew this packing out of the wall all over the people in that area of the Blockhouse. No one was physically injured, but it did scare the living daylights out of some of the guys.

After Redstone 3, my friend and supervisor, George Dannals, left our organization. George and a couple of other guys outside of our organization formed a new company. Their new company struggled for a while, but then they began to get some good contracts. The company took off and was later bought out by another company, which in turn was bought out by the giant Harris Corporation. We remained close friends with George and his family and, sadly, we attended his funeral a couple of years ago.

When George left our organization, Dr. Gruene selected me as his deputy. I could not ask for a better working relationship. I felt comfortable making any decisions in our technical and operational activities. I was very dedicated to keeping him updated on what I was doing, and he always backed me up.

In the remainder of 1953 and 1954, we went back and forth from Huntsville to Cape Canaveral. In 1955, our launch rate was increasing, and according to the original plans, it was time for the launch team to permanently move to Florida.

Kathryn and I had only been married a few months when we moved to Florida in early 1955. We were prepared for this, so it was really no surprise or problem, except for a complete lack of housing in Brevard County. There were no new housing apartments under construction, and condos were unheard of at that time. Patrick Air Force Base is located on the southern border of Cocoa Beach, and this turned out to be the solution for some of us. Since we were on a government project and we were government people, the Air Force agreed to permit a few of us to live in the officers' quarters just south of Cocoa Beach.

Five of our team took advantage of this offer: Dr. Debus, Dr. Gruene, R.P. Dodd, Bobby Green, and myself. This was not a bad deal. These were duplexes with large rooms: two bedrooms, a kitchen, a dining area, a living room, a screened porch, and a carport. These duplexes were located on A1A facing the ocean.

When you first move to Florida, living on the beach is a big deal, but for some of us, that big deal does not last that long. To get to the beach from our duplex, we crossed A1A. That was not a problem. Then we had to go a short distance through grass-covered vacant land. That did pose a problem. We quickly learned you had to run through this vacant land, because when you hit the grass you would disturb a huge storm of mosquitoes. You'd have to run as fast as you could and dive into the surf to drown all the mosquitoes on your back. If I tried, I do not think I could exaggerate how bad the mosquito problem was in those days. I cannot give the county enough credit for the super job they have done controlling it.

Another big problem we experienced in those days was the foul sulfur water. It not only tasted bad, it smelled bad, and, of course, using bottled water was a temporary solution to that problem. Fortunately, the municipalities in the county were able provide good water later. Another negative to living directly on the beach was the corrosive damage to your car from the salt spray. Cars of the 1950's did not have the protective coating like they do today. We had a new Oldsmobile. It was housed in our open carport, so after a few months the chrome looked terrible. You could obviously tell when a car had been exposed to a constant salt spray.

Overall, I would say living on the air base was not a bad deal. We were allowed to use the officers' club, gas station, and theater, but we were not allowed to use the commissary. Since there was no grocery store on Cocoa Beach, we made a trip about once a week to buy our groceries in Cocoa. We attended St. David's by the Sea Episcopal Church. In those days there were no two-car families, so it was necessary to carpool. I never did like carpools, but ours worked pretty well. I carpooled with Dr. Gruene, who lived a few houses down the street from me, and R. P. Dodd, who lived nearby. This worked out well as we could talk business—I might say problems—to and from work.

One of the happiest days of our life was on June 14, 1955, in Cocoa Beach when our son, David, was born. He was born in a hospital in Melbourne and christened at St. David's by the Sea. We were enjoying living on the air base, but we realized it was not the place we wanted to settle down and raise a family. We began to search all up and down Brevard County, from Melbourne to Titusville.

We settled on the little town of Titusville, where I bought a lot. I was especially comfortable here, since it reminded me of Slocomb. Actually, I thought I was moving to Titusville. But I found out later I was actually in an incorporated area called Whispering Hills. There were no businesses in Whispering Hills, only a few scattered houses and one paved road. There was a country club with a nine-hole golf course about a block from our home.

I designed a small two-bedroom house and had a local contractor build our little nest on this dead-end street. I think all of our family has fond memories of 1412 Bell Terrace. I should add that in those days no middle-class family started off with their first home like we see in today's housing market. We were in the very beginning of the explosive growth in Brevard County. Our surrounding area very soon filled up with new homes, and I would again say they were on a much smaller scale than in today's market. All the new homes then were being occupied almost 100 percent by young couples from out-of-state, and I would say mostly upper-middle-class incomes.

I kept adding to our little home, and we ended up with a two-story home with six bedrooms and a nice swimming pool. Thank the Lord Kathryn had a very green thumb, and she did wonders with our yard. It was not very large, but we did have grapevines and several very productive fruit trees, which we very much enjoyed. We did not have air conditioning initially, but after a couple of years we splurged and added it. Another big splurge item was a dishwasher.

SPACE HISTORY—1950S

In 1954 and 1955, the pace of our program increased significantly, especially in the building of new facilities. We grew from our little pillbox, Blockhouse 3/4, to two new larger blockhouses, 26 and 56, two new hangars, D and R, and a new office and laboratory building (E&L). This was quite a step up from our one little blockhouse, one little office in the mobile launcher, one small hangar, and one military shop truck. The frequency of our launches was increasing, and our manpower was also gradually increasing.

The Air Force came on the scene with two new programs: one was the Snark and the other was the Navajo. The Snark was an early version of a drone. It took off from an airstrip and was supposed to return and land like an airplane. The end of the runway was very near the beach and most of the Snark launches ended up in the ocean near the beach. We appropriately named that section of the beach "Snark-infested waters." This program did not last long and was canceled. The other program, Navajo, suffered the same fate as the Snark. We appropriately named the Navajo the "Never Go." This program was also canceled. Meanwhile, we were having more and more success with the development of the Redstone missiles and launching them from our new facilities, Blockhouse 26 and Blockhouse 56. However, we were still experiencing some failures.

One I remember well—I think it was Redstone 25—was a night launch. Shortly after takeoff, it tilted over and headed north directly toward the Central Control building. Central Control is an Air Force facility, and they have the responsibility to track every launch from Cape Canaveral and destroy the missile if it exceeds predetermined boundaries. Their purpose is to protect the populated areas around Cape Canaveral. Every missile launched had a destruct package on board that could be activated by Central Control operators. The destruct package would trigger an explosive charge to rupture the fuel tanks and, of course, destroy the missile.

All of our rockets, especially in the experimental flights, were heavily monitored with a comprehensive instrumentation package, and this information, through our telemetry system, was transmitted back to our telemetry station in Hangar D. The telemetry station then displayed this information on the strip chart recorders, and the launch team could analyze this data and hopefully identify the problem.

On the countdown on this flight, we experienced multiple problems that caused the launch to be delayed, so we had been up for many hours. We analyzed the telemetry data from this very short flight and the cause of the problem was not immediately obvious. Dr. Debus made the decision, saying, "We will call it off for tonight and come back early in the morning and continue our investigation into the cause of the problem."

I went home and got a few hours of sleep and then went back to resume looking at this telemetry data. I entered the lobby of our E&L building, and there were three or four people checking in with the guard. One was my friend Johnny. Johnny was a big black guy and the janitor for our facilities. Johnny had done some yardwork for me at home and we always had a friendly chat when we ran into each other at work.

Johnny came over to me and said, "Mr. Ike, I need to talk to you." I said, "Sure, Johnny, what about?" He motioned for me to come to the corner of the room and said, "I know what happened to the rocket last night." I said, "You do?" Johnny replied, "Yeah, I know, it was dem Communists. I know you and I know Dr. Debus and you would never let a rocket do that, and I want you to go tell Dr. Debus, it was dem Communists." I said, "Johnny, you are right; we would never let one do that, and I will go tell Dr. Debus what you said."

I must say Johnny had a little rationale for his assessment. First, he had the utmost faith in us—maybe a little too much. Secondly, during this period in the '50s, Russia had a strong presence in Cuba. For every launch, they had their so-called "fishing trawlers" offshore of Cape Canaveral monitoring our launches. We did have a legitimate concern that the Russians could get our destruct command code and blow up a good launch. This caused us some extra work in our prelaunch checkout of this destruct system; we could not transmit an open signal over the airways from Central Control to our missile on the pad for fear the Russians could pick up the coded signal. So, we had to establish a hardwire path from Central Control to our destruct package on the missile.

We eventually identified the cause of the failure, but I never did have the heart to tell Johnny that we could not blame the Communists for our issues on this launch. The only comfort you can take from situations like this is that you learn more from your failures than you do from your successes.

Sometime in the early '50s, scientists from 67 countries had a meeting and planned what they called an international geophysical year (IGY) in the 1957 to 1958 timeframe. The IGY was actually a period of about 18 months. They would make special studies of Earth's crust, solar activity, the Arctic, the Antarctic, oceanography, gravity, cosmic rays, and the upper atmosphere. This timeframe was selected because heavy solar activity was predicted. These scientists asked the nations of the world to launch an artificial moon during this time to study the upper atmosphere. Two nations responded to this request, the United States and the Soviet Union. Eisenhower was our president at this time, and although I was a strong Eisenhower supporter, I fault him for accepting some very bad advice on how to respond to the request to place an artificial moon in Earth orbit. The recommendation he accepted was to form a committee on how to respond to this request. Maybe in rare cases a committee is necessary, but so many times a committee just screws things up, and the committee in this case did a masterful job of screwing things up.

The committee selected three options to study. One, use the

Air Force Atlas missile to launch the satellite in orbit; two, use the Army Jupiter-C as the booster rocket; or three, design and build a completely new rocket to be called the Vanguard.

Now here is the data the committee was looking at during that time. First, the Atlas rocket was still in the early development stages and the first flight of this rocket would not be until December 1957. The updated Atlas rocket is one of the most reliable workhorses in our space program today, but in the early development of this rocket they experienced numerous failures.

Secondly, there was a warehouse at Redstone Arsenal with a Jupiter-C rocket in storage, ready to ship to the launch site. To understand what a stupid decision this committee made, you need to know a little background on this Jupiter-C rocket. Sometime in the early to mid '50s, the Department of Defense authorized the Army Ballistic Missile Agency (ABMA) and the Air Force to parallel the development of an intermediate range ballistic missile (IRBM). These rockets would have a range of 1,500 miles. Based on this authorization, the ABMA started the development of the Jupiter rocket and the Air Force started the development of the Thor rocket.

Due to the trajectory of a 1,500 mile rocket, the heat generated when the payload of this rocket reentered the atmosphere was so high that some development was necessary to come up with an ablative material that could withstand this terrific heat. To resolve this problem, von Braun and his team at Redstone Arsenal, in conjunction with the Jet Propulsion Laboratory (JPL) in California, developed a three-stage rocket that would duplicate the flight path of the military Jupiter (IRBM), testing the various ablative materials on the third stage as it reentered the atmosphere and recovered the nose cone. This program was very successful, and on one launch, we sent a nose cone 3,500 miles downrange and recovered it, which was a record at that time. A little more interesting history here: The Jupiter-C used a modified Redstone missile booster. It had an elongated tank and we used a new fuel (UDMH) that gave about 15 percent more energy. The second stage was provided by JPL, and it was a cluster of twelve small, solid rockets, and the third stage was a cluster of three of the same rockets embedded in the center of the second stage. Mounted on top of the third stage was actually an inert rocket with the nose cone on top. Now get this—if you made this fourth stage an active rocket, it would be inserted in Earth orbit. Major General Bruce Medaris, head of ABMA, and von Braun had repeatedly been to Washington to convince the bureaucrats to approve the launch of this Jupiter-C rocket with a live fourth stage. Permission denied.

The third option, as I said, was the design and development of a completely new rocket that would be called the Vanguard.

Out of the three options here, the Jupiter-C should have been a no-brainer, but this stupid committee selected the third option. It's hard to see how they came up with this position. The rationale seemed to be that this new rocket would be a total non-military version and somehow that would please the Russians. The Russians certainly didn't think like we did, because every satellite they launched used a military booster. Interestingly, the head of this committee told von Braun later that he was outvoted, and that he had voted for the Jupiter-C.

History records show what a stupid decision this committee made. On October 4, 1957, the world woke up to a *beep-beep-beep* from outer space. The world would never be the same. The Soviets had launched Sputnik, the world's first artificial moon. We were stunned, embarrassed, and I would say angry, especially those of us who knew we could have made history as the first nation to launch an artificial moon. The Soviets got tremendous mileage out of this achievement. Here we were, supposedly the greatest nation in history, and there was this third-rate Communist country making this tremendous achievement. We were in the middle of the Cold War with the Soviet Union, who was trying to impress upon all the world that the Communist system was superior to the free market capitalist system. They were proudly demonstrating this tremendous technical achievement, something their free market capitalist enemies had not been able to do.

I was at work when we received the astounding message that the Soviets had a satellite in Earth orbit. In the back room of our blockhouse we had our receivers for tracking missiles, and one of our tracking guys turned on a receiver and picked up this beep-beep-beep. I'm not sure I know how to describe how I felt. We just stood there in silence and listened to this terrible sound.

I could visualize those Soviets with their vodka bottles having a great celebration.

General Medaris and von Braun went back to Washington and pleaded for permission to launch our Jupiter-C booster rocket with a live fourth stage and payload. We had the booster rocket ready to ship to the launch site, and JPL had the fourth stage and payload sitting on ready. The idiots in Washington said, "Absolutely not; we are going with the Vanguard."

One month later in early November 1957, the Soviets added more to the humiliation and embarrassment of the Western world by successfully launching a larger satellite with a dog. Again we were astounded. We had the capability to launch a small payload, but we did not have anything in our inventory that could match the weight of the payloads the Soviets were putting in orbit.

One month later, in December 1957, the Vanguard was ready to launch. Vanguard was a much smaller rocket than the Jupiter-C, and the payload was about the size of a grapefruit. With the whole world watching, the Vanguard lifted off the launch platform and exploded. Talk about being humiliated. How low could we get? The Soviets were having a field day at our expense.

Our bureaucrats in Washington had no other options. Now General Medaris and von Braun got the "green light" to launch our Jupiter-C with the JPL payload, which was titled Explorer 1.

The ball was in our court now, and we would have to perform; the whole world would be watching. We were confident, yet we were well aware that something could go wrong.

We successfully launched Explorer 1, the first United States satellite, on January 31, 1958, at 22:48 EST. The data from our downrange tracking systems indicated everything was working properly, and then we endured a period of blackout waiting for the tracking station in Goldstone, California, to pick up the signal that Explorer 1 was in orbit. We waited in silence, and then praise the Lord, we received the words we were so anxious to hear: "Explorer 1 is in orbit." Needless to say, the silence in the blockhouse was broken and we went wild, shouting, backslapping, handshaking, and lighting up cigars.

Our satellite, Explorer 1, was not nearly as heavy as the Sputniks; however, there was no comparison in the scientific data gathered from the two systems. The scientific data from Explorer 1 far exceeded the beep-beep-beep from the Sputniks. The instrumentation on Explorer 1 discovered the radiation belt around Earth, which was named the Van Allen Belt after Dr. Van Allen of the University of Iowa, who designed the instrumentation package. This turned out to be one of the main discoveries of the international geophysical year. Another little point of interest here, Explorer 1 was the first instance of transistors in space hardware. Explorer 1 gathered data for four months and then the batteries went dead. It remained in orbit until 1970. We regained much of our prestige, but the experience made us acutely aware that we were in a hotly contested space race with the Soviet Union.

The 1950s were a very prolific period in our space history. Like every other facet of our lives, politics entered the picture. In the mid '50s there was a battle going on in the Department of Defense. It was readily apparent that the primary future offensive and defensive weapons would be missiles. The Army's position was that missiles were actually long-range artillery, and thus in the Army's domain, and the Air Force's position was that long-range missiles were like long-range bombers, and thus in their domain. The Air Force had better lobbyists on this issue, and the secretary of defense (Wilson) made the decision that the long-range missiles would be under the Air Force and the Army would be limited to missiles under 250 miles. Fortunately, the Navy was not asleep when it came to the future of missiles on submarines and ships. The Navy's first venture into the ballistic missile world was to use the Jupiter on submarines, and this explains why the configuration of the Jupiter was short and stubby. The Navy soon realized a submarine-based missile with liquid propellants was impractical, and they dropped the Jupiter in favor of a solid rocket, Polaris, which was a wise move.

When this decision was made, the Army was involved in the development of the Jupiter (IRBM) with a range of 1,500 miles, and the Air Force was on a parallel project with the development of the Thor, also with a range of 1,500 miles. The right decision was made: both of these programs would continue and be deployed by the future long range intercontinental ballistic missiles (ICBM). These would be the Atlas and Titan ICBMs and would be the responsibility of the Air Force. The Thor missile was designed and built by McDonnell Douglas and deployed in England, aimed at the Soviet Union. The first Jupiter missiles were designed and built by von Braun and his team under the Army Ballistic Missile Agency, and production was done by the Chrysler Corporation. The Jupiter missiles were deployed in Italy and Turkey, and, of course, these missiles were aimed at the Soviets.

Our launch team played a part in training the military troops from Italy and Turkey that were responsible for launching these missiles if required. The troops from these two countries went to school in Huntsville where our counterparts in ABMA taught them how to prepare and operate the various missile systems for launch. The graduation exercise for these troops was to come to the Cape and launch a Jupiter under our close supervision, and these launches were all successful. We also sent some of our launch team over to their launch site for the initial setup. The Jupiter missiles that were deployed in Italy and Turkey were a key factor in the Cuban missile crisis in 1962, and I will expand on that later.

When anyone writes about our space history during the 1950s, their story would not be complete if they did not mention a couple of real space legends, Hortense and Marilyn. Hortense was a very large white lady and Marilyn was a very large black lady and they operated the food truck. We affectionately labeled the food truck the "Roach Coach." The Roach Coach made scheduled stops at all of the launch pads on the Cape, and we were always glad to see its arrival. Everyone loved Hortense and Marilyn. Their talk, especially Hortense's, would make a sailor blush. There was a cafeteria on the Cape, but many days we would be involved in a test where we could not leave our station to visit the cafeteria, so the gourmet Roach Coach was a welcome sight. Often when we saw it was going to be a very long day we would ask Hortense and Marilyn to stay over. Most of the time one of them would stay if someone offered them a ride home later.

On one occasion, I asked if one of them could stay over for a few hours and then I would give them a ride home. Marilyn agreed to stay over. I was single at that time and I was rooming in Cocoa with Fritz Runge, one of our Chrysler employees. Unfortunately, this day we were riding in Fritz's car. I need to explain why I said "unfortunately." Fritz was a "car buff" and he had a highly modified car. It was funny looking, and the rear end looked like the front end. It was a two-door car, and if you stretched your imagination you could say it needed two rear seats. I don't recall how difficult it was for Marilyn to get in the back seat, but I will never forget how difficult it was for her to get out. Marilyn was giving Fritz directions, and we ended up in the middle of "black town" in Cocoa at a very busy intersection. Busy with people, not cars. It was a well-lit intersection, and I was surprised to see so many people out on the streets at this time, which was about 10 PM.

Now the fun begins. Marilyn could not get out of the back seat. She was struggling, and I tried to help her, but my efforts were to no avail. Now this caught the attention of all those people standing around on the sidewalk. They gathered around and started laughing, saying, "Look at old Marilyn." They were really enjoying the show. Finally, one real big guy came up, and, with his help, Marilyn finally got freed from her cubbyhole. Marilyn was laughing along with the rest of the crowd and as we pulled her out they were still laughing.

Blockhouse 56. 1957. "Ok, that didn't work.
What do we do now?"

(Sitting at consoles L-R:) Terry Greenfield, Ike Rigell, C. D. Sweat
(Standing at consoles L-R:) Bill Chandler, Bill Jaffrey, Jim Davidson,
Russ Harris, Henry Clay, John Barrow, unknown, unknown,
Bob Funkhouser

Jan. 28, 1958—Explorer 1 Launch, Blockhouse 26

(Left side, L-R:) Albert Zieler, person on the phone was Air Force Safety Officer. (Right side, L-R:) Terry Greenfield, C.D. Sweat, me, Bill Chandler. (Standing:) Milt Chambers, Bob Moser

Mercury Redstone Test Flight. We called it the "4 Inch Flight."
One of our worst days in the space program.

Pre-launch view of Juno II space vehicle on July 16, 1959.

Countdown at Complex 56.

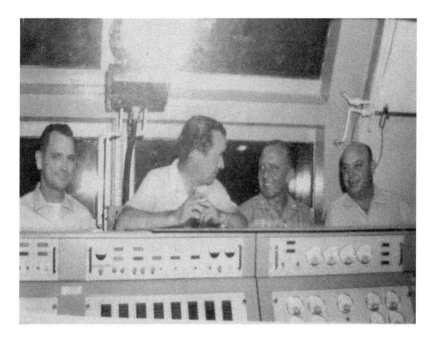

Blockhouse 26 (L-R:) Me, Edward R. Murrow, Dr. Kurt Debus, and Bill Chandler. Murrow was the Walter Cronkite of our day. He was making a documentary about the launching a rocket. We were trying to give him a good show by launching a Jupiter missile. The rocket went up and then tilted over and exploded, but we killed several rattlesnakes that day.

Ike knew a bunch about inverters
July 16, 1959

Not a good day in space!

Edward R. Murrow was making a documentary about us and we were on our best behavior to show him how good we were. This Jupiter rocket took off, went 90°, and exploded just on the edge of the pad, frying a few rattlesnakes with it. What an embarrassment.

LAUNCH COMPLEX 26 BLOCKHOUSE, JUPITER LAUNCH

March 1, 1957

1. Albert Zeiler *, 2. Dr. Eberhard Rees*, 3. Gen. Bruce Medaris, 4. Dr. Kurt Debus*, 5. Air Force range safety officer, 6. Bill Chandler, 7. Me, 8. Andy Pickett, 9. Gen. Barkley, 10. Grady Williams, 11. unknown

*Denotes original members of von Braun's V-2 missile team

This photo was taken in Blockhouse 37 at Cape Canaveral Air Force Station during the countdown for the launch of a Jupiter missile. It would have been during the late 1950s.

SPACE WORKERS - REDSTONE/APOLLO

Volumes of books have been written about our space history, but I am not aware of any that go into detail of the daily events of the lives of the space workers responsible for the tremendous success we have enjoyed.

I use the term "space workers" because that is what the local Brevard County people called us when we arrived on the scene in the mid-1950s. Among the locals some welcomed us into their community with open arms and looked upon us as an asset to the community. Others had a little different view. They viewed this sudden burst of space activity as very temporary. They thought we would leave the area in a couple of years, and they would be saddled with huge debts from the expansions of various public facilities we caused.

For example, our small church in Titusville, St. Gabriel's, quickly outgrew its walls and we needed to enlarge the building. The local old-timers were vehemently against this move just for the reasons I stated above. They thought: We expand this building to accommodate you space workers, then you leave, and we are saddled with this debt. Fortunately, these good folks were wrong, and we are still here sixty years later in even larger numbers.

I want to describe some interesting cultural changes that I

observed in these space workers and their organizations, both government and contractors, in my space career from 1951 to 1991. First, at the beginning of our space program in 1950—and I am referring to the Redstone Missile—the average age of the workforce was late 20s. For many of these young engineers, this was their first job. Dr. Wernher von Braun was 38 when his missile team was moved from Fort Bliss, Texas, to Redstone Arsenal in Huntsville, Alabama. Most of his team he brought over from Germany were a few years older, but there was no question he was their very respected leader. The Army created a new organization, the Army Ballistic Missile Agency (ABMA), molded around von Braun's team. Except for secretaries, this was an all-white, all-male team. I'm not implying at all that this was the way it should be. It was just the way it was at that time. That was our culture, and no one questioned it. I want to emphasize that I am recording history exactly as it was, regardless of how the current society would accept this. Several Mexican civilians hired for the work the von Braun team was doing at the White Sands Proving Ground in New Mexico transferred with these Germans to Redstone Arsenal.

The white males, including me, did not look upon these Mexicans as minorities. They did not look upon themselves as minorities either. One of them, Joe Gonzalez, later joined our launch team in Florida, and Joe became one of my best friends. Joe was one of our best electrical technicians. Joe was a personal friend of Dr. von Braun and several other Germans. Years later, the Germans held a special anniversary reunion in Huntsville, and they invited Joe to attend this event.

I want to make it clear that we did not have any females or minorities because we refused to hire them, but rather because these demographics just did not possess the skills we needed at that time. During these years, I personally interviewed and hired several people, but I never even had the opportunity to interview or hire a female or minority.

In the 1960s, NASA headquarters pressured us to hire females and minorities. In response to that, our personnel department toured universities and colleges in the South. Some engineers and I would come along to help sell these students on a career in space. We bombed out. Most of the students we interviewed had not taken the technical courses required for the jobs we were trying to fill, and the few that did meet our requirements did not want to settle in the deep South.

It was not until the Apollo program—I don't recall which launch—that we had the first female and the first minority, a black person, as members of the launch team. The first female was Joann Morgan. As you can imagine, as the first female in a launch room filled with a few hundred men, JoAnn attracted a lot of attention. JoAnn rolled the dice and enjoyed a long and distinguished career at Kennedy Space Center.

Remer Prince was a young black man and software engineer. Remer came in at the perfect time. We really needed him, as we were just beginning to make primitive steps toward an automated countdown. Most of us electrical-mechanical engineers did not even know how to spell *software.*

I cannot say enough good words about Remer. If any of us, because of our cultural background, had any reservations about a black person doing this kind of work, they were quickly dispelled. During one of the first Apollo countdowns after Remer joined our team, the head of computer operations, Frank Penovich, called me on the intercom and reported the computer was down and inoperative—bad news. At that time, I was chief engineer and deputy director of Launch Vehicle Operations. I was on the intercom with all of our senior NASA supervisors; all problems of this nature came to me, and I in turn briefed Dr. Gruene and Rocco Petrone. Rocco would then determine if we should brief Dr. Debus. We all sat on the top row of consoles in the firing room. Since this problem could result in a "hold" (delaying the lift off), Rocco said I should brief Dr. Debus. I gave Dr. Debus the information I had from Frank, and Dr. Debus asked me a couple of questions beyond my knowledge of the problem. Frank was still on the intercom with me, and I said, "Frank, you need to come up here and explain this problem more in depth for Dr. Debus." Dr. Debus was one of the sharpest technical guys I ever encountered; no matter how well you thought you were prepared to explain a problem to him, he always had penetrating questions that would force you to go back and get some answers.

Frank's response was, "I will have to send Remer. He knows more about this problem than me or anyone we have." So I said,

"Send Remer up here." Remer came up and I introduced him to Dr. Debus and said, "Remer, explain this problem to Dr. Debus." Remer very calmly started talking, using strange language like *flip* and *flops*, *bits* and *bites*, *inputs* and *outputs*, *gates*, *feedback* and a few other terms in this category. Dr. Debus had the same blank stare that I did; it was all going over our heads. Dr. Debus listened for a few minutes and then sort of laughed, threw up his hands and said, "That is enough, Remer. How long will it take you to fix it?"

In all my years with Dr. Debus, that is the only time I have ever seen him without a probing question to ask. I can't remember the timeline Remer gave Dr. Debus, but the story has a good ending. Not long after Remer returned to his software world, he called in, "We are back in operation." Remer later made significant contributions in the flight simulator software and software for the future shuttle. Remer transferred to NASA headquarters in DC and enjoyed a very successful career there.

The caliber of people like JoAnn and Remer paved the way for their respective groups to follow in their footsteps. They were both winners, and through their performance they did a great service in advancing females and minorities in the NASA workforce.

I think it is appropriate here to mention a dichotomy that I noticed. During several of the Apollo launches, there were organized protests led by some black leaders, and their message was something like this: "We have a 25-million-dollar moon rover on the surface of the moon, and that is wrong; we should spend that 25 million on the poor." My answer to that is this: That 25 million dollars is not on the moon—all of those dollars are still on Earth, and some of those dollars were used to pay good salaries for minorities and women. People like Remer and JoAnn.

Fortunately, these people leading the protest marches were peaceful and had good intentions, but I don't believe they could see the big picture. President Lyndon Johnson declared a "War on Poverty" back in 1964. Well, we know now that poverty won that battle. We have poured billions into this war and have more poverty and broken families than ever. I believe education is the answer. Educated people, like JoAnn and Remer, do more for their group than the people with good intentions leading these protest marches. There are many pluses that justify the cost for the Apollo program but one tremendous benefit of the Apollo program that I have never heard addressed is that it opened so many opportunities and doors for the advancement of females and minorities.

Just reflect on this: From 2009 to 2017, the NASA administrator was black, and we now have black, Hispanic, Asian, and female astronauts, and some of them have set records. Many senior positions at NASA centers are now staffed with females and minorities. That is considered a very normal situation now, of course, but less than 60 short years ago senior leadership was filled by white men.

Let me expound on minorities and females in the workforce on a larger basis. I've talked about what opportunities NASA opened up for females and minorities, but now let us include all of the space-related companies that were actually a little ahead of NASA in introducing females and minorities into the workforce. During the earlier years, when NASA was still all white males with the exception of some female secretaries, I traveled to California to visit our contractors, and we observed females and minorities in many technical positions. Also, when I went to work for USBI I found the company well balanced, with females and minorities in many responsible positions.

In addition to explaining how minorities and women came to be involved in the space program, I also want to touch on the fact that our workforce was mostly young. In my opinion, it is a great advantage to have a very young workforce in highly technical experimental work in which you do expect and do experience failures. You are not afraid of or terribly embarrassed by failure. I use the example of a young toddler just learning to walk. The toddler takes awkward steps, tumbles and gets up, tumbles again, gets up, and tries again. There could be a room full of people laughing and admiring his efforts, but he is totally not embarrassed.

Another asset of being young is that you have confidence in yourself, just like the little toddler. *If I keep trying, I'm going to make it.* Also, when you are young, you are willing to take responsibility. These are things I have observed on this subject over the long years in my career.

One day I got a call from one of my good friends, Grady Williams, a good old Auburn guy and the head of our Missile Instrumentation Division. Grady said, "Ike, do you have any job openings?"

I said, "Yes, Grady, we are looking for a couple of engineers."

Grady said, "I don't know why they did it, but Personnel sent a man over here for me to interview, and I don't have any openings. I did interview this man, and if I had an opening, I would hire him. I would like to send him over to you for an interview."

I said, "That's fine, Grady. Send him over."

Then there was a little silence, and I had a strange feeling that there must be something more to this than what Grady had said.

"Something I should tell you. This man is 52 years old."

I almost exploded on Grady. "You know we can't hire an old guy like this. He just would not fit in."

I think I was at the ripe old age of 35 at this time. Grady pleaded with me to talk to him, which I did, and I ended up hiring him, although I still had some reservations about his age.

That's not the end of the story. This man, Herman B., was a likable, pleasant man, but he could not adjust to our work lifestyle. Herman was strictly an eight-to-five workday man, and our workday was as long as necessary to complete a test or finish some other job. Herman had a lot of difficulty adjusting to this work environment, and after a few months we arranged for Herman to be transferred to our facilities organization, where they mostly worked hours more suitable for Herman. This proves my point. You needed a young workforce for the tasks that we were doing.

Herman and I remained friends, and later he invited Kathryn and me to a party at his house, where I learned something I never knew about him. He had a second, successful career as a syndicated columnist on how to fix things around the house. He showed me one bedroom that was full of nothing but file cabinets with brochures and pamphlets from commercial companies. This was the source of how he advised people to replace a faucet, patch a screen, etc.

Early in my career, I never heard the word "committee." Individuals made decisions, not committees. Neither did you need a stack of paper with a dozen signatures—some by people who had no clue what they were signing—to tell you a problem had been solved. You instead had the word of a trusted engineer.

As you get older and face some weighty decision, your thinking goes like this. *Suppose it fails, and I look bad. Maybe we need a committee to spread the responsibility.*

Organizations, like people, pick up more and more regulations, unhealthy habits, and bureaucracy as they get older. This impedes productivity.

I like to back up statements like this with real life examples. Back in the Redstone days, we were just a few days from a launch, and my friend in Huntsville, Dick Smith, head of the missile Electrical Design Group, called me. He said they had an urgent need for a small light to be installed near the top of the Redstone booster rocket, and they had a special piece of ground equipment to track this light in the early assent of the rocket.

"Can you guys come up with something?" Dick asked me.

"Sure, Dick, we will go to work on this," I said.

At that moment, I had no clue how we would do this, but I had faith in our team. I called one of our young, bright engineers, Terry Greenfield, and I told Terry what Dick Smith needed. I knew that was all I had to say.

This was prior to Kennedy Space Center. We were still operating on Cape Canaveral, and we were operating on a very low budget. In those days, there were frequent missile failures, and many did not make it to the ocean. They crashed on land, and the Air Force gathered all the debris from these failed missiles and dumped them into what we called the "missile graveyard."

Our guys, especially Terry, would frequent this "missile graveyard," looking for any parts we could use primarily or in building test equipment. Terry visited the "missile graveyard" and did come up with a small light that we thought would do the job. We designed a circuit to feed power to the light and had our mechanics cut a hole in the skin of the rocket to mount the light. Via the telephone, we described to Dick what we came up with: the light and the associated circuitry and exactly where it would be mounted. He approved it verbally, and we installed the light, which we affectionately thereafter called the "Greenville light."

In today's world, there is no way you could do this job in

the time frame in which we did it. By the way, the light worked beautifully in flight, and the Huntsville people got their data and even wanted another one for the next flight. In today's world, you would have to start in Huntsville with a formal design change request and get it approved. Then the design people would design the circuit, select and order the parts, and being late in the processing flow, it would need the blessings of higher management. Hopefully you could get all this done to make not this flight, but the following flight. Being a little sarcastic, today you might even need the approval of the EPA.

Here's another example of how bureaucracy today adds cost and impedes productivity. In 2008, several of us old-timers decided to have a fiftieth-year celebration of the launch of Explorer 1, the free world's first artificial moon. Our plan included a visit to the old Blockhouse on Cape Canaveral. We needed the involvement of the Public Relations Office (PR) at KSC. We had several meetings, and we finally agreed on the type of visitor badge we needed for the honorees, original members of the launch team, and another badge for the guests of the honorees.

At the end of the meeting, the NASA PR lady said, "I will take this to NASA headquarters for approval and will let you know."

I was strictly dumbfounded. I said, "Do you mean you are taking to headquarters the approval of these guest badges?"

She looked at me, and I know she was thinking, *You dummy, do you think we could make a big decision like this here?* But she said, "Sure, we will have to take this to NASA headquarters."

I realized then that I was living in a different world.

I want to throw in a couple of other real life stories about how having a young workforce willing to take responsibility made it possible to get the "impossible" done.

In the activation of Complex 39 for the launch of the first Saturn V, there was a crisis every day, in every area, involving meeting the required schedule. One area behind schedule was the pad facilities for loading the cryogenics, oxygen, and hydrogen. Our guy, Bill Wheeler, oversaw the electrical facilities associated with this equipment, and he was working a team of Boeing engineers. It was getting late in the afternoon, and Bill told these people they had to stay and work until the job was finished.

Their leader told Bill they could only work until dark, because they didn't have facility lights out there yet.

"Don't you leave. I will take care of that," Bill said.

He got one of his younger engineers and a stepladder and got in one of our pickup trucks and went to the NASA headquarters building. This was after working hours for the headquarters people. Bill and his assistant took the ladder, went in the hallways of the headquarters building, and removed the emergency lights. He loaded his pickup with the lights and went back and told his Boeing counterpart to get his men to unload the lights and position them in the right place.

"We are going to finish this job tonight," Bill said.

That kind of "can do" attitude is how we did the "impossible." The next morning, I heard about this from Bill Chandler, Wheeler's boss, and I felt I had to pass this on to Dr. Gruene and Rocco Petrone just in case someone in the headquarters building complained. They both laughed. They, like me, liked this kind of get-the-job-done attitude.

This kind of enthusiasm was not unusual. In fact, it was quite common. I will use another example that also involved Bill Wheeler. We were in a countdown on a rocket at Blockhouse/Pad 56 when we experienced a relay failure in our ground equipment. As I mentioned previously, we were on a very tight budget and had few spare parts, so I told Bill to go over to Pad 26 and get a relay out of the Relay Box at 26 and replace the failed relay.

Bill walked out, and in a few seconds Karl Sendler burst into the control room where I was and started almost screaming about what one of my men had done. I had no clue what he was talking about. Karl was one of the Germans, and he was the head of our Telemetry Tracking Systems and the Vehicle Instrumentation Systems. In that stage in his life Karl was a little excitable. I did not know what to say to Karl, because as I just said, I had no clue what he was upset about.

This is what happened. When I told Bill to get the relay from the other Blockhouse, he dashed out. There were several government vehicles parked outside. Bill jumped in the first government car, backed up, turned around, and took off at a high rate of speed. This happened to be the government car assigned to Karl, who'd been standing nearby talking to some people. Karl ran over to try to stop the car, and by that time Bill had gotten turned around and was taking off at a high rate of speed, peppering Karl with gravel.

I never did know if Bill knew Karl was trying to stop him. I'm not sure if that would have made any difference. Bill's thinking was getting the job done regardless of any interference.

Later, I did apologize to Karl, and I would say Karl mellowed immensely during his later years. He made a special effort every month to attend our NASA retirees' breakfast at the Village Inn in Titusville, and Karl had to get up early and come from Satellite Beach.

Karl had admiration from all of us. He lovingly visited his wife daily and fed her when she was confined to a nursing home in her later years. Karl was well-off and had no children. When he passed away, he left his money to the National Seashore Park for educating children.

Another significant cultural change from the Apollo days to the present has to do with security. What are considered to be "normal" security measures today would have been considered totally abnormal in those Apollo days. I need to go into a little background on this. In that era, we were not concerned about terrorists. They had not made their big move at this time. Our concern was about sabotage from the Soviets. They had been successful in penetrating several departments in D.C. We were at the height of the Cold War, and we knew they would do anything possible to destroy our space capability and try to prevent us from landing men on the moon before they did.

In that light, NASA created a new security background check on key positions in our launch operations at KSC. The acronym for this program was APIP. I cannot recall what this acronym stood for, but basically, we were told to identify certain key positions where an employee could secretly and deliberately take some action to damage or destroy our rocket.

The grade level of an employee had nothing to do with the "key position" classification. In fact, the technicians who made the final closeout and were the last to leave the inside of the rocket were considered the most critical positions, because they could cut a wire, unplug a connector, and numerous other things that might not be detected for launch. I don't know what department the security people worked from, but they would do the background checks and just bring the raw data into our Security Office at KSC. Dr. Debus had a small panel to review this data and decide on any questionable employees.

The main findings that would cause some concern included someone obviously living above their means, someone deeply in debt (other than a typical mortgage), and get this, homosexuals. If you're living well above your means, you could be receiving funds from the enemy. If you are deeply in debt, you could be vulnerable to bribery. In that era, being homosexual was such a stigma, you could be blackmailed.

In Dr. Gruene's area we had 400 government employees and about 8,000 contractor employees. Only a limited number of these were in the key positions for potential sabotage, but we did have some traffic in this area. I remember we had one IBM middle manager who was a cross dresser. (At that time I didn't even know there was such a thing). We brought that to the attention of our IBM manager. This man, a good worker, was transferred to the IBM group in Huntsville. One of our Quality Control Inspectors was found to be making obscene calls to women. He was removed from pad operations to a rear office position.

Now this next story is not pretty. I am just recording what life was like back then. During this same time frame, we accidentally discovered one of our long-time employees who worked directly for me and visited our home many times in Cocoa Beach was a homosexual. I won't use his name, I will call him Mr. X.

His secretary told my secretary she needed to talk with me in private. She came into my office, visibly shaken, with some papers in her hand. This was back in the primitive times when we were still using typewriters. However, we did have a one-word processing machine that plays a part in this story. The secretary had made an error in typing and had taken the paper out of the typewriter and thrown it in the trash can. Moments later, she had a question about the page she had just thrown in the trash can. She reached down to retrieve it and picked up another piece of paper. When she looked at it, she was horrified, as it described homosexual orgies. She then went further in the trash can and pulled out several pages of the same shocking material.

I calmed her down and told her to try to act like nothing had happened. I went to Dr. Gruene, and we went to Rocco and Rocco called Charlie Buckley, head of our security, and Ben Hursey, head of our personnel department. The decision was made that we needed to talk to the Center director, who at that time was Lee Shearer. We had a meeting with Lee, and the result was that security would give me a master key to Mr. X's office and a master key to open all of his file cabinets and view the contents.

I was more shocked when I found the file cabinet full of horrible, obscene material describing in detail some of the orgies. One was in a professor's home at the University of Florida, and another involved a professor at Brevard junior college in Cocoa. To show how much our culture has changed since that time, when I revealed the findings in his file cabinets to this group, it was unanimous. He would be fired immediately.

They set it up in this manner. Mr. X would be called in the next day to our personnel office. Charlie Buckley from the security office would be there, and Mr. X would be told he was fired unless he resigned immediately. Security and personnel were kind to him, in that they gave him an opportunity to save face by resigning immediately. For her safety, we felt it mandatory that he never learn that his secretary was the one who exposed him. Security and personnel would tell him they discovered this through the security survey and that Dr. Gruene and I knew nothing about this. He was to tell us he just wanted to retire.

I mentioned above our first version of a word processing machine. We had it placed in a small room off the hallway, and there was nothing else in this room. I had noticed Mr. X was spending a lot of time with the door closed, and one day I asked him why. This was just a logical question, because at that time I had no inkling anything was amiss. In answer to my question, he said he just wanted to get familiar with this machine, and he thought we could maybe save some money by using it for our test procedures. This answer had satisfied me. Of course, his high usage of the word processing machine made sense now, as we realized he was the publisher of this group's newsletter.

As planned, Mr. X came in my office the next morning and he told me he needed to be out for a few minutes as he had to take care of some things in the personnel office. He had no idea why he was being called over to the personnel office, but of course, I knew what was going to happen. I was anxiously waiting to learn the results of this meeting.

I can't recall how long he was gone. It felt like forever. He eventually came back in and said, "Ike, this job is just getting too much for me, and I've just decided I have to retire."

This put me in an awkward position because normally I would say, "Are you sure you want to do this? Why don't you give it a little time and think about it? Don't make such a hasty decision."

Of course, I could not say that, and I'm not sure what I did say. I probably wished him the best in his retirement. He cleaned his desk out and was gone that day.

Over the next few days, I had to continually answer the question: Where is Mr. X? I think some people were a little suspicious of my answer. At that time, very few people were retiring. Mr. X did marry a little later in life and had one son, and the only time I saw him after he left was when I attended his wife's funeral several years ago.

Over the years there were some extraordinary events celebrating the launches of various special flights, and many former employees would attend. Mr. X never showed up at any of these events.

PROJECT HARDTACK—1958

In 1958, our small Missile Firing Lab (MFL) group was involved in a very heavy schedule. We had just successfully launched the free world's first Earth satellite and we had more scheduled launches for the Jupiter-C and the Jupiter IRBM for that year. We were still a part of the Army Ballistic Missile Agency (ABMA) at this time, and we were told we had another very significant project that had to be accomplished in 1958. The Department of Defense (DOD) needed data from a high-altitude atomic bomb explosion. The plan was to take part of our launch team to a remote island in the Central Pacific and launch two Redstone rockets with live atomic bombs. We had made some test flights from Cape Canaveral with the Redstone rocket and dummy atomic bombs.

They first talked of the Eniwetok Atoll and the Bikini Atoll in the Central Pacific as a launch site. These locations were disapproved by the Atomic Energy Commission because of the risk that a nighttime atomic explosion could possibly blind some of the natives on the nearby islands. To avoid this potential problem, they selected the remote Johnson Island. The nearest island to Johnson was over 500 miles away. Maybe I am a little biased, but I doubt if you could duplicate today what our small workforce did in response to this added workload in 1958. I do not think Dr. Debus or Dr. Gruene had any questions; they knew that with our "can-do" attitude we could maintain our current schedule at Cape Canaveral and then send a part of our team to

Johnson Island and launch two Redstone rockets.

That we did. Dr. Debus and Dr. Gruene explained the project and asked for volunteers. We were a relatively young bunch of eager troops at that time, and the response for a volunteer team was tremendous. The skill mix worked out perfectly. We had the right skills to do the job at Johnson Island and maintain our schedule at Cape Canaveral. I must confess I was not one of the young, eager volunteers. Dr. Gruene came to me and asked if I wanted to go on this project. Ever since I first heard of this project, I knew this question would be coming, so I had been thinking hard about it and my answer to Dr. Gruene was this: "I prefer not to go, but if you want me to go, I will go." His answer was, "That is fine. Let's see who else wants to go," and it turned out we had a couple of excellent guys, Carrol Rouse and John Twigg, that could go in my place.

I do not recall how much detail I went into with Dr. Gruene, but my decision not to go was based on a couple things. The war was still fresh on my mind, and our (4th Marine Division) first offensive engagement in 1943 was in the Marshall Islands in that general Central Pacific area of the Eniwetok and Bikini Atolls. This conversation with Dr. Gruene was prior to the selection of Johnson Island as the launch site. I was so grateful for coming out alive and well from the war, I just did not have any desire to return to any of those areas in that period of my life. I might inject here, you experience major changes in your thought process as you age. For example, at age 89 in 2012, when I had the opportunity to revisit Saipan, Tinian, and Iwo Jima, I eagerly accepted it. I cannot explain why your thoughts change like this, but they do.

Another factor was my family situation. Our oldest son, David, was three, our daughter Mona was a little over one, and our daughter Amy was due to be born any minute. Our youngest son, Scott, was not on the scene yet at this time. I did not want to leave Kathryn with our young family for an unknown period.

Dr. Debus took charge of the operations on Johnson Island and Dr. Gruene ran the operations here in Florida. The troops on Johnson Island did a super job launching two Redstones on schedule, although they did experience a flight problem on the first launch. Due to a problem in the stabilized platform system, the rocket went straight up and detonated at an altitude of approximately 77 km. This meant that the detonation was a couple thousand feet closer to the launch site than if the rocket followed its intended path. On the second launch the rocket followed its intended path and detonated at the proper altitude. As far as I know, the DOD did not lose any data from the straight up path on the first launch.

In my view, these launches were of tremendous importance; they gathered very significant data and, I might add, very frightening data. Let me explain—no question these were powerful explosions, but compared to the monster bombs in the inventory of some nations today they would be considered small.

Let's look at the results of these two explosions over Johnson Island. According to the reports from these explosions, there was a violent magnetic disturbance in the atmosphere. This resulted in a layer of fission debris in the upper atmosphere, which destroyed the ionized layers of the upper atmosphere, which prevented the ability to bend radio waves back to Earth, which made high-frequency circuits in a huge area in the Pacific totally ineffective. It cut off high-frequency communications for several hours for Australia and New Zealand, and in Honolulu military and civilian air traffic communications were disturbed for several hours.

I certainly do not claim to be an expert in this area, but consider this scenario: A rogue nation like North Korea, Iran, or some terrorist organization with an atomic bomb, or even with just a crude rocket that could send a missile over the US, explodes it at a high-altitude. It could totally disrupt our entire communication system, including civilian and military air traffic, and maybe our electrical grid. They would not even need an ICBM—just bring some ship a couple hundred miles offshore and launch a crude rocket. Heaven forbid. That is the reason we cannot ignore North Korea and Iran or any terrorist group that could potentially get this type of hardware. When these people get the capability, I'm afraid you can count on them to use it.

All of our guys that were involved in this Hardtack Project were very justified in feeling pride in what they had accomplished, and I think every one of them was glad they made this trip. All in a day's work!

SPACE BARBER SHOP

There was one significant contribution I made to our National Space Program that I never did get the proper recognition for, and it has really bothered me all through the years. Here is the story.

In the late 1950s, we were on a very, very busy schedule, working six and seven days a week. One of my greatest frustrations was I only had the opportunity for a haircut on Saturdays, and Saturdays were so busy at the local barbershop. I would have to wait a long time. Our missile operations at that time were on Cape Canaveral. This was prior to the creation of NASA and Merritt Island Wildlife Refuge and prior to the NASA causeway, so to get to work from Titusville, we went across the Max Brewer Bridge onto Playalinda Road to the north entrance of Cape Canaveral missile test sites. This was all sparsely inhabited private property, and the only commercial building was one little watering hole tavern, a very popular place for the guys after work, and a one-chair barbershop.

My friend, Bert Soloman, was the barber, and one Saturday when I was in for a haircut, Bert mentioned he would sure like to have a barbershop out on the Cape. I told Bert I thought that was a tremendous idea, and I would see what I could do about it. I was just a grunt at that time, and I really didn't have any real thoughts how to make this happen. But I thought that it was worth a try. So I talked to my boss, Dr. Hans Gruene, and he was not opposed. I think he had the same thought.

I thought he would take it up from there, but he told me to go talk to Kurt. Kurt was actually our director, Dr. Kurt Debus. Dr. Gruene was the only one in our organization who addressed him as Kurt. They had a long relationship dating back to the V-2 missile days in Germany. To the rest of us, he was Dr. Debus.

I was a little apprehensive about going to Dr. Debus with this, but I called his secretary, Shirley Ferguson, a good friend of mine, and she made an appointment for me to see Dr. Debus. I went in and told him my story about my frustrations on spending my off-time sitting in a barber shop. He related to that, because I think he, as well as Dr. Gruene, had experienced the same frustrations. He said, "Ike, go talk to Jim Deese and Speedy Parker."

Jim Deese was head of our facility, and Speedy was our Chief Administrative Officer. I first went to Jim Deese and told him my story and tried to word it so that he would know that this was something that Dr. Debus was interested in. His response was very positive. He immediately said that he had an empty office trailer available and that it would be perfect for this barber shop. Then I went to Speedy and told him Jim Deese had a place for a barber shop, and again implied this was something Dr. Debus was interested in.

"How can we get it approved?" I asked.

"Well, let me work on this," he said.

Neither he or Jim Deese raised the obvious question as to why did Dr. Debus send you, a test engineer, to set up a barber shop out here. The next thing I knew, Burt was happily cutting hair in this office trailer with a long line of customers. And that is not the end of the story. Later when NASA was created and we moved our operations to the Kennedy Space Center on Merritt Island, the large headquarters building included a nice, two-chair barber shop. That still is not the end of the story. After I retired, I learned that they also established a nice, two-chair barbershop in the VAB.

I am still disappointed that they did not name these the "Ike Barbershop." There should be a sign in each one that reads, "You should thank Ike Rigell that you are able to get a haircut during working hours."

I just want my family to know about this great achievement.

TRIP TO DENVER

In the late '50s, I cannot recall the exact year, the Martin company invited von Braun to come out to Denver and view a presentation on a new rocket they hoped to sell to the government. We were still with the Army Ballistic Missile Agency at that time. Von Braun took several of his lab directors and called Dr. Debus and requested he send a couple of guys to Denver to view this presentation from a launch processing viewpoint.

Dr. Debus sent me and Bob Gorman. At that time, Bob was the deputy to Albert Zeiler, head of our mechanical group. We joined von Braun and his team in this exercise, which lasted about two and a half days. Bob and I did not make return reservations because we did not know how long these presentations would last. They wrapped up about noon on Friday, so that morning, when Bob and I knew the presentations would be over, we had one of the Martin company secretaries work on our return reservations.

At the end of the last session, Bob and I and von Braun and his team were standing around talking. The Martin secretary, who was working on our return reservations, came up and told me and Bob we could not get out of Denver to go back to Orlando before Monday, which meant spending the weekend in Denver. I should note here that this was before Mickey Mouse had arrived in Orlando. Orlando was just a small country town in the citrus belt with a very dinky airport. Bob and I were a little teed off, but von Braun said he could take us to Huntsville on his plane if that would help us. Each NASA Center director had their own Gulfstream airplane. We gladly accepted his offer as we would much rather be in Huntsville than Denver.

Before I leave the Martin story, one interesting little tidbit: Our group was picked up at our hotel each morning by an airport-type mini-bus. The top Martin guy was in the vehicle on the last day with a couple of rifles. I do not remember if he was the president of the Denver facilities or not. When we arrived at the Martin facility, this top guy and von Braun left our group and we were told he was taking von Braun to shoot wild game. They both missed the morning sessions, but I assume the Martin folks figured it would be more effective to entertain von Braun on this hunting venture than for him to hear the remaining sessions.

Now, before I go any further on what happened when we arrived in Huntsville, I need to explain something. Our launch team in Florida had constant heavy traffic with people and materials from Huntsville, so we had a small residence office in Huntsville that was run by our good friend, Jim Cobb. Jim was a good old Southern country boy that grew up in Huntsville, and he was a perfect fit for this job. While his education level may not have been very high, his effectiveness was extremely high. Jim had a network of old friends in key places around Redstone that made it possible for him to get things done that more highly educated people could not. Bob and I called Jim and told him our story. Our conversation went like this:

"Jim, we have a problem, we are stranded in Denver, but we will be coming into Huntsville about midnight on von Braun's plane. Is there anything you could do to get us to Florida this weekend?"

Jim, in his slow Southern drawl, "What's your problem?"

Bob and I replied, "We just told you our problem; we would like to get to Florida this weekend."

Jim said, "Ain't no problem. You just get on that plane. I'll take care of you."

After we took off and the seatbelt sign went off, the flight crew broke out the refreshments, both food and drinks. Each center director had his own custom layout for the seating on his plane. Von Braun's plane had seats and sofas facing each other, and you could swing the seats to face the front so you could have a rectangular layout, perfect for conversations and conducting business. I thought perhaps von Braun would want to talk about the merits of the presentations we had just heard, but his troops, all of whom were Germans, did not let him get around to that. It was interesting for me and Bob just to sit there and observe this interaction between von Braun and his troops. They were taking their turns in hitting him up for more people, equipment, and facilities. Von Braun was younger than any of his people, but there was no question—he was their highly respected leader. Sometimes it was almost like a father talking to his children. I remember one comment he made to Willie Mrazek. "Willie, you know I always take care of all of you." Mrazek was head of manufacturing at Redstone. These guys were really taking advantage of a rare opportunity to have several hours of a one-on-one session with their leader.

I never did hear any more about the Martin rocket proposal, and thinking back I believe they were getting ready at Redstone to move into the Saturn 1B program, which involved much hands-on work and was a big step up from our Jupiter missile.

We landed at the Redstone Arsenal runway about midnight. It was winter and the weather was freezing. As we stepped off the plane, Jim Cobb was there to meet me and Bob Gorman. We were a little dumbfounded when Jim told us he had a plane waiting to take us to Patrick Air Force Base (PAFB). We knew Jim was good, but we did not realize he was that good. He took us into a small hangar, and in the corner of the hangar was a potbellied stove with several people trying to stay warm. Two of the people we could tell by their flight suits were obviously Army pilots. We took our place by the stove. I heard one pilot say to the other pilot, "I wonder what is in that box over there [pointing to a box on the floor] that has to be at the Cape in the morning?"

Here is the story behind that. Jim told the transportation office that there was a missile on the launch pad (which was true) and that the launch would be delayed (not exactly true) unless they got this spare part down to the launch site. Then he added, "Since you have to go to the Cape anyway, I have a couple of people here that we could send down and save the airfare." So, Gorman and I ended up arriving at PAFB before daylight, and there was an Army driver there to pick up that precious "piece of cargo" and give me and Gorman a ride home.

The world needs more Jim Cobbs, and I have the same question the Army pilot had. What was in that box that had to get to the Cape that morning?

Interesting week. No week—not one—was ever dull in my space career.

THE COLD WAR

I reference the Cold War several times in my writing as it played a large role not only on the world stage but also on our space exploration plans at NASA. Because I refer to it so often, I want to pause for a moment to talk about it in more detail here.

My generation is noted for winning WWII by defeating two major evil empires at the same time. To my knowledge, defeating two major opponents at the same time had never happened. At the conclusion of these horrible wars we enthusiastically looked forward to a peaceful future, but in the back of our minds there was a nagging but realistic concern: Are we going to have to fight the Russians? All indications were that they were hell-bent on spreading communism worldwide. As I have mentioned, immediately after the surrender of Japan we went into a massive disarmament mode. The Soviets did the opposite; they maintained a vast military force and, in some areas, such as ballistic missile development, they increased their military strength.

The Soviets first displayed their true intentions when they established the Berlin Blockade. At the Potsdam conference with Truman, Churchill, and Stalin, there was a signed agreement that Berlin, which was in East Germany, would be occupied by the Soviets and divided into four sections: US, British, French, and Soviet. They established three designated routes for the

Western Allies to access their sectors by Autobahn, rail, and air. But in 1948 the Soviets, without explanation, closed the Autobahn and the railroad access. They wanted the Western Allies out of Berlin and their method to get them out was starvation. The Allies responded by what history now calls the Berlin Airlift, a massive, almost unbelievable plan to supply the beleaguered Berliners with all of their necessities via the airlift. This was a 24-7 operation with cargo planes landing in Berlin every few minutes loaded with precious cargo. The Soviets maintained this blockade for over a year, and then out of the blue, with no announcement, they reopened the Autobahn and railroad to Berlin.

I am convinced that had we not been the only nation with atomic power, the Soviets would have overrun all of Western Europe. At that time, they had the military capability to do this. During the Berlin Airlift we sent a squadron of B-29 bombers to Berlin on what we called a training exercise. The Soviets got the message: *These bombers can carry atomic bombs*. We had demonstrated to the world in Japan that if the stakes were high enough, we had the courage to use these bombs.

Also, during this period the Soviets made their move to establish Greece as a Communist nation, which resulted in a fierce civil war in Greece from 1946 to 1949. World communism vs. capitalism was at stake. The war was now very *cold*.

In 1950 the Korean Peninsula became the next testbed for expanding communism. Communist North Korea, backed by their Communist masters, China and the Soviet Union, moved to capture and turn the capitalist nation of South Korea to communism. In a true sense, this was a battle between American capitalism and Soviet/Chinese communism. The North Koreans were fully armed and capable of going to war, whereas the South Koreans were woefully unprepared. Obviously, North Korea thought that the South Koreans were too weak to resist their invasion. We had troops stationed in South Korea at that time but in numbers inadequate to repulse the initial onslaught of North Koreans. One thought comes to mind at this point that I must express: I am convinced that in the Korean War, the Vietnam War, and the war in the Middle East, we had the very best military troops; but we did not win these wars because we held back and did not throw the "kitchen sink" at the enemy as we did in WWII. We were stupidly very nice people and had "rules of engagement," which I am convinced cost American lives.

I do not believe our later generations have been adequately educated on the perilous periods of the Cold War. After China swarmed across the North Korean border to attack our forces, there was consideration of using our atomic power against these monsters. This was another occasion that could easily have escalated into WWIII. Heaven forbid!

During the 1950s, there were uprisings in some of the Eastern European countries with Communist puppet governments, but these uprisings were quickly and brutally crushed by the Soviets.

THE PERSHING MISSILE SYSTEM

T he Pershing missile system was our last major project with the Army Ballistic Missile Agency (ABMA). Our first Pershing launch was February 25, 1960, and in July of that year we were officially transferred to the newly formed NASA; we completed our mission in the early development launches of the Pershing missile as NASA employees. The only noticeable change in our daily activities in going from ABMA to NASA was on the military side. With ABMA, much of our documentation was classified, and on the civilian side, with NASA, all documentation except for the missile destruct system (MDS) was unclassified. The only reason the MDS was classified was the fear of sabotage from the Soviets, who were always monitoring our launches from trawlers off the shore of Cape Canaveral. These trawlers were based in Communist Cuba.

I think a little historical background on the Pershing missile system would be helpful. In the late 1950s, the Soviets were stepping up their aggressive behavior in Eastern Europe. At the end of WWII, the Soviets had established puppet governments, loyal to Moscow, in all of the Eastern European countries they had overrun during the war. In a couple of these countries, like Hungary and Czechoslovakia, some opposition to this Soviet oppression surfaced, and the Soviets immediately sent in large numbers of troops to crush any uprising. This caused great concern in Washington, and the Department of Defense asked for more offensive capability as a primary deterrent to this Soviet aggression. We had the Redstones deployed in West Germany facing these countries, but we needed more offensive capability. We needed a faster response missile system with a greater range. The Soviets only respected strength, and, I might add, they haven't changed. Today they still only respect strength. History shows they will take advantage of any show of weakness.

The Department of Defense went to the ABMA, General Maderis, and Dr. Wernher von Braun to come up with a system to meet the requirements of developing a missile with a quick response capability and 500-mile range. For the ABMA to develop a 500-mile range rocket, they needed a waiver because of a big political debate a few years earlier about whether the Army or Air Force had the responsibility for long-range missiles. As I stated earlier, the Air Force had better lobbyists and the Army was limited to missiles of 200 miles or less. On the quick response capability, one big disadvantage of a missile like the Redstone was that it required time to load the oxygen and fuel, and to overcome that problem you went to a solid propellant rocket. Stick a match to it and it was gone pronto— no pressurizing tanks, no valves to operate, and no propellant pumps; all you needed, in simple terms, was a match.

Out of this DOD directive came the Pershing, named after our top military commander in Europe in WWI. Pershing was a two-stage, solid propellant rocket capable of delivering a nuclear payload over several hundred miles. The Martin Aircraft Company was awarded the contract for developing and delivering the Pershing missile. I think the headquarters for the Martin Company at that time was in Baltimore, Maryland, but they built a large manufacturing facility just outside of Orlando, so they had the great advantage of traveling only about 50 miles to the launch pad at Cape Canaveral. Dr. von Braun selected Dr. Hans Rudolph as the government program manager for this project. Dr. Rudolph did an excellent job on this project, and I will mention more about him later.

In our initial working relationships with the Martin Company, we encountered some head-on conflicts, the same as we would encounter later in the Apollo program. Looking back now, I see one significant difference in working with the Martin Company as compared with our experience with our future contractors, Rockwell, McDonnell Douglas, Boeing Company, and IBM. With the latter companies, after some initial rough encounters we ended up with an excellent relationship and a very strong team environment, which we never achieved in our relationship with the Martin Company. Maybe if we had continued in the Pershing program we would have developed this contractor/government team spirit, but we pulled out of this program early.

Blockhouse 30 on Cape Canaveral was built especially for the Pershing missile, and we had this blockhouse built as a mirror image of our blockhouses, 26 and 56—one blockhouse serving two pads. I, along with a number of our troops, made trips to the new Martin factory in Orlando for design reviews and working out the future launch schedules. We got along better at the working levels than at the top management levels. Dr. Debus and Dr. Gruene had to strongly confront their top-level management on a number of occasions. I never saw Dr. Gruene as angry as he was one night in a countdown in Blockhouse 30, when the countdown was delayed by the Martin Company to get a piece of paper signed that did not mean anything.

The head of the Martin Company launch team, Stan Welch, was a neighbor, living just around the corner from us. Kathryn was a friend of Stan's wife. We were good neighbors and would meet socially on occasion. We were good neighbors because Stan and I never discussed business outside of work. Stan just could never adjust to our way of doing business, and I did not feel I would be doing my job properly if we were not doing business as we were. In plain language, Stan had a real problem accepting close government direction and supervision, but that was the way we worked; someone must give and it ain't us.

Maybe I need to clarify something here. On the Redstone, Mercury Redstone, Jupiter-C, and the Jupiter missile, we government employees did all of the hands-on work at the launch site. In Huntsville, the government employees designed and built all the ground control equipment and flight hardware. Chrysler did have the production contract for the delivery of the Redstone and Jupiter missiles to the military, and we did have

Chrysler as a launch support contractor in the latter stages of the Redstone and Jupiter programs, but we always maintained tight control over all facets of the operations. Many of the electronic systems in the early Pershing models were designed and built in Huntsville, like the stabilized platform and the destruct system, and that meant these systems were designed and the qualification tests were performed by our people, who had more knowledge of this hardware than the Martin people.

You should never be surprised at what strange things can happen in a routine workday. Here is my one and only example of that from our days in the Pershing program. This just proves the validity of Murphy's law: If it can happen, it will happen.

We were running a major test and, suddenly, all the lights on the consoles went out, and on the intercom the troops out at the pad were calling in, "What happened?" Those of us in the control room could not give an answer because we did not know what had happened. I cannot remember all the minute details of how we pinpointed the cause of the problem, but here is what happened: One of the Martin guys was sweeping the floor in one of the back rooms where the control cables were strung out on the floor, and he was having trouble sweeping his trash across the room. A large cable was in the way, and it so happened that this was where two links of cables were connected. To clear the path for his trash, he unscrewed the collar on this cable connector, separated the cable, swept his trash across the floor, and reconnected the cable.

He solved his problem, but he created a big problem for us test engineers. As I said, I don't recall exactly how it was determined what this guy did, but, as best I recall, he innocently did this and really did not think he had done anything wrong. The Martin Company was going to fire him, and Dr. Debus found out about it and put a stop to it. I feel confident this guy never, ever disconnected a cable to sweep his trash across the room again.

I'm proud and feel good about our participation in the early development of this important Pershing missile system. Later, after we were out of the program, there were several improved versions of the Pershing, including mobile launch platforms, and it was a primary deterrent for a number of years in the standoff with the Soviets in Europe.

MONKEY BUSINESS

One beautiful and rewarding thing about a career in space exploration is that we are always expanding our knowledge about man and the universe he lives in. Prior to the late 1950s, we knew almost nothing about how man could survive and perform useful operations in a weightless environment. Today, we have a wealth of information on the subject; back then, we were clueless but ready to take our first feeble steps to explore this area. That is when our small launch team got involved in the "monkey business."

Several primates had been flown in very short suborbital flights, including one in a V-2 in White Sands, New Mexico, in 1948. Now that we were coming up to a real manned flight in space in the near future, there was increased desire to understand how man could and would react in this environment, so several longer-ranged suborbital flights with the monkeys were scheduled. As I recall, the first primate launch our team was involved in was Jupiter AM-13 in December 1958. I should add that 1958 was a banner year for our little team. We started the year by launching Explorer 1, the free world's first satellite. Our first live passenger on one of our rockets was Gordo. Gordo was a small squirrel monkey and he survived his 1,500-mile downrange journey and performed his task well in flight. Sadly, he did not survive the reentry as the parachute system malfunctioned.

I would say having a monkey on board one of our rockets added a little extra excitement to our job, but we had no direct involvement with our monkey passengers. Our job was just to get them safely from the launch site to the recovery area.

Our next flight involving monkeys occurred in May 1959, when we launched Able and Miss Baker on a Jupiter rocket. This again was a successful 1,500-mile downrange flight and reached a height of 300 miles. Both Able and Miss Baker were successfully recovered. A sad note on Able—he died just a few days after the launch from the anesthesia used in removing the in-flight electrodes. On the other hand, Miss Baker had a long and happy life. She spent her later years as a favorite attraction at the US Space and Rocket Center in Huntsville, Alabama, and I think they have a marked grave at the Center for her. Able and Miss Baker received much media attention, and they were on the cover of Life Magazine, the number one magazine in that era. Although it was a sad event, I don't recall any negative outcry about Able's death. PETA must not have been around at that time, or we would have had the streets full of protesters and business windows smashed.

We did have some other scientific experiments on this Jupiter AM-18 flight. Seeds of various kinds and samples of human blood were used to determine what effect a weightless environment would have on them. A little speculation here . . . Hurricane Irma passed through our area in 2017, and I read in the local paper that a tree at KSC had been blown over, and this tree was from a seed that had been flown into space from one of our early missile launches. Could it have been a seed from the flight with Able and Miss Baker?

The last flight with a monkey passenger, Ham, was on a Redstone rocket, labeled MR-2 in January 1961. There were some in-flight problems; the rocket reached a higher apogee and speed and landed further downrange than planned. However, the data showed Ham performed well in flight and he was successfully recovered. These monkeys that flew in space were carefully trained and selected from a group of like monkeys. In one exercise they were trained to operate a certain lever in a few seconds when they saw a light flash or they would get a mild electrical shock; if they responded correctly, they would get a special "goodie treat." Ham demonstrated he could do this with no problem in a weightless environment and went on to live a long life at the Smithsonian's National Zoo in Washington, DC.

I do not know what all was learned from the monkey flights in regards to launching a man in space, but apparently it was all positive since just five months later, on May 5, 1961, we launched our first man in space, Alan Shepard, on Freedom 7.

All of our monkey flights were from blockhouses 26 and 56 on Cape Canaveral, and the space couch for Miss Baker is displayed in the Space Museum in Blockhouse 26.

I will take the liberty to give thanks, from all of our launch team, to Gordo, Able, Miss Baker and Ham for their contributions to our space program.

FREEDOM 7—THE WORLD'S FIRST MANNED LAUNCH

A ir Force Eastern Missile Test Range, Blockhouse 56, May 5, 1961—9:34 AM, T minus 0—Liftoff.

For a few dozen of us veteran space pioneers in Blockhouse 56, the tension could not have been greater. The media said we had a worldwide audience of 45 million, a record at that time. Keep this moment frozen in your memory and I'll explain why, in my view, this was one of the most momentous events in our history of space.

At the moment of liftoff, we anxiously peered out the narrow glass window observing a beautiful sight: Mercury Redstone 3 with the spacecraft Freedom 7 and its passenger, astronaut Alan Shepard, on his way to a 15-minute suborbital flight with an apogee of 101 nautical miles and 263 nautical miles downrange. The free world's first manned flight. Why was the tension so high when this small group of men had launched many of these Redstone rockets and other rockets larger than the Redstone? The stakes could not have been higher. Not only was this our first launch with a man aboard, but we were also in the middle of the Cold War.

About three weeks earlier, on April 12, the Soviets launched the world's first man, cosmonaut Yuri Gagarin, in one orbit around Earth. They used a rocket booster with a lift capacity well beyond anything we had. Accolades and congratulations poured into Moscow from all over the world; it was completely embarrassing, and our morale suffered greatly. Here we were, the greatest and most advanced nation the world had ever known, and this rogue Communist country had achieved something that that we had not been able to do, and they forever will be recorded in history as the first nation to accomplish this amazing feat. This was even more embarrassing than when they beat us in launching the first artificial moon, Sputnik, in October 1957. Then, two months later, in December 1957, we were again terribly humiliated when our little Vanguard missile with its grapefruit-size payload crashed and exploded at liftoff. From our experience, we had great confidence in our Redstone booster, but, remember, we experienced an embarrassing failure on our first Mercury Redstone MR-1 spacecraft launch just five months prior in November 1960.

Unfortunately, the MR-1 was a major failure and very embarrassing. At liftoff the rocket engine was operating at full thrust, and after the booster had cleared the launch pedestal about three or four inches the cutoff relay in the rocket energized and shut the engine down. The booster settled back down on the launch pedestal and remained upright. When the booster settled back down, some of the control cables in the rocket partially mated with the ground control cables, but the pins were not aligned properly and we were getting crazy indications on our control panel meters, recorders, and lights. Nothing made sense, and we had no clue what was going on. We were helpless. We had a fully loaded missile on the launch table with no control capability and no way to monitor critical components in the rocket.

When the onboard missile cutoff relay was erroneously energized, it appeared to the electrical network system rocket that we were in a normal flight mode and the fuel level was low enough to trigger the cutoff relay. The next normal event was a signal to ignite the escape rocket motor and, when that occurred, it then appeared to the parachute-release sensors that things were normal and now we were below the 10,000-foot parachute release point, so the drogue chute popped out, followed by the main parachute, which, of course, remained attached to the spacecraft. The main parachute hanging on the side of the rocket posed a potential problem; if the wind increased, the parachute could open enough to pull the rocket over, resulting in an explosion.

As I stated, we had no control over any of the components in the rocket. The lox tank was pressurized, so we had to depend on the proper operation of the vent valve to avoid an overpressure in the lox tank. Also, our destruct system on the rocket was armed and we had no control over that. The only way we could get a safe rocket was for the lox tank vent valve to continue operating properly until the tank was empty, and then for the batteries to die down so we could save the pyrotechnics.

I cannot recall exactly, but I think it was two or three days later that we were finally satisfied that we had positively identified the problem that caused the premature cutoff relay to be energized. Immediately we zeroed in on the separation sequence of the individual pins where the ground control cables mated with the flight control cables at the base of the rocket. The technicians had experienced some difficulty in making the original connections, whereas normally this was not a problem area. It turned out one of the cables was defective. In the manufacturing process, after the pins in the connector are connected to the wires in the cable, the connector assembly is potted, which means a liquid solution is poured into this area making the cable connector waterproof and securely holding the insert in place. On this cable, the connector insert was very slightly cocked, and when the liquid potting compound was poured into the connector, it solidified, holding the connector insert in this slightly cocked position relative to a parallel plane. It was so slight that with a casual view it would not be noticeable. The technicians attempted to compensate for this problem by shaving some metal off the connector brackets holding the ground cables mated to the missile cables for liftoff.

I will skip to the result of this problem. When the rocket left the launch pedestal, the ground wire in the connector separated milliseconds before some of the control wires in the connector, and one of the control wires in the missile with a positive potential sought a path to ground. In this millisecond, it found a path to ground through our ground relay box, located in a small room underneath the launch pedestal, and then back to the cutoff relay in the missile through one of those control wires that had not yet completely disconnected.

We had several guys in our group, Bill Chandler, Frank Bryan, Terry Greenville, and Ted Oglesby, who were very familiar with these circuits, and I was as knowledgeable as anyone. During this time, I made a previously scheduled trip to Huntsville and took a set of the electrical network schematics of the system with me and met with our design counterparts in Huntsville. We had been in constant communication with them for the past several days. I'm talking about two key guys, Dick Smith, head of the electrical networks design group (and director at KSC years later), and his counterpart, Bob Aden, head of the ground networks design group. We all agreed on the cause of the problem, and I called Dr. Gruene to let him know we all agreed. He asked me to get in touch with Dr. Debus, who happened to be in Huntsville on another mission at the same time. I contacted Dr. Debus and he accepted our rationale. I have mentioned before that you always learn more from your failures than your successes, and here we learned a valuable lesson. For every rocket we launched after this, we had a ground strap that followed the rocket from liftoff for about 12 inches to make sure we would never experience a premature ground connection at liftoff. Who knows? Maybe we avoided a much greater catastrophe later.

I think it is appropriate here to repeat something else I said earlier: When you examine the flight records of all of our failures, you find that many of them, like on this occasion, were almost successful—but a few milliseconds made the difference between total success and total failure. Likewise, in examining the data from totally successful flights, you can find cases where we were within a few milliseconds of a total disaster. In the rocket business, the margin between success and failure is often very narrow.

We had another in-flight problem on MR-2 that I mentioned earlier on Ham's monkey flight. In fact, after that problem on MR-2, Dr. von Braun wanted another development flight before the manned MR-3 flight. I won't go into any more detail on that MR-2 flight problem, and the purpose of talking about these problems prior to the first manned launch is to emphasize that we were in no condition to experience another failure.

Going back to my first statement above, the future of our space program depended on what happened in the 15 minutes after 9:34 AM, May 5, 1961. Just a short three weeks later, on May 25, 1961, President Kennedy would make his historic speech announcing that we would go to the moon, land a man on the moon, and return safely to Earth in this decade. I don't like to go there, but think of the unthinkable. If we had experienced a severe problem in our launch of MR-3 on May 5th and could not even successfully launch a man in a suborbital flight, do you think President Kennedy could have talked about going to the moon?

I want to go back and talk about the early history of the Mercury Redstone program. NASA originally chartered Project Mercury in October 1957; it is interesting to note that was the same month in 1958 that the Soviets launched Sputnik. NASA went to Dr. von Braun (I think we were still with the Army at that time) to provide Redstone rockets for some suborbital manned flights. This project took on the name of Mercury Redstone, and this was when the astronauts were first introduced in our space program. In April 1959, the seven original astronauts were introduced to the public. There was much excitement about this, and they immediately became national heroes. This was before Houston was Houston. Spacecraft Operations were at NASA in Langley, Virginia, and Booster Operations were assigned to MSFC in Huntsville, Alabama.

They established some very rigid requirements, and I think rightly so, for this new breed of astronauts. Some of the basic requirements were that they must be a military fighter pilot with so many flight hours—I do not recall exactly how many—and they were limited by height and weight. It was a different cultural environment in that era, and I do not think anyone was surprised or upset that there were no females or minorities in this group. Of course, we know today those requirements would have been modified and many females and minorities would have had the opportunity to make a name for themselves as astronauts.

There were four Redstone Mercury development flights leading up to the MR-3 flight on May 5, 1961. MR-1, with its disastrous "four-inch flight," was not a good start. MR-1A we launched a month later on December 19, 1960, and it was a successful flight. MR-2 we launched on January 31, 1961, and it was a qualified success. "Chimpnaut" Ham went in the space history books on this flight, but we did experience a problem in flight as I described earlier. Because of this problem, Dr. von Braun wanted another development flight. It was called MR-BD and was launched successfully on March 24, 1961.

This brings us to the preparations for our first manned launch, MR-3, scheduled for May 2, 1961. There was much speculation about which one of the seven astronauts would be the first to fly. I think it was two or three months before the flight that Dr. Gilruth, head of Spacecraft Operations, announced it would be one of three: Glenn, Grissom, or Shepard. It turned out to be Alan Shepard, but I am convinced any one of them could have done the job.

Having a human being on the top of a rocket, with all of that stored energy, adds another dimension in your daily operations. I do not know exactly how to describe it. I remember one comment made from a friend during this time, he said, "With a man on board, I guess you work harder." I replied that I could not say that, for that would mean I was not working as hard as I could on unmanned launches, and I just could not say that. I think the best way to describe how having a man on board influenced my daily work activities would be that, for any problem or issue that came to my attention, my position was, "How would I resolve this problem if I were sitting on top of this rocket?"

I do not recall any major issues in the launch preparations for MR-3. The first launch attempt was scheduled for May 2, 1961, and due to weather problems we had to reschedule for May 5, 1961. We started the countdown late in the evening on May 4th for a scheduled liftoff at 7:20 AM. As I recall, I tried to get some sleep the day before the countdown, but I had a tough time, and I went in early that evening for the countdown. I followed my normal pattern. On my way to the Cape, I went by St. Gabriel's Episcopal Church for prayer. I have mentioned that in those days the crime was not anything like it is today, and the church doors were always open for prayer and meditation. This was in pre-NASA-Causeway/Bridge days, so from the church I would take Playalinda Beach Road over the Max Brewer bridge, and at the beach the road parallels the beach to the north entrance of the Air Force missile test range. This journey took about 45 minutes, and my mind was consumed with thoughts of what the day would bring and if there was anything we should have done that we did not do. This was going to be a big day in my life.

We experienced several problems during the countdown, which resulted in a little over a two-hour delay of the launch. The first issue was the weather as it was necessary to have a cloudless sky for this launch. Then we had a malfunction in our 400-cycle power supply for our stabilized platform. We successfully replaced this unit and were back in normal operations. Then there was a hold for the Goddard Space Flight Center to correct a computer problem. I don't recall what their involvement in this launch was as we never interfaced with them on any of our test operations.

Our rocket launch team was not aware of this event during the countdown, but we learned later that, during that long hold period, Shepard had a severe urge to urinate and had a bad case of "wanting to go." Remember, he had been in the space capsule for several hours and, due to the short nature of the flight (only 15 minutes), they had not equipped his space suit with a urine collection system. The Spacecraft officials refused, due to the lengthy time required to attach and reattach the white room and open the hatch to the spacecraft to allow Shepard to come out to urinate. He told them he would just urinate in his flight suit and they said no, that would short out some of the electrodes in his flight suit. He told them to turn the power off and they did and he urinated. I guess when nature calls you must respond.

Back to the launch, on May 5, 1961, at 9:34 AM EST, tension vanished. We were euphoric. What a beautiful sight it was as we watched through that narrow-slit window our beautiful rocket lifting off the launch pedestal and ascending into the blue sky. At that moment I sort of envied what we call our "fall back crew"— these guys are the last to leave the rocket at the pad, and they retreat to a safe distance to watch the rocket or be called back in case of a problem. They are the closest observers of the flight.

In the control room we followed the flight performance by two methods. First, I was in contact over our internet with my good friend Jim Rorex, who was in our telemetry station in Hangar D, about three miles back in our industrial area. Jim was watching, in real time, several key data points in our guidance and control system. On a good flight, Jim kept a constant message on this internet—"looking good, looking good, looking good"—and I repeated Jim's words to the guys surrounding me in the control room. Our second data point was from our DOVAP tracking system. This was a real-time tracking system developed by Karl Sandler and Jim White and their team. They had a receiver in the back room of our blockhouse and it sent an audible signal on the velocity of our rocket in flight. As the velocity of the rocket increased, the frequency of the tracking signal increased until engine shutdown, and then, of course, the signal went to zero. We knew the time of the anticipated engine cut off, so we could immediately determine if we had a normal flight.

It was a beautiful, good flight, and Shepard was recovered without any problem. The cigars, high-fives, and smiles were in abundance. I like to relive those moments. There are few other jobs where you can enjoy these mountaintop experiences. I believe, and I think my colleagues share this belief, that moments like this make up for all the blood, sweat, and tears required to achieve what I would call a victory.

Now let me go back to the significance of this flight. Let me start with the old Chinese proverb, "The journey of a thousand miles starts with the first step." In this case, it would be a journey of 240,000 miles to the moon, and we had just taken the first micro-step of 101 nautical miles.

Our next step in this 240,000-mile journey to the moon was July 21, 1961, when we launched MR-4 with astronaut Gus Grissom. His flight was successful and reached an apogee of 102 nautical miles. Using higher mathematics, you can see from Shepard's flight on May 5th, with an apogee of 101, we made one more micro-advancement of 1 nautical mile toward our goal of 240,000. Our next step on this journey was February 20, 1962, when our first astronaut to orbit Earth, John Glenn, was successfully launched on a Mercury Atlas. His apogee was 261 nautical miles, so this was a big step forward.

NASA top management laid out a brilliant plan to achieve our goal of sending men to the moon and returning them safely within the decade. John Glenn's flight on the Mercury Atlas was followed by several more Mercury Atlas flights, followed by the Gemini program, which was our first two-man flight (*Gemini* means "twins"). Our launch team was not involved in the Atlas or Gemini programs. The Gemini launched on the Titian missile.

The Titian and Atlas were provided by the Air Force and were originally designed and deployed as intercontinental ballistic missiles (ICBMs). Parallel to these flights, we made progress in the Apollo program by launching the command service module (CSM), command (CM), and luna module (LM) in low-orbit test flights. These Apollo spacecraft units were placed in Earth orbit by our S-1B booster launched from pads 34 and 37 on Cape Canaveral. All our flights thus far had been limited to low Earth orbit, between 200 and 300 nautical miles.

I do not think any of us in that primitive little launch control center at Blockhouse 56 that day, May 5, 1961, could have envisioned that in a short seven years and seven months, December 21, 1968, we would be celebrating, in a totally different environment, our next great step toward reaching our goal, 240,000 miles away in the heavenly sky. I describe those events in the Apollo 8 chapter.

I want to provide a brief comparison of the progress from 1961 to 1968. The launch control room at Complex 39 was about 40 times larger than our little control room in Blockhouse 56. In fact, our computer room at Complex 39 was several times larger than our launch control room at 56. The launch pad at Complex 39 was 3.5 miles from the launch control center, whereas Blockhouse 56 was just a few hundred feet. The Saturn V rocket was 350 feet high and 33 feet in diameter compared to MR-3, which was 70 feet high and 5 feet in diameter. Saturn V had 7,500,000 pounds of thrust and the MR-3 had 78,000 pounds of thrust. The increase in size of the Saturn V launch team and in the documentation required for Saturn V compared to Mercury Redstone was truly staggering.

A few words about the astronauts on MR-3 and MR-4: Shepard developed an ear disease and was grounded until he had an operation to correct this problem. He was later the commander of Apollo 14 to the moon, which was a very successful flight. He hit a golf ball on the moon.

Sadly, very sadly, we lost Gus Grissom in the tragic fire in Apollo 1. I will cover that more later on. I want to offer my comments related to risk and danger concerning spaceflights. Astronauts are smart people, they fully understand the risk involved, and they are willing to accept these risks. Any time you are involved in expanding into a new and unknown frontier, you are accepting whatever potential risks may be encountered. That was true with people like Columbus, Marco Polo, and the pioneers who settled the West, and I think you could apply this to the men and women that sign up for the military, police departments and fire departments. They fully understand and accept that in the performance of their duty, their lives can be at risk.

May 5, 1961—Cape Canaveral Blockhouse 26. The free world's first manned flight. Alan Shepard was the astronaut aboard.

CUBAN MISSILE CRISIS

In October 1962, the world came to the very brink of Armageddon. Everyone should read about the Cuban Missile Crisis; this event will remind you of what a dangerous world we live in. To understand and appreciate the gravity of this situation, you must understand the world conditions at that time.

Late in 1959, Fidel Castro led a revolutionary force that overthrew the government in Cuba. World leaders at that time did not foresee that Castro would take over as a brutal communist dictator. There were two superpowers in the world directly opposing each other then: the old Soviet Union and the U.S. At the end of WWII the Soviet Union maintained their enormous military force. We greatly reduced ours and converted our vast wartime industrial complex into manufacturing automotive, household appliances, and other goods to advance the standard of living. The entire Soviet budget was consumed by the military and the space program, which were often strictly military weapons.

During the 1950's, the U.S. and the Soviet Union were in a desperate race to achieve superiority in missiles capable of delivery of nuclear warheads. By the early 1960's, both sides had developed a vast array of missiles capable of delivering nuclear warheads. It was obvious that to be the No. 1 superpower, you must be No. 1 in space. There was no defense against a ballistic missile. The V-2 missile launched against England in WWII demonstrated that fact.

Our little missile team (von Braun team) made significant contributions to our capability by developing the Redstone, Pershing, and Jupiter missiles. I will document the significant part our Jupiter missiles played in the Cuban missile standoff in a moment. For now, back to the old Soviet communist system.

As stated earlier, the Soviet government had no concern about the welfare of its citizens. At the time of the Cuban missile crisis, the Soviet Union was ruled by Khrushchev, a hardline dictator. The communist doctrine was and still is that communists would rule the world. On one occasion, at a United Nations meeting in New York, Khrushchev took off one of his shoes and banged the table and shouted, "Your grandchildren will live under communism."

Kathryn and I made a trip to the Soviet Union in 1982 and I recall one of our guides, a young lady, giving us a standard communist propaganda lecture. We were in a room where one entire wall was a map of the world, and there was a world map with a red pin on all Communist countries. She let us know that their goal was to someday have a red pin on every country in the world, and, of course, that would include us. She was especially proud to point out they had a red flag just ninety miles off the coast of Florida in Cuba.

Now, we go back to 1962. Kennedy was our president at that time. He was strongly opposed to Castro, and we supported some unsuccessful attempts to have Castro removed. Castro was strongly supported by Khrushchev, and Khrushchev welcomed Castro's offer for the Soviets to set up missile bases and bombers, both armed with nuclear warheads in Cuba. Our spy planes and flights over Cuba revealed this activity. This was the start of the Cuban Missile Crisis.

Khrushchev had sized up Kennedy as weak. He did not think he would take any direct action to oppose placing these weapons in Cuba. Our United Nations ambassador, Stevenson, took this issue to the UN. The Soviet ambassador denied the Soviets had missiles in Cuba. Then Stevenson pulled out very clear pictures of the Soviet missiles that proved the Soviet officer was a liar.

These pictures were from our spy planes. Unfortunately during this standoff, the Soviets shot down one of our spy planes and killed our pilot.

Over the next thirteen days, Kennedy and his advisors were in constant serious discussions. There were some direct communications between Khrushchev and Kennedy and some messages through third parties. Some of these messages were contradictive to some earlier messages, and no one knew what would happen next. The tension could not have been greater. Kennedy's message to Khrushchev was that if he did not remove the missiles and bombers from Cuba, we would invade Cuba and destroy them. Our intelligence learned there were more Soviet ships on the way to Cuba with more missiles, and aerial photos were released to the public confirming this.

Kennedy issued an order for our Navy to establish a quarantine around Cuba. He was careful to call it a quarantine rather than a blockade, because a blockade means we are at war. It was obvious Khrushchev had misjudged Kennedy. Kennedy meant what he said. For example, we in Titusville could plainly see the coming invasion. This was before we had I-95 in Brevard County; US-1 had daily military convoys traveling through downtown Titusville headed south to their embarkation ports for the coming invasion.

Our Navy would stop and search all ships headed for Cuba, and no missile or bomber could proceed. No one knew what was going to happen when our Navy encountered these ships carrying missiles/bombers. Would someone give the order to some trigger-happy Soviet officer in Cuba to pull the trigger and launch a missile? Are we about to experience a holocaust?

I want to say something about what is going on in the mind of ordinary people like myself as you watch these events unfold. With a wife and small children ages two, four, five, and seven, what do you do? Do you build some kind of bomb shelter in your back yard? It enters your mind. Some people did build some kind of a shelter. One significant point about building a shelter to survive an atomic bomb attack is the fact that a survivor in the range of an atomic blast would envy the dead due to horrible radiation burns. During this crisis period, it was hard to keep focused on your work. You are anxiously trying to follow the current news, hoping for some positive indication, no matter how small, of a peaceful solution.

We had a missile on the launch pad undergoing pre-launch procedures at complex 34. We had a couple of old black and white TV monitors in the Blockhouse, and we'd be glued to them when the Soviet ships with missiles encountered our Navy. We had to temporarily stop our test operations. Our planes were streaming live shots of the ships as they headed toward Cuba.

I am not capable of describing the sense of satisfaction, joy, relief, and answered prayers we felt when we saw the Soviet ships slowly making a U-turn and heading back east. The U-shaped wake of those ships was beautiful. They are as clear in my mind today as they were in 1962—fifty-five years ago. Praise our Lord, the Earth could now breathe again.

After all the communications confusion, the final agreement was that Khrushchev would remove the missiles and bombers if Kennedy would not invade Cuba. Kennedy also agreed to remove our Jupiter missiles in Turkey on the Russian border. For some reason I never understood, Kennedy demanded the removal of our Jupiter missiles not be made public. This policy was adhered to, and it was only learned much later that it was part of the agreement.

One final note to this story: Both sides at this time had enough missiles and bombers to obliterate each country several times over.

In 1985, Mikhail Gorbachev became the leader of the Soviet Union. President Reagan and President Gorbachev held five sessions during the late 1980s. There was an intense rivalry between the United States' allies and the Soviet Union's allies as to which system, capitalism or communism, would dominate. President Reagan had made significant progress in strengthening our military forces during his tenure in office.

He knew he could only negotiate with the Soviet Union from a position of strength and not reveal any weakness. Gorbachev was smart enough to understand he could not match our economic strength, which caused him to abandon many of the old Communist rules and regulations, and he hoped to improve Soviet economic conditions by moving more to our free market system. The Cold War finally ended in 1991 when Gorbachev introduced the policies of glasnost and perestroika, ultimately bringing about the collapse of the Soviet Union. Glasnost means openness and transparency—so, more freedom of religion and the media and other related social issues. Perestroika means restructuring, resulting in profound changes in economics, allowing some free market activities and voting rights to elect a president, and withdrawing their puppet government control of the surrounding Eastern European countries. While he was fiercely opposed by many of the old Communist gurus, his ideas won out, and in 1991 the Russians had their first elected president, Boris Yeltsin.

I cannot make this statement any stronger: It is imperative that we reach and maintain our position as the most powerful nation in the world and we negotiate from a position of power. I would add to this that our "word" must have meaning. What I mean by this is to be careful of what you say, but be willing to back up what you say with action. Now, what you have just read is history; we cannot change it, but we can change how we deal with these situations in the future, and I can assure you they will be coming. The purpose in writing this is to encourage everyone to be very careful whom you elect for public office.

APOLLO

May 25, 1961 was a great day in my life. President Kennedy stood before Congress on that day and made an awesome speech.

"This nation should commit itself to achieving the goal of placing men on the moon and returning them safely to the Earth in this decade," he proposed.

For those few of us who were in the space business at that time, you could not ask for a better statement. This was truly a historical moment, and I think you could say it kept alive that American spirit of pioneering new frontiers. Putting men on the moon and returning them safely to planet Earth has to be the number one technical event in the history of mankind. I cannot describe how blessed I have been just to have had the privilege of being a part of this great American achievement.

The only project that I can think of that even comes close to this event would be the Manhattan Project, which developed the first atomic bomb during WWII. There were some key similarities in that both organizations were created and operated by a very young workforce, and both had minimum government interference with very capable leadership at the top.

I have an interesting little story of how a few of us had advance information about this huge announcement. One day, Dr. Debus called several of us into his conference room and announced he had something to tell us. He emphatically stated, "What you hear in this room stays in this room." From his tone of voice, and just knowing his character, you could not imagine anyone in the room would ever think about violating his command. Dr. Debus started to talk, but he was immediately interrupted by one of the guys in our group. I will just use his first name: Jim. Jim was a big, gruff man with an explosive temper, who always said exactly what he was thinking, no matter what environment he was in. Jim was one of the original guys in the Missile Firing Lab (MFL), and when he was not angry he was a pretty nice guy.

It doesn't relate to this story, but here is a little background on Jim. He was a Marine on Saipan the same time I was, and he was badly wounded there. He spent months recovering in a naval hospital. I did not know this until years later when we were having lunch after our retirement. In those earlier years, we never mentioned our war experiences.

Now back to the story. Jim interrupted Dr. Debus by saying, "Dr. Debus, you can't start now," and Dr. Debus said, "Why not?"

Jim replied, "Because she is still here," pointing to Dr. Debus' secretary, Billie Fitzgerald, and saying, "You know women can't keep a secret." You could observe Dr. Debus was very annoyed, and he said very firmly, "She stays," and then he continued with his message, which was giving us advance notice of this bold announcement by President Kennedy.

I give this little story to convey how much our culture has changed since that time. Back then, the only women in our workforce were secretaries. Billie was one of the original members of MFL. She was a young Alabama girl, and single, like most of us at that time. Billie later married one of our young engineers and retired. She went on to become a leading citizen of Titusville, serving as a member of our hospital board and a leading real estate associate.

To fully appreciate this very bold new venture, you need to know where our nation was in the space race with the Soviet Union at that time. The general perception in America and around the world was that the Soviet Union was winning. Remember back in October 1957, they launched Sputnik, the first artificial moon, and in April 1961, they stunned the world again when they launched the first human in space, Russian cosmonaut Yuri Gagarin, into Earth orbit. The Soviet Union was getting a lot of high mileage out of the fact that a communist state could make these great achievements ahead of capitalist free-market countries. Clearly, we were in catch-up mode, as three weeks later, on May 5, 1961, we successfully launched our first man, Alan Shepard, in space in a suborbital flight.

The Cold War was well underway at this time in history, and the Soviet Union was making great strides in spreading communism in Third World nations. Fortunately, President Kennedy had the foresight, wisdom, and boldness to say that we were not going to accept this second-place situation. We would aim and achieve first place in the race for outer space.

I think I should add this little tidbit. President Kennedy was a Democrat, but a much different Democrat than the Democrats we see in 2015. In fact, Kennedy could not get on the Democratic ticket today. He believed in a strong military, he cut taxes, and he was capable of making bold decisions, like when he firmly stood up to Khrushchev in the Cuban Missile Crisis.

When President Kennedy made this bold announcement in May 1961, we faced the challenge of going from a mom and pop level space operation to a vast national program to beat the Russians to the moon. I would compare it to a mom and pop grocery store growing into a Walmart empire overnight. Remember that at this time the Kennedy Space Center was not on the map. All of our space operations on the East Coast were located on Cape Canaveral. The largest rocket our group had launched at this time was the Jupiter intermediate range ballistic missile (IRBM) with a thrust of 75,000 pounds, and it boggled our minds that we had to prepare for a rocket with several millions pounds of thrust to get a spacecraft to the moon and return.

The most immediate problem was where to locate this new spaceport. The Cape Canaveral missile range was not large enough to accommodate the huge rocket required for the moon operation. Several locations to launch these huge moon rockets were considered, including the southeast coast of Texas, Kings Point, Georgia, and several others.

Fortunately, there were some level heads involved, and a question surfaced. Why not buy enough land just across the

Banana River from Cape Canaveral to locate our new Moon
Port? There were several distinct advantages for this proposal.
First, we could take advantage of the vast downrange missile
tracking system operated by the Air Force. Secondly, we would
be launching in an eastern direction, which would give us some
advantage from the Earth's rotation. Thirdly, much of the land
in this particular part of Merritt Island was sparsely developed.
There were only a few orange growers and lightly scattered
housing. I believe Dr. Kurt Debus was the original author of this
proposal to locate the future Moon Port on Merritt Island.

NASA faced a huge, huge task in accomplishing President
Kennedy's charter to land men on the surface of the moon and
return them safely to planet Earth. We all realized there was
no time to waste. We had to hit the ground running. I think it
was hard for all of us close to this project to fully realize that
seven and a half years later, on Christmas Eve 1968, we would
be glued to our TVs watching and listening as Frank Borman
and his crew on Apollo 8 circled the moon and read aloud from
the book of Genesis. Seven months after that, on July 20, 1969,
we would again be glued to our TVs, watching and listening as
Neil Armstrong made his footprint on the surface of the moon.

I firmly believe that divine Providence was with us. We had
a very capable and talented leadership team in Washington. Jim
Webb (not Jim Webb, the senator from Virginia) was the head
of NASA at this time, and he brought in key men to get this job
done. The first was George Mueller, and the second was Lt. Gen.
Sam Phillips.

Their first task was to organize the vast human resources to
get this job done. That was no easy task, as NASA had strong
leadership in the three major space centers that would be
involved in this project: Wernher von Braun of the Marshall
Space Flight Center (MSFC), Bob Gilruth of the Johnson Space
Flight Center (JSC), and Dr. Kurt Debus of Kennedy Space
Center (KSC). All of these men were fighting to get as much of
this package of work in their organization as they could.

Dr. Mueller and Gen. Phillips lost no time in assigning specific
responsibilities to each of these centers, and each NASA center
faced the same task of reorganizing their resources to meet this
challenging job. Here are a few of the major problems that had

to be resolved to make this happen, and I would add it would be impossible in this bureaucratic world that we live in today.

After the issue of where to locate the new spaceport, the next most pressing issue was to determine the methods to land on the moon and return. Smart, strong-minded people had different opinions. The decision on this subject as well as many other major issues had to be made immediately. There was no time to form a stupid committee and delay the solutions. The way this system was set up was to hold a meeting with the right people, close the door, and stay there until a decision was made. Fortunately, the word "committee" was not in our vocabulary.

Next, we had to design the flight hardware-booster rocket. This responsibility was given to the Marshall Space Flight Center (MSFC) headed by Wernher von Braun. The responsibility for the design and development of the spacecraft flight hardware was assigned to the Johnson Space Center (JSC) under Dr. Bob Gilruth.

Back to locating, designing, and building the Launch Complex. The responsibility for this task was the Kennedy Space Center (KSC) under the direction of Dr. Kurt Debus. The name of the launch complex did not come until sometime later.

Listed below are some of the major problems facing Dr. Debus. Critical major decisions had to be made immediately to meet this demanding schedule. One of Dr. Debus' strong attributes was selecting the right person for the job. One of his smartest moves in this category was to recall Lt. Col. Rocco Petrone from his military assignment and give him the task of director of launch operations. Recalling Rocco to take over operations at the Launch Center was good news to me, because Rocco and I had developed a good friendship during the Redstone Program. I want to make a bold statement, and I know what I'm talking about. We would never have launched Apollo 8 and Apollo 11 on time without Rocco Petrone. And I believe anyone closely associated with the Apollo Program in those formative years would agree with me.

One of Rocco's strong points is the same as Dr. Debus. He could get the right man for the job. Rocco had Don "Buck" Buchanan, a very sharp and capable engineer, for the design and development of the launch complex facilities.

Rocco chose Dr. Hans Gruene for the development of the

launch team, which included NASA and contractors, as well as operating procedures. You could not get a better man for this job than Dr. Gruene. During this period I was promoted to chief engineer and deputy director of launch vehicle operations under Dr. Gruene.

He chose Merritt Preston for spacecraft operations. I want to cover the main events but not necessarily in a chronological order, as that would require more time and space. At the beginning of the Apollo program, Preston was head of spacecraft operations at the launch site, and he reported directly to Dr. Bob Gilruth at JSC. Dr. Debus was head of launch vehicle operations and reported directly to Dr. von Braun at MSFC. When NASA created the Kennedy Space Center (KSC), Dr. Debus was named center director.

The elevation of Dr. Debus as KSC director put him on a level with Dr. von Braun and Dr. Bob Gilruth. This move did not go over well with the top guys at Houston or Huntsville. They recognized they had lost some control over these launch site operations, but thankfully the strong, good-thinking leaders at NASA headquarters, Dr. Mueller and General Phillips, made it clear that was how it was going to be.

During this transition period, on one of his trips to the launch site, Dr. von Braun came over to Dr. Gruene's office and said, "Hans, my boys in Huntsville are giving me a hard time, and you are the one to make this thing work."

Prior to this move, Dr. Debus, under Dr. von Braun, was on the same level with Dr. von Braun's other department heads at Huntsville. They felt they had lost some control over launch site operations. Now the department heads at Huntsville would have to be dealing directly with Dr. Gruene on major issues. Actually Dr. Gruene was a reasonable man to work with, and they were fortunate he was in this position.

At this time we were having a major issue with the people in Huntsville on the concept of checking out the various stages before stacking on the launcher. The people at Huntsville proposed permanently stationing some of their people at the launch site to be in charge of the contractors preparing the individual stages prior to stacking on the launcher. Dr. Gruene made the logical case that once the individual stages arrived at the launch site, we were in charge completely. Common sense prevailed, and he convinced them to scrap this proposal.

Dr. Debus and Rocco had to make some big time decisions in a very short period of time in order to launch a moon rocket in this decade. Listed below were several major issues that had to be dealt with immediately.

First, we needed to either stack all of the stages of the rocket on the launch pad, or assemble the individual stages of the rocket in a remote facility and transfer the assembled rocket to the launch pad. If the latter method was used, how would you get this assembled rocket to the launch pad? We know now the Caterpillar tread transporter was selected. It is known today as the Crawler. I had no part in the selection of the Crawler, but I was invited by Dr. Kurt Debus to join a small group that flew up in his plane (each NASA center director was assigned a personal plane, which at that time was a Gulfstream) to a coal strip mine in Kentucky where a huge Caterpillar was operating. Dr. Debus, Rocco, and Buchanan were impressed with this huge machine, and the decision was made to use the tread type concept. A canal/barge concept from the VAB to the pad was a consideration, along with the consideration of a rubber-tired vehicle.

Then we faced the huge task of writing proposals and award contracts. We had always been a do-it-yourself organization, so we had to come up to speed very rapidly. NASA would be the integrator and manager of the various contractors. It turned out we would have much more detailed and tight management controls than the contractors had ever experienced. This caused quite a bit of friction in our initial operations. Neither we nor the contractors had ever worked in this particular arrangement before, and both sides wanted to continue to work like they had before. But that was impossible.

During previous government contracts, the government would provide the contractor with the requirements and specifications, and the contractor would take it from there, providing the final product with minimum oversight. During this program we would not do any hands-on work, but we would be in complete control, including the approval of all problem solutions, small and major. We would make all of the major decisions on manpower levels, schedules, test plans, and "go-no-go" issues.

Our contracts were structured in such a manner that the contractor management would want to please the customer. Our contracts were set up to award the contractor with a base fee and then an award fee available based on performance. We set up some basic criteria for the contractor performance, which included inputs from our system engineers embedded directly in daily activities. It is easy to see how this could get very subjective, and we had to be careful to make the contractor evaluation on an objective level. This type of contract naturally calls for the local contractor manager to be responsive to any of our concerns, since he would be in trouble with the home office if he did not bring in a good award fee.

Let me jump ahead a bit now. With a little humor, I saw these "chickens come home to roost" years later when I was on the other side as head of the USBI Florida Operations. I was doing everything I possibly could to please our NASA customer. Fortunately, we soon settled down and established a very good working relationship. I would emphasize we worked hard to achieve this strong communication system from the lowest to the highest levels.

According to the overall NASA plan, we awarded our launch site contracts to the companies MSFC selected for the design and fabrication of the various stages of flight hardware. These contracts were as follows: S-1C first stage, Boeing Company, and we added into this contract the operation and maintenance of the propellant-loading equipment and the Saturn V service arms (one of our most critical systems); S-II second stage, North American Rockwell; S-IVB third stage, MacDonnell Douglas; instrument unit (IU), IBM, and we added into the IBM contract the maintenance of the launch control center consoles and associated equipment in the ML and the RCA-110 computers.

In all of the above contracts except IBM, we immediately had a major issue. These contractors came in with a proposal for three shifts a day to meet our scheduled launch date. Dr. Gruene said, "No way are you going to work three shifts a day." They all reacted vigorously that this was the way they had always worked on other projects with the Air Force and with the Spacecraft side of the house. Now, Dr. Gruene was the most cost-conscious government employee I have ever encountered. His position on shiftwork was that you had your first team involved any time you were running major test operations, and if you required extending the day to complete a test or a major troubleshooting task, you kept as many of the first team as required to complete the task. We would authorize a limited second shift for making modifications and other non-major operations.

We did end up going Dr. Gruene's way, and we made the schedule and saved a ton of money. Our sister operations, Spacecraft, elected to go with the contractors' three-shifts-a-day proposal, and I can tell you from firsthand observation that the second and third shifts were totally inefficient and immensely added to the cost of the operations.

Management systems also had to be set up, and this included new management structures at all levels, from NASA headquarters to internal structures of the three major NASA centers in the Apollo program. In fact, it involved totally creating one new NASA Center, Johnson Space Flight Center, and making major changes in the management structures at Kennedy Space Flight Center (KSC) and Marshall Space Flight Center (MSFC). Of course, we know that JSC is located in Houston, and there was absolutely no technical requirement that the Flight Control Center be there. We all know politics come in to play when government money is involved. Lyndon Johnson was the vice president, and he was heading our space program. Common sense would tell you that it would be much more efficient if the flight control center had been located at the launch site.

Of course, you have to realize that in fighting for your budget, it is good to have the work scattered out across the country in as many congressional districts as you can. For example, it is not hard for a congressman from Harlem to vote against an increase in the NASA budget, and likewise a congressman from the KSC district could not afford to vote against an increased NASA budget. I think it significant to note that all of these activities had to be running parallel, and big decisions had to be made daily.

One of the big concerns prior to the launch of the first Saturn V was the release of the acoustical energy when we fired all five of these F-1C engines, resulting in 7.5 million pounds of thrust. Two of the big concerns were vibration in the computer/electronic racks in the ML, and the potential for structural damage in the surrounding areas. For the first problem, we did two things based on the recommendations of a contractor with experts in this particular field. First, we placed shock mounts underneath our electronic/computer racks in the ML. Second, and this was a result of some concern about vibration levels in the rocket, we constructed a large water tank on the pad with huge discharge lines from the deck of the mobile launcher to release this water from the tank instantaneously at lift off, absorbing much of the acoustical energy.

Another precautionary thing related to the acoustical energy from the Saturn V launch was to install acoustical energy instrumentation around the surrounding areas, like Titusville. This was to counter, or support, any reports of structural damage caused by acoustical energy as a result of a Saturn V launch. This was done based on the experience of MSFC during their static firing of these engines in their static firing test stand, with some reports of people alleging structural damage from these firings. Turns out we experienced no problems in any of these areas.

Another significant factor I think you should know is the Saturn-5 was designed with 1960's technology, which meant the flight hardware was full of components with moving parts, relays, stepping switches, rotating machinery, accelerometers, etc. This type of hardware by nature is not as reliable as modern day, solid-state circuitry and, of course, you pay a heavy penalty in weight. In many situations you would like to have a redundant circuit, but due to weight considerations it is not possible.

As you can imagine, it was an awesome challenge managing the many major projects at the launch site that interacted with each other. Another significant challenge was that the launch site facilities such as the VAB, crawler, mobile launcher, and Launch Control Center had to be compatible with the booster rockets and spacecraft components, which were being designed at MSFC and JSC. All of the flight hardware systems and ground support systems were constantly undergoing changes, which created a nightmare.

This is where Rocco came in. He set up a Control Center in the future Firing Room No. 4 with PERT charts on all the walls of this large room. One chart showed all of the major tasks. Each major task showed a start date, the required end date, and if the task was on or behind schedule. One individual, by name, was held responsible for that particular task being completed on time. Behind each major task bar was another chart on the wall that showed the status of all the sub tasks required to meet the schedule on time. Again, an individual, by name, would be held responsible for completing the subtasks on time. For many of the major tasks, there were a number of charts going as far down into the subsystems or component levels as necessary to ensure that your tracking was on schedule. Otherwise you would be waving the red flag that you were in trouble.

During this period, the early 1960's, our organization, Launch Vehicle Operations, was still very busy launching a variety of missiles at Cape Canaveral. We were heavily engaged in working with the design engineers on the design and development of the new launch site on Merritt Island. We were also heavily engaged with the design engineers in Huntsville, working on the design and development of the various stages of the new Saturn-V moon rocket.

One of our most challenging issues for making the first launch on time was the design, test verification, and delivery of the Saturn V service arms. They were the lifeline from the mobile launcher tower to the rocket, carrying all the electrical cables, high-pressure gas lines and propellant loading lines. At the top, the service arms provided a white room for the astronauts to enter the spacecraft.

These service arms were very large. Walking from the mobile launcher tower into the rocket across the swing arms was like walking in a hallway in a building. The KSC Design Engineering Department was responsible for the design of these arms, the Hayes Corporation in Birmingham, Alabama, had the contract to build the service arms, and they were tested at a facility at MSFC. For a period, it appeared these service arms might not be ready to meet our launch schedule. Rocco sent one of his senior guys to the contractor's facility in Birmingham and he reported back daily to Rocco. On the local scene, Rocco assigned me to head up a local working group with NASA and Boeing and our local contractor for the service arms for a design review and test plan once the arms arrived at KSC. It took long hours and a lot of challenging work between KSC, MSFC, and the Hayes Corporation, but the good news is we made it on time.

Let me explain how critical these service arms are. It is this simple: If one arm fails to eject and swing out of the way of the ascending rocket, we buy the farm. The rocket explodes, destroys the launch pad, and hopefully the escape rocket is triggered to take the astronauts out of the inferno. We cannot afford to eject and swing these arms out of the way before we fire the S-1C rocket engines, because if one of the engines fails, resulting in a cutoff signal to the other four engines, then we have a loaded bomb with all of this stored energy in the rocket on the launch pad with no means to control critical functions, like vent valves on the propellant tanks. To avoid this situation, the on-board computer in the instrument unit monitors the performance of the five S-1C rocket engines, and when the computer detects all engines are performing normally the computer sends a signal for the hold-down mechanism to operate, and the rocket lifts off of the launcher and is on its way with the service arms still attached. Then it sends a signal to release and eject the service arms and swing them back 90 degrees against the mobile launcher, clearing the way for the rocket to ascend.

Believe me, during this critical period my eyes were glued to a camera monitoring the service arms. Thank the Lord all of our hard work paid off and they worked beautifully every launch.

One of the most critical areas we were involved in at the Merritt Island launch site was the design and development of the Launch Control Center. This would be the first time we would operate from a non-fortified firing room. The firing rooms were actually a part of the Vehicle Assembly Building (VAB), and this facility was located at such a safe distance from the launch pad that a fortified firing room would not be required. We spent much time with our design counterparts in Huntsville, coming up with the number of control panels, control panel layout, and the strategic location of all the various control panels in the firing room, and it was critical that certain panels had to be located in certain positions relative to other control panels.

We had to give special attention to the computer rooms. The design of the Saturn V ground checkout and launch system required two computers, one in the back of the firing room and the other computer inside the mobile launcher. The firing room consoles communicated with the computer in the rear of the firing room, and this computer communicated with the mobile launcher computer. Due to the massive amount of cables and air conditioning ducts required for the computers and control panels, it was necessary to have a false floor in the firing rooms. We were actually doing some pioneering work in the automation of the checkout and launching of missiles/rockets with computers. Much history has been written about our space program, but I have never seen anything published on our introduction of automation in the checkout and launch of missiles until recently when my friend, Frank Penovich, wrote a good paper on this subject. Frank was the head of our RCA-110 computer operations. We were embarking on an adventure that had never been done.

It required some bold moves on the part of some people at the Marshall Space Flight Center (MSFC) and our organization at KSC. The main driver in our organization was my boss, Dr. Hans Gruene. You must understand that in the mid-1960's, none of us knew how to spell software. We were on a very demanding schedule to meet our president's objective of landing a man on the moon and returning him safely to Earth in this decade.

There was a certain amount of risk associated with this bold new venture in automation. There were some rudimentary business computers on the market, but the only input devices on these computers were magnetic tapes, punch cards, or punch paper tapes. The only output devices were line printers, magnetic tape drives, punch cards, or punch paper tapes. You had to have these devices, but the computer also had to interface with switches, lights, meters, and strip recorders. These types of interfaces were not available on the business-type computers.

To meet our requirements, the computers had to be designed to accommodate Discreet Input and output signals, and for analog input and output devices. MSFC had the responsibility to select and design the incorporation of the computer and our launch processing system. They selected the RCA computer. RCA at that time was one of the top electronics manufactures in the country. By today's standards, the computer they selected was very primitive. It required about 20 racks of equipment to house the computer. The memory storage was a magnetic drum about two feet in diameter and about three feet tall and spinning at a very high rate of speed. Of course, it had magnetic tapes and punch card machines.

If the computer shut down for any reason, which unfortunately happened frequently during these early days, we had to wait until the drum coasted to a complete stop before we could restart the computer. In fact, you could always identify the computer guys in the firing room by the punch cards they had in their shirt pockets. As I mentioned, we did have frequent shutdowns, and we did not initially understand the reason for many of them. One of our smart guys came up with one of the causes for some—a momentary glitch in the Florida Power and Light power source. The computer was very sensitive to any minute deviation in the sixty-cycle power source. These glitches were so minute, they did not disturb ordinary electronic equipment, and you probably would not even see a blink in the lights, but our computer would sense it and shut down.

Rather than redesign the computer, one of our smart guys at MSFC came up with a very practical solution. That was to install a very large electric motor with a generator attached to the shaft on the motor. So when we experienced a Florida Power and Light glitch, the momentum of this large motor would absorb it. There would be no deviation in the output of the generator, which now supplied the power for the computer.

After we fixed this problem, we encountered another, far more serious problem. The computer would inadvertently issue many discreet output commands and then shut down. This condition was very serious, because it would cause valves to open or close and relays to be energized or de-energized. The guys working in and around the missile would rightfully be very disturbed. In fact, on more than one occasion, one of them would call over the intercom system and angrily yell, "I am coming up there with an axe to destroy the computer if you guys don't fix it."

This condition developed into a very serious and complex issue, because we could not identify the origin.

One thing that complicated the investigation of this problem was the way we selected the contractors to provide and operate this equipment. That subject is too complicated to go into here, but for various reasons RCA provided the computers, but the contract to operate this equipment went to IBM. IBM was upset that we had not selected their computer, and the RCA people were upset that we did not contract with them to operate the computer. So the IBM people would let you know that you would not have this problem if you had selected their equipment, and the RCA people would say that if you had contracted with us to operate this equipment, then you would not have this problem.

It turned out both of them were dead wrong. Again I say this was a very serious problem. At one time it looked like a program stopper. Gen. Sam Philips, now the second man in charge of the Apollo program, called a special meeting at KSC, which included the top guys from RCA, IBM, MSFC, and KSC to develop a plan to find out what was wrong and identify a solution.

A double exposure added to this problem. Our ground checkout system was designed so that one of these RCA computers in the Launch Control Center was linked to the same type of computer in the mobile launcher at the pad. Of course, both of these computers had the same generic problem. It is too complicated to go into great detail, but some of our smart guys at MSFC finally identified the source of the issue.

Each computer had several hundred printed circuit boards, and they were about four inches wide and about nine inches long and loaded with transistors, resisters, capacitors, and diodes. The components were mounted on one side of the circuit board, and the leads to the components went through a hole in the board to connect to the circuit paths on the other side. It was found that after some periods of warm up, these leads from the individual components would try to expand. There was no expansion loop in this setup, and there would be a very micro separation in the leads. This would result in these erroneous discreet outputs and shut the system down. After this happened, we again had to wait for the magnetic drum to coast down before we could restart the computer. In that period of time, the components would cool down and the separation gap would close and everything would be back to normal, so now we couldn't find the problem. You'd restart the computer and sometime later experience the same cycle. This resulted in a massive workload. Every one of these circuit boards had to be reworked to install an expansion loop on each component.

Unfortunately, one nasty problem we encountered in the build-up of the firing room was with the unions. In the contracts for the launch complex, the unions would install the control cables from a terminal point at the launch pad to a terminal point in the back of the firing room. The plan was for our contractors to install the cables from the terminal boards to the control panels. Our contractor was IBM, and they were non-union. We were at a stalemate, and it ended up that some senator on the Labor Relations Committee sent some of his staff down here to assess this issue and make some recommendations. I do not remember the senator's name, but I think he was from Arkansas.

I was assigned to make a presentation stating our position to this team from Washington. I felt comfortable as we were on solid ground. I was helped by the fact that the union position was downright stupid. They not only wanted the initial installation of the cables, but a crew standing by twenty-four hours a day, seven days a week in case we needed to disconnect a cable for troubleshooting or replacing a panel. That meant we would have two or three union guys in the control room and the mobile launcher, sitting on their butts for days with nothing to do. It is nice to report that common sense prevailed, and this team from Washington took care of the problem.

Some days you arrive in your office in the morning with a well-scripted plan on what you hope to accomplish that day, and then suddenly the phone rings, your well-laid plans are out the window, and you're off to put a fire out. I'll give you an example of this. As soon as I arrived in my office one day, I received a telephone call from my friend George Faenza. George was the general manager for our McDonnell Douglas contract on the S-IVB, the third stage of the Saturn V.

George said he had a problem and needed to talk to me, and so I told him to go ahead. George said he couldn't talk to me over the phone and I said to come on over. Let me set the stage for what was going on here. George and I frequently talked, and I could detect by his tone that this was not an ordinary, run-of-the-mill problem. As I mentioned earlier, we had a team of our NASA engineers embedded throughout our contractor structure. I immediately called our lead engineer in this area, Bill Mahoney, and tried to phrase my conversation as just a casual, routine call. I said something like "Bill, I haven't seen you in a couple of days. What is going on? What kind of problems are you guys working over there now?" Bill was a very detailed guy and he started giving me a rundown on several problems, none of them with any real significance, and I thanked him and hung up. I did not alarm him that George was on the way over to discuss some apparently serious problem.

George arrived in my office and laid out several pictures on my desk, photos taken of the men's bathroom in the VAB low bay's S-IVB work area. Scrawled on the mirrors were these words: *The rocket will never fly, you will never find it, Ha-Ha-Ha.*

George said he had no idea who had done this. His security people were getting a list of all the people who had recent access to this bathroom, and he had called in his corporate security people. I immediately went to Dr. Gruene and Rocco Petrone, and we called in Charlie Buckley, head of our security office. The first thing we wanted to do was keep this as quiet as possible. We certainly did not want this in the press, and, of course, the big dilemma was: if we could not identify the perpetrator of this terrible message, what in the world were we going to do?

We had no satisfactory answer. The S-IVB in question was in its latter days of checkout before transferring to the VAB high bay for assembly on the Saturn V and rollout to the pad. We had already performed the major pre-transfer tests on this S-IVB. If we did not find the culprit before the scheduled transfer to the high bay, we were going to face an agonizing decision—to transfer this unknown stage for assembly and rollout to the pad or delay the transfer until we had uncovered the problem. That would result in a major disruption in the overall Apollo schedule as there was not a backup S-IVB stage available. Most likely there would be a delay of several months, which was unthinkable.

Our immediate plan was for a very detailed inspection of the stage, conducted by our quality control people and the systems engineers. We also decided to repeat some of our most detailed test procedures. We came up with various reasons explaining these special tests to the troops, NASA, and contractors, and amazingly the word about the situation we were in never got out.

Our detailed inspections and repeated tests did not reveal any problems. Time was running out. If by the transfer date we did not have this problem resolved, this would be big-time news, and someone at the very top would have to decide whether to accept the risk of flying with this unknown still in the system or face a lengthy delay in the overall Apollo schedule.

Prayers were answered. Just before our transfer date, George called me with some good news. One his best employees confessed that he and a couple of other guys had done this as a big joke. The employee said that he and a couple of engineers here on a visit from the home plant in California had been out to a three or four-martini lunch, came back, and did this as a joke. However, before they revealed it as a joke, it got such high-level attention that they were afraid they would be fired, so they clammed up. Because the employee confessed, he was not fired, but he was transferred back to California. I do not know what happened to the two other guys from California who were also part of this fiasco.

I slept well that night for the first time since this whole thing started. To this day, I do not know what we would have done had this guy not confessed. Just count this as all part of a day's work.

Remer Prince was our first African American employee at Launch Vehicle Operations. He was a trusted employee and a valuable asset to our team. We have reconnected with Remer and his wife, Korona, in recent years and they are good friends of ours.

LAUNCH CONTROL CENTER FIRING ROOM

This is the scene I looked over from the firing room in the Apollo program. At that time, in the late 60's, we had one African American, one White female and one Hispanic.

Launch of Apollo 12, Nov. 12, 1969--- Firing Room 2-Complex
39-KSC
L to R
1-Paul Donnelly, Chief, Test Conductors office
2-Dr. Kurt Debus, Director, Kennedy Space Center
3-Deke Slayton, Chief, Astronauts Office
4-Rocco Petrone, NASA Headquarters Office
5-Dr. George Mueller, Apollo Program Dir.
6-Al O'Hara, LVO Test Conductor
7-Dr. Hans Gruene, Director Launch Vehicle Operations (LVO)
8-Andy Pickett, Chief, Mechanical/Propulsion Division
9-Ike Rigell, Dep. Dir. and Chief Engineer LVO
10-George Smith, Manager, IBM

A few moments after liftoff of Apollo 12, we experienced one of the most traumatic moments in our launch experience. The rocket had ascended just several hundred feet when it was struck by lightning. In my 40-year career in rocket launch operations this is the first, to my knowledge, of a rocket being struck by lightning while in flight.

The flight crew reported all the displays and lights on the instrument panels in the Command Module went crazy and we received via telemetry that the booster stages sent erroneous signals. Momentarily, it appeared we had a catastrophic situation, but I am convinced by the grace of God all these erroneous indications returned to normal. We suffered no permanent damage to any of the flight hardware and it turned out Apollo 12 was a beautiful, successful flight that landed a crew on the surface of the moon and returned safely. In this picture, Dr. Mueller is addressing the Firing Room Launch Team, thanking them for their dedicated efforts in the successful launch of Apollo 12 and giving them a current update on the fly performance of Apollo 12.

Because of this near catastrophic event, NASA made an extensive study and implementation of new weather redlines for "Go" for launch. This included extensive studies on the potential for lightning in the immediate launch area, and the placement of instrumentation in the surrounding area to detect potential lightning strikes. KSC did a super job in the advancement of lightning detection and protection regarding launching of space vehicles.

DAY OF TRAGEDY— JANUARY 27, 1967

A s I write this in 2017, 50 years later, I believe I can say that for the few of us still living, the memories of this tragic event are still fresh in our minds. I would also say that no one going to work that morning even remotely thought that they would experience, before they came home that night, the worst nightmare in their career.

I think it is appropriate to set the stage for the events that unfolded during this day of tragedy. It was well known that the launch team had been experiencing problems with this first version of the Apollo command module (CSM) since its arrival at KSC in August 1966. The engineering modification traffic had been heavy and was still growing. This resulted in a much more demanding work environment for the launch team in absorbing this challenging task of incorporating engineering changes during a heavy, tight test schedule. In the preceding years, we enjoyed much success in our space program. We not only came from behind in the space race with the Soviets but also surpassed them. We had enjoyed much success in our Redstone Mercury, Atlas Mercury, Gemini, and unmanned launch programs such as the Surveyor program, mapping the moon for future Apollo lunar missions.

The scheduled activity on this day was the "plugs out" test, which is one of our major all-systems tests, and it includes the participation of the mission's flight crew. The flight crew for Apollo 1 was Gus Grissom, making his third flight, Ed White, making his second flight, and Roger Chaffee, making his first flight. The mission for Apollo 1 was a low Earth orbit and it would be the first manned flight of the Block 1 CSM. It was the first manned flight in the Apollo program, and the ultimate goal of this program was for a lunar landing. It was hoped that this would be a 14-day stay in orbit.

This first CSM was mated to our Saturn 1B booster, and this vehicle configuration was identified as AS-204. NASA later changed this identification to Apollo 1. The plugs out test was not identified as a hazardous operation; there would be no fuel loaded in the first and second stages of the booster rocket or the CSM, although the CSM would be pressurized to 16.7 psi to maintain a positive cabin pressure like the astronauts would experience in outer space. The Mercury and Gemini flights, with this same cabin environment, had experienced no problems under these conditions.

The plugs out configuration had nothing to do with the problem. The difference in the plugs out test and other all-systems tests is that during the simulated launch and flight sequence, the vehicle umbilical cables would be physically ejected at the point of lift-off and the simulated flight would be powered by flight-type batteries, whereas the simulated flight systems are powered by ground generators in all other tests.

The flight crew entered the spacecraft at 1 PM and experienced nagging problems for the next several hours, causing a delay in the test as they troubleshot a communications loop problem with the crew. Grissom got a little annoyed and remarked, "How are we going to get to the moon if we can't talk between two or three buildings?"

At 6:20 PM the count was still holding at T minus 10 minutes. At 6:31 PM, the first report of a fire in the spacecraft was heard from one of the crew, believed to be Grissom. For the next 6.8 seconds, garbled transmissions were heard from the crew—then silence. The intensity of the fire in this pure oxygen atmosphere resulted in a rapid increase in pressure, which ruptured the

CSM wall. This allowed intense heat, flames, gases and smoke to escape the CSM, resulting in severe problems for the ground crew attempting to open the hatch and rescue the crew. The ground crew worked heroically, but the damage had been done and their efforts to rescue the crew were to no avail. In fact, until the fire was extinguished, they were in a potentially dangerous situation themselves, as the escape rocket was positioned just above their heads; if the flames reached that point, it have could set off the escape rocket, and that would have resulted in a catastrophic situation with a complete loss of the ground crew.

I do not care to describe the scene in the cabin when the crew finally got the hatch opened. Very detailed comments on this tragic situation are graphically described in the NASA investigation report.

I was not in the blockhouse during this test. I had been scheduled to attend a design review with some of our design folks at MSFC at the McDonnell Douglas facility in California. I do not recall the exact time, but I was in my hotel room at Santa Monica when I received a call from Frank Bryan in the blockhouse. I knew immediately when Frank started talking that something was wrong. Frank was talking in a quivering, whispering voice.

He said, "We have a bad problem with the spacecraft." As best I remember, I said, "Frank, are we involved?" Frank responded, "I have to go. I cannot say any more, but it is bad." I learned later that those in the blockhouse were told not to make outside calls, and I do not know if this call was before or after that announcement. The reason I questioned whether we were involved was because we (Launch Vehicle) had some critical electrical circuits interfacing with the spacecraft, and Frank was our key man on those interface circuits. We call this the emergency detection system (EDS). This circuitry monitors key parameters in the guidance, control, and stabilized platform systems of the launch vehicle, and if an impending catastrophic situation is detected, it sends an abort signal to the CSM.

We did not have instantaneous news "Alerts" like we do today, and before I went to bed that night I received no news from the media. I did not get much sleep, and it was the next morning before I learned of just how bad the problem was at Complex 34.

I mentioned above that I did not care to try to describe the scene when the rescue team first opened the hatch to the spacecraft; you can get a feel for this horrible scene from a comment by one of the ground crew—when he was asked to describe the scene by the test conductor, he could only reply, "Can't describe."

NASA Administrator James Webb asked President Johnson to allow NASA to conduct the official investigation and assured President Johnson that NASA would hold nothing back and would keep the Congress informed in a timely manner. Floyd Thompson, director of the Langley Research Center, was selected to head up this team. One of the key members on the team was astronaut Frank Borman, who just 23 months later would fly the upgraded version of this CSM on a mission to the moon, including lunar orbits, and return to Earth.

The investigating board determined that this first CSM was not flight worthy. It had many flaws in design, workmanship, and procedures. The source of the fire was determined to be a spark from the electrical wiring. The flames spread intensely due to the high pressure of the pure oxygen atmosphere and the high amount of flammable material, Velcro, and nylon in the cabin. The opening hatch was very complex. It required opening the inner section of the hatch from the inside, which, with a positive pressure on the inside, they could not accomplish. Not only was there too much flammable material in the cabin, but the vast amount of electrical wiring, from a workmanship standpoint, was a disaster, with some bare wires and places where wires and cables got scuffed from frequent bending. I cannot name all the recommendations made by the investigating board, but several of the prime recommendations were to redesign the hatch to "open outside," fix the wiring design and workmanship problems, lower the cabin pressure to 5 psi pure oxygen, and give more attention to the astronauts' recommendations when they inspected the hardware.

In my view, NASA made some invaluable discoveries from the findings of this investigative board. Another failure in this time frame would probably have meant the end of the program, but instead, using the knowledge we gained from this unspeakable tragedy, we were able to forge ahead and make some remarkable accomplishments in the 30 months that followed. I use 30 months as a reference as I compare this downtime in the Apollo program to the downtime in the shuttle program following the losses of the Columbia and Challenger.

Twenty-two months after the fire on Apollo 1 on January 27, 1967, we launched Apollo 7 on October 11, 1968, on a Saturn 1B from Blockhouse 34. Apollo 7 was the first manned Apollo flight and was the first manned flight for the S-1B. This was the same booster used for Apollo 1, as it was undamaged during that fire. This was a low Earth orbit mission and was successful. Apollo 7 had one more distinction: It was the only manned flight in the Apollo program that was not made from Complex 39 at KSC. The flight crew for Apollo 7 was the backup crew for Apollo 1, Wally Schirra, Don Eisele, and Walt Cunningham. A note of interest here—Don Eisele was originally assigned to the crew of Apollo 1 and had a pre-flight training injury; he was then replaced by Ed White.

The next flight was Apollo 8 on December 21, 1968, which was the first circumlunar flight of the CSM and the first manned flight for the Saturn V. This was a successful flight as well. I go into much more detail on this particular flight in the following chapter.

Next was Apollo 9 on March 3, 1969, which was a 10-day Earth orbit flight and the first manned flight test for the lunar module (LM). This was the first in-flight rendezvous and docking of the LM and CSM. This too was a successful flight.

Next was Apollo 10, on May 18, 1969, which was the first flight to the moon with the LM. The manned LM descended to 8.4 nautical miles above the moon's surface and then rendezvoused and docked to the CSM. This was a successful flight.

Next was Apollo 11, "the big one," on July 21, 1969. This was what it was all about . . . the first time in the history of mankind that men from planet Earth would set foot on a heavenly body!!! This was a successful flight, and I go into much more detail on this flight in a later chapter.

I have listed five manned Apollo flights, with several significant "first times" in the 30 months (January 1967–July 1969) following the Apollo 1 fire. In contrast, following the loss of the Space Shuttle Challenger on January 28, 1986, we made no manned space flights for the next 32 months. Following the loss of the Space Shuttle

Columbia on February 1, 2003, we made no manned space flights in the following 30 months.

Why were we so successful and productive in the 30 months following the Apollo 1 tragedy and so dormant in the 30 months following the Columbia and Challenger tragedies? The investigative boards on all three failures did a commendable job, and the design agencies came up with the proper solutions to correct these critical failures. On the Challenger, the problem was clearly a design problem in the solid rocket booster mating joint. I would also add the recommendation, "Do not launch in freezing weather."

The readiness for the "return to flight" for the Columbia was more difficult; it required experimental testing with the design and application of the protective foam on the external tank. The readiness for return to flight after Apollo 1 required going from a Block 1 CSM to a Block 2 CSM, which involved completely reworking the wiring and cabling systems and considerable other design changes. The CSM was a complicated machine, so this involved a tremendous amount of work.

Another question to consider in addressing the above question is: Were we much more conservative in the shuttle program than we were in the Apollo program? I would say absolutely not. Ever since the birth of the space program, we have walked that narrow path of "schedule vs. risk." When you push the troops to make the schedule and at the same time you tell them that safety is the number one priority, they say, "Boss, which one do you want, schedule or risk?" These are unspoken words, but I assure you that they are hovering in the atmosphere, so management must be very careful in how much they push the troops. The best advice I can give is to go to the people you trust to speak up, ask their opinion, and then listen very carefully to what they tell you.

My unbiased opinion of why we were so much more productive in the 1960s than in the later years with the shuttle program is based on two factors. First, I firmly believe management at the top levels in NASA during the Apollo days was superior to what we had later in the shuttle program. Secondly, I believe the fact that our workforce in the '60s was younger and NASA was a younger organization meant they had not accumulated much baggage or bureaucracy, which, in my experience, all organizations are plagued with like a disease. Just like people, when organizations get older, their productivity decreases. The pattern I observed was that more and more minor issues were elevated to decision by committee, and individual responsibility was diluted. This pattern increases both cost and time. While I am extolling the virtues of our 1960s NASA team, I should mention that we launched three completely different spacecraft configurations—Mercury, Gemini, and Apollo—in that decade, whereas in the shuttle era there was only one basic configuration.

One significant advantage that the shuttle-era workforce had over our workforce in the '60s, though, is the tremendous advancements we made in the world of solid-state circuitry and software and automation. As I have mentioned previously, the Saturn V was loaded with moving parts, relays, rotating machinery, stepping switches, and other components that were later replaced with more reliable solid-state circuitry. We did make some notable advances in automation in the '60s, but compared to today's systems it would be considered primitive.

I end my comments on the Apollo 1 tragedy with these words: I believe the Apollo 1 is more indelibly imprinted on the minds of the launch team at KSC than the Challenger and Columbia tragedies. These words are not intended to minimize in any way the loss of the crews on the Challenger and Columbia; in fact, more astronauts were lost in each of those tragedies than in Apollo 1. I say this because so many of our NASA and contractor team members were physically involved in this day's events, including hearing the brief responses uttered by the flight crew at the moment of the disaster. I believe it is analogous to the comments I made about how we view wars. For example, I maintain that the Civil War was more real to people in the South than those in the North because much more of the war was fought on Southern soil. Similarly, at the time of this writing we are at war with the Taliban in Afghanistan, but the war is much more real to those people in Afghanistan than it is in the homes of America, unless you are a Gold Star mother or father.

Sadly, Grissom, White, and Chaffee never had the opportunity and pleasure of fulfilling their dream of going to the moon, but it is my opinion—and I have heard this expressed several times from people like Chris Kraft and others in NASA Headquarters—

that without the sacrifices these three patriots made, we would not have reached the moon that decade, and maybe not at all. With the faulty CSM, this problem was bound to happen sooner or later; if it had happened later, it would have had a much more negative impact on achieving our goal of landing on the moon in 1969.

APOLLO 8

In my view, Apollo 8, launched on December 21, 1968, was one of the most historic flights in our space history. Space historian Robert K. Poole classified Apollo 8 as the most historically significant of all of the Apollo missions.

As best I can recall, in August 1968, Rocco Petrone called Dr. Gruene and myself from Launch Vehicle Operations, along with John Williams and Ted Sasseen from Spacecraft operations, and his deputy, Walt Kapryn, to a meeting and told us that NASA Headquarters wanted to change the scheduled launch date and the mission for Apollo 8.

Apollo 8 had been originally scheduled for an early 1969 launch on a low Earth orbit mission to test the Lunar Excursion Module (LEM). To our great surprise, Rocco said they wanted to move the launch date forward to December 1968 and change the mission to a three-man crew to circle the moon and return to Earth. The LEM was experiencing significant manufacturing problems and was behind schedule and could not meet the planned launch date. There were some rumors and speculations that the Russians were trying to schedule a flight with a live crew to circle the moon and return to Earth. We learned later that the Russians were not as close to accomplishing this type of mission as we thought.

Rocco asked, "Could we do this? Could we safely accomplish this new schedule?"

Of course, we knew Rocco knew what our answer would be, and his question was not really a question. He was merely telling us the new challenge.

This was a very challenging schedule, but we had confidence in our NASA and contractor team as well as the hardware, and we were eager to go. In fact, we were elated. We thrived on a demanding challenge. This mission called for some things we had never done before.

I need to make this comment. It took real guts for the top NASA management to give a "Go" on this mission. Fortunately, we had some very capable people at that time running the show. This would be the first human spacecraft flight from KSC Complex 39, the first crew to leave the Earth orbit, the first to see the other side of the moon, the first crew to ride the Saturn V rocket, and the first humans to see the Earth as a whole planet and an earthrise. From August 1968 to our launch on December 21, 1968, we were solving problems, some that seemed almost insurmountable.

What a day when that beautiful rocket left the launch pad on Complex 39 headed for our nearest heavenly body, the moon, 240,000 miles away. Three days later, on Christmas Eve 1968, the crew, Frank Borman, Jim Lovell, and William Anders, were reading the first ten verses of Genesis as they circled the moon. The crew took a picture showing for the first time planet Earth rise with a portion of the lunar surface in the photo. This is still one of the most requested NASA photos from the NASA photo archives. An Apollo 8 commemorative stamp was issued, showing this photo with these words, "In the beginning God . . ."

Sadly, our deteriorated moral culture would not allow that today. In fact, Madalyn O'Hair, the atheist who brought the lawsuits against prayer in school, brought a lawsuit against NASA to ban our astronauts from public prayer in space. The Supreme Court refused to hear her case, but it did intimidate NASA, which is sad. Buzz Aldrin secretly served himself communion on the surface of the moon. He did not mention this for several years.

A little side note here. It has nothing to do with the Apollo 8, but it has to do with Madalyn O'Hair. On our second trip to

Russia in 1991 with Campus Crusade for Christ, the second man in charge of our group was one of her sons, a solid born-again Christian.

The year, 1968, was perhaps one of the most turbulent years in our history. That year saw the assassinations of Martin Luther King Jr. and Bobby Kennedy, President John Kennedy's brother, and we were bogged down in the war in Vietnam and a number of serious riots in our major cities. President Lyndon Johnson was quoted as saying it was like living a nightmare. The successful flight of Apollo 8 gave a positive lift to our country and to the Western world. We needed something like that after all the disturbances in 1968. It could best be summed up in this short telegram Frank Borman received from some unknown person after the flight: "Thank you, Apollo 8. You saved 1968." Frank Borman said out of all of the congratulations he and his crew received for this historic Apollo 8 flight, this one short message "said it all."

Every Christmas Eve since 1968, remembering the Apollo 8 flight, I think of and read the first ten verses of Genesis. Another earthly event that I always recall on Christmas is Washington crossing the Delaware River. I firmly believe these two events were successful because of Divine Providence.

"Earthrise."

The crew of Apollo 8 read the first nine verses of Genesis Chapter 1 as they orbited the moon. This is one of the most requested photos from the NASA archives.

25th Anniversary of the
launch of Apollo 8.

APOLLO 11

July 16, 1969, must be the number-one day in my entire career in space exploration. If you looked at some of our previous achievements, you would find a number of very big days, so to classify this day as the most memorable means it had to be a super big day. This was the day for which we had dreamed and worked so hard over a number of years. During these years, we overcame major setbacks and many serious, challenging problems. By far the most serious setback we overcame was the tragic fire on Apollo 1 that cost the lives of three of our brave astronauts. In this context, when I say "we," I am referring to the entire NASA Apollo workforce and our contractors. On a local level, the "we" was our Launch Operations directorate under Dr. Hans Gruene, which was comprised of 400 NASA employees, mostly engineers, and 8,000 contractors, also mostly engineers.

I want to go a step further and make this as personal as I can. Please do not interpret my story to imply that I am saying, "Gee, look what I did." I am very proud and satisfied with my role in our very successful space programs, both from a military and a civilian standpoint. I feel comfortable that I did my job well and my colleagues can proudly say the same thing. In fact, I have attended a number of funeral services for my space colleagues where I could personally testify to the families involved that they would be well justified in having a sense of pride for what their loved one accomplished in our space program.

Briefly, I want to recap some of those other big days I refer
to above. First was the Redstone 1 launch 15 years prior on
August 20, 1953. Why was that little primitive rocket, just 5
feet in diameter and 70 feet tall with a range of 150 miles and
a thrust of just 150,000 pounds, such a big deal? Back in 1953,
nothing of that size had been launched in the Western world.
In fact, the largest rocket I had ever witnessed launched was a
military rocket back on Saipan and Iwo Jima, about 5 inches
in diameter and 5 feet in length with a range of a few hundred
yards. I will repeat something I said earlier about this Redstone
rocket—during the countdown, I made the short trip from the
blockhouse to the launch pad and looked up at this giant rocket
and my thoughts were, *This thing is just too big to fly; it can
never disappear over the horizon.* Sometimes it is so good to be
so wrong. I can tell you, when we finished the countdown on this
primitive rocket, the tension and anxiety in the blockhouse was
there in spades.

We experienced the same level of excitement, tension,
and anxiety in the blockhouse when the firing command was
initiated for the Jupiter (IRBM) on March 1, 1957. In that era,
the Jupiter was an awesome giant, with a thrust of 150,000
pounds and a range of 1,500 miles.

I would say that there was an elevated level of excitement,
tension, and anxiety when the firing command was issued for
our Jupiter-C rocket that inserted the free world's first satellite
into orbit on January 31, 1958. The prestige of our nation was
at stake. The Soviets had embarrassed us by launching the
first satellite, Sputnik, on October 4, 1957, and a month later,
in November 1957, they launched a larger satellite with a dog,
which doubly embarrassed our nation. This was a moment of
truth for us, and we were blessed with a very successful flight.

Then, on May 5, 1961, we experienced another historical
event. The excitement, tension, and anxiety of issuing the firing
command with a man on board a primitive but still complex
rocket, on a scale of 1 to 10, approached a 10. Having a man
on board certainly added another dimension to the preparation
and launch process.

I was selected by Dr. Gruene and Rocco Petrone to present
the launch vehicle directorate flight readiness review for all of

our manned and unmanned launches. I explained this process in some detail in a previous section of the book. This was serious business, and I took it as serious business. If I erred, I wanted to be on the conservative side and, again, my thought processes progressed as if I myself were on a couch sitting on that loaded bomb—was I comfortable with the disposition of all the problems as presented?

As stated in the review writeup, you are talking to the review board, made up of the very top men in NASA, and they are making the decision, based on the information given by the presenters, on whether we are ready to safely launch the rocket under review. You must be honest, open, hold nothing back, and be ready to answer any questions the board might raise.

I cannot recall any "show-stopper" problems in the Apollo 11 prelaunch processing or countdown. I've questioned a couple of my friends involved in the countdown, and they had no memory of any key issues. This does not mean we had no problems—we were always working a backlog of what we considered routine problems, and by this I mean problems we could resolve without a scheduled delay. I remember well Rocco always reminding us that we did not distinguish between *major* and *minor* problems. The only place for major and minor is in music; in other words, all problems are major. Also, Rocco frequently reminded us that the rocket we were processing did not know the last rockets we launched were successful.

In the firing room during the countdown, things appeared to be just like any other countdown, but we were all very much aware that we were on the verge of accomplishing something that had never been done before in the history of mankind: men from planet Earth walking on the surface of another heavenly body, the moon. There was something special in the firing room's atmosphere, but I do not know how to describe it.

I sat on the top row of the consoles in the firing room along with Dr. Gruene, MSFC Program Manager Rocco Petrone, Dr. Debus, Walt Kapryn (Rocco's deputy), and the Spacecraft managers. I could look out over this huge room with our NASA and contractor engineers glued to their displays on the consoles, and then swivel my chair around and observe this beautiful Saturn V rocket on the launch pad. With the oxygen vapors, it appeared to be alive and breathing. My mind would go to these three brave astronauts and I'd visualize two of these astronauts making footprints on another heavenly body before they put their feet again on the good Earth. Awesome—almost unbelievable.

All several hundred console operators and the engineers watching the pens moving on the strip chart recorders in the firing room had an awesome responsibility. They had to judge, in the seconds before the firing command was initiated, if one of the critical parameters exceeded its predefined "redline" limits. By the Apollo 11 launch, we had made good, measurable progress in automation, but we were still far from the automated countdown we enjoy in today's world.

In the days prior to the launch, the excitement and tension increased daily with the uptick in media coverage and arriving VIPs from entertainment, sports, business, and politics. People with tents and campers staked out their observation sites along the river banks in Titusville and the coast on Cape Canaveral and Cocoa Beach. People with small boats anchored in the Indian River just west of the KSC. I read that one in four people on Earth were watching the Apollo 11 launch on TV or listening on the radio. It was estimated that one million people from all over our nation and the world were present in our county. My biggest fan in these one million observers was my precious mother, bless her soul. She was very much a people person, and she really enjoyed mingling with the people along the riverbank in Titusville.

There was some concern at the KSC about traffic bottlenecks as result of this huge crowd, which could potentially delay some of the launch team from coming to work on time. As a result, they had helicopters on standby, but as far as I know they were never needed. I always went in early for the countdown, and on this particular launch it was still dark when I headed in. I stopped at our church, St. Gabriel's Episcopal Church in downtown Titusville. I knelt, completely in the dark, and prayed. I felt good about this and I had no problem getting to work. Down US-1 there were large crowds along the river bank, and many of them were still up and in a festive mood in the middle of the night.

We always had built-in "holds" at strategic points in our countdown to work out problems without delaying the launch time. As we approached the final two minutes after the automatic sequencer started, everyone in the firing room was very calm, but the tension was there. At this point my eyes were glued to a large display board on the wall just above the VIP viewing room, which was to my left. Key events in this final two minutes were displayed in sequence, such as fuel tanks pressurized, and one key light that I looked for was *Vehicle on Internal Power*, which meant the vehicle electrical systems were now totally on the flight batteries and ground power had been removed. This was a very critical point.

As the last light on this sequence board came on, I swiveled my chair around and viewed the rocket with binoculars. After the first stage engines fired, the next critical event was the separation and swinging back of the service arms. I explained in another part of the book that these service arms are still attached when the rocket lifts off of the launch platform. If these service arms did not eject and swing back against the mobile launcher as planned, then we would have a very bad day. In other words, that would be an unthinkable, catastrophic situation.

After liftoff, we at KSC were essentially out of the picture and all communications were between Houston and the flight crew. However, our launch vehicle hardware had to perform perfectly for the next 2 hours and approximately 50 minutes. The first burn of our third stage, S-IVB, along with the instrument unit (IU), placed the service module (SM) and command module (CM) in Earth orbit. At the proper time after liftoff, around 244 minutes with all systems go, was the second engine start— the S-IV, which burned for about 5 minutes, propelling the spacecraft into Earth's escape velocity. The next major event was the separation of the CM/SM from the S-VB/IU and the mating and extraction of the lunar module (LM).

Thus far in the flight of Apollo 11, we had been there before with Apollo 10; however, on Apollo 10 Stafford and Cernan descended in the LM within 50,000 feet of the moon's surface, as planned, so once Apollo 11 passed this point we were in new territory. Things went according to plan until moments before touchdown when Armstrong and Aldrin realized they were not in the smooth landing area they had anticipated—instead, they were over an area with large boulders and craters. Armstrong took over the controls in an effort to find a smooth place to touch down.

This was really about as tense a situation as you could imagine. During these decisive moments they received repeated alarms about a computer overload, and the fuel indicator said they were approaching empty. Aldrin called out their forward speed and descent parameters and things were not looking good. In fact, they were on the verge of having to abort and fire the moon liftoff engine to return to the CSM.

Can and getting within a few feet of your destination and having to abort and return home? I've said this several times in my story, but I must repeat it here—I believe that Divine Providence was with us, because in a few moments Armstrong had maneuvered LM to a safe spot and they had a soft landing on the surface of the moon. Praise the Lord.

Armstrong calmly stated, "Tranquility Base here. The Eagle has Landed." Mike Collins, alone in the CM/SM, was circling the moon 70 miles above the surface.

Several hours later, the world watched as Armstrong slowly descended the ladder from the LM and made the first human footprint on another heavenly body. The date was July 20, 1969, and as the world watched they heard these very appropriate, history-making words: "One small step for man and one giant leap for mankind."

I am thoroughly convinced that had a Russian boot made that first footprint, the world we live in today would be different, and not for the better. Armstrong and Aldrin planted an American flag on the moon, but they did not claim it as American territory. Had this been the Communist Soviet Union, this territory might have been claimed by the Soviets.

I have read books on the Soviet space program during this period, and they were desperately trying to beat us to the moon. They did accomplish some "firsts" regarding the moon, such as the first flyby (it was unmanned) and the first soft landing (it was unmanned as well). Another interesting thing: during the Apollo 11 mission, the Soviets had an unmanned spacecraft, Luna 15, in orbit around the moon and hoped to land on the surface, scoop up some moon soil, and return to Earth before the return of Apollo 11 crew. Luna 15 crashed on the surface—again, Divine Providence.

Since the early days of the space program, there have always been arguments about man vs. robotics in space. The scenario

I just described was a big winner for the "man in space" people, because if Armstrong had not taken over the controls, the LM would surely have crashed just like the unmanned Luna 15, which had no human to correct the problems it encountered.

I want to say a little more about the competition to be the first to land men on the moon and return them safely to planet Earth. The stakes were enormously high; the winner of this contest would truly be the leader of the free world. From what I have read, the Soviets had many more problems in their 1960s test program than we were aware of. Remember, we changed the flight plan for Apollo 8 from an Earth orbit mission to a moon flyby mission because there was some real concern that the Soviets were going to beat us to the moon.

The Soviet space program had a brilliant leader, but he died young in a botched operation in 1966 and his deputy was chosen to replace him. This deputy had a bitter rivalry with another leader, and both had their staunch supporters. The deputy was finally ousted, but in all of this commotion several of their projects were delayed. In fact, it appeared the Soviets had a completely dysfunctional management system. I don't see how, but in spite of all of this they did accomplish some notable achievements in space.

Fortunately, we could not have had a more competent management and technical team in the 1960s. There is no way we could have accomplished the moon mission in this timeframe without the very best management. I am referring to the NASA administrators during this period: Jim Webb, Dr. Paine, Dr. George Mueller, General Sam Phillips, Dr. Wernher von Braun, Dr. Kurt Debus, Dr. Bob Gilruth, Rocco Petrone, and Dr. Hans Gruene. I say more about our leaders in another part of the book. Everyone should read the details of this historic Apollo 11 event and teach it to their children when they are old enough to comprehend what it means.

On the journey from the moon to planet Earth, Buzz Aldrin read from Psalm 8:3–4, "When I consider the heavens, the moon and the stars, which thou hast ordained; What is man, that thou art mindful of him?" Remember, on Christmas Eve 1968, the crew of Apollo 8 read the first nine verses of Genesis as they circled the moon. It is sad, but in today's world reading aloud from the Holy Scriptures would be unthinkable—it would be politically incorrect and might possibly offend someone. Ugh!

One event we and the launch crew always looked forward to after a manned launch to the moon was when the flight crew would come to the VAB, and we would assemble the launch team to hear the crew's first reports of their exciting journey. After the return of the Apollo 11 crew to KSC, there was a smaller briefing in Dr. Debus' conference room, and someone commented that this must have been somewhat like it was when Columbus returned to Europe to report the strange things he had observed in the new world across the ocean.

I think man will always be reaching for the stars; like a small child at the foot of the stairs, he *must* see what is at the top.

Dr. Hans Gruene
Dir. Launch Vehicle Operations

Lee James
Apollo Program Manager
Marshall Space Flight Center

Ike Rigell
Dep. Dir. And Chief Engineer
Launch Vehicle Operations

July 16, 1969—Firing Room 1—Apollo 11 countdown

In this scene we are looking down on the control consoles manned by several hundred NASA and contractor engineers. We can wheel our chair around and view the rocket on the launch pad.

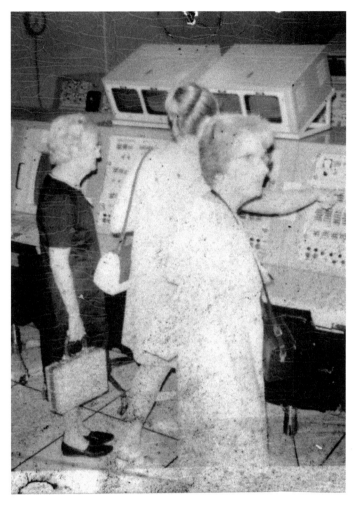

(L-R): My mother Attie, my wife, Kathryn, and my sister, Mary Jo, at Complex 39, Firing Room 1, after the launch of Apollo 11.

APOLLO 17—
LAST MAN ON THE MOON

Rockets, like people, have their own individual stories, and of course there is not time or space to tell of all the rockets I had the distinct privilege of working on. The Saturn V moon rocket was an amazingly successful program, and I am telling the stories of three of the thirteen Saturns that we launched. First, Apollo 8, the first manned Saturn V, with the crew Borman, Lovell, and Anders, which circled the moon December 24, 1968. Second, Apollo 11, July 16, 1969, was the first mission to land men, Armstrong and Aldrin, on the surface, while Mike Collins orbited the moon. Third, Apollo 17, December 7, 1972, was sadly the last mission to send a crew— Cernan, Schmitt, and Evans—to the moon and return safely.

December 7, 1941, was a very significant day in my life as an 18-year-old Marine on Midway Island. My duty that quiet Sunday morning was to operate our small combat telephone switchboard, and I awkwardly obeyed the officer of the day's command to be connected to our commanding officer, Lt. Col. Shannon, to inform him that the Japanese had bombed Pearl Harbor. Later that night, Japanese naval forces attacked our Marine garrison on Midway, and Midway is so small that no matter where a shell or bomb landed, it was too close for comfort. To put it mildly, that was an exciting day.

Now what does this have to do with Apollo 17? Exactly 31 years later, on this same date, December 7, I experienced another very exciting day. Now, an exciting day can come in two vastly different packages, one very unpleasant and one very pleasant, with anxiety in abundance in both situations. Contrast the two December 7s: one, I was thinking about survival; the other, I was on a real high, enjoying the fruits of my labor—it could not be better.

On December 7, 1941, I could never, ever imagine being in such a different world on December 7, 1972. You never know what the future will bring, but my advice is to look to the future with optimism. Maybe I have mentioned this before, but I like Hall of Fame baseballer Yogi Berra's quote about the future: "It is hard to make predictions, especially about the future." Thanks, Yogi, for that brilliant thought.

My subject is Apollo 17, but since this was the last Saturn V mission to the moon, I want to get a little nostalgic and make additional comments, related to but broader than this specific launch.

Three more missions to the moon were scheduled when the decision was made that Apollo 17 would be the last. Unfortunately, Congress had lost their enthusiasm for space, and public interest in the space exploration programs had significantly tapered off. Here is a little data point to back this statement up: for the Apollo 11 launch, it was estimated that we had one million visitors watching the launch; on Apollo 17, we had 500,000 watching. That is still a lot of people but half the number from just three years prior. Our scientists had a wealth of experiments ready to go, and we had three Saturn Vs to transport these experiments to explore and learn more about the moon, but with no money all of this good stuff was earthbound.

My mind is so full of thoughts I would like to express, but I hardly know where to start and stop. One thought comes to mind now—we have a short but very rich history in space, and our history in space has been very well documented, but almost 100 percent of that documented history commenced after the rocket left the launch pad. The launch teams' dedicated work in the long periods of preparation receive only a minor mention. The prime focus is—as it should be—on our courageous astronauts as they advance our knowledge of the universe. There is no question that it requires a certain type of person to understand and willingly take the risk and welcome the opportunity to venture into the hostile environment of outer space.

The book *Rocket Ranch* by Jonathan Ward, a friend of mine, does an excellent job of telling the stories of the guys "in the trenches" at KSC during those exciting days in the Apollo program. Jonathan spent many hours interviewing the workers who were still alive and able to share their stories. Jonathan's work was extensive and required two volumes. He asked me to write the foreword for one volume, and my friend, Bob Siek, wrote the foreword for the other volume. Many interesting stories are contained in those volumes, and I highly recommend reading them.

Back to the countdown of Apollo 17. This was the first and only night launch of Apollo. It was also the first Saturn V launch countdown where we experienced a technical problem that resulted in a countdown delay. At T minus 30 the launch sequencer failed and we recycled to T minus 22 minutes, and this resulted in a launch delay of 2 hours and 40 minutes. I can tell you the adrenaline was really flowing during this period. The launch sequencer is a critical part of the ground launch system, and it takes over the last two minutes of the launch countdown. There is one positive thing here: if you are going to have a technical problem in the countdown, you would much rather it be in the ground equipment than the flight hardware.

This type of problem required the right experts from NASA and our contractor (in this case IBM), along with MSFC Apollo Program Manager Dick Smith, Launch Director Walt Kapryn, Dr. Gruene, and Center Director Dr. Kurt Debus, to retreat to the "woodshed" to come up with a troubleshooting plan and hopefully a solution to the problem. The MSFC program manager had direct access to a team of MSFC design engineers who followed the countdown in a special launch support room with an RCA-110 computer, the same as we had at the launch site. Their computer was connected to a crude missile simulator. I sat by Dick Smith in the firing room, and we had already discussed this problem in some detail. I had worked with Dick (years later he was center director at KSC) since I first came to Huntsville with the old ABMA organization. I was very familiar with the ground sequencer and the associated circuitry, and it helped that I knew my counterparts in Huntsville. We both had the same electrical schematics, so we could easily follow each other as we developed a workaround for the problem. In some similar countdown situations like this, the people at MSFC could install our proposed fix in their RCA-110 simulator and verify it before we installed it at the launch site. I do not recall if we were able to do this on the Apollo 17 countdown or not. Anyway, we came out with a workaround that bypassed the problem and, in the end, we had a good day, and I think we earned our pay.

I will add a little note here about the atmosphere in the control room in situations like this one. When the several hundred people at the firing room consoles see a group with solemn faces enter the "woodshed," they know there is a genuine problem. They anxiously keep an eye on the door and try to judge by the faces coming out whether the news is good or unwelcome. Fortunately, on this occasion it was smiles.

I just mentioned that this was the first time in the Saturn V program that we had to hold for a technical issue. This just boggles my mind. I can visualize, from all of these launches, the thousands of components, pieces of ground equipment, and flight components—many with delicate moving parts that had to operate perfectly—working 24-7 during the countdown to achieve the tremendous success we enjoyed. The lack of technical launch issues is especially amazing when you consider the almost insurmountable problems we encountered on our initial operations. Our first attempt at a countdown demonstration test (CDDT) on Saturn V required 17 days to get all the "green lights" on the consoles "on" at T minus 0, whereas the process should take 24 hours. We had to recycle and start the countdown over so many times that I honestly questioned whether we would ever get all systems on a "go" mode at the same time.

I practically lived at the VAB during this period. Dr. Debus had a special room at the VAB equipped with a nice leather sofa, a toilet, and a small conference table. He seldom used this room, and Dr. Gruene and I had a key, so it was my hideaway comfort room during those long hours.

A CDDT is a full-bore rehearsal for a real launch countdown; it includes tanking and counting down to T minus 0 with the full countdown team, including management, on their assigned positions. Whenever we got close to T minus 0, Rocco would look over at me and say, "Ike, are you sure the igniters are not installed?" Of course, my answer had to be, "Yes, I assure you they are not installed."

Come with me now as we resume the count at T minus 22 minutes, and anxiously follow as the clock ticks down to T minus 30 seconds—where the sequencer failed on the first attempt. We were literally holding our breath until we had a positive indication that our fix worked. We did not have any time for any outward high-fives, but inwardly I had a very brief high-five. It had to be brief because in a few seconds I had to be ready to witness the moment of truth, when those huge F-1 rocket engines fired, and absorb that beautiful sight of the service arms ejecting and swinging out of the path of the ascending Saturn V.

As I mentioned previously, we at KSC were essentially out of the picture once the rocket cleared the mobile launcher. Houston took over, but us launch-vehicle folks had flight hardware, the third-stage S-IVB and the IU active in flight for almost three hours. After liftoff, I would remain at my console and switch to the Houston and flight crew communication circuit to follow the performance of the flight until the second ignition of the S-IV engine and engine cutoff, which occurred about five minutes later. Then the S-IVB and IU separated from the spacecraft, and only once this occurred could we in Launch Vehicle Operations know we had done our job, light up our cigars, and head home for some sleep. Of course, we followed intently the remainder of the Apollo 17 voyage to the moon and their stay. We loved to see, at the end of these ventures into outer space, those three beautiful, open parachutes lowering the Command Module in the water.

It was sad that Apollo 17 had to be the last Saturn-V flight to the moon, but this was one of the most rewarding flights of this series. This was the first flight with a professional geologist—Harrison Schmitt—as a crew member, and they had a record time operating the lunar rover. One little story here about the rover: They damaged one of the fenders, resulting in a moon dust problem, which was solved by using some good ol' "missile tape" to attach one of their maps to the fender.

Gene Cernan, the commander of Apollo 17, was one of only three astronauts that made two trips to the moon. Cernan said these words as he made his last step on the surface of the moon: "As we leave the moon at Taurus-Littrow, we leave as we came, and God willing, we shall return, with peace and hope for all mankind. Godspeed the crew of Apollo 17." I did not personally know Gene Cernan, but I have met him and heard him speak several times. Cernan passed away January 16, 2017. I also greatly admired astronauts Deke Slayton and John Young.

After his retirement, Cernan was a motivational speaker and TV commentator and one of the best and most articulate speakers for a strong space program. Unfortunately his efforts, as well as other astronauts', including Armstrong, fell on deaf ears during the administration of President Obama. They made a compelling case for keeping our country number one in space by not canceling the Constellation program and keeping the shuttles flying. The opposition argues that President Bush shut down the shuttle program. My answer to that is that under President Bush's plan to phase out the shuttle, the Constellation, if kept on schedule, would have been the next rocket generation, replacing the shuttle. President Obama should not have canceled the Constellation and he should not have permitted the phaseout of the shuttle. To me it is sad and humiliating for our country, the leader of the Western free-market countries, to be at the mercy of an unfriendly country ruled by a thug, paying them large sums of money to get our specialist to the International Space Station. How did we let this happen?

Back when we first received the word that Apollo 17 would be the last Saturn V launch, we had a little concern that we might lose some of the key contractor launch team members before the launch; they might seek employment elsewhere rather than be laid off immediately after the launch, because all of these contracts would be greatly reduced or canceled. I am happy to say, I do not know of one case where this happened. I think it started with Grumman, the contractor for the lunar module, with the slogan "Let us make the last one our best"—that attitude was picked up, and it prevailed throughout our workforce.

There was a massive layoff after the launch of Apollo 17, and it was a hard hit on the economy in Brevard County. At our peak, we in Launch Vehicle Operations had five major contracts—Boeing, Rockwell, McDonnell Douglas, IBM, and

Chrysler—totaling about 8,000 contractors. The Boeing and Rockwell contracts would be immediately downsized, but we would require a downsized crew to prepare and launch the first Skylab workshop scheduled for May 1973. Skylab would be launched from Launch Pad B using the Saturn V S1-C first stage and the S-11, the Saturn V second stage. We would retain a downsized IBM team to prepare and launch one unmanned and three manned Skylab flights in 1973 and the Apollo-Soyuz launch in July 1975. The McDonnell Douglas contract would be downsized, but we would retain a reduced launch team for the three manned Skylab launches and the Apollo-Soyuz launch.

Fortunately for McDonnell Douglas and us, we were awarded the support contract for processing our new project, the European Space Agency Spacelab at KSC, which picked up after the Apollo-Soyuz launch. I say fortunately for us because we had developed a very good relationship with the McDonnell Douglas team on the S-IVB contract and they would retain their key people for this new contract. Our contract with Chrysler was for the prelaunch processing and launch of the Saturn 1B, the booster stage for the Skylab and Apollo-Soyuz launches. Chrysler had previously had the contract with MSFC for manufacturing the tactical Redstone and Jupiter missiles and, of course, they were our support contractors for the launch of these military rockets. Chrysler also had a small support contract during the Apollo program.

Among all of these companies, IBM stood out as far as taking care of the people who were laid off. At that time, IBM had a strict hiring policy that any person hired at any of their locations needed the right qualifications for a position at one of their other locations if that project folded. We had a little issue with this policy when we were activating Complex 39. In our IBM contract, they had the responsibility for the onboard instrument unit (IU) and all of the electrical systems in the launch control center, computer rooms, and the mobile launcher, and this included a vast amount of specialized cables of all sizes, lengths, and shapes.

Cables were not IBMs "thing." They vastly underestimated this task and, before we knew it, we were in deep "yogurt." In other words, we were on the verge of a real showstopper. Cables warranted a big red flag on one of Rocco's PERT charts in the master control room (Firing Room 4). We had a technician,

Jim Finn, who had been our cable man on previous blockhouse activations, 26, 56, 34, and 37. We talked to Jim and he was willing to work for IBM. They refused to hire him because of their policy. When this contract ended they could not transfer Jim to another location because IBM had no locations that needed a cable expert, and at that time they had a reputation of never having a layoff. In later years, due to economic conditions that "no layoff" policy went out the window.

My brother-in-law, Jim Teply, had a brother who worked as a computer technician for IBM in the control room, and when he was laid off there, he had three IBM locations to choose from, and that was typical of all IBM employees.

Most of the senior guys in these various other contracts were relocated to their home bases, mostly on the West Coast. Dr. Gruene scheduled one very nice final get-together with the senior management of our contractors. One at a time, our senior NASA managers met with the various contractors in Firing Room 1 for a final photo op and farewells. Sadly, some of these guys we had worked so closely with for several years we would never see again. At one of our recent NASA meetings, someone brought these old pictures out, and strangely we had trouble identifying some of these guys.

The economic impact on Brevard County for these layoffs was severe. Every street had *House for Sale* signs, including our next-door neighbor, who was laid off from Rockwell. It was strictly a buyer's market.

I have to admit we could have reduced our NASA numbers at KSC, but, as I mentioned earlier, that is not the way the government system works. However, we did have a suitable work load for the next three years. From 1973 to 1975, we prepared Complex 39 to launch three manned launches on Saturn 1Bs, which had been designed to be launched from Complex 34 and 37 on Cape Canaveral. Adapting the mobile launcher to accommodate the S-1B service arms was one of the big issues. After the Skylab launches, we had one more manned launch, Apollo-Soyuz in July 1975, before we unfortunately had a long dry spell of manned launches—six years before the first shuttle launch in 1981.

Complex 39, Firing Room 1—Last countdown for Apollo 17, we have a problem. (Bottom, L-R:) Bo Corn, Dr. Hans Gruene, Dick Smith. (Top, L-R:) Dr. Debus, John Williams, Walt Kapryn, Bob Gray, Rocco Petrone, me.

NIGHTTIME LAUNCH OF APOLLO 17

NATIONAL AERONAUTICS AND SPACE ADMINISTRATION

APOLLO 17 LIFTOFF—The huge, 363-feet tall Apollo 17
(Spacecraft 114/Lunar Module 12/Saturn 512) space vehicle is
launched from Pad A, Launch Complex 39, Kennedy Space Center, Florida, at 12:33 a.m. (EST), December 7, 1972. Apollo 17,
the final lunar landing mission in NASA's Apollo program, was
the first nighttime liftoff of the Saturn V launch vehicle. Aboard
the Apollo 17 spacecraft were Astronauts Eugene A. Cernan,
commander; Ronald E. Evans, command module pilot; and Harrison H. Schmitt, lunar module pilot. Flame from the five F-1
engines of the Apollo/Saturn first (S-1C) stage illuminates the
nighttime scene.

December 7, 1972—"We have a problem."

There was a problem with the ground sequencer, but we
managed to fix the problem without delaying the launch.
This was the only night launch of the Apollo program.

READINESS REVIEWS

In the early space years, our flight readiness reviews were very informal. When we began our manned flights, these became a major event. Here is the difference. In the old days, Dr. Debus would schedule a visit to the launch complex three or four days before the scheduled launch. He would conduct a one-day, informal one-man launch readiness review.

We would begin our discussions with Dr. Debus in the Blockhouse, and our discussion would break down into three parts. The first was Electrical, Guidance, Control, and Ground Support Equipment. The second was Mechanical Systems, which included propellant loading. The third was Instrumentation, Telemetry, and Tracking Systems. Germans—Dr. Gruene, Albert Zeiler, and Karl Sendler—were head of these departments, but they always had their second man giving presentations. I gave the presentation for Dr. Gruene's area. Andy Pickett gave Zeiler's. Grady Williams gave Sendler's.

I might note here that Alabama was well represented in this process. We were all good old Alabama country boys. We used no sit-down presentation material for this review; in the Blockhouse we just gathered around the consoles and had a general discussion on our processing history of the flight hardware. This included any significant problems and their resolution, modifications since the last flight, and any concerns we might have regarding the flight hardware. Dr. Debus was like Rocco. No matter how much you boned up on a subject, he would come up with a question you'd have to go find an answer to.

One thing I knew very well that some guys had to learn the hard way was that if you get a question from Rocco or Dr. Debus that you did not know the answer to, just say "I don't know, but I will get you the answer."

Never, ever, ever try to fake it. From the Blockhouse, our little group would walk out to the launch pad and up the mobile gantry, discussing any particular features or problems we had experienced during our launch preparations. As I said, this was a very informal type review, but I can assure you Dr. Debus did not miss a thing. He knew what he was doing.

In the Manned Flight Programs, it was a very formal meeting in a very large room in the Operations and Control Building (O&C). This room was designed for this purpose and was called the Mission Briefing Room. All of the top brass from JSC, MSFC, NASA Headquarters, Air Force (Eastern Test Range), and KSC were in attendance. The top men from these organizations would make the decision if we were "go" or "no go" for the scheduled launch.

These men were seated at tables arranged in a horseshoe configuration with the presenter's podium at the open end of the horseshoe. Surrounding these tables would be rows and rows of chairs occupied by the next level of NASA managers and the senior level management of our contractors: IBM, Boeing, Rockwell, McDonnell Douglas, Rocketdyne, North American, Chrysler, and GE.

A typical lineup for the management team making the decision for "go" or "no go" included Dr. von Braun (MSFC), Dr. Bob Gilruth (JSC)—later this would be Chris Kraft—Dr. Kurt Debus (KSC), Dr. George Mueller, and Lt. Gen. Sam Phillips (NASA headquarters), Deke Slayton, Chief of the Astronaut Office, the Astronaut Medical Doctor, the Air Force Range Safety Officer, the Chief Range Meteorologist, and the Recovery Task Force Officer. I think it is obvious that the presenters were talking to some of the brightest minds in the country, so you had to be very sure you knew what you were talking about.

Presentations covered all facets, from the manufacturing of the hardware to the present preparation of the flight hardware and ground support systems involved in the next flight. These presentations would describe all problems encountered during the processing of the flight hardware and how these problems were resolved. Also included were discussion and resolution of any in-flight anomalies experienced on the previous flight. One of the biggest nightmares we presenters had to deal with was what we called an unexplained anomaly. Unfortunately, we did encounter a few of these.

A typical anomaly would be a component such as a relay, valve, regulator, etc. either failing to operate on one occasion or cycling "on" when it should not operate. After that occasion you could not make it repeat the failure no matter how many times you tried to repeat it. Now your problem was to convince these very smart people (this anomaly could be in a very critical circuit) it was safe to fly this vehicle with three astronauts aboard. You must have very good rationale to support your "go" position. This would certainly include describing all the suspected hardware you replaced. Very likely you had installed a completely redundant path for this suspect hardware.

A typical agenda included the MSFC Program Manager giving the status of the booster rockets, their development history, and new modifications. It was the same thing for the JSC Program Manager for the Command Module and the Luna Landing Module. The KSC presentation was in two parts. First came the Launch Vehicle Operations, which covered all our test and prelaunch activities since the arrival of the flight hardware at KSC. I made these presentations for all of the Mercury-Redstone, Apollo, Skylab and Apollo-Soyuz flight readiness reviews. My counterpart on the Spacecraft side, Ted Sassen, made the presentations for the Command Module and the LUNA Landing Module.

My package included the S-1C (1st stage), S-II (2nd stage), S-IVB (3rd stage), Instrument Unit (IU), all the Control Consoles in the Firing Room, the RCA ground checkout computers (one in the Firing Room and one in the Mobile Launcher), the ground support equipment located in the MLP and on the launch pad, the status of all our Launch Countdown Procedures, and the readiness of the launch team, NASA, and contractors. At our peak in the Apollo program, we had direct control of about 8,000 contractors and 400 NASA employees in our work area.

I felt honored that Rocco Petrone and Dr. Gruene assigned me this task of preparing and presenting our part of the overall flight readiness review process.

I think it is fair to say this was an awesome task. Our Problem Tracking System documented every minute or major problem we encountered during the processing of the flight and ground hardware and software under review. This meant you had to deal with several hundred problem reports for every flight readiness review. It was up to me to recommend to Dr. Gruene and Rocco Petrone which issues we would take to the Readiness Review Board. On one hand, you did not want to waste the Board's time on a bunch of trivial stuff. On the other hand, you for sure must not leave out something that could contribute to a problem in flight that they had not been briefed on.

All of us presenters used view graphs, which was the standard method of presentations during that era. Normally I would have a one-sentence statement to introduce the problem, and I would talk from that. If necessary, I would call up backup charts. You had to be prepared to go into any depth necessary to convince the board we had resolved the problem.

Prior to the presentation to the Launch Readiness Review Board, I had gone through all of my material with our contractors and with Dr. Gruene and Rocco Petrone. And I can say after I had successfully gone through my material with Rocco, I felt I was in good shape for the presentation to the Review Board. In my view, Rocco was the most capable person I have ever known to probe and ask the right questions to understand the problem and come up with the right solutions.

At the conclusion of my presentation, I like that the other presenters had to make a statement concerning our readiness status. My typical statement was something like this: "With the successful completion of our remaining schedule tasks, the flight hardware, the ground support equipment, the countdown procedures, and the launch team, NASA and contractors are ready for launch."

Dr. George Mueller would poll the Board members for their "go-no go" position, and he would also ask for a readiness statement from each of our contractor managers.

Since the FRR was scheduled several days before launch

when there were many preparation tasks still underway, there were some issues still in work, and the "Go" position had to be qualified with the successful closeout of any open issues. The final "go-no go" position would come out of an L-1 meeting attended only by the MSFC, KSC, JSC, center directors, Dr. George Mueller, Gen. Sam Phillips, Air Force weatherman, and Rocco Petrone. Rocco was the main speaker for this meeting.

Here is a little gem I want to add, and it is good advice for anyone who might happen to read this. In my career with NASA and United Technologies, I had the privilege and pleasure to observe and interact with some of the most successful and smartest people in their profession. I observed one attribute they all possessed: They surrounded themselves with very smart and capable people, and they received counsel from them. Maybe there is some truth in the old axiom that if you hire people smarter than you are, you are smarter than they are.

I learned early in life it is mandatory that you surround yourself with the smartest, hardest-working people you can find. Fortunately, in all my career in the missile and rocket business I was well surrounded with the best. NASA people included Ed Fanning, Frank Bryan, Bill Chandler, Carrol Rouse, Milt Chambers, Carl Whiteside, Frank Penovich, Norm Carlson, Remer Prince, and many others just too numerous to mention. Contractor managers included John Culley and Bill Holms of S-1C; Al Martin of S-II; George Faenza, Ed Scully, and Hal Eaton of S-IVB; George Smith and Bob Ehrhardt of IBM; and Pat Yount of Chrysler. We made a great team. In my career I also had the opportunity and pleasure to bring in the next generation of talented space workers like Al Koller and Enoch Moser.

SKYLAB PROGRAM— 1973-1979

What do you do for an encore after the Apollo Earth-to-Moon program? As I said earlier, Apollo extended man's environment from a very narrow band about 8 miles above Earth's surface to about 240,000 miles. I had a deep sense of satisfaction being part of this historical event that allowed man to break the bonds of Earth's gravity and make human footprints on another heavenly body. So, what should be next? You ask Dr. Werhner von Braun and any of us guys, NASA or contractors, and we all with one accord would say, "Let's go to Mars." Ask Congress and the general American public and, sorry to say, you would get a completely different answer.

Take a view of our solar system and you will immediately zero in on the Red Planet, Mars. *Yep, that's it; let's go to Mars.* Dr. von Braun and his colleagues had this vision for many years. We proved man can live and work in space, and we have the technical and manufacturing capability to design and build hardware to safely travel and live in space. I am positive that if we put out a call for astronaut candidates to travel to the Red Planet, we would have a tremendous response of highly qualified men and women anxious to be the first human to set foot on another planet.

Going to Mars would extend man's venture from Earth from approximately 240,000 miles to a minimum of approximately

39 million miles, and it could be as far as approximately 249 million miles. Since Earth and Mars trace different elliptical orbits around the sun at different speeds, the distance between Earth and Mars is constantly changing. Every day we are learning more and more from the International Space Station (ISS) about how to live and grow food in outer space. Maybe we do not have all the answers, but I believe it is well within our grasp. All we need for this exciting venture would be the support of Congress and the American people.

Unfortunately, at the end of the Apollo program we did not have the support of Congress or the American people for a bold program to Mars; it was still only a dream for space-minded people. The next large space program on the books was the shuttle, and on the most optimistic level it was still several years away, but in the intervening years we did have two very interesting and valuable programs, Skylab and Apollo-Soyuz. Skylab was very valuable in extending our knowledge of the solar system and man adapting to a spacecraft environment. The interesting aspect of Apollo-Soyuz was more on the human side than the technical side. There was nothing new or exotic about placing our astronauts in low Earth orbit, but to link up with the country with which we were heavily engaged in the Cold War created a certain amount of interest.

We barely had the support of Congress for Skylab. Years earlier, I think it was in the early 1960s, von Braun made serious proposals for using some of the future elements of the Saturn V rocket, like the S-1C or S-11, not as a propulsion stage but as a space workshop. Due to funding problems, he finally got approval to use an S-IV as our first space workshop. It would be launched, unmanned, with a Saturn V S-1C first stage and the S-11 second stage from Complex 39. This would be followed by three manned launches using the Saturn 1B booster with the S-IVB to place the Apollo CM and SM in low Earth orbit to rendezvous with the space workshop. All previous S-1Bs had been launched from blockhouses 34 and 37 on Cape Canaveral, but we had decommissioned these facilities and it required some significant modifications to accommodate launching a S-1B from the Saturn V Complex 39.

We launched the Skylab workshop from Pad B, Complex 39 on May 14, 1973. The launch was successful, but in flight we suffered a severe problem when the meteoroid shield inadvertently opened due to aerodynamics. This in turn damaged one of the solar panels and resulted in some communication problems. There was extensive work between the experts at MSFC and KSC and the flight crew to recover as much as they could from this problem.

We launched Skylab 2 (SL-2), the first manned crew to occupy the space workshop, on May 25, 1973. The launch was successful, but we came within milliseconds of a total disaster.

We successfully launched SL-3 on July 28, 1973, and SL-4 on November 16, 1973. All manned Skylab launches had three-man crews. The Skylab program was considered very successful, and the scientific experiments performed and long-range crew survival data proved very valuable. A record of 84 days in orbit was set, which of course was later surpassed in the ISS program. Due to some solar activity, the decay of the space workshop began earlier than anticipated. NASA planned to use what was called an inertial upper stage (IUS), which would be placed in low Earth orbit by a future shuttle flight, and propel the Skylab into a higher orbit. Unfortunately, that never happened.

1973—Skylab Launch, Complex 39, Firing Room 1,
Dr. Kurt Debus and me.

The following is the official caption from Kennedy Space Center shown on the back of this official photo: "A happy Dr. Kurt H. Debus, Kennedy Space Center director, appears to be indicating that NASA's manned Skylab launch record is now two for two with today's successful liftoff of Skylab 3 astronauts. Dr. Debus is shown in the launch control center speaking to Isom A. Rigell, KSC's deputy director of Launch Vehicle Operations. A Saturn 1B rocket broke through heavy cloud cover over Complex 39B, sending the space pilots on the first leg of their planned 59-day mission aboard the orbiting Skylab space station."

Complex 39. Saturn 1B. We built a "milk stool" to adapt
Saturn 1B at Complex 39 where we also launched the
larger Apollo rockets.

AMERICAN ASTP LAUNCH
СТАРТ "АПОЛЛОНА" /ПРОГРАММА ЭПАС/

This was a historical flight, as it was a joint flight with NASA and the Soviet Union, during the height of the Cold War in 1975. It was the last manned flight before the shuttle six years later in 1981.

NEAR MISS

Skylab 2 was the first launch of a Saturn IB from Launch Complex 39. It was launched from atop a pedestal carrying the Apollo Capsule/Service Module with three astronauts bound for orbit. The MSFC supplied Saturn IB Electrical Ground Support Equipment (ESE) and used generally the same components and system used at Complex 37 and 34 for the Saturn IB launches, with modifications. The very complex relay logic used in the ESE had an effect not well understood, which almost caused a disaster on this launch.

During the final automatic sequence during the SIB launch, the ESE generated a "commit" signal after a check that all eight SIB engines were running. The commit signal starts the sequence of releasing the hold-down arms, allowing the vehicle to start rising from the launch pedestal. As the vehicle rises, "liftoff" sensing switches are actuated, causing the vehicle ESE umbilicals to disconnect.

It was in this period that a poorly understood electrical phenomenon occurred. The relays used to build the interlocked logic in the ESE are electromechanical, consisting of a wound magnetic coil and a spring-loaded arm with electrical contacts. One of these "re-contacted" due to an unforeseen current in the coil caused by a diode. The re-energized circuit caused the cutoff sequence to start.

At approximately .1 seconds after commit, the thrust failure cutoff circuit was momentarily energized for only a fraction of a second. If the erroneous cutoff signal had been sustained long enough to energize the cutoff relay, an improper automatic cutoff sequence would have been initiated. Vehicle power would have been transferred from internal to external without engine cutoff, resulting in launch without vehicle electrical power.

Translation: If the signal had been slightly longer, the vehicle would have been transferred to external power with the umbilicals out, which meant powering down. The S1B H1 engines require no power to keep running, so they would have kept running. The hold downs were released, so the vehicle would have flown uncontrolled without electrical power. The crew would have to abort, a very dangerous action. We found this after the launch when we were reviewing the digital records which recorded the pulse. After we realized what had almost happened, I was "elected" to tell Walt Kapyran, our launch director. I've never seen him turn ashen before.

We were very fortunate to have dodged this bullet. The good Lord was watching!

ABMA—NASA
LEADERSHIP LESSONS

I t is a good feeling when you are serving in an organization where you have complete confidence and respect for your top leaders. Fortunately, I have been very blessed in this area all of my career, in both my military and civilian service. In the military, I served under Adm. Nimitz, Gen. Cates, Gen. Schmidt, and Col. Shannon. I was never in the real presence of these leaders but I, along with our country, benefited greatly from their professional expertise and wisdom.

In my civilian space career, I served under Maj. Gen. Medaris, Dr. George Mueller, Gen. Sam Phillips, Dr. Hans Gruene, Dr. Kurt Debus, Rocco Petrone, and Wernher von Braun. I am convinced our country would never have enjoyed the tremendous benefits, technology advancements, national security, and world prestige had we not had this leadership team at the very time we needed them. As a brief survey of our history reveals, I think by Divine Providence the right leaders surface at critical times of need. For example, during the Revolutionary War there was George Washington, during the Civil War there was Abraham Lincoln, during WWII there were Franklin Roosevelt and Harry Truman, during the Cuban Missile Crisis there was John F. Kennedy, during the Cold War there was Ronald Reagan, and during the Space Race with the Soviets the team listed above was ready and willing to serve. We must also recognize the wisdom of the first NASA administrator, Jim Webb, who formed this NASA leadership team.

I started my space career in the Army Ballistic Missile Agency (ABMA) under Gen. Bruce Medaris, who was the top man, and under him, Wernher von Braun, the top civilian leader. Gen. Medaris was 100 percent "spick and span" military, and, in my view, he was the type of leader we needed at that time. He and von Braun made a great team. In his first visits to the blockhouse and launch pad, he reminded me of Gen. Patton with his polished cavalry boots, swagger stick, and his lieutenant aide closely following him.

He made no bones about it—there was just something in the air that told you he was the man in charge; however, I did not ever observe that he tried to micromanage or interfere in any of Dr. Debus' decisions regarding Launch Operations. He would ask questions of the launch team and seemed interested in learning more about the details of the rocket. I remember on one occasion he wanted to understand more about the guidance system in the Redstone, and one of our system engineers was explaining how the guidance system worked. The general kept asking questions about how this system worked, and while this engineer was technically very smart, diplomatically he was not so smart and he just blurted out, "General, you are just not getting this." By the way he said it and the tone of his voice, one could interpret him as saying, "General, this is just above your head." The general smiled and passed over the comment, but later this guy's boss, Carl Whiteside, chewed him out for what Carl considered being rude to the general.

I want to comment further on the statements I made about having the right leaders at the right time and this formidable team of Gen. Medaris and von Braun. In the mid 1950s, before the Soviets launched the first Sputnik on October 4, 1957, Gen. Medaris and von Braun made several trips to Washington to convince the bureaucrats there to give them permission to launch an Earth satellite.

In other parts of this book I go into some detail on the facts supporting their position that we could have launched an Earth satellite before the Soviets. Sadly, we see many times that common sense does not prevail when you get enmeshed in the bureaucratic, political world in DC.

Another turf battle raging in DC during the mid '50s was the role of the Army and the Air Force regarding short and long-range missiles. I discussed this issue in another part of this book, so I won't repeat it here, but we all in ABMA were proud of the leadership displayed by Gen. Medaris and von Braun and their efforts in Washington to try to prevent the pending decision to severely limit the range of missiles developed by the Army. They made some very strong testimonies before Congress on the prediction that future wars could be prevented or, if there were a war, the surviving nation would be the country with the most powerful missile capabilities.

I do not recall the exact year, but Gen. Medaris retired around 1960. A few years after his retirement, he was diagnosed with terminal cancer. At this time, he was living in Winter Park, Florida. His many friends from Huntsville wanted to have a special dinner in his honor. Dr. Debus invited Dr. Gruene, myself, and a couple of others whom I cannot recall from our launch team to accompany him. Other than Dr. Debus, none of the rest of us, including Dr. Gruene, were real close to Gen. Medaris, but I guess they wanted some attendance from the launch team. We went to Huntsville in Dr. Debus' plane, which at that time was a JetStar; later the NASA center directors switched to Gulfstreams. We flew from PAFB to the Orlando airport, which today is the Orlando Executive Airport, and picked up Gen. Medaris. A JetStar is a very fast plane but also a small plane with all seats facing forward. Dr. Debus and Gen. Medaris sat in the front two seats, so the rest of us had no conversation with the general on the trip. This dinner, in essence, was a farewell to a respected friend.

You never know what the future holds, though, and several years later I heard a powerful testimony from Gen. Medaris. I cannot quote it word for word, but here is a good summary. He was invited to a prayer meeting in his neighborhood in Winter Park. He did not want to go, but somehow he was persuaded to attend. This prayer group was from the Episcopal Church in Orlando, and a lady named Virginia Lively was the leader of this group for that evening. Virginia was from some town on the Gulf Coast around Naples, and she was well known in Episcopal circles for having the gift of healing. She prayed over Gen. Medaris during this meeting and he felt a powerful surge through his body and his cancer went into remission. I might add here, a year or so prior to this event, Kathryn and I attended a healing service at St. Gabriel's Episcopal Church in Titusville conducted by Virginia Lively, so we were not at all surprised to hear this wonderful story.

From this point on, Gen. Medaris' life took a new direction and he studied for the ministry. He was ordained and later served as the rector of the Episcopal church in Maitland, Florida. As best I can recall, he was given about 18 months to live when he was in his mid-60s, but after this divine healing occurred he lived many more years before passing away at the age of 88.

Dr. George Mueller was the head of the Apollo program and, in my view, the right man at the right time for the job. He and his deputy, Gen. Phillips, organized and established a management plan for this enormous task of landing men on the moon and returning them safely during the 1960s. As I said in another part of this book, Dr. Mueller had to take charge and direct this strong-willed group of talented men from the various NASA centers, assign specific responsibilities for each, and define the overall management structure. This was no simple task, but he did it. He was not afraid to make bold decisions and stand by them. One bold decision I recall was early in the Apollo program when he stated we were going with the "all up configuration." This was strongly opposed by the folks in MSFC. What this means is that rather than flying a first stage with a dummy second and third stage, on the initial flight we will have all three live stages. The MSFC plan was the opposite: verify the live first stage with dummy upper stages; in other words, verify one new stage at a time. Turned out Dr. Mueller was right—just look at the tremendous success we had with Apollo 8, an "all up" configuration that successfully sent a crew around the moon and safely back to earth.

Along with his professional talents, Dr. Mueller was a gentleman. One very thoughtful and positive thing he did was periodically holding a "tea" for the wives at the various NASA centers. Kathryn enjoyed these events, as Dr. Mueller expressed his appreciation for their support for the space program and gave them an interesting update on where we were in our efforts to reach the moon and what was projected for the near future in NASA. I did not have a personal friendship with Dr. Mueller, but I did present the flight readiness reviews for all of our manned flights where he was the head of the review board. On one occasion when he was down in Florida, I invited him to speak at a civic event here in Titusville and he graciously accepted.

Gen. Sam Phillips was Dr. George Mueller's deputy and he was a very well respected and capable man. He had a significant role in the formation of the management system for the Apollo program. The first time I saw Gen. Phillips was when he and Dr. Mueller visited Blockhouse 34 during the launch of a Saturn 1B. We experienced a significant problem during the countdown. I cannot recall the details, but it was some small, unique electrical component and we did not have a spare to replace it. We were on the phone to MSFC looking for a spare and Gen. Phillips came over to one of the consoles and said he wanted to use the outside phone. I was standing nearby, and I do not know who he was talking to, but it was one of his colleagues in the DOD and he was describing this part and telling the person he was talking with to get one down to Cape Canaveral as soon as possible. I sized him up right there as a man of action, and he turned out to be a tremendous asset to NASA.

Sometime later, we were having severe problem with our RCA-110 computers, and although I discuss this in another part of the book, I want to briefly mention it here as it relates to Gen. Phillips. Four parties were involved in our computer operations. RCA designed the computer along with MSFC. KSC had awarded IBM the contract to operate the computers and there was a certain amount of "It's the other guys fault that we are having so much computer downtime." Gen. Phillips called some of the top people in these four organizations together for a summit meeting at KSC. He ran the meeting and he made it very clear, in no uncertain terms, he wanted a team effort to identify the source of the problem and a solution to fix it. I admired his management style. He did not yell, pound on the table, or use any vulgar language. He simply made his point, and made it very effectively, using a very calm but deliberate voice. I can say the same thing about Dr. Mueller's communication. Come to think about it, I could say the same thing for the other men on this management team I am discussing, von Braun, Dr. Debus, Rocco Petrone, and Dr. Gruene. They all commanded respect without being loud or vulgar.

I can say the same thing about General Phillips as I said about Dr. George Mueller. He was the right man for the right job at the right time. He was truly an asset to NASA and our nation.

I have mentioned this before, but I want to say it again. One of the outstanding attributes that I observed in our top leaders was that they surrounded themselves with very capable people and listened to their counsel. There is an old saying, and maybe it has some merit, that says, "If you hire people that are smarter than you are, then that proves that you are smarter than them." In the early years of our space activities in Huntsville, all of the first-line technical management were Germans from the old V-2 program, and in fact all of the second-level management in the technical areas were Germans as well. I never did see that this presented a problem, as the vast majority of the workforce were young male engineers just out of college with no work experience.

The top civilian in the ABMA was von Braun, and when the Florida Launch Operations group was formed, which was identified as the Missile Firing Lab (MFL), von Braun selected Dr. Kurt Debus to head up this group, which was an excellent choice; he could not have picked a better man.

Dr. Debus in turn selected Dr. Hans Gruene as his deputy and as head of the guidance control and electrical networks systems. Again, the right man for the right job. Then Dr. Debus selected Albert Zeiler as head of the mechanical and propulsion systems and Karl Sendler as head of the instrumentation, telemetry and tracking systems. These three men were, of course, from the old von Braun team and excellent choices for these jobs.

I had a daily working relationship with Dr. Gruene, and later I became his deputy and took his position when he retired. I could not have asked for a better boss. In all my years with Dr. Gruene, I never had to ask for a raise. As best I recall, I received promotions as soon as the system would allow it. Over the years we developed a very good rapport. I could make any technical decision or schedule changes, and he would back me up. I always kept him up to date on any issues or problems we were working on.

Notice, I left out one thing in my decision-making power:

spending money or hiring new people. Dr. Gruene was the most conscientious person I have ever known in government work concerning fiscal responsibility. In the civil service system, all organizations have an organizational chart that specifically defines the grade levels, job titles, and the number of people in the various skill levels. It is common for many managers to fill every vacant slot and plead for more people. With Dr. Gruene, it was the opposite. He liked to operate below his authorized strength, and you had to convince him of the need before you could hire someone.

One good example of his thriftiness comes to mind. When the time came for us to move from our engineering and laboratory building on Cape Canaveral to our new office building on Merritt Island, we were given a floor plan of our future office. The personnel office, who would be occupying the executive offices in the new building, came to us with a catalog to select our furniture and carpet. The walls in these offices were nice wood panels. Dr. Gruene told them he did not need the wood panels or the fancy, expensive furniture. Dr. Debus said, "Hans, you must take it."

Dr. Gruene earned his money, big time, in the structuring of our launch service contracts. We initially had some big issues with the aerospace contractors McDonnell Douglas, Rockwell, and Boeing. We had similar launch service contracts with IBM and Chrysler, but due to their different background we did not face the same big issues as we did with the aerospace contractors. The aerospace contractors were accustomed to working three shifts a day on projects like these, and their initial proposals came in with the position that the only way they could meet the launch schedule we provided them was to work three shifts a day. Dr. Gruene let them know that there was no way we were going to accept a three-shifts-a-day work plan. Dr. Gruene's plan was the same concept that had been so successful with the Redstone, Jupiter, Jupiter-C, and Pershing programs. The concept was that we had one first test team and we would go as long as necessary to complete a major test, and then we would authorize a limited second shift for modifications and other offline work. Dr. Gruene did not want a second or third team performing major test operations.

Dr. Gruene's wisdom paid off in spades. I do not want to go into too much detail, but our Spacecraft counterparts accepted their contractors' three-shifts-a-day proposal and, from my observation, it was a huge mistake.

Here is why I say this. Rocco's daily early morning staff meeting was most of the time consumed trying to figure out what kind of screw up or problems the Spacecraft second and third shift experienced during the night. Finally, Rocco got so irritated with this that he had the Rockwell contractor manager attend his morning staff meeting. On the Launch Vehicle side, if we had to run overtime during the night to complete a major test, I was usually there and did not need a third-hand report of what happened. Another thing that convinced me this second and third-shift plan was a waste of money was that one of my neighbors, a Rockwell employee, worked the second shift, and he would brag about sleeping much of the time so he had plenty of free time during the day.

Another area where Dr. Gruene taught us a lesson in fiscal responsibility was in the budget process. Toward the end of the fiscal year, if we had not spent our entire budget allocation, the word would come down from Washington to "spend that money and buy anything," because if you did not use all of your budget one year, it would make it harder for them to justify a larger budget for the coming year. Dr. Gruene would not play this game. It's sad that you get penalized and not rewarded for doing an excellent job in the fiscal world. If every federal employee worked on the same principles as Dr. Gruene, we would have a surplus rather than a deficit at the end of the year.

Another area where Dr. Gruene had a profound influence on my thinking was is in the area of automation. He was one of the first to envision how automation could advance the checkout and preparation of missiles and rockets. He was a primary thinker in defining the requirements and the layout for the launch control center at Complex 39.

If there were any negative comments or opinions concerning Dr. Gruene, I never heard them. The very few times I ever witnessed him get really angry he said, "I give a damn." That was the limit of his expression of anger.

He had a good sense of humor. In one of our discussions he said his young son, Peter, who must have been about six or seven at the time, came running into the kitchen all out of breath and sweating and wanted a drink of water. Dr. Gruene said, "What are you doing Peter?" Peter answered, "We are playing war and I am chasing those mean Germans."

When Dr. Gruene retired, we gave him the best retirement party I have ever witnessed, and in these latter years I have attended many. I had lunch with Dr. Gruene at least once a month after he retired, and I sought and received much valuable guidance from him during the transition period after the termination of the Apollo program.

Dr. Gruene passed away suddenly of a heart attack, and sadly we were up in the Maine woods on vacation and I did not learn about it until we returned home. He was a good man, and I enjoyed my close association with Dr. Gruene for many years.

Dr. Kurt Debus was the original head of the ABMA Missile Firing Laboratory (MFL), which first came to Cape Canaveral in 1953 to launch the Redstone missile. Later, when the MFL was transferred to NASA and the Kennedy Space Center (KSC) was created, Dr. Debus was named the first KSC director. Dr. Debus was in the von Braun group that was brought to the US after WWII.

Dr. Debus turned out to be an excellent choice to head up the launch operations in Florida. We, MFL, were such a small organization in the beginning that we all got to know each other, including our leader, Dr. Debus. He had the initial appearance of being somewhat aloof, but that was really not who he was. I want to describe a few of the personal, one-on-one, friendly encounters I had with Dr. Debus over the years.

On one of our very early launches on the Redstone, I got very sick during the countdown, and I told Dr. Gruene that I was going out of the blockhouse for a few minutes. I laid down in our emergency medical vehicle, which at that time was an old army vehicle. Fortunately, there was a mosquito net in the ambulance or I would have gotten sicker by the loss of blood from the mosquitoes. Yes, they were that bad. Dr. Gruene mentioned to Dr. Debus that I was out in the ambulance. Dr. Debus came out there and said, "Ike, you need to go home. You should not be out here. I am going to get Smitty to take you home." Smitty was Dr. Debus' personal driver. I replied, "No, Dr. Debus, I will be okay in a few minutes." He said, "No, I think you should go home. You should not be out here like this." I pleaded with him, "Let me stay a few more minutes and if I do not feel better I will go home." He finally agreed. In a little while I did return to the blockhouse feeling a bit better, and, while certainly not well, I did make it for the rest of the countdown. The real message here is that Dr. Debus demonstrated a real concern for the troops.

Another little dialogue I had with Dr. Debus was during the Explorer 1 countdown. We had to scrub the first launch attempt due to unfavorable high-altitude wind conditions, and I proposed running an all-systems test prior to the next countdown. Dr. Debus told me he did not think we needed it, and we got into a friendly discussion there in the blockhouse as I tried to convince him we should run the test and he was telling me we didn't need it. Then he proposed something that backed me in the corner, saying, "I will bet you a dollar I can go to any switch on these panels and operate it and it will work." What could I say? I could not take that bet. Dr. Gruene was standing there listening to all of this, and I said to Dr. Gruene, "Help me out here." He laughed and said, "That is between you and Kurt." The result: Dr. Debus finally said, "Okay, go ahead and run your test."

Another very pleasant memory I have of Dr. Debus occurred during the Christmas holidays, and I should add that when this event started out I did not think it would be such a pleasant memory. This Christmas we did not have a missile on the launch pad, which was a little unusual as some Christmases we were under pressure to get a launch off before the year ended. I received a call from Shirley Ferguson, Dr. Debus' secretary, and she told me Dr. Debus wanted me in his office the next morning at 10. I asked Shirley, "What is this all about?" She said, "I cannot tell you." I knew Shirley pretty well, and I tried to probe her to give me some hint. She played it cool and just kept telling me she could not say anymore. Needless to say, the rest of the day, I had my mind more on this telephone call than I did on Christmas.

The next morning, I was still full of anxiety as I headed out for our office building, which at that time was still on Cape Canaveral. I arrived there a little before 10, and as I entered the lobby I saw Andy Pickett. Andy was one of the top guys in the mechanical group and, like me, he was one of the original members of the MFL. I found out Andy received the same call that I had, and he did not know any more about why we were there than I did and was as nervous as me. We went on into Dr. Debus' office and had to wait in the lobby outside for a few minutes. We tried to work on Shirley a little more about why we were there. No luck. The only comfort I could muster was that if I *were* in trouble, I had some company with Andy.

I cannot recall the exact exchange of words between me, Andy, and Dr. Debus at that moment, but he presented me and Andy each with a $300 bonus check. We were both astounded, going immediately from anxiety mode to euphoria. This was in the 1950s, and I can tell you $300 was a lot of money back then. In a recent launch preparation period, we experienced a very complex and difficult problem. Andy and I spent several days devising special tests to identify the source of the problem. It was an electro-mechanical problem, and the answer kept eluding us, but finally we were able to identify and solve the problem—we saved the day. Dr. Debus happened to be out at the launch pad one day when Andy and I were poring over schematics, and he joined us for a few minutes in discussing this problem. Back to receiving the bonus check: of course, we exchanged Christmas greetings with Dr. Debus and gave a big "Happy Holidays" to Shirley as we left. I could not wait until I got home to tell Kathryn that I did believe in Santa Claus. One little footnote about Andy— he and Kathryn attended the same high school at one time, and then the University of Alabama at the same time.

One of Dr. Debus' management attributes was that he liked to play the "devil's advocate" to determine how well you could defend your position or how strongly you felt about it. He was so good at this that I was never able to figure out if he really agreed with what I was saying or the opposite.

I will describe one event to illustrate this. Toward the end of the Skylab program, the Skylab was going into a lower and lower orbit than had been anticipated, and there was a real concern that large chunks of this hardware could eventually plunge to Earth in populated areas. One plan to avoid this was to launch a booster rocket into orbit, link up with the Skylab, and boost it into a higher orbit. This booster stage would be launched in the space shuttle. MSFC was responsible for the Skylab and the booster rocket. They selected the booster rocket, which they identified as the Inertial Upper Stage (IUS). The IUS was designed and built by the Boeing Company, and I think it was originally going to be used by the Air Force. I have to say all of this to get to my "devil's advocate" topic. Our program office at KSC scheduled a meeting with Dr. Debus to describe how we would process the IUS at KSC. I should add that things changed after Rocco left KSC for Washington. In his day, we, Launch Operations, would be making that presentation and not the program office. I could write a whole chapter on this, but I will just leave that one statement.

I was invited to this presentation being made to Dr. Debus by the program office, and during their presentation I voiced total disagreement with just about everything they said. It was a complete bunch of garbage, and those people did not know what they were talking about, but that was not my main problem. Dr. Debus seemed to challenge my comments and agree with the program office. I left the meeting pretty discouraged, and when I returned to my office building I went to see Walt "Kappy" Kapryn. He took Rocco's place after Rocco left KSC. I was telling Kappy how discouraged I was that Dr. Debus was agreeing with the program office. He laughed and said, "Dr. Debus' secretary just called and he wants you to give him a presentation of how we, Launch Operations, would process the IUS."

I do not care to use his name, but the head of the program office found out about this presentation I would be making and said, "Let me know when you make this presentation and I will go with you." I said, "Dr. Debus asked me to this meeting. He did not ask you." I left it at that. I made the presentation to Dr. Debus and he accepted our plan, and I learned he had actually been in agreement with me the whole time. Note, I used *our* in the above sentence. Before I made the presentation to Dr. Debus, I had several of our guys get together and work up a plan. We had much smarter guys in Launch Operations than the program office.

The story with the IUS did not end well, as the space shuttle suffered such a long delay due to a number of problems that Skylab fell out of orbit and crashed before we could use the IUS. Before the cancellation of the IUS, I made one trip to Seattle for a design review on the IUS, and I had the opportunity and pleasure to visit and have dinner with my old friend John Culley and his wife. John was the manager for our Boeing contract at KSC (S-1C, swing arms, and propellant loading facilities), and after the Apollo program ended he was transferred back to Boeing Operations in Seattle.

In all my years with Dr. Debus, I only had one negative experience. One day during the Apollo program he called me and Dr. Gruene over to his office. He was a little upset, and I must say rightfully so. I should provide a little background for this meeting. Periodically, the NASA Headquarters quality control audit team would pay us a visit. To justify their position, they always had to find something to report, no matter how trivial, and most of their findings were in this category. However, on their recent visit they did find one discrepancy that needed some attention. We were maintaining two "cable disconnect" books, one in the firing room and one at the launch pad. Anytime it was required to disconnect a cable for any purpose, it had to be documented in these books, explaining when and why it was disconnected and verifying the reconnection. The audit team found on one occasion these two books did not agree, which was a legitimate finding. At the completion of the NASA audit team's visit, they would send their report to the head of our quality control group and he would reply to their findings with our solution to the problem. We knew there was some bad blood between our quality control people and these audit people from NASA Headquarters, but we did not know it was as bad as it was.

The head of our quality control group included a somewhat sarcastic response to this finding in the report he submitted back to them, essentially saying, "You will never be able to find this problem again because we will just eliminate one of these books." That did not go over too well with the Headquarters folks, and they sent a letter directly to Dr. Debus stating they did not feel this was a satisfactory answer to their finding. This was the first time Dr. Gruene and I were aware of what was going on here, and we had no defense; we could understand why Dr. Debus was so upset. This reply letter should have been prepared by our quality control for Dr. Gruene's signature to be sent to NASA Headquarters, and you can rest assured this letter would have never gone out in that form. Dr. Gruene had a long talk with our quality control manager, who was generally a very capable man, but on this occasion his emotions overcame his common sense.

In my view, Dr. Debus never did get the recognition and credit for the tremendous job he did in developing the concept and implementation of the Kennedy Space Center, or Moon Port, on Merritt Island. I'm talking not only of the physical facilities, such as the VAB, crawler, mobile launcher, launch pad, laboratories, and other support buildings but also of the organizations, both NASA and contractor, that had to be molded into one cohesive launch team. I also give him credit for the first version of the visitor center at KSC, which is a tremendous national asset and draws international as well as domestic visitors.

One more recent story comes to mind. Several months ago, Delaware North, the contractor for the KSC visitor center, invited several of us old space pioneers to make a video presentation about life in the early Space Age that would be used in the attractions at the visitor center. Delaware North hired a professional PR company to make the videos. Each of us took our turn in a real barber chair, went through the "makeup" procedure, and then took our place in the recording room. The young lady in charge would ask leading questions and we would respond. Midway through my session she stopped and asked, "Who is this Dr. Debus you keep referring to?" I was shocked. I thought that in our community Dr. Debus was a household name. I said, "He was the first head of a permanent missile launching team at Cape Canaveral, he was the chief designer of our moon port, and the first director of the Kennedy Space Center." Then it dawned on me that I lived in a different world.

It was sad to see Dr. Debus suffer so much in his later years. I recall one visit when he was in the hospital, and Bill Chandler, Don Buchanan, and I visited him and he said, "I never expected to be in this condition." Bill Chandler and I visited him one more time at his home before he passed away. He was a good man, a good American, and he had a lot of influence on my life.

When Dr. Debus brought Rocco Petrone back into our organization at the beginning of the Apollo program, it was a common expression among those of us who knew Rocco that when he came back, no matter if his title was "head of the motor pool," he would still be the man in charge. That gives you some measure of how much we respected Rocco's capability and strong personality. I do not remember his initial job title, but he was definitely in charge of bringing Complex 39 to an operational readiness state on time and in charge of all Launch Operations activities. Later his title was director of Launch Operations, but, as you will find out below, his influence was prevalent throughout the vast Apollo program.

Interesting little side note here, as I was writing this portion of my chronicles in August 2017, I was connected through a mutual friend, Dr. Al Koller, to a man in Texas who was writing a story about Rocco Petrone. This man's name is Ed Manton, and Ed told me that based on his research he concluded that Rocco never did get properly recognized and given the credit for the tremendous job he did in the successful launch of Apollo 11, our first moon rocket. Ed had read a statement I made when I wrote the foreword to the book *The Rocket Ranch*. I'd made a statement Ed latched onto when I said, "We would never have launched Apollo 11 on schedule without the efforts of Rocco Petrone." Ed asked me if I would be willing to talk to him about my experience with Rocco, and I assured him I would be most honored to help in any way I could with this objective of telling the complete, true story of Rocco's achievements in the Apollo program. Ed and I have had several telephone conversations on this subject, and I am anxious to see his finished product.

I want to say a little more about Rocco from a more personal viewpoint. I first met Rocco in Huntsville in the early 1950s on the Redstone program. He was a captain in the Army assigned to the Redstone missile program. Rocco, like almost all of the young engineers on the Redstone program, was single. He later married about the same time I did, 1954. Rocco was a no-nonsense person and a strict disciplinarian, but with my Marine background I had no problem with his leadership style. I established a good friendship and working relationship with Rocco; however, toward the end of the Redstone flight development program, Rocco was reassigned and I lost contact with him.

When President Kennedy chartered the Apollo program in 1961, Dr. Debus, then head of Launch Operations at Cape Canaveral, faced what appeared to be an insurmountable problem:

how to design and award the contracts, construct a moon port, and develop the procedures and management structure for a launch team. This planning was on a scale that had never been done before in order to launch a moon rocket that had not yet been designed. This was an awesome, awesome challenge. I have stated previously that one strong attribute that I observed in all of our top managers was their uncanny ability to select the right person for the right job and give them the authority to do their task. I cannot think of a better example of this than when Dr. Debus called for Rocco Petrone to be reassigned from his current military duties to be his right-hand man. Rocco was a lieutenant colonel at that time. Sometime later, Rocco retired from the military and assumed an executive civil service position.

Most successful managers have strong attributes, but they also have some identifiable weakness. If Rocco had any managerial weaknesses, I do not know what they were. His memory was the envy of us all. For example, he would say, "Ike, you remember that meeting with so and so? You were sitting there, Dr. Gruene was sitting here . . ." I could barely remember the meeting, much less where people were sitting. Rocco always asked the right probing questions to understand and get to the root of any problem. I have been exposed in my career to many very smart people, but two people that stood out, by far, were Rocco and Dr. Debus.

Rocco had the same strong attribute Dr. Debus possessed of selecting the right man, and here I'm talking about NASA and contractors. With Rocco, if you did not "cut the mustard," you were out. With NASA being civil service, it was almost impossible to fire someone, but you could reassign them, and that happened to several people who did not measure up to Rocco's standards. With the contractors, and I am talking about the top local contractor management, Rocco would go up to the corporate level and have the local management removed. Rocco had to do this with Rockwell, Boeing, and McDonnell Douglas. The aerospace companies had apparently never worked in an environment with the government as it existed in the Apollo program. It seemed to be a cultural thing that the initial management for the contracts at KSC were more attuned to the financial aspects of the program and not deeply involved in the day-to-day problems.

Of course, the "day to day" problems were, much of the time, very significant. Rocco's modus operandi was to stay very, very current on all of our major problems. He would call a contractor manager concerning a particular problem he had identified, and the contractor manager would not even be aware there was a problem because he was not as dialed in as Rocco. After this happened a few times, that contractor manager would no longer be around. Rocco would let the corporate leader know what kind of a manager he expected, and in the end he got what he was after. We ended up with an excellent management team on all our contractors—Rockwell, Boeing, McDonnell Douglas, Chrysler, and IBM. I need to clarify that with Chrysler and IBM we did not have this problem. Chrysler and IBM came in from the beginning with excellent managers, and they remained with us throughout the Apollo contracts.

Rocco was the most efficient time manager I have ever known. He started the day off with a short briefing from Paul Donnelly, chief of the test conductor's office, on the status of the testing and problems that occurred during the second and third-shift operations on the spacecraft. This was followed immediately by Rocco's staff meeting, which included Launch Vehicle Operations, Dr. Gruene, myself, Spacecraft Operations, John Williams, Ted Sassen, Rocco's deputy, Walt Kapryn, and Paul Donnelly. As I mentioned earlier, later on Rocco got so frustrated trying to get accurate information on the status of spacecraft problems occurring on the second and third shift that he had Tom O'Malley, the head of Rockwell, attend these meetings. There was definitely a communication problem in this area. These meetings occurred in Rocco's office, and immediately after this meeting there would be several NASA employees and contractors waiting in the lobby of Rocco's office to discuss a major problem. At the end of this meeting there would be another group waiting in the lobby to discuss another issue, and this same pattern would go on throughout the day.

These problems and issues ran the gamut. The problem could be an issue in the crawler steering system, stress corrosion in the rocket structure, contaminated lox lines, printed circuit cards in the computer, or labor issues. There were really an endless variety of problems. No matter the subject, though, Rocco had the uncanny ability to probe and ask the right questions. One thing some of the guys learned the hard way was that you should never, never try to fake it if you did not know the answer to a question. You could say, "I don't know, but I will get the answer," and that was okay, but it was not okay to attempt to fake the answer.

One funny thing I remember was that we were all amazed at how Rocco could sit at his desk and conduct these sessions all day long and never go to the bathroom. We would laugh and say, "Rocco has a multi-gallon bladder." He had a private bathroom in his office, but he never seemed to use it.

It was not uncommon at the end of the day to have a long teleconference with MSFC on some significant issues. Usually on the other end of the line would be the MSFC program manager and his technical support people. Early in the Apollo program, the program manager at MSFC was Dr. Hans Rudolph. He was a good, capable manager and well respected at MSFC and KSC. Sadly, years later he was deported back to Germany due to some alleged prisoner activities during WWII. He had strong support from the Alabama senators as well as other prominent people, but it proved to be of no help. Earlier, we had worked with Dr. Rudolph when he was manager of the Pershing missile program, and in the early days of the Apollo program I sat by him in the firing room during the launches.

Take note, I said above that Rocco had frequent teleconferences with the MSFC Apollo program manager. Our KSC Apollo program manager was not participating in these sessions. At this time, our KSC program manager was a general and Rocco was a lieutenant colonel. At JSC and MSFC the program managers had a lot of authority, but not so at KSC. Rocco made the decisions. He worked the same way with our KSC Engineering Design directorate. We had much traffic in this area, and Rocco would go not to the director of this group but rather most of the time directly to Don Buchanan. Don, who we called Buck, was well recognized as the engineering brains of this organization. Rocco had a solid relationship with Buck.

Rocco never attended a meeting he was not well prepared for. In fact, at Dr. Debus's weekly staff meetings, Rocco many times knew more about problems in the other departments than their leaders did, which made them look not so good. I think it is fair to also say that Rocco was not all that popular at the other NASA centers, especially JSC, because he kept their feet to the fire. What I mean by this is that according to the overall Apollo schedule, there were specific dates for delivering the various flight elements—CSM, SM, LEM, S-1C, S-II, S-IVB, and IU—to the launch site. The design centers, JSC and MSFC, and their contractors desperately wanted to maintain these dates for two reasons. First, the contractors would be financially penalized for not making this scheduled date and JSC and MSFC would be in trouble with NASA headquarters; and secondly, once the flight hardware was at the launch site, the focus would be on KSC, and then a launch delay would be attributed to KSC. Rocco learned a bitter lesson on Apollo 1 when JSC and Rockwell shipped the CSM and SM to KSC when it was faulty to the point that it was not flightworthy. There also turned out to be over a hundred open engineering changes to be made at the launch site. This would be comparable to buying a car with a trunk full of parts like a radio, heater, turn signal, cruise control, and maybe a leaking windshield, all to be installed and fixed by you in your garage.

After this disaster, Rocco demanded a very clear status of the flight elements to be shipped to KSC. He made it clear that NASA Headquarters was to be fully informed of the open work to be transferred from the manufacturing site to the launch site. At the launch site, we would have a well-prepared schedule for the assembly and testing of the flight hardware for launch. We expected, and were prepared, to absorb a certain amount of engineering changes, as we knew this would be the nature of a new program, but we were not prepared to receive a "basket case" and still maintain the launch date. Some of our biggest problems in the past resulted from making major changes in the flight hardware while still maintaining a tight test schedule. Rocco's point to NASA Headquarters was if we must receive this flight hardware and complete this transferred work that should have been done at the manufacturing site in the first place, then the launch date would have to change. Now it was up to NASA Headquarters to put the pressure on the design centers to do a better job in delivering flight hardware without a huge amount of open work. I think the worst case of delivering flight hardware prematurely was on the first shuttle. That hardware was at KSC for over a year of work at the launch site that should have been done at the factory. Rocco was not at KSC on this program, and I am positive had he been there he would not have accepted that flight hardware in the condition it was in.

Rocco liked to "walk the stack," which was a phrase we used when we visited the flight hardware. You went up the elevator on the mobile launcher to the various levels, where you could walk across the swing arms to the rocket, if the mobile launcher was in the VAB, or on the pad. This tour also included the work areas in the VAB. On one occasion, Rocco and I were visiting the VAB and for some reason we were going up the stairwell and not the elevator. The stairwell was dirty and Rocco was not pleased. As soon as he could get to a telephone, he called the head of the facilities management office and told them he wanted these stairwells cleaned. He was a stickler for a clean work area. His theory was: The cleaner your work area, the better job you will do. This makes sense to me.

Rocco did not miss a thing. On one walkdown on the pad he found a non-flight streamer on the concrete. A non-flight streamer is a red cloth tag with the words *Remove Before Flight*, and it has a number on it. The purpose of the non-flight streamer was to make sure we removed any special, non-flight hardware used for ground testing, like a dummy flight-code connector for the real flight item, which had a secret code we could not use during daily test operations. Our procedures called for a non-flight streamer to be entered in a logbook, and then before launch it had to be verified that the non-flight item was removed.

The immediate action was to go to the logbook and see where this number was installed. Adding to the embarrassment, the number on this non-flight streamer was not in the logbook. The question we faced was: Was there a dummy non-flight item installed someplace in this giant rocket without the non-flight streamer attached and not listed in the logbook? Rocco was not a happy person at this moment, and none of us were happy about this dilemma. Rocco wanted an answer and he wanted it sooner than later. Needless to say, we applied all appropriate resources to understand this problem and, as best I can recall, this lasted a day or two before we reached the conclusion that this non-flight streamer was never used. One aspect that really teed Rocco off was the fact that he was the one that found the streamer; workers had been all around that area and none of them observed this obvious discrepancy. I was particularly anxious to get this issue resolved because I certainly did not want to have to address this at the flight readiness review.

Rocco set up a system where he knew exactly where the major problems were that threatened the schedule, and then he would apply all the pressure and resources necessary to overcome the problems. For example, early in the program it looked like the service arms would not be ready to make our schedule. The service arms attach to the mobile launcher at strategic elevations and can be rotated to mate with each flight stage, and they carry the electrical cables, high-pressure gas lines, and propellant loading lines that attach to the rocket. These service arms are massive. Walking from the mobile launcher to the rocket in one of these service arms is like walking down a hallway in your home, they are that big. You can appreciate how critical these service arms are when you realize that when all the first-stage engines are full thrust, the takeoff signal is initiated, and the rocket lifts from the launch pedestal, these service arms are still connected. At this point they must be released and then swing 90 degrees back to the mobile launcher and clear the path for the ascending rocket. Too much detail is required to describe why this particular sequence is necessary, but I just want to convey how critical these service arms are. They must work or you have bought the farm, so to speak.

During this period when the problems with the service arms were threatening the schedule, Rocco was not satisfied with the daily progress reports from the manufacturer. They were being built in Birmingham, Alabama, by the Hayes Company. To get a better handle on this problem, Rocco sent one of his senior staff members to Birmingham to report daily to Rocco on the progress of getting this hardware back on schedule. Along with this, Rocco assigned me to head a small group of our mechanical and electrical engineers, along with members from our Design directorate, to conduct a design review and develop a test plan for certifying these service arms at KSC. The service arms did make it on time and worked beautifully on every launch. You always need a few miracles.

Another almost show-stopping problem we experienced in the activation of Complex 39 was the delivery and installation of hundreds of cables connecting the electrical equipment in the launch control center and the mobile launcher. Again, Rocco came to the rescue. He assigned one man to make an accurate inventory of the cables we had received and the delivery date of the missing cables. Rocco received a daily status report on this issue and, while it was close, we did turn this problem from red to green just in time to meet our schedule. Just another typical "insurmountable" problem we solved during this activation of Complex 39. We were told these type of insurmountable situations were not problems, they were just opportunities. Looking back, I think we just thrived on insurmountable opportunities. My office was two doors down from Rocco's and many days, late in the evening, I would drop by his office, and if he was not tied up I would bring him up to date on any issues we were working on. At the end of the session Rocco liked to unwind, rest, and have a relaxed discussion about the overall status of the program. On most of these occasions Paul Donnelly and Walt Kapryn were also present.

After the successful launch of Apollo 11 in July 1969, Rocco was moved to NASA Headquarters in Washington. His able deputy, Walt "Kappy" Kapryn, took his place and, of course, Kappy inherited a superb organization, both NASA and contractors. Kappy knew that he was stepping into some big shoes, but he also knew he had a super team of dedicated people, well organized with all of the procedures and know-how to get the job done. I need to throw in a little note of interest here. No pun intended, but Kappy's first launch, Apollo 12, was a little "fiery." Shortly after liftoff, lightning struck the rocket and all of the displays in the CSM went crazy, but again we were blessed with a little miracle. Everything settled down in a normal manner and we had a most successful flight to the moon and back.

As I recall, from his new position in Washington, Rocco did attend the remaining launches in the Apollo program. Later he was transferred from his position in Washington to Huntsville, Alabama as the new director of MSFC. Rocco remained the director of MSFC until his retirement from NASA. Rocco then took a position with Rockwell and later he became the president of Rockwell's space shuttle operations. In this capacity, he would come down to KSC for the shuttle launches, and when I moved into the position as head of the Florida USBI operations, I joined Rocco in the backup firing room for the launch. There were four firing rooms in the launch control center, and KSC would set up the firing room adjacent to the active firing room for the visiting management personnel from the JSC and MSFC and their contractors. We had an assigned position at a non-operative console, but we did have access to the various intercom channels. We could listen but not talk on these intercom channels, and we had a monitor where we could select the various cameras positioned around the launch pad. I enjoyed some good visits with Rocco on these occasions. At my retirement, Rocco sent me a nice letter, which I have included in these chronicles, and he reminded me in that letter of a little thing we had going. Many times, when I went to inform Rocco about new bad news, I would ask him, "Rocco, do you want to take this medicine as a pill or liquid?"

Several years ago, when I first learned Rocco had passed away, it was a little difficult to accept; I remember Rocco as a very robust, energetic individual, and I treasure my memories of my friend. I tried to learn all I could about the management style of successful people like Rocco. Rocco could, and did, get angry at times, but I never observed him raise his voice in anger, shout, pound the table, or use vulgar language. He did not need to do this; he just looked at you and you got the message, loud and clear.

I think it is fair to say, in my space career I benefited significantly from being closely associated with Rocco. I explain this statement in this manner: whether people liked Rocco or not, they respected him. I could get my telephone calls answered and a favorable response from all of our NASA contractors and NASA management personnel at KSC and MSFC, because they knew if they did not respond to me they would probably receive a call from Rocco. I could say the same thing about my relationship with Dr. Gruene.

The last person I want to highlight in detail in this chapter is Dr. Wernher von Braun. Early in the last century, about 1920, a few years before I was born, a mother in Germany gave her eight-year-old son a telescope. He became fascinated with this instrument and had a vision that mankind someday would travel to these distant heavenly bodies that he could view through his telescope.

What in the world does this have to do with me, here in 2017, trying to document my journey on the good planet earth? Well, it has everything to do with me. If this young child had not become obsessed with a passion to reach for the stars, there would have been no von Braun missile team in Huntsville in 1950, which was the catalyst for drawing me and many other young engineers to the Huntsville rocket center. To make this even more personal, I would never have crossed paths with the beautiful and loving Kathryn, as she was also drawn to this rocket center. I cannot imagine life without my Kathryn. This just had to happen then and there. In the Christian community there is a common saying that "God has a plan for your life," and I believe this. I am convinced that Divine Providence was active in these happenings.

I have already documented Dr. von Braun's involvement in the V-2 program, but here I want to talk about his very significant role in our country's space exploration program with the Army Ballistic Missile Agency (ABMA) and NASA. When I first went to work with the Redstone missile project in 1951, Dr. von Braun was the civilian head of the ABMA under General Bruce Medaris. I had heard about von Braun, but I knew little about him. I did know he was considered the number one space authority in the world, and I guessed there could be nothing better than a new job where the top guy is considered the number one expert in the missile and rocket business.

The more I learned about von Braun, the more I respected and admired him, and I observed this to be true of my fellow colleagues. Jump ahead a few years later, one evening I was in Rocco Petrone's office at KSC with several other people and von Braun's name came up. Rocco stated, "von Braun is the nearest thing to a genius that I have ever seen." Rocco was always very careful about uttering accolades, so I thought this was very significant.

I heartily agree with Rocco. I have been exposed to some very bright people in my lifetime, but I don't know of anyone I would call a genius. I think my inherent concept of a genius is someone who is extremely brilliant in a particular area, but maybe a little eccentric or lacking good social skills. Dr. von Braun was not in that category. He was a super well-rounded individual. His management and social skills matched his enormous technical capacity, he had incredible vision for future space explorations, and, from all I have learned, he possessed a strong spiritual foundation. Put all of that together and you come up with what Rocco said: "Closest thing to a genius that I have ever seen."

I put Dr. von Braun in the category of a natural leader. Natural leaders are born with a certain type of charisma that inspires people to follow. I'm thinking of people like George Washington, inspiring those loyal patriots without adequate clothes or shoes to cross the freezing Delaware River, or the loyal troops that followed leaders like Patton, Grant, Lee, and Alexander the Great. I think this country was very fortunate to have Dr. von Braun when we were facing a serious Communist threat in the Cold War.

I mentioned he possessed strong social skills. Here is an example of what I am talking about: when he visited the launch site, he would visit and carry on conversations with the test engineers, the mechanics on the pad, and a little later he would be briefing the president of the United States on the status of our space program.

Unfortunately, there are two negative things that Dr. von Braun had to contend with. There were certain individuals at NASA Headquarters and JSC who were extremely jealous of von Braun. In big meetings with government officials and the press, Dr. von Braun, although he did not seek it, was the center of attention and these people did not like that. In my opinion, von Braun should have been appointed as the NASA administrator following the Apollo program. I believe there are three main requirements for a top-notch NASA administrator: first, have a bold vision for the future of NASA; secondly, possess the skills to sell this vision to Congress for the necessary support and funding; and thirdly, have the courage to make tough, bold decisions like NASA administrator Tom Paine did when he advanced the schedule of Apollo 8 in August 1968, and made it a mission to the moon when there was a credible concern that the Russians were going to beat us there. Dr. von Braun possessed those attributes more than any other candidates on the scene at that time.

The other unfortunate situation von Braun faced was the resentment many people felt toward him for bringing other Germans with him to work in our country after WWII because of their past involvement in the V-2 program. I think the attitude of the few people that made this an issue was shortsighted and stupid. Do you want these talented people working for us or do you want them working for our Russian enemies? Place yourself in their shoes—you might have done the same things they did.

I experienced a long, hard struggle with "forgiveness" of the Japanese after WWII. Two events solved this issue for me. First, it dawned on me that when I repeated the Lord's Prayer, I was clearly saying, "Lord, if I cannot forgive others, then do not forgive me." That was a real revelation to me. I ask you, the reader, to recite the Lord's Prayer and ponder on those words of forgiveness. Secondly, I was greatly influenced when I read and absorbed the powerful forgiveness story of Jacob DeShazer, a member of General Doolittle's team that bombed Japan in 1942. If you need a lesson in forgiveness you should read or re-read DeShazer's story, which I described earlier in the book.

These Germans became solid American citizens and were a tremendous asset to the security of our country and society in general. I will share another von Braun story in this vein. When he was with ABMA, he gave a presentation to the secretary of the Army, and at the end of the presentation the secretary said, "Dr. von Braun, we appreciate what you are doing for our country." Von Braun replied, "You know, this is my country too." Good response. Dr. von Braun had a good sense of humor. He once received a letter from a lady in Alabama saying, "If God wanted a man on the moon, he would have put him there, and besides that, I will bet you $10 that you will never make it." Von Braun replied, "My Bible does not say anything about God not wanting to put a man on the moon, but it does say something about gambling."

Von Braun also once issued some words of wisdom to the troops along with a touch of humor that said, "The reliability of a missile should be such that it is more dangerous to be in the impact zone than it is at the launch site." I believe this was after Redstone No. 3, which flew about three inches and blew up on the launch table, sending a pressure wave down a cable tunnel and blowing some debris into the blockhouse. That day you would have been perfectly safe in the impact zone and in more danger at the launch site.

I guess the most notable legacy of Dr. von Braun is the mighty Saturn V rocket that won the Space Race for our country. Here it is 50 years later and there has not been a new rocket equal to or even close to the size and lifting power of the Saturn V.

It was my distinct honor and privilege to prepare and present every one of the launch vehicle flight readiness presentations in which our Launch Operations organization was involved to the manned flight review board, where these leaders I have just discussed were the audience. Neither I nor any of the other presenters were ever challenged with a "gotcha"-type question. These were serious men and very much gentlemen.

Dr. von Braun was a man of faith. He was obviously a student of the Bible by his many quotes regarding the relationship of science and religion, and the idea of a creator as opposed to a series of haphazard events called evolution. One of the early astronauts had dinner at von Braun's home and said he was amazed at the number of books on religion there.

Here is one of von Braun's quotes about religion: "The ethical guidelines of religion are the bonds that can hold our civilization together. Without them man can never attain that cherished goal of lasting peace with himself, his God and his fellow man."

Here is another quote, and it is powerful: "It is no longer enough that we pray that God may be on our side. We must learn to pray that we may be on God's side."

I will leave this chapter with one final quote from von Braun: "But I can't help feeling at the same time that this space effort of ours is bigger even than a rivalry between the United States and Russia. The heavens beyond us are enormous beyond comprehension, and the further we penetrate them, the greater will be our human understanding of the great universal purpose, the Divine Will itself."

I am certainly proud and glad that Dr. von Braun, and all of the men mentioned above, were part of our incredible team.

Me, Kathryn, Florence Petrone, and Rocco Petrone,
sometime in the '50s.

Dr. Gruene's retirement in 1973.
(L-R:) Dr. Debus, Edith Gruene, and Dr. Hans Gruene.
I was honored to be the emcee for this event.

Retirement Party for
DR. Kurt Debus

Dr. Debus' retirement party. We played a joke on him, saying that the model above was a model of the telemetry station in the VAB that we had secretly built without his permission. We had been asking for this station for several years and he had always denied it, so we all enjoyed this good joke at his retirement.

Thought You Might Like to See the People

1st Row (L-R:) George Mueller— Dir. Apollo Program
        Gen. Sam Phillips—Dep. Dir. Apollo Program
        Dr. Kurt Debus—Dir. KSC
        Dr. Bob Gilruth—Dir. JSC
        Dr. von Braun—Dir. MSFC

2nd Row (L-R:) John Williams—Dir. Spacecraft Operations
        Rocco Petrone—Dir. Launch Operations
        Paul Donnelly—Chief Test Conductor's Office
        Dr. Hans Gruene—Dir. Launch Vehicle Operations

3rd Row (L-R:) Ted Sasseen—Chief Engineer Spacecraft
        Operations
        George Page—Chief Spacecraft Operations
        Joe Bobik—Chief Spacecraft Quality Control
        Ike Rigell—Chief Engineer and Dep. Dir. Launch
        Vehicle Operations

NASA—SPECIAL ASSIGNMENTS

NASA always had a policy to form a panel for any major problem, staffed from outside the organization where the problem occurred, to investigate the cause and make recommendations to avoid such a problem in the future.

I was assigned to several of these failure investigations on the "unmanned vehicle" side of the house. Most of those failures occurred in the early period of our space program, and it was a challenging task. Our rockets today are very reliable, and this remarkable reliability can be traced back to the lessons learned from our failures. In all walks of life and in any endeavor you learn more from your mistakes than your successes.

I found this assignment to be a very rewarding task. In a thorough investigation of the processes and events that led up to a serious failure, you learn things that you can go back and apply to your own operations.

These panels were composed of a diverse group, with expertise in all facets of technology. You were associating with the very best in their field, NASA or contractor. These investigations usually required several weeks of intense work and included trips to contractor facilities and other NASA facilities. Normally, in a missile failure there is more than one contractor involved, and each contractor desperately tries to prove his hardware was not the cause of the failure.

In the earlier days of our space program, serious failures were not uncommon, and I am reminded of one of the first questions the reporters would ask: Was the cause of this failure a human error? If you examine this question closely, you realize it is a very stupid question because all failures are the result of a human error, either design, manufacturing, assembly, test, or human judgment. The Challenger tragedy was a combination of several of the above areas.

I know of no failure in the history of space that was not the result of human error. The only other option is divine intervention, and as far as I know that has never happened. The closest thing in this regard would be Apollo 12, when shortly after liftoff lightning struck the rocket, traveling down the rocket through the conductive engine flames to reach ground. The displays in the command module went wild and the first thoughts were, *We are in big trouble*, but things settled down, no equipment was damaged, and Apollo 12 went on to a highly successful mission. Monday morning quarterbacking that event, you could question the wisdom of launching that day due to the proximity of clouds. Since then, KSC has made tremendous progress in identifying and predicting the proximity of potential lightning clouds, and elaborate lightning towers protecting the rocket on the launch pad have been installed.

In one investigation, the missile failure was finally traced back to a welder who innocently selected the wrong welding rod to weld a critical missile assembly. Examining the welder's work environment, you could understand why it was so easy to make a mistake and select the wrong welding rod.

My last and final special assignment for NASA occurred a couple of years after I retired from USBI. This would be in the early 1990s. Dan Golden was the NASA administrator at that time, and he asked Chris Kraft, retired director of JSC, to form a panel and give him options and advice on more efficient operations between KSC, JSC, MSFC, and their contractors. I did not know Dan Golden, but I did know Chris Kraft, and he asked me to represent Launch Operations on his panel. Others on the panel were Frank Borman, astronaut and commander of Apollo 8; a retired president of Rockwell; and one member from MSFC and one from NASA headquarters whose names I do not remember.

We worked hard for several weeks on this panel and had extensive presentations from the NASA centers. On key issues, we as a panel were all together, and I was convinced that we had made some valid recommendations that would reduce the cost and improve efficiency in the areas that we addressed. It required some time, but I believe the major elements in our report to Golden were eventually implemented. Unfortunately, I lost my copy of this study, along with my little Bible that I carried in my pocket all through WWII, in one of our moves.

I enjoyed my work on this panel, but I was glad when it was over. I was ready to return to my strenuous role in retirement.

SPACE SHUTTLE PAYLOADS

The completion of the Apollo-Soyuz launch in July 1975 marked the end of an era. I doubt we will ever exceed the accomplishments made in this period. It was gratifying to end this era in a highly successful mission. This joint effort with the Soviets was a very significant and historical event. We now faced the same painful exercise we experienced after the last Apollo launch in 1972—cancelling contracts and the resulting layoffs. This time our workforce was smaller than it was in 1972, but it was still just as painful to the people involved and still a sizable impact on the business community in Brevard County. The primary contractors involved in this layoff were Chrysler, McDonnell Douglas, Rockwell, and IBM. The civil service employees in both layoffs were not impacted like our contractors were. I offer my opinion that with the workload we faced for the next few years, we did not need all of these civil service people, but that is not the way the system works.

From 1953 to 1975, we phased out several missile and rocket projects, but the major difference was that, in the past, when we phased out a missile or rocket program we had an overlap. We always had the next-generation space vehicle on the launch pad before the last launch of the previous generation.

A little overview is needed to explain what I am talking about in this 22-year span. We launched the following missiles and rockets in this sequence, and there were always overlaps, and at times we were launching three different configurations: Redstone, Jupiter-C, Jupiter (IRBM), Juno (non-military version of the IRBM, used to launch probes to outer space), Pershing (military missile), Mercury-Redstone, and Saturn 1B. In addition to those mentioned, in 1958 part of our launch team went to Johnson Island in the Pacific and launched two Redstone rockets with live atomic warheads for the DOD. In the 60s, we were up to our ears in alligators, struggling to meet our deadlines for organizing our local management structure, and developing procedures and design reviews for the awesome task of being prepared for the first moon rocket.

Now, here we were in July 1975, with a very capable launch team and nothing to launch. In earlier years, when we first learned that the shuttle would be the spacecraft of the future, the schedule for the shuttle coming online was very optimistic. At the time, we did not know that it would be such a long dry spell; it would be six long years before we experienced the next manned launch.

Several factors contributed to this long hiatus of the manned flight program. First, the Apollo program was terminated earlier than we had anticipated due to funding. Secondly, the shuttle program suffered from funding issues, which resulted in delays. Thirdly, there were technical issues, some very serious, which resulted in a significant delay in the launch of the first shuttle. No matter how optimistic you are, I think you can always count on some major surprises with any highly technical program like the shuttle program. In my opinion, no matter how smart the people are, the unexpected happens, and the only way to minimize the impact of these surprise issues is unlimited funding.

On Apollo, Launch Vehicle, Spacecraft, and in activating Complex 39, we had these surprise problems out the wazoo, and fortunately we had the funding to recover from them. Two things worked in our favor then. First, we had a more receptive Congress in the Apollo era than we did in the shuttle era; secondly, and this is very significant, in the Apollo era we had James Webb as the NASA administrator. He had the talent, the know-how, and the contacts to work with Congress, and the executive office to obtain the funding necessary to meet our schedule. We had some good men as NASA administrators later in the shuttle era, but in my view, they were not in the same class as James Webb.

We knew that after the Apollo-Soyuz launch our launch operations directorate would have to be totally reorganized due to the vast differences in processing the space shuttle configuration, rather than the launch-vehicle-spacecraft configuration we were accustomed to. After Apollo 11, Rocco Petrone was moved up to a position in NASA Headquarters and his deputy, Walt Kaprayn, took his place. Under "Kappy," as we called him, and me (Dr. Gruene had retired in 1973), we had the Launch Vehicle Operations, and Spacecraft Operations was under John Williams.

I was now 52 years old, and a few pages back I made some pretty strong statements that an old, 52-year-old guy did not fit in a work environment where the work hours were long and daily problems were in abundance. Bringing the space shuttle online would not be as difficult as bringing the Apollo online, but it would still be a formidable task. Now, the major facilities were already in place but did require some modifications. We had paper systems to track problems, prepare schedules, and perform various other tasks that we had to learn the hard way on Apollo. Even with these advantages, I saw the next several years would be very similar, though on a smaller scale, to the early days of Apollo. I felt I had paid my dues, and I was not ready to continue in that environment.

After Dr. Gruene retired, we met for lunch at least once a month, and I always sought advice from him on various issues. I asked his advice on which direction I should go in the future. He strongly came across as wanting me to "get out of Launch Operations and go into Shuttle Payloads." I took his advice and it turned out beautiful. For the first time in my career with ABMA or NASA, I worked a normal eight-hour, five-days-a-week schedule. I almost felt I was on a continuous vacation. The shuttle was experiencing more and more delays, and, of course, if the shuttle is not flying, you cannot be processing payloads.

At this time, there were only two major payloads on the horizon; fortunately, one of these, the European Space Agency's (ESA) Spacelab, was a sizable project—over one billion dollars— and just getting underway. The other future payload, also a sizable one, was built by the Boeing Company for the Air Force.

NASA planned to use it to move the Skylab to a higher orbit.

The ESA Spacelab was an interesting program, and we became heavily involved with this project. Ten nations of the European common market contributed to the building of the Spacelab and the supporting equipment. The Spacelab was a very versatile system. It had a habitable module loaded with experiments that would fly in the cargo bay of the shuttle, and there were also combinations of pallets with experiments that would fly on missions without the habitable module. The Europeans were excited about this venture as it would afford them the opportunity to participate in a manned flight program. From the NASA side, the Spacelab program was managed by the Marshall Space Flight Center (MSFC) and the program director, Jack Lee, was a friend of mine. We had worked together for several years when Jack was head of the MSFC office at KSC.

The way ESA was required to manage this program was very inefficient. For example, the overall funding pie was divided among all 10 countries. Spain, for example, was allocated so much money to build the ground support equipment that the funds they received were more than enough, but they had to—and wanted to—spend all of this money. We described this ground equipment as "gold-plated," meaning it was more massive than required. Of course, this is not unlike some of the things we did in the Apollo program, like locating JSC in Houston.

The ESA headquarters is in Paris, and the main center for the assembly and construction of the Spacelab was Bremen, Germany. I said above we became heavily involved with the Europeans through our friends at MSFC who were on this project. As with MSFC, we sent several of our people to Bremen as permanent residents to work with the Europeans. Our good friends, Eldon and Georgia Raley, and their family were the first to make this move to Bremen and work with the ESA team on the assembly and checkout of the Spacelab. We had a number of other people from our office join Eldon.

At KSC, we designated the operations and checkout building (O&C) for the prelaunch processing of the Spacelab. This was the same building where we prepared the spacecraft and lunar module for the Apollo program. The O&C would also be the building to house the European Spacelab team that would set up permanent residence here. Our NASA contractor for processing the Spacelab was McDonnell Douglas, with my old friend George Faenza as the general manager. George and I worked together for years on the Saturn 1B and Apollo program.

Several members of our NASA management team, including me, made many trips to Europe on this program. Most of our trips were to Bremen, but we did visit other sites where some of the components of the Spacelab were built, including Holland, France, and other cities in Germany.

From the beginning, Spacelab was running behind schedule, and this did not seem to bother the Europeans. They maintained what we viewed as a very relaxed attitude and work schedule. From the NASA side, maintaining the schedule was the responsibility of MSFC. One time, they made a special trip to Europe to push the ESA people to meet the schedule. I was with them on this trip, and the day the MSFC people arrived, the German, who was head of the production, left to go on a month-long vacation to an island off the coast of Spain. Europeans take their vacations very seriously; a vacation is a higher priority than the schedule. The people in northern Europe really like to travel where the sun shines, and I can understand why. Most of the time we were in Bremen, it was overcast, never much sun. Regarding the Spacelab schedule, they were saved by the long delay in the shuttle schedule.

We had the opportunity, on several occasions, to visit the homes of the Europeans. One thing you had to be impressed with was their children. Even the little ones could speak more than one language. That reminds me of a little language story.

One of the ground rules in the ESA-NASA agreement was that all meetings involving NASA would be in English, and all the top documentation would be in English. The meetings among the ESA people would be in any language they chose, and the lower level documentation could be in the vendor's language. Now, since I am a native of Alabama, I can tell this story. I mentioned before that the MSFC in Huntsville was in charge of the Spacelab program, and, as I have stated already, MSFC was staffed primarily with good old boys from Alabama and adjoining states. Technologically, they are unsurpassed, but in the usage of the "king's English," they might come up a little short. When you are in a heated discussion trying to make a point, it is easy to slip into your native tongue, as you can more adequately make your point that way. This is true of any nationality, and we saw a little bit of this in the Redstone program with the Germans. In this instance, one of the good old Alabama boys was running the meeting, and there were some heated discussions happening. At one point, a couple of the Europeans reverted to their native tongue and our Alabama boy said, "Listen here, you all, we are supposed to speak English in this meeting." A very proper British man at the table said, "Why do you say that, you do not speak English."

Kathryn accompanied me on several trips to Germany, my daughter Amy came on one trip, and my son Scott on another trip. We had a little extra excitement on the trip with Scott. One of the ESA facilities I had to visit that trip was in Friedrichshafen, in southern Germany, on a very large lake, Lake Bodensee. Scott was free during the day when I was working, and one day he told me he wanted to take the ferry boat across the lake to visit the little country of Liechtenstein. I said okay and I thought that would be an interesting trip for him, which it was, but later in the afternoon I had second thoughts about that. I left work a little early and went down to the dock to meet Scott when he returned on the ferry. A couple of ferry boats came in and Scott was not on them. It was getting late in the afternoon, and as best I could translate some of the German signs there was only one more ferry scheduled to arrive that day, but I was not 100 percent sure of that. So, I anxiously had my eyes glued to the horizon and finally I saw something in the distance and I thought, *This has got to be it.* This was pre-cell phone days, so if Scott was not on this approaching boat, I had no means of communicating with him. We were scheduled to leave that night in a rental car for another German city to catch a train to Paris, and then fly out of Paris the next day. I got as close as I could to the dock to scan the faces on the ferry. It was a full boat. Finally, I spotted Scott and my heart dropped back to a normal beat.

My map of Germany showed a main highway between Friedrichshafen and the town where we were to catch the train to Paris, so we were not concerned about making this trip at night. But a few miles out of Friedrichshafen, we faced a barrier blocking the road, which we interpreted to be a detour. Let me add, the countryside was covered in snow. This detour took us for miles on small country roads through farmland making some 90 degree turns, and sometimes I was not sure we were on the official detour road. But Providence was with us and we arrived at our destination. We turned in the rental car and were very happy when we noticed we were just across the street from the train station. We made our train to Paris and early the next morning we got up to catch our bus to the airport.

Our NASA resident office in Bremen was very good about taking care of us when we made side trips out of Bremen. They knew the right places to stay and the more interesting places to visit. They always booked us in places more like a bed-and-breakfast than a commercial hotel, so it gave us more opportunity to see how the local people lived. At times, this office could arrange for a trip to the American sector in West Berlin, which was in East Germany, and East Germany was under the strict control of the Soviet Union. The Berlin Wall was in full force at that time, and traveling between East and West Germany was a real problem. The trip to West Berlin was via a military train that was only permitted to travel through East Germany at night. They referred to this as the Duty Train.

We left Bremen, and when we reached the border of West and East Germany the train had to stop and change engines from a West German to an East German locomotive. This stop was in the middle of the night, and we were told not to leave the train. We were in a nice, comfortable Pullman coach. I raised the shade on the window by my sleeper and observed a soldier marching back and forth on this dimly lit platform. I assumed he was making sure no one left the train, or maybe more likely he was making sure none of the dissatisfied East Germans were trying to sneak on the train to West Berlin and freedom.

As soon as the train picked up speed on the East German side, it was obvious the tracks were inferior to the train tracks in West Germany. In West Germany, from Bremen to the border, we enjoyed a real smooth ride. However, in East Germany it was a rather loud *clickety-clack* all the way. In fact, I think everything in East Germany was clickety-clack. The office in Bremen arranged for everything. We stayed at a super wonderful place; it had been taken over by the military, and I'm not sure what the original building was—either a huge mansion or a nice residential type hotel. I found they had booked us into a nice suite because my civil service grade in their books was equivalent to a major general. There was a good restaurant in the building, and from the lobby there was a very wide marble stairway up to a large ballroom. One night the military officers were having a big Western theme party, and they did a very excellent job of making it authentic. They had a little donkey loaded with backpacks, and a guy dressed up like an old prospector trying to get this little donkey up the stairway from the lobby to the ballroom. The little donkey did not want to go up the stairs, and this old prospector had to get some help to pull and push this stubborn donkey up to the ballroom.

One of the interesting sites in Berlin was the famous "Checkpoint Charlie," where you saw elaborate barriers set up to prevent East Germans from crashing through the border to freedom in West Germany. Several ingenious contraptions and methods of escape were on display, evidence of what people had done as they desperately sought freedom. We do not appreciate how fortunate we are in our country to have never lived in a repressive dictator state. Freedom is a precious commodity, and we should thank our God every day that we live in freedom.

A little reminder here in history. The first major crisis in the Cold War was when the Soviet Union closed all land traffic to West Berlin in 1948. This meant that the Berliners had no source of food or fuel. Fortunately, we had a president then, President Truman, who was not afraid to make a tough decision, and he initiated what history records as the Berlin Airlift. Joined by Britain and Australia, we sent planes around the clock, loaded with food, fuel, and other supplies for the desperate people in West Berlin. Stalin wanted all of Berlin to be under Soviet control. This blockade lasted about a year. If the Soviets had tried to shoot these planes down, we would have had WWIII.

On one of my trips, Kathryn and I took a long side trip through Germany in a rental car. Late one evening we stopped at a family-type German restaurant. It was off the main road and I do not recall how we found this place, but it was an interesting stop. Kathryn was impressed with this restaurant. The kitchen was visible from the dining area, and in the kitchen you could observe a very high ceiling, and all of the walls were covered in very small tile. It was really a work of art. The restaurant was part of an L-shaped building and the other part of the L was an antique shop.

The antique shop was closed but, peeking through the window, Kathryn observed some things she was interested in. Now, get this: Kathryn could not speak German, and the proprietor of the restaurant could not speak any English, but somehow Kathryn communicated to this German that she would like to go in that antique shop. In just a few minutes, the owner of the antique shop came in, opened up her shop, and Kathryn bought something, I can't recall what. The good news is we enjoyed a fine meal, and more good news is that just a little later we safely negotiated traveling the wrong way on a one-way street. We learned at the end of the street why those people we met were all loudly blowing their horns.

In summary, I enjoyed my work on the Spacelab program. It added another dimension to my overall work in our space program. Due to the delay in the shuttle program, I retired before the first Spacelab launch in 1983. Various configurations of the Spacelab flew in over 20 shuttle flights. However, the ESA launch team arrived before I retired and we did receive and set up some of the ground support equipment before I left. The leader of the ESA launch team was a very capable, very smart English engineer named Alan Therkittle. Alan and I became good friends, and I had the pleasure of having dinner one evening in Alan's home in England. Initially we had some thorny issues to resolve as to the specific responsibilities of ESA, NASA, and our contractor McDonnell Douglas in the prelaunch processing of the Spacelab. Fortunately, we had reasonable people involved— Alan, George, and myself—and in spite of some interference from our program office, we came up with an agreement that all parties were pleased with.

I will sign off on the Spacelab program with this little tidbit. Alan told me one day that they had found a very nice little restaurant on Merritt Island that served very good European food. I had never heard of this restaurant and I asked Alan for directions. Kathryn and I found this small restaurant on North State Road 3 on Merritt Island and we verified that Alan knew what he was talking about. It became a favorite restaurant of ours. I cannot remember the name of the restaurant. We always just referred to the owners, George and Odette; they were from France. George was the chef and his wife, Odette, was the waitress. When our order came out, George would come out of the kitchen with his high-top chef's hat and, in his heavy French accent, ask how we enjoyed the food. Odette was always a very pleasant lady as well. They were not young people. They had been in this business a long time. I told Alan it was very embarrassing that we had to have someone from Europe come over here and tell us locals where to go for a super delicious meal.

The Spacelab in Breman, Germany was a joint venture with NASA and the European Space Agency. This was my last major project with NASA.

USBI

I retired from NASA in May 1982 and went to work the next day with USBI as a consultant. I need to give some history on USBI. It was a newly formed company, a subsidiary of United Technologies (UTC), a very large international corporation. Some of their companies included Pratt and Whitney jet engines, Carrier Air Conditioners, Otis Elevators, Sikorsky Helicopters, and several others, which I do not remember. UTC was vehemently opposed to unions, and I have some comments on unions later.

The company was created to bid on a NASA contract worth about $1.2 billion. The contract was for major flight elements and launch operations support for the solid rockets for the Space Shuttle Program. MSFC was responsible for the portion of the contract providing major elements of the solid rocket motors for KSC. KSC was responsible for the portion of the contract to assemble the various segments of the solid rocket booster systems and to check out and prepare them for launch.

At the time I went to work for USBI, they were in pretty serious trouble at MSFC and KSC in meeting their contract requirements. The top guys at UTC sent down from their headquarters to run this contract with MSFC were clueless. It was a disaster. Fortunately, someone up the line in UTC had enough wisdom to make some necessary changes. They hired some very capable NASA retirees at Huntsville to replace them. These key NASA retirees—Gene Cagle, Frank Batty, and Don Reid from Teledyne Brown—took over. They turned this organization into a first-class operation. These people were old friends of mine. At KSC, UTC hired one of my NASA retiree friends, Paul Donnelly, to run the KSC portion of this contract.

My contract was with the MSFC portion. USBI headquarters was in Huntsville, where all of the design activities were located. The physical activities, which included manufacturing, assembly, and refurbishment, were located at KSC. It was a little unusual for one NASA center to have a completely independent operation at another NASA center. MSFC had a fenced-in area about one mile south of the VAB, which included the USBI Florida Operations, Headquarters, and Manufacturing Facilities. We had a separate facility for packing and refurbishing the parachutes used in the recovery of the solid rocket boosters. Our refurbishment activities were located at Hangar S on the Cape Canaveral Air Force Missile Base.

USBI under the MSFC contract operated the two solid rocket booster's recovery ships, *Liberty Star* and *Freedom Star*. The boosters parachuted down to the ocean about 150 miles off the Florida East Coast, were brought back into the Cape Canaveral Harbor through the locks, and then up the Banana River to our dock at Hangar S.

Our manufacturing building was a modern state-of-the-art facility specifically designed for our mission. One neat feature was the use of air bearing platforms to move our large flight segments from one station in the building to another station without having to use overhead cranes.

I had been working with USBI a few weeks when MSFC decided they wanted USBI to establish a Field Engineering Office at the KSC location. I was offered the job of heading it up as a permanent employee of USBI, which I accepted. I had good people in this office, and by this time the home office in Huntsville was staffed with several of my old NASA friends who were now permanent employees of USBI, so I enjoyed a good relationship working with these people.

Later, I don't remember which year, our General Manager, George Murphy, of the overall USBI operations, suffered a heart attack and died suddenly. Al Reeser, the head of the MSFC operations at KSC, replaced him. I was then offered the position of vice president of USBI Florida Operations to replace Al Reeser. I accepted this job. Fortunately, I inherited a very talented and capable secretary, Shirley Brewer. I think capable secretaries are the most underrated people in the workforce.

I encountered a few "blips" along the way, but I could take care of them. One little blip occurred immediately. A smart and talented man named Bernie was also a little obnoxious. He felt he should have been selected to head up this organization. Bernie had been hired to head up our Manufacturing Division by one of the corporate executives at UTC Headquarters, in Hartford, Connecticut, and the word was that he promised Bernie he would later head up the MSFC activities at KSC. UTC headquarters did the same thing at the USBI organization in Huntsville, which also caused some problems.

Bernie and I clashed several times, but he eventually settled down and we became friends and worked together very well. Before I leave Bernie, here is one little tidbit. Every morning we had a telecom with our counterparts in Huntsville with all of our key guys on the line at each location. Bernie was a very foul-mouthed individual, and in giving his report, it was loaded with vulgar language. I never said a word to Bernie about this, but immediately after I became the head man at KSC, Bernie stopped using this type of language.

One of the first things I did in my new position was to have a meeting with all our department heads, and then make a tour of all our facilities to explain in some detail what was going on in their area. I knew some of these guys didn't talk to each other. On our tour, we started out in the Manufacturing Facility. We would walk along slowly and talk, and when I saw a piece of trash, paper, metal, or whatever, I didn't say anything, but I would pick it up and at the next opportunity drop it in the trash can. I did this several times and then found I could not do this anymore because one of these managers would beat me to it. That proved the old saying, "action is more effective than words."

Not long before my former boss, Al Reeser, left to go to Huntsville as the general manager of USBI, he started a little unique management tool that I observed to be very effective, so

I continued using it. Al had Human Resources select 15 people at random from the lowest to the highest grades. They were invited to a working luncheon in our conference room. A box lunch would be provided, and Al would announce, "This is your meeting. You can say anything you like. You will not be penalized for anything."

Most of the time this announcement would be followed by silence. People were a little hesitant. I followed Al's pattern by saying, "If you do not have anything to say, then I will start talking about my grandchildren."

That usually got a response. After the first person began talking, it would be like trying to drink from a fire hydrant. Everyone wanted to air his or her problem. I am a firm believer that management should listen very carefully to what the troops say. Here are three good examples of some issues that needed attention that we were able to resolve immediately.

It was our standard procedure for the launch team to spend two days before the delivery with a team of USBI and MSFC NASA Quality Control people going through all the paperwork, and a very detailed hardware inspection before we delivered it to KSC. KSC spent two days with a team of contractors and KSC NASA Quality Control people doing the same thing that our people had done when they received it. At one of these lunches, one guy suggested having the KSC Contractor/NASA team join us to do this inspection as a join team and resolve any issues on the spot. I thought this was a great idea. I asked him why he had not brought this up before now.

"I have, but no one would listen," he replied.

Our people got with their counterparts at KSC, and the next scheduled transfer of this hardware was accomplished in two days with the combined team effort. We saved two days in the schedule of processing this hardware.

Here is another little issue that cropped up, and in this scenario, you can see how dedicated some of our people were. One of our mechanics aired his frustration that he needed a certain tool to accomplish his task of installing a piece of hardware in a difficult location in the rocket. He went to the tool crib to get this tool, was told they did not have it, they could not order it, and that the mechanic should be able to do the job without the authorized tools. This was not an exotic tool; in fact, the mechanic went down to Sears and bought this Craftsman-made tool to do his job. He paid for the tool himself. It so happened that the head of the department, that included the tool crib, was in the meeting. We got the problem solved right there and assured him it would never happen again.

Another problem was brought up that needed fixing. We had a good "Suggestion System" in operation where an employee could submit a suggestion for improvement in cost, safety, or efficiency, and if the suggestion was approved and implemented, the employee would receive some monetary award and recognition. In this case, an employee made a valid suggestion that was later implemented, but he never received credit for it. We initiated action immediately to resolve this problem.

One key note here. My secretary, Shirley Brewer, always attended these meetings and made a record of our action items. We made it mandatory that all issues that surfaced were resolved and feedback provided to the originator of the problem.

One lesson I learned at NASA was never underestimate youth. I was vividly reminded of this shortly after I took over my new position. We were in the process of checking out a flight assembly, and we were using a new automated ground checkout system. A problem occurred early one morning, and all our experts worked on it all day. They were in constant communication with the design people of this equipment, and they just could not resolve the problem. Several times I heard the comment, "I wish Eric was here. He could solve this problem."

I finally asked, "Who is Eric, and why is he not here?"

I was told Eric was the smartest guy regarding the software. He was on second shift and would be in later. Obviously, this was an urgent problem, and if we did not get it resolved soon, it could affect our schedule. I decided to stay for the second shift. I wanted this problem solved. Eric came in, and I was introduced to him. I could not believe it, and I am not exaggerating, Eric looked like he should be in junior high school.

All of these senior experts have been working on this problem all day, and now they expect this young kid to come in and fix it? I thought. *We are in deep, deep doo-doo.*

The people who said they'd wished Eric was here obviously

knew what they were talking about, because after they spent some time briefing him, he went to work. It was not very long before the problem was solved. Believe me, I knew who Eric was now, and he was my hero.

One lesson I quickly learned in this position was what it was like to be a contractor and please our NASA folks, including the lowest-level NASA engineer. As I mentioned earlier, as a contractor manager, you must earn that award fee above your base fee to keep your job. Sometimes, you have to eat a little humble pie.

I can't go into too much detail to cover nine years with USBI, but here are several little events that come to mind to give you a flavor of my work environment during this period. One significant difference in NASA and the contractor world is that in the contractor's world, you get much more involved in community affairs. UTC had a strong, community-oriented program that encouraged giving back and making a positive impact in your community. We had a generous budget for participating in and sponsoring community activities such as United Way and other, similar programs. One such event comes to mind. It's a little embarrassing for me, but here goes.

We were asked to be one of the sponsors of a special event to honor the parents of the teacher and astronaut, Christa McAuliffe, who lost her life in the Challenger accident. Sometime during the mid afternoon on the day of the event, my secretary, Shirley Brewer said, "Ike, you better get home and get ready for that event tonight."

I said, "Thanks, Shirley, I had forgotten about that."

Kathryn was out of town attending a Garden Club Convention, so I called my daughter, Amy, and asked her if could go with me to this special event in Cocoa Beach. She said she could.

So I went home and proudly dressed in a new, nice brown suit, and Amy had on her nice cocktail dress, and we headed out.

When we walked in the door, I said, "Oh my gosh, this is a black tie event."

I could not go off in the corner and hide, because USBI was one of the sponsors of this event. We were seated at the head table, and later the sponsors had to have pictures taken with the parents of Christa McAuliffe. To add to the embarrassment, this picture was in the paper the next morning. What an embarrassment, but you know, maybe there is a lesson to be learned here twenty-eight years later. "What difference does it make today?"

I mentioned earlier that UTC was vehemently opposed to unions, and in my view, they were correct. The company and the employees greatly benefited from this policy. In my time with TVA, I had some firsthand experience with the abuse of union power. Our Human Resources people did a super job of evaluating and comparing our employee benefits and salaries with the other aerospace companies operating in our area. We always maintained our position as the best compared to these other companies. We enjoyed a very, very low turnover rate and had very good morale. If we had job openings, we had no trouble finding highly qualified people.

At our peak, we had about 1,200 employees, and in that number, you are bound to have a few nerds. We had three, and I wanted to fire them, but they did perform just above the threshold that would give me clear justification for firing them. They were always trying to stir up support for a union. Every year, union gurus from up north would come down and try to organize unions. They would make a mass distribution of union literature and place signs at all the gates to the Space Center and the Air Force Station on the Cape, inviting employees to attend meetings at a local motel on Cocoa Beach. These three nerds would always attend, lapping up that garbage from these union thugs.

I did not ask him to, but one of our technicians, a good non-union guy, would attend these meetings and come back and tell me what went on and who from our company was in attendance. He described these union organizers, and it sounded like the Mafia. Fortunately, these three nerds could never get any support, and we happily remained non-union.

Another thing UTC had to counter the union threat was a good grievance procedure. Any employee could file a grievance, and it would go up the management chain as far as necessary to resolve the complaint. Very few came up to my level for a resolution.

One sad case I recall very well. The head of our Human Resources Office brought me a case they had not been able to resolve to the employee's satisfaction. I read his complaint, or I might say I tried to read it. The grammar and spelling were so terrible, it was hard to make sense out of what this guy was saying. He had applied for, and was turned down, for an open supervisor position in our cable manufacturing shop where he worked. He felt he should have been selected. I interviewed this young man, and his speech was like his writing, almost unintelligible. He pointed to a piece of paper indicating he had graduated from some sort of trade school.

"Looka here. I is educated," he said.

I had talked to his immediate supervisor, and it was clear to me he was hardly qualified for the job he was in. The supervisor said if he had a work order to fabricate a cable eighty-four and three-fourths inches long, he could not read the tape. I felt sorry for this young man. He sincerely thought he was educated and qualified for this supervisor position. Of course, I had to rule against him.

One of the most stressful periods I experienced in my USBI service were the days immediately following the tragic loss of the Challenger space shuttle on January 28, 1986. All contractors that have hardware involved in a space vehicle problem immediately are concerned. "Did our hardware cause or contribute to this problem?"

Until you receive the answer, you must be deeply concerned. You immediately must impound all of the paperwork and the complete history of the hardware in question. We worked twenty-four hours a day, seven days a week within our own company, and we had several of our people assigned to other teams working with NASA and the other contractors. Fortunately, it was learned later our hardware was not an issue in this tragic event, but I would say in a thorough review like this, you do identify some problems. Even though they did not contribute to the problem, they did require some attention.

One event I recall from my days at USBI was when NASA gave Jane Fonda a VIP tour of KSC. To those of you too young to remember, Jane Fonda was a famous movie star back in the Vietnam War era. As an antiwar protester, she made a trip to Vietnam. There was a famous picture made with her in an antiaircraft gun pit with the North Vietnamese crew celebrating shooting down an American plane. In my book, this is treason of the highest order. The reason I mention this event is because we had several Vietnam veterans in our workforce, and they refused to come to work that day. I sympathized with them, and we gave them administrative leave.

Another event I recall from my USBI days was a very pleasant event. Four of my old WWII Marine buddies, Jerry Foley, R.P. Wood, Larry Mason, and Joe Bonifer, and their wives came down to visit Kathryn and me. I was able to give them a VIP tour of KSC. USBI owned a nice, three-bedroom condo in Cocoa Beach which was used for our VIP visitors. I was able to put my friends in this condo right on the ocean and they enjoyed it very much. During this period, prior to the September 11, 2001 terrorist attacks, each contractor at KSC was issued ten guest badges we could use any time. We did not have to go through KSC to bring guests to the Space Center.

One day, I had an unpleasant visit from two government workers from the EOE office in Orlando. I think it was called the EOE office. Anyway, it was the office that takes care of discrimination issues in the workforce. They presented me with a thick report that one of our employees had filed. This was a young lady in our parachute packing and refurbishment facility.

To understand this situation, you need to know something about the working environment in this building. Our parachute crew was located in a separate building several miles from our main operations building. The parachute crew was very dedicated and highly skilled in their profession. They always received excellent ratings from our NASA people, and I never had to spend any time over there working out any problems. I made regular visits to the parachute crew, but as I said, I never had any problems in this area. There were several women in this crew, and during their lunch hour and break periods, most of them were engaged in card games. I learned from the women as well as the men that their conversational language in their work and card games was rough. This had been going on a long time.

I interviewed our manager, Bruce Rutledge, and several of the workers, and they all said the same thing. This young lady who filed the complaint had one of the foulest mouths in the crew. She got into a personal issue with Bruce and made these outlandish charges. All of her co-workers told me she was the problem, not Bruce.

My account of the situation did not cut any ice with these "yo-yos." They preferred her story. In my view, these EOE employees were not all that bright. In the end, to wrap this thing up, we had to set up a "sensitivity training program" for all employees. How stupid. Ugh!

Now a more pleasant thing. One day, I received a notice from the UTC Headquarters in Connecticut that one of the UTC Board of Directors from England was coming to the US and wanted a tour of KSC. I had his itinerary. He was flying the Concorde to Miami, where a UTC executive helicopter would pick him up and bring him to our local Ty-CO airport. Along with my friend Bernie, and the head of our Public Relations office, we met this gentleman at the Ty-CO airport. He was a very distinguished gentleman with the title of Lord. I cannot remember his name, but he was a very pleasant and friendly man. We gave him an excellent tour of the Space Center and a very detailed tour of our USBI operations. We enjoyed a box lunch in my office. When we returned him to the airport, he asked if we would like to take a little spin in his helicopter. We said we would, and we enjoyed about a twenty-five minute flight over the Titusville area. It was an enjoyable day.

UTC was also very strong on education and training. Several of our technicians continued their education, got a degree, and moved up to an engineering position. I had the opportunity to attend several management seminars conducted by some of the top motivational speakers in the country. One I particularly recall was a seminar by Dr. Edward Deming. Dr. Deming was the man Gen. MacArthur called to Japan to straighten out the Japanese industrial complex after WWII. Dr. Deming is credited with the Japanese economic miracle which occurred at that time.

We experienced the results of his work when Japan started exporting quality automobiles, appliances, and other goods, which destroyed our industrial complex. Based on what he did in Japan, our companies began to pay attention to his message. When he returned to the U.S., Ford Motor Company was one that listened and benefited from his program.

I enjoyed my days with USBI. Just as I was in NASA, I was privileged to work with so many nice, talented people both in

Florida and Huntsville. I could easily add a whole bunch of people here, and I know that I'll get in trouble for naming but a few, but here were some of my talented friends at USBI: Larry Clark, Jim Carlton, Joe Kinsley, Jim Seaman, Joe Lessey, John Smith, Ben Glenn, and I can never leave out my super secretary, Shirley Brewer. I should add I had a wonderful working relationship with the MSFC resident office at KSC with people like John Key and Jimmy King. I was now 68 years old and had enjoyed about the best career I could ever imagine. It was hard to leave this work environment, but I was convinced it was time to retire. Kathryn and I had a dream to RV and travel the world. Now we would make it come true.

This is the aft skirt for the solid rocket boosters on the shuttle system. We (USBI) manufactured this assembly and transferred it to the KSC launch team. The solid rocket boosters were recovered after each shuttle launch and refurbished at our facility, Hangar S, Cape Canaveral Air Force Station. The entire shuttle assembly, comprised of the solid rocket boosters, external tank, and the shuttle, rest on the aft skirts.

This was the forward assembly of the solid rocket booster that USBI delivered to Kennedy Space Center, after they resumed flights after the Challenger accident. The people pictured above were the USBI Management Team at the time. (I am in the center, in the tan coat.)

As the air is pumped into the booster, it slowly tilts over into the log mode, and then it is strapped to the recovery ship and towed back to our refurbishment facility on the Banana River.

Recovering the solid rocket boosters for the Shuttle System. Boosters land in the water in the spar mode (upright), parachute removed, and divers go down and pump air into the booster.

Brown suit at a black tie affair. Not my best fashion choice. Especially at an event honoring the parents of Christa McAuliffe, the teacher killed in the Challenger explosion.

My retirement party from USBI in 1991. (L-R:) Astronaut Steve Oswald, Jim Teply, my sister, Mary Jo Teply, Diane Gossard, my sister, Florence Cothren, Kathryn, and me. And in the front row, my grandson, Tim Dennard.

REFLECTIONS ON MY SPACE CAREER

Man has always gazed in wonder and awe at the heavenly bodies we view in the night sky and has always pondered, *How do I fit in this vast universe? Who am I? Why am I here?* I do not know precisely how to answer these questions, but here is a "go" at it. During my service in the Marine Corps in WWII, I had a deep inner satisfaction that I was doing something positive, not only for my family and country but also for mankind. The world we would be living in if the enemy won the war was unthinkable.

The more I was engaged in our space exploration program, the more I had the same comfortable feeling that what I was doing was not just a job. I was engaged in a mission that was very positive from two aspects. First, from a personal standpoint, the more we expanded our knowledge of the universe, the more I marveled at and appreciated the perfect creation of the universe. The more I learned about the perfect order of the universe, the more convinced I was that there had to be a Creator. In my view, and I am convinced absolutely that I am right, there is no way— it is totally impossible—that the perfect order of our universe resulted from some stupid "big bang theory." I am in very good company when I make this bold statement, and I think you will agree with me when you read the following:

"For me the idea of a creation is inconceivable without God. One cannot be exposed to the law and order of the universe without concluding that there must be a divine intent behind it all." This is a direct quote from Wernher von Braun. I know of no one more qualified to make that statement than von Braun. I like other statements von Braun made related to this subject, such as his debunking the idea that science and religion are not compatible: "Science and Religion are not antagonistic. On the contrary, they are sisters. While science tries to learn more about creation, religion tries to better understand the Creator."

Secondly, from a less personal but more of a "greater good" perspective, I felt my work in our space program was not just a job but a mission that was absolutely necessary for the good of my family, my country, and Western civilization. As I mentioned earlier, from the end of WWII in 1945 until the disintegration of the old Soviet Union in 1990, we were engaged in the Cold War with the Soviet Union. To paraphrase presidents Kennedy and Johnson, you cannot be the number one nation in the world without being number one in space. Fortunately, presidents Kennedy and Johnson actively backed those words with the Apollo program. I have read about the Soviet space activities during those years and I am convinced that had the Soviet's version of the Apollo succeeded, and had we failed in our Apollo program, today we would be living in a different world.

The Soviets were very serious about bringing all the nations in our world under a Communist banner. Our counterparts in their space program referred to themselves as "Cold War soldiers." I realize the term *cold war* does not mean anything to today's generation, but I would advise everyone to become familiar with this part of our history. I believe, and I say this with great sadness, that we are likely (as of 2017) headed for a serious cold war situation with the current Russian president, Vladimir Putin. I am concerned about the future my grandchildren and great-grandchildren will experience. Again, I want to loosely quote President Reagan when he said, "For peace you must prepare for war." Basically, this means if we are not number one in space and in the military, we are in big trouble. Sadly, you must question if we are number one in space today when we must depend on Russia to ferry our astronauts to and from the International Space

Station (ISS), and use Russian rocket engines on our rockets to transport cargo to the ISS.

I think all my colleagues also saw what we were doing as not just a job but also a vital mission for our country. Invariably, today when some of us old guys get together, someone will express how fortunate we were to spend our entire working career in our space program. Never a dull moment. A successful launch was always worth the "blood, sweat, and tears" it took to witness that beautiful rocket lift off. This reminds me of the old axiom, "You cannot have a victory unless you have experienced a battle."

Thinking back over my 40-year space career, I must say I would not change a thing, and that is a very good and satisfying feeling. Almost 100 percent of the young engineers I was associated with in the beginning, 1951, remained in the program until they retired. There were some internal transfers, but the turnover—that is, leaving the space program—was almost zero.

The more our venture into space revealed the perfect order of the universe, the more my thirst to learn more about God's creation increased. In the 1950s, when we first started talking about launching a man-made moon to orbit Earth, I was excited to learn more about celestial mechanics. I had to start from ground zero. I am not implying that I made a scholarly study of celestial mechanics—I only scratched the surface. I did read some works of ancient astronomers like Kepler, Copernicus, and Galileo with much fascination and awe on how knowledgeable these men were on planetary movements and other aspects of the heavenly bodies. They had to be very brilliant to make these discoveries with the very primitive tools available in those ancient times.

When you are first exposed to the space program, your mind starts expanding. Every day you increase your space vocabulary and learn new meanings for familiar words like *roll, pitch, thrust*, and unfamiliar words like *apogee, perigee, perihelion, escape velocity, inclination, geosynchronous orbit*. You also learn a whole new world of acronyms. My heightened interest in my expanded world prompted me to buy a couple of books on astronomy, and I subscribed to one of the leading magazines on astronomy. I also bought a five-inch telescope, and I was so excited when I first viewed the moons orbiting Jupiter and Saturn. At that time, there were no bookstores in our local area, so when I made trips to Huntsville I would often head to the bookstore after work. Huntsville had an excellent bookstore, especially for technical books, and that was a common pattern for all of our local guys when they traveled there.

My generation is the only generation that has lived through the entire history of our space program. In this relatively brief period of history, we have experienced tremendous progress. Just a quick snapshot of my own involvement in our space history: our early primitive Redstone; Jupiter-C and Explorer I (the free world's first satellite); Jupiter (IRBM, deployed in Turkey and Italy during the Cold War); Juno (space probe, the non-military version of the Jupiter IRBM); Pershing (ballistic missile, 500-mile range, deployed in Germany during the Cold War); MR-1 (first US manned flight, suborbital); Saturn 1B (used in early Earth orbit testing of the Apollo CSM and LM, and later used in the Skylab and Apollo-Soyuz programs); Spacelab (joint program between NASA and the European Space Agency); and finally, on the contractor side, USBI (providing the forward assembly and aft skirt for the solid rocket boosters on the shuttle system).

I still try to keep current on our space activities, and one of the most encouraging things I see is the vast increase in commercial launches. It is very encouraging to see some business tycoons with very deep pockets and a passion for extended space travel. The future looks very exciting.

At one of our recent NASA Alumni League meetings, our speaker was the KSC director, and he gave us a glimpse of the future activities at our beloved KSC. I commented, "I just wish I was 50 years younger." What we could accomplish in the next 50 years in space exploration just boggles the mind. I am convinced there will be a lineup of bright young men and women eager to climb aboard the spacecraft to Mars. Who knows? One of them might be one of my great-grandchildren. We only need the will of the people, which is Congress. I'm sorry I will not be on the banks of the Indian River in Titusville, along with a million others, intently looking eastward across the river for that first puff of smoke indicating ignition, and then witnessing that historic liftoff. I will be watching from above.

I cannot begin to document all of the benefits we have enjoyed from our brief (about 60 years) space history. Just scratching the surface, I would say we have experienced significant benefits in the following areas because of our space program: satellite communications; TV; GPS; weather; general knowledge of the universe; and medical advances. These are all awesome, and I am one of the thousands that have enjoyed an extended life because of these medical advances in particular.

My career in space exploration has tremendously expanded my world and enriched my life, and I am reminded daily what a mighty, omnipotent God I serve. This reminder can come in many forms. Here is just one example: We have a room with one wall, all windows, facing the western sky, and many times in the late evening, one of us, Kathryn or myself, will happen to be in this room and view the indescribably beautiful sunset. We will immediately call the other, saying, "You must come see this sunset." Only God could be the artist of this picture.

If you have read this far, I ask the reader to do two things. First, go out one night with a full moon and gaze intently at the moon. Try to visualize one of your loved ones walking on the surface of this distant heavenly body. Secondly, Google the Hubble Space Telescope photos of the outer universe; these will truly boggle your mind.

I'll repeat this quote from one of my favorite philosophers, Yogi Berra: "It is hard to make predictions, especially about the future."

Space club honors former KSC employee

The National Space Club – Florida Committee recently honored a former KSC employee with a Lifetime Achievement Award.

NASA astronaut John Young presented the award to Isom "Ike" Rigell on Sept. 22 during a luncheon in Cocoa Beach.

Rigell's career spanned the early days of the American space program through the Space Shuttle program's first decade.

He was director of Shuttle Payload Integration for all

LIFETIME ACHIEVEMENT awardee Ike Rigell, left, with astronaut John Young.

non-Department of Defense payloads when he retired from NASA at KSC in 1981. He later worked for USBI and retired from the space program in 1991.

This article was published in the *Florida Today* paper.

The 50th anniversary of the Explorer 1 launch
in Blockhouse 56, Cape Canaveral, Florida.

(L-R:) Terry Greenfield, Ike Rigell, Kelly Fiorentino,
Frank Bryan, Milt Chambers, and Bill Chandler.

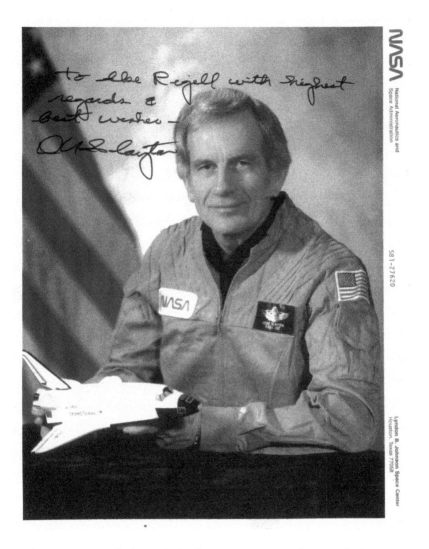

Deke was one of the original astronauts and one of the most popular of the original 7 astronauts. He was sadly grounded for many years for medical reasons, but was cleared to fly again on the joint NASA/Soviet ASTP Launch. We worked closely together on the Readiness Review Board for many years.

National Aeronautics and
Space Administration

Lyndon B. Johnson Space Center
Houston, Texas
77058

Reply to Attn of: LA15 (81-93A)   July 9, 1981

John F. Kennedy Space Center
Attn: CO/Ike Rigell
Kennedy Space Center, FL 32899

Dear Ike:

Tommy Walton informs me that you are on the verge of retiring from
Government service after 35 dedicated years. I am sorry to hear that,
since I have become accustomed to listening to your presentations at
countless Flight Readiness Reviews over the years. Your talent and
companionship will be missed by all of us. However, I wish you well
in all of your future endeavors and hope they will include a copious
quanity of relaxation.

Best of luck,

Donald K. Slayton
Astronaut and Manager
for Orbital Flight Test

Letter from Astronaut Donald "Deke" Slayton to
me upon my retirement.

NATIONAL AERONAUTICS AND SPACE ADMINISTRATION
JOHN F. KENNEDY SPACE CENTER
KENNEDY SPACE CENTER, FLORIDA 32899

REPLY TO
ATTN OF: CD

OCT 9 1974

Mr. Isom A. Rigell
LV/Director, Launch Vehicle Operations
John F. Kennedy Space Center,
Kennedy Space Center, FL 32899

Dear Mr. Rigell:

We have shared failures and successes since the by-gone
days of the Missile Firing Laboratory. As you know the
triumphs far exceeded our disappointments due, in great
measure, to your unflagging loyalty and devotion.

Prior to 1960 we contributed to the development of guided
missiles which strengthened the national defense while out
of the same progress we established the basic technology
which carried the United States into space. Since 1960
we shared the problems inherent in the growth of this
organization and its recognition as NASA's major launch
arm. Along the way your personal contribution grew in
complexity and stature.

As I now take my leave, with mixed emotions, I have a keen
appreciation of the rigorous schedules and sacrifices required of you and a deep gratitude for the willingness
with which you accepted the inevitable hardships and
responded in the fullest measure. You helped this country
obtain a predominant role in the exploitation of space
technology from the first satellite through our participation in Project Mercury, and the historic Apollo launches
to the Moon, climaxed by the extraordinarily successful
Skylab Program. I shall always cherish the memories of our
association and wish for you every success in your future
endeavors.

Sincerely yours,

Kurt H. Debus
Director

Letter from Dr. Kurt Debus to me upon my retirement.

Rocco A. Petrone
Executive Vice President

Space Transportation &
Systems Group
12214 Lakewood Boulevard
Downey, CA 90241
(213) 922-2466

**Rockwell
International**

Dear Ike:

Upon your departure from government service after over 35 years
of service to our Country, I want to take this opportunity to
commend you for the many years of dedicated service to the
Missile and Space Program and the leadership you personally
demonstrated in taking our Nation into the Space Age.

Progress has been made by leaps and bounds since the time that
we both participated in the first Redstone launch in August, 1953.
It is probably impossible to count all the hurdles and obstacles
that had to be overcome from that time through the many programs
you worked on up through the Apollo/Saturn Program and beyond.
However, I must sincerely state that on all the projects that I
served with you, I always valued most highly your incisive recommendations upon which action could be taken. There are few
people in the Space Program on whom I relied more heavily during
the buildup and operations of the Apollo/Saturn Program and I will
always have the warm memory that you met the test whenever we
had a serious problem to solve.

Ike, I never will forget the expression you used when you would
come to me with a particularly knotty problem -- "Which hand do
you want to drink the poison with - the right or the left?". That
expression in many ways epitomized the problems that you faced
and then had to make recommendations to those of us who leaned
so heavily on you. You always met that test and the success of
the programs you worked on show the positive results.

I hope the years ahead will bring you many more rewards which
you so earnestly have earned with your dedicated efforts over the
past 35 years. I also hope that the future will bring the opportunity
for us to stay in contact as the Nation's future in space continues
to grow on the foundation you did so much to help establish.

Best regards,

R. A. Petrone

Letter from Rocco Petrone to me upon my retirement.

1991
RETIREMENT

RETIREMENT

I retired at age 68. This was a tough decision. I had contemplated retiring the preceding couple of years, but I was enjoying my job and it was tough to leave. I admit, it wasn't as exciting in the space business in 1991 as it was in the first 25 to 30 years of the space program. We had settled into a mode of mostly repeating the same thing. In the rocket business there are always challenging issues, but not to the extent of the early years when every launch brought something new and exciting.

To those of you still young and in the workforce, I have these words of comfort: "Some of your best and most enjoyable days are ahead of you." I have heard the expression "Never, never lose the child in you," and I believe these are true words of wisdom. Always think young, go out and see and enjoy the world. Make your world much bigger. Travel, travel. Prior to my retirement, Kathryn and I made several trips, domestic and overseas, but due to my work I was limited to a maximum time of about two weeks, and we desired to make more extensive trips.

Let me jump back and talk about our early, primitive travel days. We started tent camping, as best I can recall, in the early to mid '60s. We first ventured out to the Florida state parks and then boldly took our young children to the Maine woods. We became addicted to this environment, and for several years this was our main—no pun intended—destination: the coast and the woods of Maine.

Years later, as our children were older and on their own, Kathryn and I decided to go for a motor coach. At that time, we were driving a large Ford SUV and a large Mercedes, and neither was suitable for towing, so we bought a small Ford pickup truck. This was fine until we had some grandchildren that were old enough to travel with us. We decided to go back to an Airstream, and then a Ford Excursion (the largest SUV Ford made at the time) was necessary to tow it. We fell in love with this combination and attended many Airstream rallies over the years. I remember one in particular held on a large farm in Canada where we had over one thousand Airstreams. We found Airstream people to be the friendliest people in the world.

I think it is beneficial for everyone to travel overseas as it is enjoyable and educational to observe various cultures, and it is especially interesting if you make the effort to learn some history of the areas you are visiting. One thing you come away with from your foreign travels, whether you express it openly or not, is that you are very aware of how blessed you are to have been born in the USA.

I think it was in 1982 that we took advantage of a tremendous travel offer to fly from Washington, DC, to London on the Concorde, stay several days at a first-class hotel, and then sail back to New York on the *Queen Elizabeth II*. What a trip. We flew over the Atlantic at 55,000 feet and the speed of Mach 2. Having broken the sound barrier at that speed in just a little over three hours, we set foot in England. Remember, Mach 1 is the speed of sound, which is 758 miles per hour, so at Mach 2 you are really moving out. We dined almost the entire trip. As soon as the seatbelt sign was off, the flight stewardess started serving the food. I thought this was a tremendous dinner, and a little later I learned this was just the appetizers. The main dish followed and then our choice of desserts. It is sad that Concorde is no longer in service. So now when you fly from the USA to Europe on a Boeing 747 you must poke along at about Mach .84, and you finally get there about eight hours later. One very nice thing about flying the Concorde: When you land, you have just enjoyed a super meal and you are ready to take on the day. It is so nice realizing that you do not need an entire day to recover from a mostly sleepless, uncomfortable overnight flight.

Two of the most meaningful trips we made were to Israel. I know, everything is so commercialized and tourist-oriented there, but I still maintain that you cannot travel around Israel without experiencing a deep spiritual realization that our Lord once made footprints and taught where you are standing. Israel is the only place we have visited that I still have a really deep desire to return to today. The more I understand about Israel, the more convinced I am that God has had His hand on this very small piece of biblical real estate. First, biblical prophecy was fulfilled in 1948 when the world recognized Israel as a sovereign country. Secondly, this tiny little nation has only 8.5 million people. The neighboring Arab countries combined have several hundred million people. Israel successfully defended herself against major attacks by some of these Arab countries in 1948 (in 1948 Israel only had 2.3 million people), 1967, and 1973. Numerous smaller attacks are still occurring on a regular basis. When you understand just how small this country is, you must marvel at the fact that they still exist as a nation, they are prosperous, and they are still making major advancements in the technical and medical world. You also must marvel at how ingenious they are in the conservation of water in their agricultural industry.

During the 1980s, we were active in the Full Gospel Business Men International (FGBMI), and for a couple of years I was the president of the Brevard chapter. We attended several world conventions, in Hong Kong, Rio de Janeiro, Montréal, San Francisco, Nashville, and Orlando. These were powerful spiritual events with dynamite speakers, and several thousand businessmen and women from all over the world in attendance. On the overseas conventions, we always enjoyed side trips in the surrounding areas. For example, from the convention in Rio de Janeiro we visited Iguazu Falls and Argentina, and from Hong Kong we made our first of three trips into China.

Through our FGBMI contacts in Hong Kong we scheduled a trip through a local church that smuggled Bibles into the interior of China. This church provided an escort and made all the arrangements for the trip: hotel reservations, intercity travel, and sight-seeing. We paid the church, including the expenses for our escort, who was a very impressive young man from Minnesota.

He was serving as a missionary from his home church. He made these trips into China on a regular basis and we went to places the ordinary tourist tours would not visit. Our luggage was loaded with small Bibles to be delivered at designated points in China. They had a system set up that distributed these Bibles to towns and villages deeper in the interior of China. They called these people that went further into the interior "donkeys for Jesus." What we were doing was, I might say, "spiritually" legal, but since the Chinese government is not "spiritual," what we were doing was illegal in China. I was a little apprehensive about this venture as I never did get a clear answer on what happened if the Chinese discovered you were smuggling Bibles into the country. Somehow, I suppressed my concerns and we signed up for this trip.

From Hong Kong, we flew to a town in inland China, the name of which I cannot remember how to spell, and as we exited the plane we faced two check-in stations. The same type as in our country when you go through security to get to your departure gate. My thoughts were, *This isn't good, we are in deep yogurt.* However, as we got closer we observed that the belts on these check-out stations were running, but the two uniformed Chinese girls attending these machines were very busy chatting with each other and paying no attention to the incoming passengers. Some passengers were putting their baggage on the belt, walking along, picking it up, and leaving. Our guide said to just stay with him, so we walked right on by these two girls. *What a relief*, I thought. *Someone is surely looking out for us.*

Our guide suggested we take a boat trip down the Lei River. I would consider this one of the most interesting days we ever experienced in our world travels. This was an all-day trip. We passed Chinese peasants on tiny reed floats fishing a type of bird called a cormorant. These cormorants had rings around their necks so that they could dive down, catch fish, and bring them back up on the raft but they could not swallow them. At noon, several of these fishermen pulled alongside our boat and sold their fish, and the boat's chef cooked out on the open deck. It was delicious. We observed Chinese peasants harvesting water plants in the river for their water buffalo, and farmers plowing their fields with wooden plows pulled by oxen. The scenery down the river was spectacular. At the end of the day we boarded an old, dilapidated bus and made the trip back to our hotel.

In our foreign travels, Kathryn and I frequently disagreed over the question "Do we want to eat where the locals eat?" My answer was almost always "No," and hers was always "Yes!" She always won and I carried a pocket full of energy bars, as I usually passed when I saw the local "stuff."

On this particular trip we had been taking our meals at the hotel where we were staying. The food was barely passable, but you could tolerate it for a day or two. Late that afternoon, after we arrived back at the hotel from the boat trip, Kathryn asked the hotel clerk to recommend a restaurant where the locals ate. He called the bellboy over and conversed in Chinese and told us to follow the bellboy. The bellboy spoke no English, but we followed him down the street through a couple of alleys and stopped in front of a restaurant. The front of the restaurant was all doors, and they were folded back so the restaurant was completely open, and it was full of people. There was a wide sidewalk, and the maître d', a woman, was standing there with her menus. But what really got our attention was a guy—I assume he was one of the cooks—on the sidewalk skinning a snake about 4 feet long. There was blood dripping on the sidewalk from the snake, and we noticed several wire cages against the wall with large rats and snakes. We later learned this was a typical scene. Our bellboy conversed in Chinese with the maître d', and by this time Kathryn had lost her appetite for the local cuisine, so we quickly turned around and started walking away. The maître d' ran and caught up with us and said in broken English, "You like snakie, you like snakie?" We said, "No thanks," and could not get out of there fast enough.

What I initially thought to be a negative on this trip I would now call a positive. As I stated, the church in Hong Kong made all the travel arrangements, and obviously they were very conservative. Our hotels were in the "el cheapo" category, but the China we got to visit was far more interesting than the normal tourist routes. For example, in one hotel, from our room we could raise our window and look down over a group of locals doing their early morning tai chi. There were all ages participating and they were obviously very serious about this. A few feet from this group were some wide steps leading down to the river, and on the steps were fish peddlers holding up their "catch of the day," and people were taking their morning baths and brushing their teeth in the murky river water.

In this village, apparently they weren't accustomed to seeing Americans. Whenever we walked down the street, several people would follow us. On one occasion, I stopped at a little roadside food cart to buy some bananas. I was trying to communicate with the Chinese lady on how much to pay, and one of the bystanders told me in English that the lady was trying to cheat me. He intervened and settled on a price and I still don't know if I got cheated or not. During this discussion a number of the locals closely gathered around us to the point that they were literally pressing up against us. I discovered a few minutes later that some guy tried to pick my pocket. As we walked away I felt something in my back and I turned around and this guy ran off. I felt my back pocket and discovered several slits about ¾-inch long. My pocket was bulging, but the poor pickpocket did not realize my back pocket was full of toilet paper. I am sure he thought I had a wallet stuffed with $100 bills. Our guide had instructed us to take toilet paper with us as it was not available in any of the Chinese public toilets. We always kept our money and passports in pouches under our shirts.

On this trip, we delivered our Bibles to the designated distribution point. We did not meet anyone at this distribution point, but our guide knew where the key was hidden, so we deposited our Bibles and left.

Our next trip to China was about a year later and our daughter, Mona, was with us. On this trip we also smuggled Bibles into China from the same church in Hong Kong.

I should say a little about this church we were working with. The pastor was an American and a Vietnam veteran, and he spoke fluent Chinese. He preached two sermons every Sunday, one in English and one in Chinese. In all of our visits to this church, we were always impressed with the number and dedication of these young missionary volunteers from the USA, female and male. On this trip, the church fitted Kathryn and Mona with skirts to wear under their dresses, and these skirts had row after row of small pockets, which held the small Chinese Bibles we were delivering.

The church gave us very detailed instructions on how to get to the city in China where we were to deliver the Bibles and the transportation schedule.

This city, I cannot remember the name of it, was not very far inland, and we traveled in an old bus loaded with Chinese and their boxes and luggage. The details of how we entered China on this trip are a little vague in my memory, but we encountered no problems. We had instructions on how to find the building and we had the key to enter the distribution point, which was an apartment in a large apartment building. There was no one present when we made our delivery. It appeared that no one lived there and it was strictly a distribution center. There were Bibles stacked everywhere, on and under the beds; even the bathtub was full of Bibles. Mission accomplished.

We felt really good about what we had done, and then we enjoyed the remainder of our tour in China and Hong Kong, including a "high tea" at one of the five-star hotels in Hong Kong. I should qualify this last statement—I enjoyed this high tea until I got the bill. Next time I will just order the egg foo young.

Our third and last Bible-smuggling trip into China was totally different. We worked with the same church, but we booked a first-class, tourist-type tour covering several major cities in China, including a trip to the Great Wall. On a trip such as this, your traveling companions are whoever the travel agency books for the same trip on that day. Our group was small. We had an American family comprised of a Boeing 747 pilot for United Airlines, his wife, and their two daughters, both college students. The other member of our group was a single guy from Australia. We were very compatible with our new friends. I did not tell our fellow travelers that we were illegally bringing Bibles into China because if there was a problem, they could truthfully state they were not a part of this event.

The first leg of our flight was to Xi'an, the location of the famous terra-cotta warriors. We were flying on a Chinese airline and, as we checked in, I thought that it might be the end of the trip for me and Kathryn. We were checking our luggage in, and when the Chinese guy picked one of my bags up, I observed he realized it was extra heavy. Apparently, his English was not very good, and he looked at us and pointed at my bag and said,

"Who?" I stepped up and he picked up my bag and motioned for me to follow him.

My thoughts were, *I'm about to find out what happens to you when they discover you are bringing Bibles into China.* This bag in question was loaded with Bibles and very little clothes. He started to open the suitcase, but I had it locked. He pointed to the lock and uttered something I interpreted to be "unlock," which I did. He opened it up and all he could see were Bibles. He stirred them around as if he were looking for something else, and then he closed the bag and motioned for me to lock it up and get back in line. Many times your prayers are answered long after the actual prayer, but in this case my prayer was answered immediately. I needed the divine intervention right then and there. *Amen!* I will mention this incident again a little later.

Our instructions from the church were to wait for a call from one of their contacts in that city after we checked into our hotel, a five-star hotel. Everything went according to plan. We received our call and the caller said he would be up to our room in a few minutes. We heard a knock on the door and when I opened the door there was an American, about 6'10", standing there. We invited him in and we enjoyed a nice visit. I told him about the incident when I was checking in at the Chinese airline, and I told him I was dumbfounded that he let me go without any problem. He had two theories. One theory was that the Chinese are very sensitive about being embarrassed and he might have been embarrassed to ask about these books and my luggage. The second theory was that he could be a secret Christian and supported what we were doing. I do not know if one of these theories fit the situation or not.

Another interesting thing was that I told this man we had some friends back in Titusville who had a friend teaching at a Chinese university. We had his telephone number and they wanted us to call him. I told our new friend the name of the man we were supposed to call and our friend laughed and said that some of the Bibles we had were set to go to this man. He then explained how this guy used these Bibles. He was hired by the Chinese government to teach American government to graduate students. The Chinese economy was accelerating their push to enter the American market. This American teacher taught the

Chinese about how our government works. He told them our Constitution was based on a little book, and then he would show them a Bible and say he would give them one of these little books. This teacher was a Christian, and this was a clever way to have the Communist Chinese government unintentionally support some missionary work.

One clear message I learned on these trips to China, and on our first trip to the old Soviet Union, was how cleverly and thoroughly evil dictators shape and control a vast population. It is scary. The more I observed communism, the more convinced I was that it was an evil force and kept people under total suppression. Every place communism has been tried, it has failed; just look at Cuba today.

The following story is an example of how inept the Communist system is. Our group was traveling via Chinese airline from Xi'an to Beijing. We boarded a little two-engine plane during a violent thunderstorm. I did not like this situation at all, but fortunately we sat in that plane for several hours until the storm passed. On this tour, we visited several cities, always via the Chinese airline, and when our friend, the United Airlines pilot, entered the plane, he showed the pilot his credentials and was always invited to spend some time in the cockpit. While we waited on the tarmac at Xi'an, our friend was in the cockpit. When he came out of the cockpit he came over and said, "Ike, you know what kind of plane we are flying?" I said, "No, I do not have any idea." He replied, "This is an old 1955 Soviet Tupolev." My initial thoughts were, *I knew I was right. I should get off this cotton-picking piece of junk.* But then I thought, *This guy with all of his experience is still willing to fly on this so-called airplane. I guess I will stay.* I should add, the upholstery on the seats was dirty and tattered and the floor was dirty.

After the storm passed we took off and safely landed in Beijing about midnight, which was about four hours later than originally scheduled. The travel company agent had patiently waited for us, and, at this late hour, she was about the only one in the airport. She was a professor at a local university and this was a second job for her. We exited the airport and it was very dimly lit outside. All of a sudden someone in our group shouted, "Watch out! There is a hole there." One of us was about to step in an open manhole.

There were no kind of safety barriers around this open manhole. This is communism and pride in workmanship at its best.

We arrived at the hotel, again a five-star, and our tour guide left us and said she would pick us up in the morning. We went to the check-in counter and we and our Australian friend told the American family to check in first, which they did, and they got their luggage and went to their room. Kathryn and I and the Australian stood there at the checkout counter for several minutes, and there were a couple of Chinese hotel staff members shuffling paper and just completely ignoring us. Finally, I said to these yo-yo's that we needed to get checked in.

One came over and we were completely astounded when he said, "We do not have a room for you." We could not believe this, and I said, "What are we supposed to do?" In his broken English he said, "You may sleep on there," pointing to some sofas and chairs in the lobby, "and tomorrow we get you a room." I cannot recall all of our back and forth conversation, but I did tell him that this was not acceptable, and I showed him my travel company schedule, which clearly stated that we had reservations for that night. He went back, conversed with the other guy, and came back and said, "You sleep in the house next door tonight." I told him that was not acceptable either, and that we demanded a room in the hotel as we had reserved. He went back and I noticed he made a telephone call. Then he came back and said they had another hotel, also five-star, and we could stay there tonight. We were out of options, so we agreed and the check-in guy said, "Follow bellboy." This little bellboy, with his nice bellboy uniform, loaded our luggage on a cart and headed out the door and we followed. As soon as we were out the door, we observed about half a dozen taxicabs lined up. The driver of the first taxicab jumped out and opened his doors and the trunk. We expected to get in this cab to go to the next hotel. The bellboy, pushing the luggage cart, kept moving, and we thought, *He does not want this cab he wants another one*, as the other cabdrivers did the same thing, opening their doors and inviting us in. But the bellboy just kept walking past these taxicabs. We did not know what to expect, and since the bellboy did not speak English we just silently followed him down a dimly lit street.

We could not see anything in the distance that looked like

a five-star hotel. At the first intersection, we looked to our left and, about a block away, there was a well-lit building that looked like it might be a five-star hotel. The bellboy turned left. The building was uphill. It became immediately obvious that this little bellboy could not push this luggage cart up that incline, so my Australian friend (he was a real big guy) and I pushed the cart up to this building, and we were very pleased to find this was more of a five-star hotel than the one we had just left. They were expecting us, so everything went smoothly from there. The next morning, we tried to get our reservations for the reminder of our stay in Beijing changed to this hotel, but that did not work, so we were back to our original hotel. Other than our check-in problem, our stay at that hotel was very pleasant.

Now, here is a lesson I learned about communism from this experience. If things go according to plan, they can make it, but if unexpected events crop up they do not know how to deal with it. We learned that the same company owned both hotels and they finally figured out a way to get us a room in their sister hotel, but they did not have the authority to use a taxi to transport us to the other hotel, which explained us having to walk there. Thinking about how to best treat their customers meant nothing to them; the pay was the same. Any credible American company would have immediately made reservations in their sister hotel and provided a taxi to get their customer there. Going back to the original encounter, after the American family went to their room these two guys at the front desk just ignored us. I assume they were thinking that if they ignored us long enough the problem would go away. They were not trained to deal with unexpected situations. An example of communism at its best. Like I said earlier, when you travel in foreign countries and return home, you must think how blessed you are to be a citizen of the USA. One thing I should mention: the church in Hong Kong always gave us strong warnings to not pass out any Bibles on the streets or to any unknown individuals. This turned out to be the total opposite of what happened later when on a Bible mission trip to Russia, which I will describe next.

One summer after glasnost and perestroika, I think it was in 1992, we responded to a request from Campus Crusade for Christ (CCC) seeking volunteers for packaging toys and medical supplies for orphanages in Russia. I explained glasnost and perestroika in the Cuban Missiles section of the book. The collection and distribution point for these toys and medical and pharmaceutical supplies was Lancaster, Pennsylvania. I was very much impressed by the CCC leadership and the way they organized these volunteers. There was a production line processing plan for receiving this vast quantity of medical and pharmaceutical supplies and toys from all over the country, and then packaging this material for shipment to Russia.

Kathryn and I decided we would like to be a part of this venture, so we took off for Lancaster. We felt good about volunteering for this mission. We were in our Airstream and discovered a first-class campground not far from our work area. Several of our campground neighbors, from all parts of the country, were there on the same mission with CCC as we were. This was our first visit to Amish country and we enjoyed many side trips in this beautiful area. Late every evening, after we returned to our campsite from our work, we would listen for the welcome sound of horse hooves and a ringing bell to let us know there was an Amish couple in their Amish buggy with fresh baked bread to sell. What a treat!

The response for volunteers for this project was tremendous, and it included many people from the local church. We became friends with some local Mennonites and visited their home and church. It was a valuable experience.

During this work period with CCC we were told about the planned mission trip to Russia to deliver these goods to the orphanages, visit churches, and distribute Bibles on the streets in some Russian cities, including Moscow. Notice, I am using the word Russia and not the Soviet Union as this was not long after glasnost and perestroika. The Russians were enjoying a freedom that they had never experienced.

Back in my discussion of our space program, I described a trip we made to the old Soviet Union in 1982 when the Cold War was very cold. Kathryn and I decided we would like to make this trip with the CCC and see what changes had occurred.

We had close to 300 volunteers on this trip and our first stop in Russia was Moscow. It required several chartered buses to get our party to our hotel, and each bus had a Russian guide. Immediately we observed one enormous difference from our trip in 1982. On the route to the hotel, the Russian guide, a lady, stood in the front of the bus facing the passengers and she was explaining the scenery as we passed. One of her first comments was, "Look at all this ugly stuff built under Stalin." She was referring to the ugly, huge, drab apartment buildings. They were unpainted, and almost every balcony was covered in laundry hung out to dry. There were almost no cars in the parking lots. If someone had made a negative comment like that back in 1982, they would have been carted off to jail as soon as the bus stopped.

We literally hit the ground running. Early the next morning we were loaded on the buses headed to Red Square, where we were given a shoulder bag stuffed with Russian Bibles to be distributed to anyone passing. I can tell you I was a little apprehensive about this. I was still heavily influenced by the repression observed on our previous trip. To my delight and surprise, the word spread among the locals. They were coming up to us, and many times not waiting for us to hand them a Bible but instead reaching into our shoulder bags and getting one. Each one of us had an empty bag in just a few minutes and had to return to the bus to refill. It was not long before we did not have any more Bibles. I vividly recall one old Russian lady coming up to me after we were out of Bibles and asking in broken English, "I want bible, I want bible," with tears in her eyes. I tried to explain to her we had no more Bibles, but she was not fully understanding me, so I got our Russian guide to interpret. I asked our guide to explain that we had no more Bibles but to get her address and we would have a Bible sent to her. I gave her address to one of the local CCC helpers and I trust this sweet old lady did receive a Bible.

Red Square and the Kremlin were interesting as they represented the center of power for the old Soviet Union. Thinking back to our visit in 1982, I could never, in my wildest dreams, imagine that 10 years later I would be standing in Red Square distributing the gospel. Maybe there is a lesson here. Remember, the Bible states, "God can do anything."

Later, we were dispersed to street corners passing out Bibles and again the reception was tremendous. We observed streetcars passing by with people intently reading our Bibles, and when we gave people on the street a Bible, they would immediately go over and stand against the wall and start reading. We never saw one of our Bibles discarded on the ground. One day we stationed ourselves outside of a huge factory when the workers were leaving for the day and we had the same eager reception. One day on the Moscow subway Kathryn gave an old lady a Bible and the old lady responded by giving Kathryn her lunch, which was in a small paper bag. Kathryn tried to resist, but to please the old lady Kathryn had to take the lunch.

One large city we visited was Kiev, which at that time was still part of Russia. We had an experience there that I can never forget. We were scheduled to depart from Kiev early in the afternoon. We departed our buses and entered the airport on time. Let me say this airport was sub-substandard for a city the size of Kiev. All the seats were occupied, and Russians were sprawled all over the floor. Many of them looked like they were sleeping, and you had the feeling they had been there a long, long time. Most of the luggage we observed was cardboard boxes.

Our leader checked in and was told our chartered plane was a little late and would be ready for loading in a few minutes. A few minutes turned into many minutes, so our leader checked in again and was assured the plane would be ready shortly. We all got tired of standing and there was just no place to sit down, so we went outside and waited and waited. Our leader repeatedly checked in and got the same answer of "just a few minutes," and "a few minutes" turned into several hours. In the meantime, a plane landed and taxied nearby, and we were told that this was the plane of the newly elected president, Boris Yeltsin. Several of our more aggressive CCC party took off and went over there. When they came back, they reported that they were well received and had given Yeltsin a Bible and he accepted it.

As we waited outside the airport, we tried to make the best use of our time, so we did not let anyone pass in or out of the airport without giving them a Bible. Suddenly, we heard a loud crash. The front of the airport was mostly glass from the ground to the ceiling, and a large part of this glass wall had collapsed for no apparent reason. Seemed like a saying we had picked up from our local Russian friends was involved here: "We pretend to work and they pretend to pay us." In the Communist world, they did not seem to take any pride in what they were doing.

Finally, after several hours we received word the plane was

ready, and we could hardly believe it. I do not know what the original problem was, but this is another example of communism at its best: When things don't go exactly as planned, they don't know how to deal with it. Our flight from Kiev was to Leningrad, and we had the same experience in passing out Bibles in Leningrad as we did in Moscow. We were given a touristy tour of the city, and the only thing of beauty they could point out was actually built by the Russians czars—there were zero beautiful structures built under the Communist regime.

We had the opportunity to visit several small churches in Russia, and you had to admire these people that maintained their faith throughout the Communists' reign. During this trip, we had several social events and dinners with local Russian officials, including one with a couple of cosmonauts in attendance. I do not know whether they were Christians or not.

Kathryn and I felt good about this trip, and I think we are justified in believing that our group made some impact on the people we encountered. One negative thing we observed on this trip was that we encountered several events that were sponsored by the Jehovah's Witnesses and a couple of other cult organizations, and I think this did confuse the Russian people.

Most of the overseas trips Kathryn and I made had a purpose greater than tourism, and the last trip I will discuss falls into this category. We retraced the travels of the apostle Paul in Turkey and Greece. Among many other stops on our tour, we visited the place in Corinth where Paul preached, and we visited the sites where the seven churches recorded in the book of Revelation were believed to have been located. This tour was by bus throughout the countryside of Turkey and Greece, and I need to mention one little miracle we received in Turkey.

I mentioned earlier that Kathryn was always eager to eat the local food and I was more energy bar oriented, and on this occasion my energy bar paid off. At a little village in Turkey, we stopped for lunch and Kathryn headed straight to the local food counter. As for me, I stuck with my energy bar. That night in our hotel Kathryn got deathly sick—I mean really super sick. I went down to the hotel desk and told the young lady at the front desk that I needed a doctor. She said no problem, she would get me a doctor. A little later, we had a knock on the door and our doctor arrived. He had a little brown bag exactly like our doctor in my younger days in Slocomb.

I was encouraged when I learned this doctor was a retired Turkish air force doctor and had studied in the US. He examined Kathryn, wrote me a prescription, and said to take it to the girl at the desk. His fee was $100. I went down to the desk and asked the clerk to get me a taxi as I needed to get a prescription filled. She said to give her the prescription and she would take care of it. The way she said it, I trusted her and went back to the room. A brief time later she personally came up to the room with my prescription. I asked her how much it was and I was shocked when she said it was $8. I then asked her about the taxi and she said the $8 included the taxi. I could not believe it was that cheap. I gave her a generous tip.

I was prepared to go down early the next morning and tell our tour director that we could not continue with the group as I could not see how Kathryn would possibly recover by morning.

Well, thanks to some heavy prayer and whatever was in that pill the doctor gave Kathryn, she unbelievably was 100 percent the next morning. It was a true miracle. As usual she was ready to go. This was a great trip, but had it not been for this miracle it would not have been so great. I now have completed my travels and thankfully have many precious memories from them. Again, I recommend you go out and see the world and marvel at what God has created.

KATHY'S ANTIQUES

I did not know until several days after we were married that Kathryn had been keeping a deep, dark secret from me. Maybe she had been sending me signs, but they passed right over my head. When we got married I was living in an apartment with two other guys and they graciously agreed to move out and leave me with this nicely—I thought—furnished apartment. I guess you could say our apartment was not furnished in early American or Victorian style; it was more like "El Cheapo" and "Early Halloween." The dark secret Kathryn had withheld from me was that she had a bad case of the "antiquities." To put it mildly, our décor was not exactly what she admired.

As I said earlier, we made a trip to Chattanooga and bought several nice pieces of furniture, but we needed more as nothing other than a few forks and knives was worth keeping. So here was the next step to solve our furniture problem. Kathryn has always been an avid newspaper reader and she found an ad in the local paper for an antique furniture auction. She insisted we go as this would be a fantastic opportunity to get some good stuff. I had never been to an auction and I had no clue how much to bid for an item. I delegated the responsibility of bidding to Kathryn and before I knew it we had the high bid of $12 for an old dresser. My first thought was that this was $12 down the drain, but Kathryn was very excited about her new purchase.

She explained to me that it had a beveled oval mirror, dove tailed drawers, marble top, ornate drawer pulls, a hidden, secret drawer and some other notable features she pointed out. Let me jump ahead a little—it took a while, but the "antiquity" disease Kathryn had was contagious, and I came down with a bad case of "antiquity" myself. Back to the dresser, it still occupies a prominent place in our bedroom and is worth many times its original cost. As you will learn, that was the first of many, many antique auctions for us.

One big disappointment for us, or rather for Kathryn that evening, was the bidding for an old, high four-poster antique bed. The price just got too high for us. Kathryn was very disappointed, but she did not stop there. She found a picture in a magazine for a four-poster bed and took that picture to a local woodworking shop and asked this old Alabama redneck if he could make a reproduction of the bed. His answer was "Yes ma'am." He got the job and Kathryn was very pleased with his work. Later, when my buddies visited us and saw our high bed, they passed the word to our other friends that our bed was so high we needed oxygen to sleep.

Not long after this, we moved to Cocoa Beach, and we had enough furniture for our apartment at Patrick Air Force Base, so we were dormant on the auction scene for a while. When we later moved into our new house in Titusville, we needed more furniture, and again Kathryn found an ad in our local paper for an antique furniture auction in Port Orange. We just had to go, and by this time I had this "antiquity" disease as bad as Kathryn. We completed furnishing our house from these auctions, and as we kept adding rooms to our house, we kept up our trips to the auction house. Our children were small and they enjoyed the auctions; they could get hot dogs and other goodies from the snack bar. Some nights at the auction we were very fortunate as we seemed to be the only ones interested in the old stuff, but most of the time we had one serious competitor, an antique dealer in New Smyrna Beach. When he was there, he wanted the same stuff we did, and we knew we would have to pay more than normal to get what we wanted.

If Kathryn spotted an old piece of furniture she really liked, she would let nothing get in her way to get it. In the late 1950s and early 1960s, we took vacations up in New England. We should have had a sign on the back of our station wagon that said *This vehicle stops at all flea markets and antique shops*, because that is what we did. We brought back a number of small treasures from those trips.

Here is the story of one I like the best. On the trip home from New England we would stop in Spartanburg, South Carolina, to visit my mother and sister. They told Kathryn about a place that had lots of architectural antiques from demolished old buildings. Kathryn had to go and immediately spotted something she could not live without—an antique commode with a water tank that mounted on the wall, and flushed with a nice ivory handle on the end of a chain. At that time, we were making another addition to our house that included a third toilet. We were traveling in a station wagon with our camping equipment in a small clam-shell trailer. Like I said, if Kathryn wanted something, she was determined to get it, so we came home from Spartanburg with the water tank in the trailer and the commode on top of the station wagon. I do not remember how many cars almost ran off the road when they passed us.

After we completely furnished our house, we occasionally attended an auction just for the fun of it, and, of course, most of the time we could not resist bringing home some little treasure.

When I retired from NASA, I went to work for USBI as a consultant and I was not thinking then about spending the next 10 years at the space center. We decided that when I retired we would go into the antique business, and we got started while I was still working. We rented a place on Highway 50 and set up Kathy's Antiques. We initially furnished the store from auctions and estate sales, and later we got established and became good friends with a wholesale antique dealer in Albany, Georgia. He had a huge brick warehouse, two stories with a freight elevator, full of antiques. Most of his goods came from England via large shipping containers. He would call us when he had a new shipment and we would go up in our van and come back loaded. We looked forward to these trips and enjoyed them immensely. We would leave about midnight on a Friday and be at his warehouse when he opened Saturday morning. All his goods were marked with the retail price and a coded number for the wholesale price. He would give us the code for the wholesale price and we would spend most of the day selecting our load. After we were loaded, we would go to our favorite restaurant in Albany and check in at our favorite motel, and then Sunday we would take a leisurely trip back to Titusville. When we arrived back in Titusville, we would go by the recovery house and pick up a couple of guys to unload our van.

On one of these trips to Albany, we almost had a little incident. Maybe "little" is not the word; maybe calling it a "big event" would be more suitable for what almost happened. That Friday, Kathryn had a customer from Orlando who wanted to buy a nice wicker Victorian baby buggy, but it was too big for the customer to put in her car. Kathryn told her that we would be going through Orlando later that night and we would take it over there and meet her someplace to deliver it. The customer was happy with that arrangement, and she and Kathryn agreed to meet at Steak 'n Shake at midnight. We arrived at Steak 'n Shake on time and our customer was there waiting for us. We made the transfer and then I told Kathryn, "I am going into Steak n' Shake to get a cup of coffee. Do you want anything?" Her reply was, "No, I am going to take a nap." This was normal. She would take a nap for two or three hours for the first part of the trip and then she would take over and drive. We had taken the seats out of the van and it was entirely open, and we had several blankets, so it was comfortable.

I got my coffee, pulled out of the parking lot at Steak 'n Shake, and turned left on Highway 50. It was just a short distance from where I entered Highway 50 to a traffic light, and fortunately the light was red. I stopped at the red light and happened to glance back in the rearview mirror. I saw a lady in front of Steak 'n Shake frantically waving her arms. I thought she looked familiar and I glanced back in the van and it was empty. As soon as I could, I made a U-turn and went back to pick up my passenger.

Here's what happened. When I went in to get my coffee, she decided she needed to go to the bathroom. I did not see her and she did not tell me, so when I took off from the parking lot I thought she was sound asleep in the back of the van. If it had not been for that red light, I would have been about two hours up the road before I pulled into a rest stop and found I did not have my passenger. I can imagine what the people passing by thought about this lady frantically waving her arms on the side of the street. Needless to say, after that I always verified I had my sweet passenger safely on board before I moved.

We enjoyed our antique world, but it placed more restrictions on us than we had anticipated, especially with regard to traveling. We decided we should either go in it big time where we could afford to hire some help, or get out of the business. We were operating in the black and business was improving, but it was still hardly worth our time.

To investigate going big time, like our friend in Albany, we made a trip to England to learn more about buying and shipping containers. We hired an agent in London to take us around the country, visiting a number of establishments that shipped containers to America. They provided us detailed examples of the cost of different items and the shipping and insurance cost. This was an interesting trip, and at a couple of places they took us in the back rooms where they manufactured antiques. Here is the way that worked: They would take an old piece of furniture like an armoire and use that wood to build a more expensive piece of furniture, like a desk. The craftsmanship was superb, and unless you had a very trained eye, you would never know this desk was not original.

One factor we did not like was that unless you personally made a trip to England every time you needed a shipment and selected each item to be shipped, you were at the mercy of your agent to ship whatever he wanted to fill the container. Taking all these factors into account, especially our lack of freedom if we did this, we decided not to go big time in this business.

More and more we felt this was not as much fun as it used to be, and one day I got this message in spades. After a very busy day at the space center, I stopped at Kathy's Antiques as I normally did, and Kathryn pointed to a nice piece of furniture, a china cabinet, and said, "I sold this today and told them we would deliver it when you came in." I wasn't ready for this, and then I said, "What street do they live on?" She said, "They live in Cocoa Beach." I could not believe it. I said, "Cocoa Beach? We got to deliver this piece of furniture to Cocoa Beach today?" This was a good sale, but I was not a happy delivery boy.

Not long after that, we had one of our auctioneer friends from Orlando come over and take our inventory to his auction. Overall it was an enjoyable experience, but it was time to close that chapter of our life.

RAMBLIN' THOUGHTS

Today's old-timers seem to enjoy talking about how tough life was when they were growing up compared to the easy life of the present generation. I want to go in another direction. I want to focus on what we had and not what we did not have. The environment in which I grew up lacked, I would guess, about 95 percent of the luxury items we consider necessities in today's world. However, the things we did enjoy that are sadly lacking in today's environment are many. For example, stable, loving, two-parent families, usually with a non-working mother at home, very low crime rates, safety in your home and walking the streets at night, no filthy garbage in the media or movies or music, integrity and respect for authority, and no drug problems. We had pride in our country, our flag, and in our Christian heritage. The school environment was very pleasant, with no violence, no need for counselors or truant officers, and no need for metal detectors. Teachers were highly respected and their authority in the classroom was never challenged.

Prior to WWII our population was very stable. Most people married and settled in the same community in which they were born. Frequently changing jobs was not a common thing. Many men retired in the same occupation as their first job. Most of my high school graduating class had been together since the first grade.

As we get into the sunset portion of our lives, when our

involvement in events, projects, and other physical activities is greatly diminished, we spend more time just thinking. I am constantly thinking about a wide range of situations. I am reminded of a quote from Yogi Berra: "You can observe a lot just by watching." Here is a current observation that concerns me. In the past few years we have made tremendous progress in improving our health and extending our life span. We see a new exercise machine advertised daily, gym and fitness centers are readily available, and so are nutrition stores. Using these available health assets, we are living longer and with healthier bodies. Here is the negative: We remain far, far behind in maintaining our mental health. We have a growing number of physically healthy old people who do not know where they are. I live in a retirement community, and sadly I see this situation every day. Alzheimer's disease is reaching an epidemic state. This situation results in a tremendous burden on the families involved and the economy. We hold much more control over the condition of our physical body than we do of our mental health. There is very little we can do to maintain our mental health. The only answer that I can see to this problem is to greatly increase the research in mental health, and we all hope that increased awareness of Alzheimer's will result in greatly expanded resources applied to finding a solution to this dreaded disease.

Another thing I think about frequently is what kind of world my grandchildren and great-grandchildren will live in. We live in a world that could provide ample resources for the world's population to live in comfort, yet due to totally senseless wars we have massive numbers of starving refuges with no safe place to go in many parts of the globe.

We are in a totally different kind of war today with radical Islam, and I see no end to this conflict. With radical Islam, we can never simply end the war with a surrender ceremony like we did in 1945 on the deck of the battleship *Missouri* in WWII. I have seen war up close and I know how utterly senseless war is, but I also realize we will always have evil men with a thirst for power that will unfortunately lead to war.

My greatest fear is that one of these evil men gets possession of an atomic bomb and uses it. Heaven forbid; I pray this will not happen.

Let me give an excellent example of how mankind can live and prosper in peace. Let's go out in space, low Earth orbit, to the International Space Station (ISS). The ISS is one of the most marvelous engineering achievements in the history of mankind. It was designed, manufactured, and placed in orbit by a diverse group of male and female engineers and scientists from several different countries working in harmony. We marvel at what they achieved. The crews of the ISS have demonstrated for years that they can live and work together in peace. Their achievements are remarkable. What they are learning in their scientific research is beneficial to mankind. They represent just about every ethnic group in the world. The ISS is a microcosm of Earth and its inhabitants. These brave occupants know they must get along and unselfishly share their space and resources to survive.

Why can't mankind, on our beautiful planet Earth, follow the example of the brave and diverse crews of the ISS? Recently I was watching the NASA channel featuring the ISS when they were having a direct conversation with the pope in Rome, and part of their conversation centered around just what I am talking about. Why can't mankind on planet Earth live in peace?

I hold real mixed emotions as I think of the future. On the plus side, I predict miracles in the medical field that will eliminate many of the prime medical problems that result in so much suffering and pain in today's world.

I try to be optimistic, but I must face reality, and I see potential dark clouds in the future. The filth and garbage this present generation is exposed to from the entertainment world is normal for them, as they have no reference of a world without this garbage. We seem to ignore or accept gradual changes until "the camel has his nose under the tent," and then it is too late. If the moral decay of our country continues at the rate it has for the last 60 or 70 years, I don't think I would be comfortable living in that environment.

Other considerations. Do I want to live in a completely robotic world? I recently read about a new computer coming that will revolutionize the way we live. All computers today, as far as I know are binary, either a 1 or a 0, and this supercomputer can have a 1 or 0 or both. I do not understand this, and I am not sure I want to understand this monster.

Do I want to live in an immoral world where the fear of God is completely obliterated? With great wisdom, our Founding Fathers based the foundation of our nation on solid Judeo-Christian principles. Sadly there is a growing number in our country who are desperately trying to dismantle our Constitution, the greatest document in the history of mankind next to the Holy Scriptures.

I repeat what I said above: I try to be optimistic, and I do take great comfort in knowing there are some very smart and capable young people out there who, by the grace of God, have the value system necessary to counter these far-left radicals. They need all the support, including prayers and encouragement, we can provide them.

This work started out to be for my family only, but when the publisher sent me the contract to sign it included the potential for my book to be marketed to a much larger audience through avenues like Barnes and Noble and Amazon. I thought, *Wow, this can't be*, but it is, and how far this goes I have no clue.

I firmly believe these thoughts have great merit, and, as mentioned, they were originally aimed for my immediate family, so I feel I must include them even if this work reaches a wider audience. I would like to add that I consider anyone who reads this, even a stranger, to be an extended member of my family, and I would be pleased for any reader of this work to seriously ponder the thoughts I express here.

The very moment any of us are born, we immediately start a physical and spiritual timeline. On this timeline, the physical length is finite, but on the spiritual side the timeline is infinite— it extends to eternity. Our finite physical mind cannot even grasp the enormity of living for eternity.

Our finite physical timeline at the outside is about 100 years, which is but a micro-blip on the eternity lifeline, and the question is: How do we use this very brief, finite time in our physical world? One thing we do, if we are wise, is plan for our eventual retirement. I encourage everyone to plan early in life for their retirement years, which according to today's lifespan would be about 15 to 20 years, or about 20 percent of your total lifespan. When the commercial world finds out—and they are very good about this—that you have reached retirement age, you will be inundated with massive amounts of advice on how you should enjoy your retirement years. For example, you will receive information on the best cities to retire in, how to make your money last, when to start social security, the best retirement communities, how to stay healthy, and it goes on and on, but remember that this period you are planning for is only a blip on the eternity timeline.

Now, the big question: What are you doing in this very brief physical timeline here on planet Earth to prepare for eternity? I am absolutely convinced we have a Creator and He has given us the choice of where we will spend eternity. Also, I am absolutely convinced there is a place called Hell and a place called Heaven. In the physical world, we decide what city and street we live on, and likewise on the spiritual side we make our choice, and I remind you that eternity is a long, long time.

Each one of us is making that decision—*Where will I spend eternity?*—every day. Even when we think we are doing nothing, we are making the biggest decision of our lives. I encourage you to ponder the question, *What am I doing to prepare myself for where I will spend eternity?* I repeat, this is by far the greatest decision you will ever make in your life!

2012
GREATEST GENERATION TRIP

Me and Nick at Iwo Jima.
Mt. Suribachi is in the background and
the beach where we landed is on the left.

On Saipan, I guess I was on the receiving end
of this wicked cannon at one time.

Captured Japanese miniature submarine on Saipan.

Marpi Point on Saipan, where hundreds of Japanese leapt
to their death at the end of the war.

Memorial park on Saipan with me, Cotton, and Nick.

A captured Japanese gun on Saipan.
At one time these were pointed at me.

On the beach at Iwo Jima. There was no cover
for the troops once they landed on the beach,
and it was almost impossible to build a foxhole.

This is a picture of the very narrow beach on Tinian that I landed on July 24, 1944. This picture was made on my return trip to Saipan, Tinian, and Iwo Jima in March 2012. This trip in 2012 was my first view of this nice little narrow beach, a perfect picture of tranquility. July 24, 1944, I landed on this beach in an AmTrac. That day it was a far different scene than the peaceful tranquility we were experiencing this day in 2012. Coming in an AmTrac you can't see where you are going and as soon as you exit this vehicle you are desperately looking for cover. Can you look at this picture and visualize several thousand Marines pouring in here in one day with a well-armed unwelcoming party waiting for you. The same scene was repeated several hundred yards south of this little narrow beach as part of our landing force came in on a similar beach that was very slightly wider than this beach. As you read in the chapter on Tinian, this was one of the most brilliant invasion plans of the war. The thought comes to me, in war or peace, beaches are some of the most valuable real estate, location, location, location. Beaches can be the most pleasant and enjoyable real estate in the world or they can be the most dangerous places to be. I am thinking of the beaches like Omaha, Anzio, Saipan and Iwo Jima and all because of the evil in mankind- WAR is SENSELESS.

Runway on Tinian where the "Enola Gay," a Boeing B-29 Superfortress bomber, took off to drop the first A-bomb on Hiroshima.

GREATEST GENERATION TRIP

In March 2012, I made a return trip to Saipan, Tinian, and Iwo Jima. This was an all-expenses paid, first-class trip sponsored by The Greatest Generations Foundation (TGGF). This is a nonprofit organization that takes WWII veterans back to their battle sites in Europe and the Pacific. There were twelve veterans in our group: eight Marines, three sailors, and one Seabee. A college student was assigned to accompany each veteran. These students, male and female, were from Ohio State University. Two professors from OSU also joined our group.

I was impressed with the students. They were serious about their assignment, and they seemed keenly interested in gathering our thoughts and experiences during WWII. The students were also very helpful in assisting with our luggage and navigating our walk over some rough terrain.

These students were required to write a daily report. The student assigned to me, Nick Brill, of Cleveland, Ohio, was a very smart student. He was a junior majoring in economics and history. I was very impressed with his knowledge in both subjects. Fortunately, he had a strong body, as I will mention later. I do not think I could have made it without his physical assistance.

Our journey as a group started in Los Angeles, where we first met at a hotel. Our group came from all over the country. The only one I knew in this group was my old buddy Cotton Billingsley. In fact, Cotton was the one who informed me about this trip. He had already signed up and wanted me to accompany him.

I roomed with Cotton. He arrived at the hotel not long after I checked in. As instructed, we went down to the lobby early the next morning to meet the other guys and the staff of TGGF. We found the lobby to be crowded with sixty or seventy bikers, including a few females. They were a tough-looking group, with all the biker leather and bandannas. I thought maybe one of the motorcycle gangs was having a reunion. Then we learned this motorcycle group is called the Patriot Riders. They were there to escort us to the airport. They loaded our luggage in the shuttle bus to take us to the airport, and when we were ready to go, they revved up their bikes. Ahead of the bikers were several police cars with their blue lights flashing. It was still dark as this impressive convoy headed for the airport. None of us expected any special attention, but we were pleasantly surprised when we received this treatment throughout the remainder of the trip.

When we entered the airport, there were large banners on the walls welcoming our little group. Apparently they had announced our arrival on the PA system, as there were many people in the airport lined up and clapping their hands as we headed for our check-in station. There was a special check-in just for us.

We were seated in first-class, and as our plane taxied out to the runway, there were fire trucks on either side that sprayed the plane with their large water hoses. When the seatbelt sign went off, the airline stewardess wheeled out one of their food carts with a cake as large as the top, decorated with the flag raising on Iwo Jima. I think everyone on the plane received a piece of cake.

The first leg of our trip was to Honolulu, and again there were some banners welcoming us on the wall in the airport. We changed planes there, and several of us needed wheelchairs to get to our departure terminal. Now here is where a little prayer was answered. When we arrived at our departure terminal, I suddenly realized, in all of the excitement, I had left my walking stick on the plane to Honolulu. It had belonged to my grandfather Rigell and was very special to me.

There were several airline employees accompanying us, and I mentioned to one of the young ladies that I had left my walking stick on the other plane. She took off, and a little later she came back with it. I cannot thank her enough. I also thank my Lord for hearing my prayer. Amen.

Our next destination was Guam. I did not participate in the battle for Guam, but there were two or three in our group who had, along with a couple of guys in our group who were evacuated to Guam after being wounded on Saipan.

A short history on Guam. Prior to December 7, 1941, we occupied Guam and several thousand Marines were stationed there. Later in December, the Japs came with an overwhelmingly strong force and captured it. Shortly after we invaded Saipan, the 3rd Marine Division, after a tough battle, recaptured Guam. We still have a strong military presence there today.

We were given a good tour of Guam, including the invasion beaches. We met the leading government officials and enjoyed a lunch and a general discussion with them. That night, our group joined a much larger group organized by a military tour company for a nice banquet in our hotel. I should add we were in a five-star hotel. We were the honored guests.

Our next destination was Iwo Jima. We flew in a chartered plane. When we arrived over Iwo Jima, the pilot made a couple of passes in a figure eight pattern to allow people on both sides of the plane to get a clear view of the island. Every one of us was in total shock. The island was covered in green, and I cannot recall anything green. We were told the Navy sowed seeds from an aircraft all over the island after they took over.

I do not know how to describe my feelings as we flew over and landed on Iwo Jima. We were given a good tour of the island. I did not recognize any of the detail areas from the battle except the black volcanic ash beach.

Our tour included a trip up to the top of Mt. Suribachi. I tried to imagine how the Japs felt as they looked out over the vast ocean and saw hundreds of ships and observed thousands of Marines scrambling up those terraces on the beach. I was never on Mt. Suribachi during the battle. In fact, our landing beach was the furthest away from the mountain.

This was a one-day trip on Iwo Jima, and it was well planned and coordinated between TGGF and the military tour company. They had two large tents with chairs set up in the middle of the island, and some dignitaries from our side and the Japanese government gave a number of shorts speeches with this message: "We were enemies then; now we are friends."

One of the guests was the widow of the Hollywood actor Lee Marvin, a Marine wounded on Saipan. After the ceremonies, we were free to go down to the beach. As I mentioned above, we were in the center of the island. Looking down at the beach, our elevation seemed higher than we recalled. I was standing there with my student Nick.

"Nick, I really want to go down to the water, but I just don't think I could make it back," I said.

"You are going to make it even if I have to carry you on my back," Nick said.

"OK," I said. "Let's go."

So with Nick holding on to me, we made it down to the water's edge. I stood there looking up at those volcanic ash terraces and to the left, Mount Suribachi. I just don't know how to describe my feelings. I stood there a few minutes and told Nick I was ready to go back up. Surprisingly, it was not as difficult as I thought it would be. I would never have made it without Nick's strong assistance.

As we rode around the island, I could never get reconciled with all of this greenery. At times, the foliage on either side was so thick we could not see anything else. We flew back to Guam late that afternoon. One day proved to be enough. I'm glad we did not spend the night there.

Some years after the war we returned Iwo Jima back to the Japanese. I don't think we should have done that, as they allow visitors only one day a year.

I could sum up the return trip to Iwo Jima like this. On the physical side the main observations were, first, the greenery. Secondly, the silence of the guns. During the campaign the noise of the ongoing battle—machine guns, mortars, artillery, and bombs—were twenty-four hours a day. Now there was silence— only the wind. Eerie. I guess I could add a third dimension, and that is in 1945, I was scared all the time. Now, of course, I was completely free of fear.

I originally did not plan to mention the following story. It is very sad for me to discuss this, but I feel like I should include it. Cotton was one of the closest and best friends I ever had. We played baseball on our company team, and we kept in close contact until he passed away a couple of years ago. After a couple of days on our trip, I realized, sadly, Cotton was suffering from dementia.

His wife, Kay, had called me before the trip and said, "Make sure Cotton takes his medicine on schedule."

Kay did not mention dementia, and in all the excitement I failed to check on Cotton's medication. The Greatest Generations Foundation staff told me they had to send Cotton home.

"You can't do that," I said. "I will take care of Cotton."

They reluctantly agreed to let me try it. It turned out to be a challenging task, but I am glad I did it. I know Cotton would have done the same for me. Physically, Cotton was in better shape than most of the men in our group, and it was hard for me to keep up with him.

Cotton had a remarkable memory of the events during our operations on Saipan, Tinian, and Iwo Jima. Several times on our tour, I would have a vague memory of some of our experiences, and I would talk to Cotton and he could go into great detail of these events that occurred sixty-seven years ago.

On our return trip, when we landed in Los Angeles, we all went our separate ways. Cotton was from Richmond, Virginia, and he had to change planes en route to Richmond. Fortunately, one of the other guys in our group was from Richmond, so the Greatest Generations Foundation staff made sure this man would take care that Cotton safely got back. I cannot remember this man's name, but he was on the administrative staff at University of Richmond. Cotton was a graduate of University of Richmond, and he was in the University of Richmond Athlete Hall of Fame for baseball and football.

After we got back, Kay told me that she was sorry she let Cotton go on the trip. I tried to assure her it had been the right thing for Cotton. The positives outweighed the negatives. I want to conclude this chapter with the report my student Nick wrote about his trip. I think it offers a unique perspective on our trip, and I wanted to share his experience with you in his own words.

RETURN TO IWO JIMA
By Nick Brill

In March 2012, I had the opportunity to travel with seven other students, and professors Hahn and Mansoor, on a once in a lifetime World War II study abroad experience. We accompanied twelve WWII veterans as they returned to the battlefields on the islands of Guam, Saipan, Iwo Jima and Tinian, the battle sites they fought on over 67 years ago. The trip was coordinated in conjunction with the Greatest Generation Foundation. We also had the honor of traveling with two United States congressmen: Representative Bill Braley and Representative Ed Perlmutter. Each student was assigned a personal veteran to whom we served as both an aid and a chronicler of their wartime experiences over the 10 days we traveled throughout the Pacific. I think I may speak for all of the students in saying the trip had a profound impact on our lives. Not only did we learn a great deal about the war from our veterans, but we also learned a great deal about life. Here are a few of the many memorable moments I experienced while visiting the battlefields.

The first was the tour of Asan Beach and the overlook areas on Guam. These sites stick out because Asan Beach was the first experience we had with the battlefields on the trip. As I looked down from the overlook area and tried to imagine 20,000 American soldiers storming the beach, I was overcome with a sense of awe. It really was hard to imagine numbers like that, not to mention the machine gun fire, mortars, and artillery that would have been pounding the soldiers as they made their way up the beachhead. This was the first time I tried to imagine what it would have been like for the soldiers, and I determined that I'm just not capable of emotionally connecting with the soldiers on that kind of level; my experiences in life just cannot match the realities of a wartime battlefield.

The second moment was our visit to the island of Iwo Jima, and specifically my journey to the beaches with Ike Rigell, my veteran for the trip. As we flew into Iwo Jima, Ike leaned over and told me, "Never in my wildest dreams did I imagine coming back to Iwo Jima in a modern jet." I could tell that the experience was a surreal one for him. At the age of 89, Ike can no longer move like he used to. Therefore, getting down to the beach and back up again was a challenge that he might not have been able to overcome on a normal day. Obviously, his return to Iwo was not a normal day for him. When we made it back up from the beaches, he told me that he must have had super human strength from the extra boost of adrenaline he received from returning to the island where he lost so many friends. Later, he would tell me that making the trip down to the beaches was the highlight of his trip. Accompanying him on his journey back to the beaches and watching him overcome a challenge he wouldn't normally be able to complete was truly inspiring for me.

I would like to conclude with one last personal reflection about the trip. As I talked with Ike and he told me about his experience in the war and in life thereafter, I came to realize one thing. The war stories are not simply stories about what occurred in the Pacific during World War II. Yes, listening to these veterans' stories has been a great experience, and honoring their actions was a very important aspect of this trip. But, to me, these stories are not just memories of actions past; they are windows into a way of life. This way of life was forged on these islands, on the beaches and in the jungles where these men fought and died for each other. This war defined their generation's character, a character cultivated by what these men went through here in the Pacific. Hidden within Ike's stories, I discerned courage, humility, an acute sense of empathy, honor, and selflessness, all trademarks of a virtuous life. These stories have taught me not just about the war, but also about how to live life, and I believe this will be the greatest legacy of this trip. It is because of men like Ike that their generation has truly earned the designation of the Greatest Generation, and I am truly grateful to have been able to accompany him on this trip.

THE BEGINNING
OF THE END

I began this project about 20 years ago at the encouragement of my family. My plan was to document my journey through life on this planet Earth. It would be very personal and would include some words of wisdom aimed directly at my family. I would have just a few copies put together at the local Staples store. But, the next thing I knew, some of my family had talked to a publisher and I received a contract to sign authorizing that this publication could be distributed by Amazon and Barnes and Noble. I thought, *Wow, what is going on here?* and I guess I am still overwhelmed wondering where this is going from here. I have no clue. With this change in direction, I had to do a little editing of what I had done, like not using first names and nicknames, which would be familiar to my family but a complete mystery to those outside our family.

Another thing I had to consider was passing on some timely "words of wisdom" that I thought would be appropriate for my immediate family audience. Then I thought, *Maybe, if this thing goes any further, I should abandon these thoughts.* Then I got a "zinger"—why not just consider everyone who might read this as a part of my family? So, okay, family, here goes. My hope would be that these "words of wisdom" enrich your life.

Never lose the child within you. According to statistics, a child laughs many times a day, while an adult laughs just a few times a day.

Never fear or be embarrassed by failure. A little child learns to walk by many tumbles; he just gets up and tries again until he gets it right.

Set goals, and when you set a goal, develop a system where you can measure your progress toward the goal.

Remember the glass is half full and not half empty.

Do not wait until someone is dead before you eulogize them. Express appreciation to those who have been a positive influence in your life before they pass on.

As Proverbs 3:5–6 says, acknowledge Him in all of your ways, lean not on your own understanding, and He will direct your path.

Be thoughtful and careful of who you choose to be your close friends. Parents, watch this for your children—you can tell exactly where a child is by the company he keeps. This is true also for an adult.

Parents, be and act like you would want your child to be. (This is a favorite of Kathryn's.)

Forgiveness—this is a must. Remember, in the Lord's Prayer we say, "forgive us our debts, as we also have forgiven our debtors." In plain English, we are saying, "Lord, if I do not forgive others, do not forgive me." For some time after WWII, I had trouble with this.

Never, never stop learning

Use your time wisely. We all have the same amount of time, 168 hours per week. You can never recover lost time.

Never go to bed angry.

Communicate, communicate, communicate. In my view, the lack of good communication is a major problem in all facets of our lives: families, marriages, relationships between children and parents, business, sports, the military and other organizations. Unfortunately, many families are dysfunctional simply because they do not communicate. In the military, we worked desperately to maintain communications, and we worked desperately to disrupt the enemy communications.

I go back to the example of a little child. They are excellent communicators. They can let you know immediately, at about 125 decibels, if they have a need. Also, do not forget we are spiritual as well as physical and we cannot neglect spiritual communications with our Creator.

Expect some battles in life. Remember, you cannot celebrate a victory unless you have experienced a battle.

Go that extra mile; do your part and a little more.

Remember the poor and needy. Share your good fortune.

Have a kind word for the waitress and give a good tip.

Make reasonable choices to maintain your health and work on preventable health issues.

Always, always tell the truth and then you never have to try to remember what you said last time.

If you make a mistake, admit it.

Find the good in others. Do not concentrate on their faults. Remember, they are putting up with some of your faults.

Remember, you can learn more when you are listening than when you are talking. Unless you can improve the silence, keep your mouth shut. This reminds me of the lion story. The lion had killed and eaten a bull. He felt so good, he just sat there roaring. A hunter heard the lion roar and headed in that direction. The lion kept roaring and the hunter slipped up on him and shot and killed him. The moral to this story is, "If you are full of bull, keep your mouth shut."

Work is a virtue. Let me repeat this: Work is a virtue. Find a job you enjoy and have fun. I have said many times that I was at the space center 40 years and never worked there a day in my life, because if you enjoy what you are doing, "it ain't work."

Gossip: just never go there.

Patience is a virtue. Remember it took Noah 120 years to build the ark.

Be careful; someone is setting their clock by you. This requires the telling of a little story I have used many times. In the early 1900s, it was common in many small towns in the South to have one major employer, usually a textile or garment factory or something along these lines. In my small town of Slocomb, it was a large sawmill. In those days, most people did not have a watch, and if they had a watch, most of the time it was running slow or fast, nothing like the accurate time pieces we have today. These workplaces had a very loud steam whistle that could be heard in the surrounding area. Most of the workers had no automobile and lived close enough to walk. The foreman at one of these small factories walked to work, and on his way to work every day he passed a little jewelry store. This little jewelry store had a large clock in the window, and the foreman would stop, set his watch, and continue to the factory. It was his job to blow the whistle during the day to let the workers know it was time to work, time for lunch, time to go back to work, and then time to go home. One morning when he stopped at the jewelry store to set his watch, he panicked. The clock was missing. He peered in the glass window and observed the owner was in the store. He knocked on the door and the owner came to the door and said they were not open yet. The foreman said, "I must come in and talk to you. I am the foreman down at the factory and it is my job to blow the work whistle every day and it must be blown at the correct time. I take my job very seriously." The owner said, "You better sit down friend, I have something to tell you. Every day at 5 PM when you blow that whistle for people to go home, I set that big clock."

Now the moral to this story is that someone is setting their clock by you. We all preach a sermon, good or not so good, every day without saying a word. I gave two excellent examples of preaching a silent sermon in my USBI story: when I picked up trash off the floor in the presence of the department heads, and in the fact that I did not use vulgar language in our meetings.

Finally, be thoughtful and careful of what you seek. You just might find it. I am reminded of the following wisdom. Take a honeybee and a tumble bug out in a beautiful meadow and release them. The honeybee will seek and find the sweet nectar of a beautiful flower and the tumble bug will seek and find the droppings of a cow or horse. They found just what they were seeking.

So, to both my immediate and my newly extended family, I have enjoyed my conversation with you. I close with these words, and my immediate family, I assure you, will be expecting this, as I always end my conversations this way, either in person, by email, or via the phone: BLESS YOU!!!

FAMILY

Grandpa Rigell sitting in front of his house in
Slocomb, Alabama.

My sisters, Florence and Mary Jo, and me.

Me in front of Aunt Etta's house in Slocomb, Alabama.
She was my daddy's sister.

Grandpa Rigell and me.

Our family at our home at 1412 Bell Terrace in Titusville, sometime in the '60s. (Front Row, L-R:) David, Amy, Kathryn, Scott, and Mona. (Back Row:) Me.

My four kids and I on a camping trip.
(L-R:) Scott, Amy, Mona, David, and me.

Living off the land. (L-R:) David and Scott.

We enjoyed going hunting in our beloved Land Rover.
(L-R): Me, Scott, and David.

A time when we couldn't afford a barber.
(Bottom row, L-R:) Kathryn, Scott, Amy, and me.
(Top row, L-R:) Mona and David.

The two women in my life. My mother, Beatrice "Attie" Rigell, and my wife, Kathryn, at 1412 Bell Terrace.

God is good. Our family home for many wonderful years.
1412 Bell Terrace in Titusville, Florida.

Sweethearts.

Tranquility.

Me and Kathryn at LaGrange Church at a Sons
of the Confederacy memorial service honoring
Confederate soldiers.

You need to travel, at least one time in your life, first class. In 1982, Kathryn and I flew from Washington, D.C. to London on the Concorde and returned to New York on the QE2. This is a scene from our flight on the Concorde, and note on the displays, our speed of Mach 2 at 56,000 feet. As soon as the seat belt sign was turned off, the flight attendants started serving food. We dined all the way to London, which was about a 3 1/2 hour flight. When we landed in England, no jet lag for Kathryn, she was ready to hit the town.

Queen Elizabeth 2   Photographed on board 1986

Great trip. We flew over to London in the
Concord from Dulles, spent three days in London, and
sailed back to New York on the QE2.

Red Square, Moscow—1991. We passed out many Bibles in
Moscow on this trip.

Cappadocia, Turkey
This beautiful place has some of the most
magnificent scenery in the world.

Grandchildren in wagons.

Me and Kathryn and all of our grandchildren.
The Lord is good.

All my grandboys.

All of my talented granddaughters at our old home at Fawn Lake in Mims, Florida.

On the road again in our Airstream.
We travelled all over the country in her.

Our four grown children. How the Lord has blessed us.
(L-R:) Scott, Mona, Kathryn, me, Amy, and David.

Me and Kathryn surrounded by family at our Rigell family reunion in New Smyrna Beach, Florida, in 2017. We are truly blessed.

CPSIA information can be obtained
at www.ICGtesting.com
Printed in the USA
BVHW022025150919
558469BV00028B/55/P